Urban and Regional Planning in an Age of Austerity

Pergamon Policy Studies on Urban Affairs

Laska & Spain Back to the City
Meier Urban Futures Observed
Moss Planning for Urban Waterfronts
Perry & Kraemer Technological Innovation in American Local Governments
Savitch Urban Policy and the Exterior City

Related Titles

Bernstein & Mellon Selected Readings in Quantitative Urban Analysis
Blowers The Limits of Power
Bromley The Urban Informal Sector: Critical Perspectives
Carter & Hill The Criminal's Image of the City
Catalano Health, Behavior and the Community
Chadwick A Systems View of Planning, 2nd Edition
Davidson & Wibberly Planning and the Rural Environment
Fagence Citizen Participation in Planning
Faludi Essays on Planning Theory and Education
Geismar & Geismar Families in an Urban Mold

Urban and Regional Planning in an Age of Austerity

Edited by
Pierre Clavel
John Forester
William W. Goldsmith

Pergamon Press
NEW YORK • OXFORD • TORONTO • SYDNEY • FRANKFURT • PARIS

Pergamon Press Offices:

U.S.A	Pergamon Press Inc., Maxwell House, Fairview Park, Elmsford, New York 10523, U.S.A.
U.K.	Pergamon Press Ltd., Headington Hill Hall, Oxford OX3 0BW, England
CANADA	Pergamon of Canada Ltd., 150 Consumers Road, Willowdale, Ontario M2J 1P9, Canada
AUSTRALIA	Pergamon Press (Aust) Pty. Ltd., P.O. Box 544, Potts Point, NSW 2011, Australia
FRANCE	Pergamon Press SARL, 24 rue des Ecoles, 75240 Paris, Cedex 05, France
FEDERAL REPUBLIC OF GERMANY	Pergamon Press GmbH, 6242 Kronberg/Taunus, Pferdstrasse 1, Federal Republic of Germany

Library of Congress Cataloging in Publication Data

Main entry under title:

Urban and regional planning in an age of austerity.

(Pergamon policy studies)
Bibliography: p.
Includes index.
1. Urban policy—United States—Addresses, essays, lectures. 2. City planning—United States—Addresses, essays, lectures. 3. Regional economics—Addresses, essays, lectures. 4. Radicalism—United States—Addresses, essays, lectures. I. Clavel, Pierre. II. Forester, John, 1948- III. Goldsmith, William W.
HT167.U7 1980 309.2'12'0973 79-21416
ISBN 0-08-025539-6
ISBN 0-08-025540-X pbk.

Printed in the United States of America

Contents

Preface

Historically, planning has served mostly to benefit local, regional, and national business rather than the broader public. It was not always meant that way, but that has been its effect. It began in the United States in response to mushrooming urban problems, as part of a larger movement to reform city governments and take graft out of the hands of city hall. It was also, in part, a reaction to the public attention that social workers and writers such as Jacob Riis brought to slums and urban decay. Early city planning was in addition influenced by the Beaux Arts atmosphere that surrounded the Chicago Exposition of 1899. The early dominant figures in planning, for more than a half-century, were those interested in cleaning, straightening, beautifying and rationalizing the cities of America.

This kind of planning, this regard for the city as a physical mechanism with mechanical needs, suited downtown merchants, land developers, auto makers, and the construction industry. The best example of such planning was the dismantling of literally scores of profitable and popular municipal streetcar systems, whose demise made way for the more profitable sales of buses, autos, gasoline, and rubber tires.(1) The market-serving nature of planning, through massive subsidies for highway construction, suburbanization of industry and housing, and renewal of downtown business property, has been prevalent ever since. Under conditions of recession, planners are called upon to an even greater degree to forge weapons to serve private interests, to protect property and privileged neighborhoods.

At least a part of the planning profession has never been happy with sponsorship by powerful corporate interests. There has always been a radical minority and a probable majority who considered themselves "liberals" – while hoping to gain leverage within the existing political system through incremental means. These planners have had to face the problem of how best to conceive and organize an alternative position.

One strategy has been to move outside the established professional structures and work actively within the community to build political pressure and alternative centers of power. During the period of the 1960s and the great upheaval in the nation's ghetto communities, progressive city planners urged their colleagues to resist the large financial interests that dominate urban development and become instead advocates for the oppressed. Local groups, often staffed by "advocate planners," who either diverted time away from city hall or found federal funds available to neighborhoods, sprang up in cities to fight against housing demolition, highway construction, and inadequate programs for residential relocation.

At the national level these progressives, though often confronted with hostility or stony silence in official professional circles, formed an organization called Planners for Equal Opportunity (PEO) in the early 1960s, which served for a time to pull together many of the planner-activists within and outside of official agency jobs. By the mid-1960s, the idea of advocacy planning for disadvantaged groups had caught on with an influential segment of the profession. It was much discussed in journals, supported both academically and through urban internship and assistance units in many schools, and spread rapidly outside the profession – both to other professions and among urban activists who felt confined within formal planning circles. It was perhaps inevitable that the use of planners for direct contact with client groups became part of the official planning process, particularly in big cities. Formal participation requirements multiplied with the grant programs of the 1960s and early 1970s – first in housing and urban reconstruction, then in economic development, poverty, highway construction and environmental legislation; and many big city planning agencies established neighborhood planner units with at least the trappings of the advocacy model.

In the 1970s this activism had touched thousands of professionals, and many were evaluating the experience. On the one hand, cities were in worse shape than ever. Pluralist political processes had opened up, only to reveal deeper layers of resistance to the activists' programs. On the positive side, many more planners were sharply aware of these deeper, institutionally rooted issues than a decade earlier, and the overall level of sophistication had increased. One issue was how best to organize within and outside the profession. PEO had officially disbanded in 1976, but many of its members had participated in the formation of a new group, the Planners Network, in the summer of 1975. One of the Network's founding members, Chester Hartman, a planner and community activist in San Francisco, became the editor of the Planners Network newsletter, an irregularly published communications organ shared by about 1,000 planner-activists – mostly in the U.S. In various cities Network chapters held periodic forums and provided technical assistance for community groups. In general though, the Network was more an association of like-minded individuals than a functioning organization, largely at the members' own preference.

Network communication supported the proposition that, aside from an organization, conceptual advances were necessary before the Left within planning and urban movements could gain the necessary cohesion to move ahead politically. A number of developments outside of the planning profession suggested that this cohesion might be possible. In the academic disciplines, the well-organized Union for Radical Political Economics (URPE) and other leftist organizations within geography, sociology, public administration, and political science, opened up new connections between the universities and working class and poor client groups. New radical groups among professionals and activists in such fields as housing and health sprang up, and established ones continued to thrive. The Conference on Alternative State and Local Public Policies, among other national organizations, began to explore alternatives to mainstream, that is, both liberal and conservative, urban policies. A new unity was being sought among political groups in the democratic Left, as indicated by the growth of the Democratic Socialist Organizing Committee, the New American Movement, the Progressive Alliance, and the Campaign for Economic Democracy. The radical Left was joining together with the working class Left in more effective alliances.

In this context, leftist academic planners began to think in terms of broader clienteles and new opportunities for their professional training programs. One element of this was the infusion of new personnel, in which persons with organizing experience made their way through Ph.D. programs and into planning faculties by the late 1970s. Another was the recognition by literally scores of planners who earlier had been touched by organizing and advocacy planning experience, of a need for a theory to guide city planning. The specific relevance of Marxist theory to their experiences and for formulating future planning roles also crystalized. By the end of the 1970s these developments were bearing fruit. A small conference at Rutgers University in 1977 was followed a year later by a somewhat larger gathering at Virginia Polytechnic Institute. At VPI the participants, after intense discussion about papers that were both theoretically penetrating and practice-oriented, became enthusiastic about the prospect of building a broader base among radical planners.(2) The papers that comprise this book were selected from a conference on planning theory and practice, held at Cornell University, in April 1979. The Cornell conference, which attracted some 300 academics, planning students, professional planners, and community activists, was organized around the three connected topics of this volume: economic conditions, emerging political coalitions, and new roles for planners. These themes were developed in a paper first drafted by Sander Kelman and then worked over by a group at Cornell (included as Chapter One of this volume.)

The ideas of emerging coalitions and "new roles" for planners were based on observation and involvement in planning practice as well as neighborhood, community, and labor organizing by persons who would not formally define themselves as planners. As we write this, in November, 1979, links between academics and practitioners, and between community and labor organizers, continue to develop. Planners

Network people organized a lively series of sessions at the annual meeting of the American Planning Association in Baltimore in October, have scheduled a series of regional conferences, and look forward to a more formal national organization.

At the Cornell conference, and in preparation of this book, we were assisted by many people. Pat Cross did the key work in coordinating all conference arrangements. Professor Barclay Jones and the Program in Urban and Regional Studies provided valuable advice and administrative support. The Department of City and Regional Planning and its Chairman, Sidney Saltzman, and the College of Architecture, Art and Planning and its Dean, Kermit C. Parsons, contributed materially and generously to the conference and the book. We thank, in particular, the staff of Left Sibley Hall – Verlaine Boyd, Cindy Coleman, and Jeff Coleman for substantial editing, Lynn Coffey, Helena Wood, and Donna Wiernicki for numerous administrative and secretarial services – and Susan Jacobs for the indexing.

We also thank the following scholars, whose research and discussion at the conference helped make this book possible: Jeff Armistead, Allen Baird, Larry Bennett, Joe Biber, Richard Bolan, Major Clark, Miguel Cordova, Chris Cotant, Paul Davidoff, Ernest Erber, Norman Fainstein, Susan Fainstein, Nancy Gilgosch, Richard Glance, Edward Greer, Bertram Gross, Britton Harris, Linda Hollis, David Houston, Frank Kendrick, Richard Klosterman, Jackie Leavitt, Charles Levine, Peter Marcuse, Robert Mier, John Nettleton, Paul Niebanck, Alan Rabinowitz, Thomas Reiner, D.A. Seni, Rick Simon, Kusum Singh, Judith Stoloff, Raymond Studer, Thomas Vietorisz, Robert Warren, and David Wilmoth.

Organizing and running the conference was in most respects a cooperative venture. Phil Snyder and Marian Howe helped us in Anabel Taylor Hall. Numerous members of the Department of City and Regional Planning and friends donated time and provided accomodations for conference participants: Lucia Andrade, Bill Baer, Denise Balkas, Christie and Jeff Barnes, Steve Brower, Michael Brown, Betsy Dietel, Kerry Dyer, Trina Eadie, Betty Falcao, Bob and Phyllis Fenneman, Sherry Fontaine, Paula Ford, Stephanie Foster, Glenn Gibbs, John Green, John Greenwald, Paul Gregory, Bob Grose, Steve Hall, Susan Hansen, Fran Helmstadter, Jim Himel, David Jacobs, Harvey Jacobs, Candy Kane, Brenda Kleysen, Kerry Korpi, Mano Kumarasuriyar, Jill Lawrence, Peter Lilienfield, Dick Lourie, Wendy Lovett, Betsy Lowe, David and Sandy Lyons, Laura Malakoff, Dwight Mengel, Tony Opalka, Paulo Penteado, Gerry Pfeffer, Michael Philips, Gary Pivo, Michael Raffe, Donna Shusterman, Amy South, Godfrey Spragge, Harry Sterling, Francesca Verdier, and Eric Won.

NOTES

(1) Bradford Snell, American Ground Transport, 1974.

(2) The papers presented were published in Harvey Goldstein and Sara Rosenberry, eds., The Structural Crisis of the 1970's and Beyond, 1978.

1 New Opportunities for Planners

Sander Kelman,
Pierre Clavel,
John Forester,
William W. Goldsmith

The context of planning in the United States is changing: fiscal crises and an unhealthy economy promise a decline in planning efforts focused upon growth of the market and federally funded programs. The demands planners will face in the coming years will be new ones. Many planners will be pressured to be hatchet men – streamlining programs and eliminating clients. If they are to resist, they will need to begin to work together with progressive political coalitions or territorial groups in opposition to threatened cutbacks. The skills required of planners will thus be different from those needed in the past. As progressive coalitions and organizations present special needs, planning education must change accordingly.

AUSTERITY: THE CONTEXT OF A WEAKENING ECONOMY

Since the end of World War II, comprehensive, goal-directed approaches have been eclipsed by planning oriented predominantly to enhance economic markets.(1) Two assumptions gave a certain plausibility to such planning. First, liberals and conservatives alike spoke of harnessing the resources of the private sector based on what they presumed was a basically stable, healthy, and growing economy. The country was seen to be gradually absorbing its "marginal" elements so that everyone, however gradually, would climb up the ladder of success.(2) Second, even skeptical, publicly minded planners could be market supporting as long as they thought that questions of redistribution would be solved by the trickle-down effect: let the private sector build houses for those who can afford them, for example, and everyone else will move until an equivalent unit opens up for those not able to afford new housing. However attractive these assumptions may have appeared a decade ago, they are no longer tenable.(3) Planning for the foreseeable future on the basis of these assumptions promises only failure. How, then, are we to understand the situation we face in the years ahead?

The process of growth of the American economy is very uneven. Cycles of expansion and recession or depression are frequent. Severe territorial inequalities persist. Recent booms and busts of the economy have greatly aggravated fiscal inadequacy in central cities, have resulted in decline in employment in large areas such as the Northeast and Midwest, and are related to massive transfer of manufacturing employment to areas outside the country. Future changes in the cycle are awaited with much trepidation.

Still more ominous than the short-term cyclical problems, Western economies today generate insufficient private investment to employ all, or nearly all, people actively seeking work. Thus even without cyclical aggravation, fiscal and unemployment problems appear to be with us for some time to come.

The Conventional Response: Austerity Policy

The reasons most commonly given for the failure of our economy to generate sufficient private investment are well known: taxes (to pay for social expenditures), interest rates (at which to finance investment) and wages are all too high; regulations of the use of land, of conditions at workplaces, and of pollution of the environment are too stringent. As a result, profits are too low to warrant the levels of domestic investment necessary to generate full employment without severe inflation. This interpretation underlies economic policy making in virtually all Western countries.(4)

What is significant for our purposes is that this explanation of insufficient investment, when coupled with a widespread attack on government spending, becomes an austerity policy. Such economic logic promises that an austerity policy will provide the national context for planning in the immediate and foreseeable future.

Why an austerity policy? If the problem of the national economy is seen as the absence of investment incentives, the prescribed solution will be to increase those incentives by lowering taxes (by lowering expenditures on social programs), thereby lowering pressure on money markets and thus interest rates; lowering wages (relative to prices) by maintaining high rates of unemployment indefinitely, and relaxing regulatory standards. The intended result, and ultimately perhaps, the real effect, may be to raise the anticipated return on domestic investment to create more employment. But the adjustment is paid for by wage earners and social service dependents, the presumed beneficiaries of the past 25 years' expansion. This is one way to interpret the significance of Proposition 13, the Supreme Court's ruling against OSHA factory inspections, and the Carter administration's reluctant position on the Humphrey-Hawkins bill.(5)

In a modern economy, a more pagan ritual would be difficult to imagine. Everyone depends upon income and the productivity of our collective labor for survival. Most people depend on employment for income, and on private productive investment for employment. Consumer and government expenditures are relatively stable when compared to private investment, so the major fluctuations in employment come from fluctuations in private investment. And such investment, according to the dominant economic school, depends upon incentives: inadequate incentives=inadequate investment. When the incentives are not sufficient, so the argument goes, sacrifice is required on the part of those (generally working people) already most dependent for their livelihoods on the investment of the corporate sector.

This is more ideological than scientific. Through the inspiration of fear and awe, investment is assigned characteristics that it does not in fact have.(6) The requirement of the incentives listed above is not intrinsic to investment; it follows from the logic of a game in which the roles and powers of the players are unquestioned. Such incentives seem necessary only in the context of a situation in which powerful institutions not only intervene between the productive members of the population and what they produce, but also where a fitting payment is demanded in return for the "service" of withholding part of the annual product for privately directed investment.

The illusion that such incentives are necessary cuts two ways. First, it reinforces the willingness of the population to suffer regressive measures so that the economy may once again be "healthy," thus perpetuating a situation in which the productive members of the society are continually and structurally its victims. Second, the political and social consequences of such beliefs are debilitating and dependency-promoting. If the majority of Americans are to believe that services and social programs must be cut back and that they must suffer willingly so the economy may revive, the circumstances that have made planning necessary in the first place will never be altered. To alter this belief, a new diagnosis and therapy for the economic crisis will be necessary, in particular, a therapy that promises economic recovery without austerity. While the particulars of this program remain to be clearly defined, they would have to overcome the hegemony of private capital and involve a major national commitment to planned public investment. The misleading focus upon austerity, or more euphemistically, "creating necessary incentives for private investment," threatens to distract our attention from demands we need to face – as planners and citizens – in the years ahead.

NEW DEMANDS FOR PLANNING

The strategy for producing such a national commitment depends upon the existence of widespread political support. Fortunately, in the face of attempted national retrenchment, it is not likely that the legacy of the past twenty years of social action will be political silence. Instead one may expect a pendulum effect of workplace efforts and popular organizing, and a further proliferation of consumer, neighborhood, and environmental organizations, setting a potentially more progressive context for planning in the years ahead. Instead of the appeal to expertise and the "end of ideology" that once promised to make such organizations obsolete, it is now apparent that conflicts among technical experts result in the political education of the public. Energy and health issues are common examples. Experts speak on both sides, and the message of the conflict is clear: resolution will be a matter of political debate, organization, and power.(7) The public's political sensibility no longer allows blind trust in expertise. Certainly no one coherent "consciousness" in any broad segment or class of our society has developed over the past 20 years; but a far greater familiarity with liberal political movements has. Two examples are the effects of the diverse environmentally focused groups and the politically educating character of the women's movement.

All of this means that the social and political context in which planners are working is changing. In the early 1970s, when Nixon dismantled the federal OEO effort, planners shifted their attention to community development block grants – and the politics and possibilities of local planning shifted too. Those possibilities are continuing to shift. Whatever degree of federally sanctioned austerity is forthcoming, planners can expect a continued, increasingly important response of local organizing efforts oriented to such issues as neighborhood preservation, municipal power, housing, locally controlled economic development, programs for the elderly, local tax reform, human rights, alternative technology, worker management, public land acquisition, redirection of energy use and production, environmental management, community health, occupational health and safety, and others.(8)

If planners are to do more than carry out austerity measures and reconcile the public to live with them, they must understand the changing context of their work and devise strategies, organizational forms, and skills accordingly. The Cleveland efforts reported by Krumholz and his associates may be increasingly typical:(9)

> In Cleveland experience indicates that planners can have considerable impact on public policy if they will do two things. First, they must become activists prepared for protracted participation and vocal intervention in the decision-making process. Too often, planners have been content to assume a passive role. Second, planners must offer something that decision-makers want and can relate to, not rhetoric but information, analysis, and policy recommendations which are relevant to decision-making. Local politicians must confront growing problems without adequate information, a long-range perspective, or even a clear idea of what they wish to achieve. This presents a great opportunity for the goal oriented activist agency. An agency must have patience, persistence, and the ability to attack on a variety of fronts. It must also seek out potential allies, including politicians, community groups, and other elements of the government bureaucracy, and show them how their interests are affected.

There have been many attempts to use federal resources to promote such local activity, including community owned or controlled enterprises.(10) Urban Development Action Grants, CETA, and Community Development Block Grant moneys have also been channeled to support wide ranges of local organizing activities and community groups. Proposals have even been made for such use of food stamp funds,(11) and, more ambitiously, for multibillion dollar pension funds.(12) There are coordinating lobbies and agencies serving these groups as well. Some of the most widely known are Massachusetts Fair Share, the Ohio Public Interest Campaign and other public interest groups, ACORN (now branched out from its beginnings in Arkansas), the National Training and Information Center, the National People's Action Coalition, and California's Campaign for Economic Democracy.(13) In addition, federal funds support the Center for Economic Development in Cambridge and the Research Center for Community Economic Development in Palo Alto, among others, to expand research and training in precisely these areas.

One of the most important nationwide organizations oriented along these lines is the National Conference of Alternative State and Local Public Policies, which held its fourth annual conference in 1978, attracting numerous state legislators, city council and union members as speakers.(14)

One illustration of the political interest that these movements have aroused is the 1978 sponsorship by 54 Congresspeople of a collection of policy papers (many related to urban policy) called the Federal Budget and Social Reconstruction, produced by the Institute for Policy Studies.(15) What this suggests is not bureaucratic entrenchment but the existence of an active, if diffuse, politically progressive population, organizers and organizations, with whom planners might ally themselves. Successful opposition to austerity will require these alliances to develop a reasonable and coherent economic recovery strategy, e.g., an aggressive commitment to a planned public investment program.

POLITICAL SKILLS FOR PLANNERS

As budgets contract there will be less money for comprehensive studies and large-scale model building. There will be less money for full-blown evaluation studies. There will be less money for elaborate plans detached from implementation. And with less money around, planning staffs will have to pay more attention to mobilizing community resources, building coalitions, organizing support for particular proposals, and organizing resistance to others in the everyday scramble of a local planning agency's work.

Krumholz clearly locates the planner's technical abilities within a context of necessary political skills.(16) We might call such planning "lobbying," but much more than this takes place. Planners do lobby decision makers and those close to them; they mobilize community groups to build their power; they selectively shape citizen participation and access to information as they work through contracts, networks, and supporters to bring about policy changes. The planner's work is organizational, political, educational, interpersonal, and technical – all interwoven together.

This new pragmatic but critical role will be less rationalistic than the old comprehensive planning, more politically sensitive and astute than a market-centered model. Interorganizational politics will become increasingly the planner's province, as the divorce of planning from implementation becomes less tolerable. To be more pragmatic and effective planners will be increasingly involved in both business and politics. Questions of local resources, coalition building, bargaining and negotiation, mobilization and coordination will become more central.(17) As the federal presence becomes less innovative and direct and maintains instead an increasingly regulative posture, the planner's political and organizational skills become all the more important.

The demand planners face, then, is to formulate a political role encompassing their technical skills. Local constituencies will ask planners to avoid simply "smoothing out" cutback measures. Instead planners will need to support and foster local progressive organizations and broader coalitions through which a politically sensitive, critical and responsible public might act. All of this suggests the encouragement of planning in which organizing skills, responsive organizations, and democratic politics are primary,(18) and markets and incentives are secondary.

No less important than before, technical skills will need to be complemented by the political and organizational skills demanded by the present political-economic context. To reiterate, the demands calling for these skills will continue to be: 1) the necessary integration of democratic participation with technical analysis and review; 2) the mobilization rather than preemption of community skills and resources; 3) the cultivation and support of emerging progressive groups and coalitions; and 4) the interorganizational need for planners to work not only as technicians but also as skilled organizers. They must be capable of skilled, technical work, astute at working in complex organizations, pragmatic in their approach to local politics, and informed of and attentive to the national political economy.

KNOWLEDGE AND TECHNIQUE IN THE CHANGING ORGANIZATIONAL ENVIRONMENT OF PLANNING

Because, as we have argued, the context of planning in the U.S. is changing, many planners will be facing new demands in their professional practice. These expectations lead us to propose a shift in the form and content of planning education – toward the orientations, theoretical perspectives, skills, and fieldwork and case study experiences necessary to serve these changing demands. The institutions, organizations and clientele with which many planners must work today differ from those of the classical market context. Accordingly, new skills and new programs of study are called for.

Large public bureaucracies provide an important environment for contemporary planning practice. Unless planners understand these institutions and know what to expect from them, both they and their clients are likely to suffer. Exposure to administrative practices and theory in planning curricula will clarify how formally defined responsibilities coexist with networks of power, influence, and trusted contacts. Recognizing that bureaucracies are themselves in internal conflict over competing goals,(19) that they too are politically dependent upon others for support, information and cooperation – all this begins to suggest that there are indeed ways to work effectively with the larger public agencies.

Local consumer and community organizations tend to be young and not yet institutionalized. Planners must be able to anticipate and address the needs of these organizations – from block clubs to city-wide food cooperatives to regional environmental organizations, or regional coalitions and alliances such as the recently formed Appalachian Alliance.(20) Field experience and study of group mobilization and institutional development can be fruitful here.

Local organizations that strive to organize and provide services inevitably become entangled in vast webs of regulations. For example, a local housing organization encounters a whole structure of finance and regulatory machinery, both private and public, finds it useful to ally itself with other organizations similarly obstructed. In such a situation planners can serve to help others navigate the bureaucratic maze.

The progressive groups with whom planners may work are not always highly visible. Networks of progressive professionals within existing bureaucratic structures and individuals dispersed throughout community and neighborhood organizations can be effective in part precisely because they are invisible to the media and politically sensitive officials. To be effective, these invisible networks must be recognized, appreciated, and cultivated – not exposed.

Equally important to these areas of skill and knowledge will be the ability to relate to the development of national institutions that can support these local phenomena. The development of public banking, to cite one example, can scarcely operate at the local level, yet the form such a regional or national institution takes will be crucial to many progressive local efforts. Shifts in the form of the federal system are similarly important, as in the case of the development of revenue sharing and related block grant programs. Local planners have often been alert to these larger developments. But the transition from traditional to new local roles will require keener attention to both existing and potentially alternative national institutions and policies.

NOTES

(1) Local planners held steadfastly to the ideal of planning as an alternative vision, subordinated neither to market forces nor to existing power structures. Rexford Tugwell argued for this in its most extreme

form, but Jack Howard's famous defense of the independent planning commission also had a considerable following. Only with the development of the federal grant system in the 1960s, with the opportunity to get into local policy making directly, did planners drop this apparently independent stance in order to work where they thought the power lay. This shifting perception of opportunities moved planners away from the comprehensive planning position – a move justified also by an increasing sense of conflicting and contradictory political and economic interests of diverse segments of our society. Planning activities then became diffused into a rather fragmented program analysis set of tasks, in response to the proliferating availability of programs. See Clavel, "Planners and Citizen Boards," 1968. The literature is extensive. See, for example, Altshuler, The City Planning Process, 1965, Beauregard, "The Occupation of Planning: A View from The Census," 1976, and Hemmens, Bergman, and Moroney, "The Practitioners View of Social Planning," 1978. Most land-use planning has also been market-oriented. See Kravitz, "Mandarinism: Planning as Handmaiden to Conservative Politics," 1970 and Fitch, "Planning New York," 1977.

(2) This is a central tenet of liberal "development economics." See Goldsmith, "The War on Development," 1977.

(3) For examples of the weakness of such homeostatic, equilibration hypotheses, see Goldsmith, "Marxism and Regional Policy: An Introduction," this volume.

(4) In the central economies of the world market – e.g., the U.S. – official unemployment may stay at oppressive but apparently politically acceptable levels, between five and ten percent. In closely related peripheral areas it is higher – e.g., persistently about 20 percent in Puerto Rico, about 40 percent in Mexico. True unemployment and underemployment are higher still in all areas. See Vietorisz, Mier and Harrison, "Full Employment at Living Wages," 1975.

(5) Such an austerity policy may be more covert than explicit, taking its toll more by the omission of effective and progressive policies than by the commission of particular acts.

(6) This is fetishism in the most literal sense.

(7) See Kelman, "Toward the Political Economy of Medical Care," 1971.

(8) See also recent issues of journals such as Working Papers for a New Society, Self-Reliance, Journal of the American Institute of Planners, In These Times, Social Policy, among others.

(9) Krumholz, Cogger, Linner, "The Cleveland Policy Planning Report," 1975.

(10) Cizman, "Steelyard Blues," and Brous, et al., Democracy in the Workplace, Washington, D.C.: Strongforce, 1977.

(11) Goldsmith and Vietorisz, A New Development Strategy for Puerto Rico: Technological Autonomy, Human Resources, A Parallel Economy 1978, and "Operation Bootstrap, Industrial Autonomy, and a Parallel Economy for Puerto Rico," 1979.

(12) Jeremy Rifkin, The North Will Rise Again, 1978.

(13) Perlman, "Grassrooting the System," 1976, Shearer, "Catalog," 1978.

(14) St. Paul-Minneapolis, July 13-16, 1978. See Lee Webb, ed., Public Policies for the 80's, 1978.

(15) See Raskin, ed. The Federal Budget and Social Reconstruction, 1978.

(16) See Galper, The Politics of the Social Services, 1975; Martin and Carolyn Needleman, Guerrillas in the Bureaucracy, 1974; Meltsner, Policy Analysts in the Bureaucracy, 1976; Benveniste, The Politics of Expertise, 1977.

(17) These political, nonmarket aspects of planning practice are likely to become more crucial in the years ahead precisely because of the looming austerity measures of national economic policy. Planners will be asked to rationalize, streamline and assist in the administration of austerity-related policies. Consenting to these tasks would violate the traditions of the profession calling for public service before public management, for democratization before technocratic administration. See also Dewey, The Public and Its Problems, 1927.

(18) See Forester, "What Do Planning Analysts Do?" and "Questioning and Shaping Attention as Planning Strategy: Toward A Critical Theory of Planning," 1978.

(19) See Booth, "The Adirondack Park Agency: A Challenge in Regional Land-Use Planning," 1975.

(20) See Pierre Clavel, "Opposition Planning," in this volume.

I

Regions, Corporations and the Economy

Introduction

Problems in the American city reflect changes in the U.S. economy. Briefly, the economy is locked in a period of slow to nonexistent aggregate growth in which high unemployment and high inflation seem without remedy. Opinions vary on the nature, causes, and possible solutions to this unhappy combination of events, but few doubt that the effects on cities are severe and long term. One outcome, the austerity effect on policy and politics, was described in the previous chapter and is touched on in many of the chapters comprising the rest of this volume. In this section, several of the chapters focus on another outcome, the spatial effect, as government and major corporations attempt to adjust to their economic problems.

It is now apparent that there are major shifts of jobs and investment from northeastern cities to their suburbs, to the south and west, and to other countries. These shifts often have disastrous effects: fewer jobs, smaller tax bases, abandonment and deterioration of private facilities. Schools and social services are not adequately funded. At the same time, public facilities are obsolete; streets, buildings, and utilities are in need of repair. Furthermore, there are badly placed political boundaries, inherited from a time when the city, not the metropolis, encompassed most of the economy. These boundaries make long-term fiscal solvency a near impossibility. Central cities also have a disproportionate number of people in need of public services and subsidies; this would be so even if there were full employment for others. Left over are the aged and infirm, single parents, and the handicapped. Finally, many cities are centers of racism, expressed in segregated neighborhoods and schools and in open political antagonism.(1) These factors affect not only physical blight and the well-being of the population, but also fiscal, managerial and political capacity, with the result that some observers have begun to characterize central cities as "reservations" of diseased and dependent populations, governed by political techniques reminiscent of the most primitive colonial empires.(2)

There is thus a superimposition of shifting corporate activity on top of more general reductions in public services caused by tight budgets, hardships imposed by inflation, and unemployment due to inadequate programs of new productive investment. Some understanding of corporate territorial behavior and its ramifications is necessary to intelligently explore the roles for progressive planners in American cities.

What is perhaps most interesting about this set of spatial effects is the extent to which regional scholars, social scientists, and policy makers failed to anticipate the shifts, particularly their institutional and political ramifications, just a few years before they happened.(3) Locational forces and movements of population, jobs, and capital were certainly studied and reported, but the curious nature of these studies was that they were conducted as if spatial shifts were mysterious aggregate effects of a multitude of individual, autonomous decisions. In fact, one of the concepts in regional geography that has been most popular – and sometimes useful – makes use of analogies between movements of population and the gravitational attractions among bodies in the heavens. Nowhere, however, was there an effort to consider the movements of economic and political forces as more important than individuals. Instead, politics was considered separate from individual decision making, reflecting that our general ability to think about politics in a systematic way, as related to spatial phenomena, was very limited.

Characteristic of the chapters that follow, in contrast, is a consciousness of politics and major economic forces, e.g., the corporation, and an awareness that urban problems and policies to solve them are properly set in the context of regional economics and politics. The authors are aware that dramatic shifts in this setting have been taking place and probably will continue. Even more important, the authors delineate their assumptions about relations between politics and economics, and between corporations and government. They distinguish between forces directly involved in production, such as labor, financial resources, and technical innovation, and the relations that govern productive organization, such as laws, wage contracts and labor unions.

In the next chapter, Goldsmith details the widely different interpretations of corporate behavior in spatially arranged markets. Conservatives rationalize the problem by expecting shifts in prices, wages and other mechanisms of exchange to remove disparity between one place and another. Liberal economists assert that these mechanisms must be aided by government action. Because of implausible assumptions and inadequate performance, the conservative and liberal views seem to mystify; the alternative – a radical (Marxist) perspective – seems to clarify.

Using a series of examples from Latin America and Western Europe, it is argued that regional inequality arises from personal inequality, which is generated, reinforced, and protected by market structures and the power of private corporations. In more general terms, basic regional and urban problems are unsolvable because they arise from the normal operations of capitalism. The government – what Marxists more specifically refer to as the capitalist state – is itself in part a creation of capitalism; as such, its policies are normally inadequate to the task. Insofar as social and economic problems may be expected to grow from geographically dispersed operations of private markets and the needs for corporate profitability and expansion, these problems will thus appear in regional concentrations and shift from time to time.

In chapter three, Ann Markusen makes an important elaboration by distinguishing among three arguments. The first is that capitalism needs to make or keep territories unequal as its businesses look for profits by exploiting labor, gathering natural resources, or expanding markets. The second argument is that, although a capitalist order may produce regional inequality, such unevenness is not necessary for the generation or circulation of surplus value (profits, rents, interest). Finally, one may hold the position that regional unevenness may be produced or eliminated, depending on conditions. Corragio, in a 1973 paper, posed the issue more generally in an analogy with cell structure.(4) Patterns of location of cells in a body would not be understandable without theories of biology and physiology. Similarly, patterns of industrial, commercial, housing, and public facility location cannot be understood without a theory of society. It is for this reason that specificity about assumptions must precede analysis.

Present Discussion of Spatial Effects

With the decline of older, northeastern cities, regional disparity has now become part of political debate. Discrepancies in national urban policy between sunbelt and northeastern cities have led frostbelt mayors, governors, and senators to speak "bluntly about their cities' needs."(5) As the issue has become more openly political, so the analyses have become more hotly debated, their assumptions more openly examined. A series of very different (but possibly compatible) notions have been used to explain major regional shifts. One is that changing prices, particularly rises in prices of basic commodities such as oil and foodstuffs, have favored the South and West, which produce or control production of such items, inducing industrial growth in those areas and relative decline in the Northeast, which produces other, less favored items.(6) Some believe that shifting investment and migration will take up the slack; others think the government must rechannel resources to the declining areas. Thus a classic debate in regional economics – jobs to stranded people, or people to available jobs – has surfaced.

A second notion is that shifts in the national industrial structure, such as an increase in tourist services compared with a relative decline in the production of basic metal products, or an increase in the production of electronic calculators (requiring low-skilled labor) compared to the production of electromechanical calculators (which require highly-skilled machinists), have been played out with marked geographic unevenness. In these terms, the " 'problem of the city'. . . can be related to an analysis of the changing structure of the national economy."(7) Unless one advocates public planning of innovation and control of the economy, however, there remains no more than the possibility of predictive "planning," to warn of upcoming trouble spots.

Another notion is that patterns of corporate expansion have followed increased differentiation between head office and line operations, the former becoming more and more concentrated, usually in the biggest and richest cities, the latter spreading across the globe, in search of low wages, compliant labor forces, and minimal government interference. Such tendencies, which may lead to ever widening gaps between central areas and their distant peripheries, may also reinforce the tendencies of some major regions to grow at the expense of others. Hymer suggested, not entirely in jest, that this globalization of corporate planning requires highly coordinated and strongly enforced programs of international regional planning by public bodies.(8)

A fourth notion, at a subsidiary level but important for present purposes, is that these industrial shifts, which have generated much growth, have nevertheless provided little help for the dependent populations of the southern and southwestern U.S. cities which, without the aid of either strong unions or public service traditions, find themselves still without a decent standard of living.(9)

Whichever of these hypotheses is true, there is general agreement among professional economists, regional scientists and planners that the industrial, corporate and population shifts now taking place are costly in terms of job losses in the northeastern central cities.

Although important regional differences and rivalries in America arose partly from basic economic differences, these are neither consistent nor irreversible across regions. On the contrary, the needs of capitalist expansion lead corporations to ignore regional economic boundaries. But regional politics in the U.S. go beyond direct response to economic differentiation. Markusen – in this volume – argues that in order to hide the real influence of giant corporations and their public allies, the government and the corporations have reinforced and manipulated regional differences, creating a false politics that inhibits organizing and obscures "the basic class and corporate dynamics of the actual economic situation." The role of the government in the new regionalism has been significant. "While ubiquitous capitalist economic relations, culture, and ideology homogenize American society /public/ power is employed to preserve and create new regional differentiations." (While discussing this subject as a respondent, Bertram Gross added a new word, "placism," to go with "racism" and "sexism" in our dictionary of perjoratives.)

Corporations and Cities

The large number of regional shifts that depend on corporate structure and business location decisions suggests not only the politics of a new regionalism but also a rather direct role for the corporations in metropolitan areas. Far from being disinterested actors separate from politics and involved mainly in the private market, as the classical liberal economists suggested, the mature economy finds corporations deeply enmeshed in government and politics.(10) It follows that a major part of this interaction is applied to the management of government in the metropolis. The relationship between corporations and cities and metropolitan economies is, however, ambiguous.(11) On the one hand, corporations have pressing reasons to engage with governments; on the other hand, engagement has become increasingly difficult for them. Corporations need to secure social order to do business, yet this order has become difficult to achieve, particularly in central cities. They need a trained and loyal labor force, yet the institutions supporting these workers, including schools and neighborhood environments, are of doubtful quality. They need local government to provide services and capital facilities, yet this has also become complex, not only because of the fiscal limitations but more profoundly because of the increasing complexity of the federal system.(12)

An option for businessmen has always been to disengage from local public affairs. Each of these problems of local public management would, if confined within the firm, seem to merit constant and persistent attention from management personnel. The government, however, gets inconsistent treatment. As Schumpeter commented on this critical failure of capitalist management: they were good at creating firms, and they were good at adapting the political system they inherited to their ends; but they had no talent for creating political systems once the old system decayed.(13)

The disengagement of the business class from public institutions has accelerated with the transition to absentee management, as corporate executives have shifted from heavy, if paternalistic, involvement in politics, to superficial involvement aimed only at public relations.(14) Even the development of suburbs has been, in part, an effort at related class segregation and the avoidance of the most important urban public issues by the managerial classes.(15) Recent development of the monopoly sector at the expense of competitive business suggests exacerbation of all this.(16)

In Schumpeter's terms, the problem was in the "civilization of capitalism": dominated by profit motives, businessmen have no stable motivations to commit them consistently to solving urban, and particularly central city, problems. Motivated by profit, they engage public programs when it profits them rather than for long-term reasons, and many of their public activities have varied with the business cycle.(17)

In a somewhat broader sense, business participation in urban political coalitions has been prominently related to rather narrow profit motivations. There is a sequence of urban political regimes in which the more recent transition has been from one dominated by real estate and construction interests in urban capital improvements, to one of corporate enclaves dominated by a motivation to maintain order in a surrounding dependent population.(18)

Government Response

These shifts in the national economy and in corporate relations with cities have, of course, not gone unnoticed by public officials or citizens; on the contrary, there has been a variety of responses. At the city and metropolitan level, there have been concerted activities by neighborhood groups (developing into national coalitions), by ward politicians, and by city halls. State governments have responded with new legislation and with their own forms of coalition politics, in attempts to reorient programs of federal spending and to attract increased industrial investment. Markusen documents seeds of progressive use of this new regionalism. Michael Stone, in the last chapter of this section, notes the relationship between a strained economy, the housing sector, and organized politics on the Left. Finally, the federal government has, for the first time, tried to formulate a unified national urban policy from its many problematic elements.

As Mark Weiss shows in his discussion of public housing, urban renewal, and other programs (chapter 4) there has been a distinct evolution of policy toward the cities, as the government has tried to follow a path of resolving the most difficult of urban problems while maintaining effective alliances with business.(19) In the 1950s and early 1960s, federal policy focused on aid for physical construction: urban renewal, massive highway programs, and housing subsidies for the suburbs. This policy fostered the patterns of urban expansion so elaborately documented in the New York Metropolitan Study and in many others of the period – a multiplicity of neighborhood governments, costly but comfortable suburban sprawl, enormous investments in physical infrastructure. Beginning in the middle 1960s there were large increases in maintenance and direct social programs that particularly affected central cities.(20) More recent emphasis in federal urban policy has tended to be oriented directly to business development involving incentives for investment projected to create jobs in the inner city. Direct job creation strategies, such as CETA and public sector employment programs, after a brief flurry, were deemphasized in the late 1970s (in the Carter budget). Overall, expansion of federal programs for the cities has been strictly limited since about 1973.(21)

There was some hope, throughout 1977, that the Carter White House would innovate and dramatically improve programs of federal aid to cities. Even Treasury Secretary Blumenthal said that "there is probably no issue that will concern this administration more and concern the president more than the question of jobs and the question of cities." Unfortunately for the unemployed and for the cities, there has been little evidence of this professed concern. Furthermore, even if it were White House policy to back a program of urban revival, lack of interest from an increasingly suburban and southwestern Congress would be an obstacle.(22)

Although the picture is complex, the overall urban strategy seems oriented to a corporate business clientele with a few small, selected programs targeted to specific urban populations (for example, the Legal

Services Administration, and the Minority Small Business Administration. The new urban impact statements may, in the distant future, provide help, but there is good evidence that they will not help now.(23)

The combined effects of national austerity and regional corporate shifting do not bode well for the American city. It is only realistic to view private business needs as frequently in conflict with public needs. Profitable private business implies activity harmful to groups living in cities.

> To make profits, business must buy cheap and sell dear. Buying cheap means either paying low wages or buying inputs made by low-wage labor elsewhere. Several elements of the urban problems of the U.S. are thus created or exacerbated: ethnic groups, especially blacks and illegal aliens, easy targets for discrimination, provide very cheap labor; the existence of a poor, welfare population serves as a mechanism to keep down the general level of wages since welfare payments are a subsidy to employers and to weaken unions since the existence of a large unemployed population can be used as an alternative source of labor. Lower levels of service in schools, transportation, child care and other areas of public life mean lower business taxes. Production overseas to cut costs means not investing at home, thus increasing unemployment and decreasing productive income. In all these ways and many others, rational business pursuit of profit creates urban problems.(24)

When austerity and regional decline are included, any attempt by the government to resolve urban problems within the bounds of the privately dominated economy are virtually guaranteed to fail.

Housing and the Economy

In the last chapter of this section, Stone points to housing as a particular aspect of the urban problem that is intimately related to the economy. Shelter poverty, which is defined as a condition resulting from the squeeze between incomes and housing costs, appears as a contradiction Stone claims will not go away, but will become more severe. Twentieth century evolution of the housing sector in America, comprised of giant growth of the mortage system and government intervention, is seen as an attempt "to manage the contradiction between the housing and labor markets in the interests of capital." Housing is such a big part of the economy that it cannot be ignored. It is important as a cost for labor, which must somehow be met within the constraints of low wages, necessary in the economy for building, banking and real estate. According to Stone's analysis, attempts to resolve these inherent conflicts will necessarily fail. As we shall see in subsequent sections, this leads to arguments for using housing programs, rent control, and urban planning as organizational strategies for advocating change to socialism.

NOTES

(1) Kain, "Failure in Diagnosis: A Critique of Carter's National Urban Policy," 1978.

(2) See, e.g., Nathan and Dommell, "The Cities," 1977.

(3) Vernon, Metropolis 1985, 1960.

(4) Coraggio, "Towards a Revision of the Growth Pole Theory," 1973.

(5) Goldsmith, "Is There an Urban Policy?" 1979.

(6) Rostow, "Regional Change in the Fifth Kondratieff Upswing," 1977.

(7) Massey and Meegan, "Industrial Restructuring Versus the Cities," 1978.

(8) Goldsmith, "Marxism and Regional Policy: An Introduction." See also Hymer, "The Multinational Corporation and the Law of Uneven Development," 1972; Gordon, "Capitalist Efficiency and Socialist Efficiency," 1976; and Therkildson, "Regional Development in Western Europe: A Study of the Locational Behavior of Large Industrial Enterprises," 1976.

(9) Perry and Watkins, eds., The Rise of the Sunbelt Cities, 1977.

(10) The argument for thinking of business and politics as separate is made in Milton Friedman, Capitalism and Freedom, 1962. The alternative view, that business and government are subject to increasing interactions, is more common, as presented by Charles Linblom in Politics and Markets, with a long list of works documenting the development of the mixed economy in western countries. See Andrew Shonfield, Modern Capitalism, 1965.

(11) There have been several contrasting theoretical formulations of how corporations relate to city politics, but the empirical literature on corporate positions, structure, and public behavior is thin. We have been stimulated, but not convinced by various studies. These include Lynd and Lynd, Middletown in Transition, Hunter, Community Power Structure, Dahl, Who Governs? Crenson, The Unpolitics of Air Pollution, O'Connor, The Fiscal Crisis of the State, Domhoff, Who Rules New Haven, 1979, and numerous case studies in article form or unpublished.

(12) On "business" requirements one such listing is contained in Form and Miller, Industry, Labor and Community, 1960.

(13) Schumpeter, Capitalism, Socialism and Democracy, 1942, Chapter XI.

(14) Schulze, "The Bifurcation of Power in a Satellite City," in Janowitz, Community Political Systems, 1961.

(15) Sennett, The Uses of Disorder, 1970.

(16) O'Connor, The Fiscal Crisis of the State.

(17) Piven and Cloward, Regulating the Poor. Cloward and Piven attributed the ebb and flow of poverty and welfare programs to variations in unemployment and consequently labor scarcity.

(18) Elkin, "Cities without Power: Transformation of American Urban Regimes," paper presented for Conference on Urban Choice, Western Societies Program, Cornell University, Ithaca, N.Y., June 1977.

(19) Also see Goldsmith, "Is there an Urban Policy?"

(20) Sundquist, Dispersing Populations and Rodwin, Nations and Cities.

(21) Anton, "Outlays Data and the Analysis of Federal Policy Impact," in Glickman, ed., The Urban Impacts of Federal Policies, forthcoming, and Goldsmith, "Is There an Urban Policy?"

(22) Moynihan, "The Politics and Economies of Regional Growth," 1978.

(23) Glickman, "Methodological Issues and Prospects for Urban Impact Analysis," in Glickman, ed., The Urban Impacts of Federal Policies, forthcoming; also see the article by Congressman John Conyers in In These Times, Feb. 21, 1979. p. 16. Also see Danziger, Haveman, Smolensky and Taouber, "The Urban Impacts of the Program for Better Jobs and Income," Edel, "'People' versus 'Places' in Urban Impact Analyses," and Markusen, "The Urban Impact Statement: A Critical Forecast," all in Glickman, ed., The Urban Impacts of Federal Policies, forthcoming.

(24) Goldsmith, "Is There an Urban Policy?" p. 101.

2 Marxism and Regional Policy: An Introduction*

William W. Goldsmith

This chapter identifies technical, liberal and radical approaches to regional planning, applies the radical approach to some very broad issues of regional policy, and finally, focuses on a particular project in some detail.(1)

THREE DEFINITIONS AND APPROACHES

Regional planning is a widely accepted and growing public responsibility for addressing problems of geographic inequality, lagging regions, and inefficiencies of concentration.(2) Technocrats (conservatives?) tell us of the existence of an interregional economic market system that is equilibrating in the most important senses: labor shortages or surpluses are reduced through migration from low-wage to high-wage regions; returns on regional investments are equalized when banks of the rich regions invest in projects of the poor ones; prices are equalized through trade; information and technology continuously diffuse from the leading to the lagging regions. Liberals (the establishment) react to this view, pointing out that the market malfunctions. Migrants are misinformed and migration is selective, thereby increasing wage differences between regions. Investors, likewise, seem to over value already productive regions, respond to agglomerative efficiencies and in other ways contribute to the disequilibria. Finally, diffusion of information is very slow, national backwaters always lagging behind the centers of invention and innovation. The result is that mechanisms for interregional market equilibration are rusty; they need both oil and applied force. The standard approach to regional planning provides special incentives

*Reprinted with slight editing from The Review of Radical Political Economics 10, no. 3 (1978): 13-17.

for industrial location, protection for local business, promotion of exports, establishment of industrial complexes and, in general, aids to make the market function smoothly and more equitably.

In the radical view, however, it is the market and its arrangement of production that generates and guarantees inequality and imbalance. To fully appreciate the contrast it is necessary to set the scene.(3)

Prior to capitalism, workplaces were organized, without much plan or hierarchy, in guilds of loosely connected individuals, each doing more or less the same thing, with little division of labor. At the same time, the overall society, where goods were exchanged for other goods, was very formal and carefully arranged. Hierarchy of class, caste and guild guaranteed that people would work at all occupations in a setting of political and social stability – in effect an authoritarian rigidity. Within this rigid feudal society work proceeded autonomously in small informally run groups – generally families.(4)

Market capitalism turned this inside out. The shell of the new society, deceptively as rigid as the old, takes obvious shape in the workplace. In the marketplace, objects of equivalent value are exchanged voluntarily, without a hierarchy of command, with no conscious form.(5) As Alfred Marshall wrote early this century, in the modern world we find "work within each trade so divided up that the planning and arrangement of the business, its management and its risks, are borne by one set of people, while the manual work required for it is done by hired labor."(6) Marx had earlier written, this "division of labor within the workshop implies the undisputed authority of the capitalist over men that are but parts of a mechanism that belongs to him. . ."(7) Today multinational corporate responsibility is even more clearly divided between top management goal-determination and planning, middle level responsibility for coordination, and lower level responsibility for day-to-day production, sales and other operations. The shell of society has thus become further obscured by the anarchy of markets.(8)

The implications of these changes for geographic patterns of society, and regional planning, are profound. Fundamentally, the capitalist organization of work, reinforced by the marketplace and by legal, religious, political and social institutions, generates inequality as one class of people accumulates surplus produced by others. This process, called by some the Law of Uneven Development, is one in which market competition for more efficient production is continually superceded by mergers and market intervention, so that, by the logic of surplus accumulation, those who have been successful continue to succeed, defeating and swallowing their competitors. As markets spread from localities to regions and across nations, opportunities for accumulation through exploitation increase along with productive efficiency. Inequality grows and is expressed geographically. Capital is invested not only where it is most profitable, but where the businessman can most effectively guard his control over appropriation of surplus.(9) Public spending reinforces private, and there is a cycle of feedback that reinforces the efficiency of major centers of growth. Many orthodox theorists claim that massive efficiencies are bound to come hand in hand with imbalances and concentrations, just as apologists of early capitalism explained that concentration of money in the hands of a small class of people was required for rapid investment and development.(10) More recently, with the growth of multinational corporations, the geography of surplus value has become much more complicated, but, as we shall see, it still arises from the requirements of a productive system designed to insure transfer of surplus to a minority.

INTERNATIONAL CAPITALISM AND REGIONAL DEVELOPMENT

The impotence of liberal reform in a capitalist society is obvious when one talks about the need for schools to produce winners and losers, the requirement of restraint on the part of a responsible journalism, or the need for the clear separation of authority in the workplace. Though problems of regional development would seem to be much less important to the maintenance of the order, it is not difficult to show that even regional reform is strictly limited by the needs of capitalist production.

When the military took over in Peru in 1968, it clearly hoped to implement far reaching social change. One of its objectives was industrial decentralization, which aimed to incorporate outlying peoples and regions, to productively utilize the nation's resources, to limit growth and diseconomies of metropolitan Lima, and to insure national security. As Patricia Wilson has shown,(11) such reforms were basically incompatible with a system of capitalist production, in which multinational corporations sought to exploit surplus in three ways: from mineral and agricultural extractions, from cheap labor that would process the raw materials prior to export, and from a Peruvian market for technology and machinery. How were these needs for surplus expressed geographically? – by sierra mines, coastal plantations, and selva oil wells; by coastal urban-industrial development, complemented by cheap sierra food; and by expanding markets for imports in Lima. This produced Peru's geography – a rich urban coastal area with a vastly impoverished interior, pocketed with mining enclaves.

Reform was impossible because the local manufacturing firms' need for foreign exchange, supplied by multinationals, supported this very pattern of geographical exploitation. None of the government's programs – subsidies, tax incentives, direct expenditure and investment – could balance the need or power of the continuing capitalist base.(12)

Perhaps, the liberal critic retorts, capitalism _is_ the culprit in situations like that of Peru, where a history of colonialism and imperialism continues even today, where dependency and underdevelopment are pronounced. But what of regional problems in, say, Western Europe, where governments are highly sophisticated, where autonomy is more practical, and where class divisions are much less pronounced? In this case, the liberal critics argue, problems of regional inequality and backwardness can certainly be attacked with some success. If the radical argument holds, it must be able to demonstrate that these critics are wrong. It must show that once again the structure of the market and the productive system itself give rise to the inequality that is expressed regionally, and that, though policy may sometimes appear effective, it is only accidentally so, when it happens to coincide with the needs and patterns of expansion of capitalism. Research on recent development in Western Europe, much of it directly focused on the potential or actual impact of the EEC and EFTA on backward regions such as southern Italy or Wales, very strongly suggests that what counts is not regional policy of countries or of European communities (13) but the pattern in which giant corporations are expanding. As in the Peruvian case, for example, when the British government tries to encourage firms to locate outside London, the result seems more often to subsidize those who would relocate anyway, with no effect on the dominant position of London, which gathers corporate headquarters at a more rapid rate in spite of the policy.(14)

Again, the notion of the division of corporate responsibility into planning, coordination and operations is very useful. With big companies, and in Europe these are nearly always international, responsibilities are practically, as well as conceptually divided by place. Activity location quotients show, for example, a vast concentration of planning activity (head offices) in Brussels, London, and along the spine running from Bonn to Amsterdam. At the same time, it is probable that operations (factory production, e.g.) are spread throughout the continent, searching for low wages, weak unions, and special tax incentives.(15)

The liberal expectation about lessening regional income inequality is not found in Europe either. On the contrary, at least from the crude indicators available, we see that inequality between regions in the most rapidly expanding national economies is increasing, as opposed to the apparently random patterns it follows elsewhere. Why is this so? The answer is relatively simple: corporate expansion has certain requirements. One of these is that head offices be located in a few rich and well developed centers, whose average incomes thereby rise, leading to worsening income distributions. Another is that production can be located almost without regard to the head office location, so that considerations of efficient surplus extraction can be followed. This means that while the location of head offices becomes more and more concentrated geographically and is reinforced by mergers, ever increasing size, and rationalization of conglomerates, production plants can be more and more dispersed, according to changes in local conditions, world markets, and other variations important to minimization of production, particularly labor costs. Thus the pattern appears random, shifting, and bewildering. Even the formation of the EEC and EFTA provided little relief. Indeed, the question is whether they were forced on Europe by exigencies of corporate expansion (requiring lowering of national barriers to migration of capital and labor), or these needs were anticipated and facilitated by the market mergers.

The conservative theories are wrong – market mechanisms obviously do not help diminish regional inequality. In fact, the most common concern about market expansion (especially in the case of the dropped international barriers of the Common Market) is that regional inequalities will be increased. But the liberals are wrong, too – even with strong policies (and there are well-defined regulations of the Common Market concerned with lagging regions), regional inequalities don't change in any predictable way. Certainly, they are not seriously reduced. The only plausible explanation is that, opposing policy notwithstanding, capitalist expansion and change produce regional inequality insofar as it is necessarily a by-product of personal inequality, the basis of capital accumulation. As others have asked in the Latin American context, How can we talk of policy to integrate marginal citizens in a society that produces marginality?

REGIONAL DEVELOPMENT UP CLOSE

This large-scale interpretation of regional inequality as a response to the needs of capital accumulation is given meaning only when we see how it actually takes place – how policies of regional development are frustrated by the requirements of the system within which they are embedded. There are many well-documented cases. Perhaps the most prominent is that of Ciudad Guayana in Venezuela, a massive program of regional development thoroughly documented in English by a research team from the Joint Center for Urban Studies and ably criticized by Lisa Peattie in her View from the Barrio.(16) For the moment, though, I shall review the much smaller program of development of the Tepalcatepec River Basin in Mexico, a project with some $50 million invested over 20 years (versus $16 billion U.S. private investment in Mexico). This program has also been thoroughly documented by David Barkin and Timothy King.(17) The 7,000 square mile river basin, with over half a million people living there now, was the recipient of irrigation and other investments that led to a six-fold increase in irrigated acreage, an increase of all cultivated area by 2.5 times, a shift from subsistence corn to commercial cotton and melon farming, and a tripling of the value of product per acre. Altogether, production (at constant prices) increased six-fold from 1950 to 1970, yielding, by conservative standards, a 13 percent return on the government's capital investment. By any standards, these statistics indicate tremendous success at regional planning, with increases in production and incorporation of a subsistence area into the national economy.

But this traditional cost-benefit calculation must be qualified. The objectives of regional planning include reduced income inequality (both between the region and the rest of the country and within the region), a regime of self-sustained growth in the region, and reduction of pressure on more crowded areas of the country. On these counts the project failed. Income inequalities increased, the region's residents lost control over their subsistence economy, which was now tied to a fickle market responding to conditions elsewhere, and local population showed little growth. Why and how did this happen? In brief, because the process of private capital accumulation conflicted with these interests of the region. The development program led to an increase in the surplus extracted from the region, rather than either a transfer to the region or stimulation of some self-generated growth. Specifically, most of the agricultural profits (subsidized by the development program) were channeled into industrial investment in the wealthier and more urban parts of the country. The hydroelectric power was and is utilized almost exclusively for industry in other regions. Credit, subsidized and otherwise, was more available to large operations, so small landholders and other local people found themselves squeezed out. Processing of crops for market, such as grinning, grading and packing, is more profitable than growing, and here, too, concentration and investment by outsiders was the rule. And, in the end, even national urban migration was not diminished, because once private investors had capitalized on the initial subsidies, then the region stabilized rather than continuing to grow. As Barkin writes:

> To be sure, the region continues to help finance development in other areas by providing huge surpluses which the capitalists are able to extract from the highly profitable farming activities but most of the people. . . continue to fulfill the role they played before development began providing labor and living at levels materially below those prevailing in the rest of the country. Under present arrangements they are being more effectively exploited because their labor power is being mobilized to produce cash crops for the national and international market.(18)

Thus we come full circle. Conservatives and technocrats who view markets as mechanisms for equilibration, however right they may be about minor adjustments and the multitude of individual decisions made in the economy, are clearly wrong about processes of regional development. There is no evidence that the concentrating forces of market development ever give way to forces for equalization. Why should they, when the process for growth makes those who benefit from it more powerful? The establishment liberals, in turn, seem unable to explain the failure of their programs. As is evident, regional development does not work in Peru, Western Europe or elsewhere. Somehow, the markets, incentives and subsidies never seem to be enough. Only when we turn to examination of the market and production processes themselves do we see what gives rise to the regional problems – the very nature of capitalism and its drive to accumulate private profits, through the production and gathering of surplus value.

NOTES

(1) For discussion of the promise of regional development under radical governments in the Third World, see the review by Goldsmith and Siy, "More on Third World Development," 1978; Barkin, "Confronting the

Separation of Town and Country in Cuba"; Sawyers, "Cities and Countryside in the Soviet Union and China"; and the comment by Hans Blumenthal in the June 1978 Monthly Review.

(2) For elaboration, see Goldsmith, "Some Thoughts on Teaching Regional Planning," presented at the Conference of the American Society of Planning Officials, Chicago, May 13, 1974, or a revised version in the Proceedings of the U.C.L.A. Colloquium on Comparative Urbanization, 1974.

(3) See Hymer, "The Multinational Corporation and the Law of Uneven Development," 1971, p. 116.

(4) See Laslett, The World We Have Lost, 1965.

(5) Cf. Emmanuel, Unequal Exchange, 1972.

(6) Principles of Economics, pp. 744-745, quoted in Hymer, p. 137.

(7) Capital, quoted in Hymer, p. 137.

(8) Doubters should look at contemporary discussions of work in America by Braverman, Labor and Monopoly Capital, 1975, and Terkel, Working, as well as the descriptions of multinational corporations in Global Reach, by Barnett and Mueller, 1974.

(9) Gordon, "Capitalist Efficiency and Socialist Efficiency," 1976.

(10) See, for example, Hirschman's Strategy of Economic Development, 1958; and Williamson's "Regional Inequality and the Process of National Development." Also see the review by Goldsmith, "The War on Development," 1977.

(11) For the case of Peru see Wilson, "From Mode of Production to Spatial Formations: The Regional Consequences of Dependent Industrialization in Peru " (Ph.D. thesis, Cornell Department of City and Regional Planning, Ithaca, 1975); or "The Political Economy of Regional Development in Peru: 1968-1977," forthcoming.

(12) The situation was, of course, more complex. Political support for the junta came principally from the local business class. Among other things, this local bourgeoisie wanted to expand production and sales to include potential mass agricultural markets. But growth of this internal market would require still further commitment of resources, to rural infrastructure, in competition with the direct needs of the urban manufacturers themselves.

(13) For a review of literature on Western Europe, see Ole Therkildson, "Regional Development in Western Europe: A Study of the Locational

Behavior of Large Industrial Enterprises," October, 1976, (unpublished M.R.P. thesis, Cornell Department of City and Regional Planning).

(14) Westaway, "The Spatial Hierarchy of Business Organizations and its Implications for the British Urban System," 1974.

(15) Harnappe, "Spatial Aspects of Industrial Development in Western Europe: Economic and Political Areas," 1975.

(16) Peattie, The View from the Barrio, 1968.

(17) For details on the Mexican study, see various papers by Barkin, e.g., "A Case Study of the Beneficiaries of Regional Development," International Social Development Review, 1973, "Regional Development and Interregional Equity: A Mexican Case Study," 1975.

(18) Barkin, "Case Study of the Beneficiaries of Regional Development."

3 Regionalism and the Capitalist State*

Ann R. Markusen

Regionalism – the existence, consciousness, and significance of territorial differentiation – is a prominent feature of modern political life.

It arises from uneven economic, political, and cultural development of territories. Four theoretical questions concern the nature of uneven development. Is there a law of uneven development and what is its nature? What is the meaning of the concept "region"? What are the historical origins of regional structure? Finally, what is the nature of contemporary regional differentiation?

The basic argument arises from these theoretical concerns. While the boundaries of regions are inherited from past events in the political economy, the significance of contemporary regionalism derives more from the evolution of political power and structure. Capitalist production relations are spaceless, in essence, since the basic dynamic of capitalist expansion is to overcome regional barriers to exploit labor power wherever it resides. Furthermore, capitalism, because of its need for socialized wage labor and a mass market, destroys ethnic and cultural differences that attempt to impede capitalist penetration. However, these differences are the foundations of nation states and their subdivisions. Thus the political and legal inheritance of these original state structures, based on culture and ethnicity, conflict with the spaceless needs of the economy. Thus, while ubiquitous capitalist economic relations, culture, and ideology homogenize American society, state sector power is contested in order to preserve, create, or destroy regional differentiation.

*A previous version of this paper appeared in Working Papers on the Capitalist State, vol. 7, Winter 1979. I wish to thank members of the Bay Area Kapitalistate Collective, my students in the Regional Planning Seminar at Berkeley, John Mollenkopf, Steven Cohen, Susan Christopherson, James Greenfield, and William Goldsmith for their helpful comments.

The last parts of this chapter address the political questions raised by regionalism. Class interests and class coalitions may form to lobby the state for political favors to aid regional accumulation needs. Working class and other progressive groups may become involved in such coalitions, which may bring limited gains but obscure the long-run dynamics of the economic situation and the culpability of capital. The contradictions in contemporary regionalism allow us to identify situations that can be used regionally for political organizing.

THEORETICAL ISSUES

Capitalist Uneven Spatial Development

Uneven development was Marx's characterization of the process of capitalist expansion. Marx applied it primarily to the specialization of labor within industries, although his description of the antagonism between the city and the country echoes a spatial dimension.(1) Marx's emphasis was dynamic: it was the process of capitalist development that he characterized as uneven, not its outcomes. More recent Marxist social scientists – who unwittingly mimic the tendency within bourgeois social science to assign characteristics to places and things, rather than sticking to the dynamics of a process as the analytical focus – have incorrectly transferred this notion to the characterization of outcomes (i.e., "spatial unevenness").

Three types of uneven development have been most noted in recent Marxist literature: temporal, sectoral and spatial. Sectoral uneven development involves the uneven expansion of industries, some faster than others, with consequences for employment, profitability and interindustry links. Temporal uneven development refers to the short- and long-run cycles of capitalist expansion, where overproduction crises stunt expansion and create periods of unemployment, low profits and restructuring of the economy. Spatial uneven development refers to the uneven progress of capitalist social relations and sectors across territories. It has been used to characterize the relationship between city and country, and the more rapid development of certain regions than others. In all of these cases, the characterization of the process as uneven remains descriptive. In order to understand the causation in each case, Marxists have had to delve deeper into the structure and dynamics of capitalist social relations.

The spatial array of capitalist social relations has never received the attention that the sectoral and temporal dimensions have in Marxist theory, with the exception of still immature theories of imperialism. Many bourgeois and Marxist scholars alike, drawing on the apparent correlation of capitalist development with uneven spatial phenomena, have concluded that capitalist development necessarily requires or necessarily produces spatial unevenness. For instance, Walker writes "The kind of development operating throughout the United States today is not chiefly a consequence of barriers to capitalist transformation, development, and convergence, but of capital's own internal logic-working itself out in space."(2) Three positions on the inevitability of uneven regional development seem to emerge from Marxist work on uneven regional development.

1. Capitalism requires uneven spatial development as a condition of accumulation.

2. Capitalism produces systematically uneven spatial development, although it may not require it and may even suffer from its consequences.

3. Capitalism may produce, as well as eliminate, uneven regional development.

According to theoretical plausibility and empirical evidence, I would argue the third of these positions. First of all, there is nothing in the logic of capitalist accumulation that requires spatial differentiation. Capital, the motive force in the expansion of production, pursues the extraction and realization of surplus value, e.g., profits, through the organization of the production and distribution processes. As such, it is always in search of wage labor, the source of surplus value. As many of the accounts of imperialism assure us, precapitalist modes of production, including feudal agriculture and peasant subsistence farming, have provided impediments to capitalist expansion by withholding wage labor from the capitalist sector.(3) Such prior modes of production had their own class structure, cultures, and state formations, each of which provided elements of resistance to capitalist incursion. This line of reasoning suggests that it is not capitalism per se, but the environment that capitalism encounters on its expansion path that renders the process of expansion "uneven." Certain capitalists and corporations may be able to exploit conditions existing in any one region at a particular point in the process, but the system as a whole has no stake in ensuring uneven development. This interpretation of uneven development also permits convergence and reversals in the positions of different regions. (My argument here, and that of Brenner's as well, parallels Schumpeter's on imperialism: "Imperialism is thus atavistic in character. It falls into that large group of surviving features from earlier ages that play an important part in every concrete social situation. In other words, it is an element that stems from the living conditions, not of the present, but of the past – or put in terms of the economic interpretation of history, from past rather than present relations of production.")(4)

Secondly, the arguments about the necessity or systematic occurrence of uneven development operate at too aggregate a level. In order to understand why uneven development results in a particular region lagging behind others, we have to know the specifics of the particular region relative to other regions. Many features have retarded or accelerated capitalist expansion across different regions.(5) They include differences in the degree of militance of various classes in pursuing or fighting capitalist incursion; differences in ownership patterns of both land and the means of production; differences in the degree of competitiveness or oligopoly in industrial structure; differences in nature (existent but overplayed in the non-Marxist literature); and differences in the adjustment of various sectors to crises in the accumulation process. However, these various features are not peculiar to regional distinctions, since they also characterize neighborhoods, cities, and conflicts or differences within regions.

Finally, the empirical evidence on regional experience suggests that different regions' fortunes within capitalism rise and fall with the evolution of capitalist social relations and their expansion across the world. Most recently, the rapid growth of resource-rich (especially oil-rich) Third World nations belies the conventional wisdom that resource-based economies are necessarily on the losing end of uneven regional development. At the same time, the woes of the British economy and hard times in the European Economic Community suggest that nationally-based capitalist hegemony may not be permanent. And within nations, the rapid growth of previously laggard regions, such as the southern U.S., suggests that once precapitalist and sectoral barriers to incursion are removed, capitalist production will indeed move to areas where immature capitalist relation of production results in less militance, lower wages, and a less expansive welfare state. Thus generalizations about the systematic nature of uneven regional development are dangerous unless they are disaggregated to specify the precise set of forces operating in each case.

In this disaggregated analysis, the role of the state and political conflict becomes clearer and more significant. While economic specialization does create potential regional differences, it is the establishment and operation of State machinery along regional lines that gives regionalism both its framework and contemporary significance. Political economists give too little credit to both culture and politics as sources and perpetrators of regional differentiation. While I acknowledge the cultural forces at work, the focus of this paper is the significance of politics and State structure in the evolution of contemporary regionalism.

The Concept of "Region"

The concept of region has no precise, universal, analytic definition. In the U.S. planning curriculum it is sometimes defined as everything that is complementary to and superceding the "urban." In popular usage, region refers to everything from the metropolitan through the state and multistate levels, to Third World countries and continents. Castells, Feldman and others have recently begun to question the usefulness of the urban notion, correctly pointing out its ideological function as the reification of certain spatial consequences in the sphere of reproduction under capitalist economies and the prescriptive treatment of them, separate from capitalist dynamics and social relations.(6,7) Capital mobility undermines urban viability so that it becomes increasingly clear that urban problems cannot be dealt with in isolation from regional and interregional forces. The renewed U.S. controversy at the regional as opposed to urban level may be a direct consequence of imperialism and urban crises coming home to roost.

Abstractly, "region" is a conceptual category that connotes a physically definable and contiguous geographical area with some political status. Membership in a region may be multiple ("I am a Minneapolitan, a Minnesotan, an American"), but it is primarily determined by political status, not by class or cultural circumstance. Regional membership generally extends to all those who reside within the region. It does not distinguish residence from membership, although access to power may be very different across groups within the region and there may be strict controls via immigration on who may thus "join." Regions may have multiple cultures and economic activities within their boundaries. In a nation state with multiple levels of power, such as a federal system, regional groupings may arise from cultural affinity or common economic problems, but remain political aggregates (e.g., the Appalachian Regional Commission or the Western Governor's Policy Office) or political derivatives (federal regional councils).

The essence of state power is the monopoly of force in a territorial unit. Because of the changing nature of the capitalist economy and the existence of resistance to cultural and political oppression, many regional delineations are frequently under attack, through conflict over the political structure or control of the existing state apparatus (Northern Ireland, Cyprus, northern Michigan, Quebec). Thus, the form and content of regional divisions and groupings change over time as an indirect function of capitalist dynamics and a direct function of class, political and cultural struggles. But the target of such changes is always political structure and power. Therefore, we are justified in identifying the political as the primary determinant of regional divisions, even though at any given moment we may have to seek the roots of political conflict over regional boundaries in internal cultural and economic events. But no consistent relation between cultural and/or economic status can be found to empirically justify the primacy of either as the definer of region. I argue that a consistent relationship can be found between state boundaries, State power, and the content of regionalism. An operational definition of region therefore incorporates subdivisions and aggregates of existing political jurisdictions.

The Evolution of Regional Structure

Regional spatial structure coincides with political boundaries. The history of these political boundaries explains why contemporary nation states may have serious internal regional problems or threats to their territorial sovereignty from without. Original political boundaries were drawn as a result of conquest, unification, separation, or incorporation.

Each region has its own unique history, where its political structure can be traced to the dynamics of the dominant mode of production. This political structure now wields power that may no longer correspond to the underlying economic or cultural dynamics and may therefore be the subject of conflict.

For instance, in the colonial era, mercantilist capitalists enlisted the aid of their own nation states to break down barriers to capitalist expansion, through military, economic, and ideological means. Imperialism and its predecessor, colonialism, were thus propagated by an inextricable mixture of State and private institutions. In fact, the major protagonists were seen to be Spain, France, England, etc., not the primitive accumulators or industrial capitalists behind each. As part of world expansion, these nation-states replicated themselves by imposing nation-state political structure on the Third World. These political divisions remain as the primary regional identifiers today.

U.S. regional structure parts dramatically from the European tradition because its territory was resettled during the era of mercantilist capitalism, not feudalism, and its native population was exterminated rather than incorporated as under classical imperialism. Furthermore, its settlers came from many different cultures and political and economic experiences. Of all the advanced capitalist nations, it thus has the most youthful political structure, in the sense that its evolution was less constrained by previous indigenous social relations and cultural traditions than most other nations. Nevertheless, it has a political structure with a strong regional base and has had many regional conflicts, even one – the Civil War – that was a full-scale insurrection.

From the outset, U.S. political structure granted regional sharing of power within the nation. Its federal system derived from the different colonial political structures in the original thirteen states, each one a function of a different franchise or charter granted by a European power, and each possessing a different culture and economy.

As the new nation expanded across the continent, at first to facilitate primitive accumulation, later to aid exploitation of farmland, and still later to engender industrialization, several features determined the boundaries and size of new political units. At first, requirements of defense (from other European powers and from Native Americans) made rivers and mountains convenient boundary lines, regardless of the fact that a river frequently dissected a natural economic and cultural unit – the water basin. Second, the emerging dominant regional conflict between the slave based cash crop economy in the South and the wage labor manufacturing and commercial economy in the North required additional states to enter as slave/not slave pairs, resulting in smaller states than might otherwise have been carved out of existing territories. Third, the boundaries of many states were inherited from the older claims of European colonial states, which devolved in chunks on the American nation (the Northwest Territory, the Louisiana Purchase, Texas and California). Finally, the demands of new settlers for protection and control of resources were also granted in some cases, especially if contiguous territory was not already incorporated into another state.

East of the Mississippi, the dominance of the defense motive produced an array of states strongly outlined by rivers. The middle western and plains states were drawn on both river and "equal population" criteria. California's boundaries were drawn by several causes. Her northern and southern boundaries were inherited from previous colonial settlements; her mammoth size can be credited to her strongly organized internal politics (although a counterproposal could have made the five southern counties into a separate state); and her eastern boundary was charted by settler greed for the timber on the east slope of the Sierras and control of the lower portion of the Colorado River.

Both economic motives and cultural identities were thus important shapers of the original political units in the United States.(8)

Following the establishment of the fifty states, the political endowment of power in the lower tier of the federal structure began to reorganize regional affinities. Concomitant with the formation of states in the Western U.S., strong regional identities emerged on a state by state basis. Settlers, encouraged by provincial newspapers, took great pride in their states. In the West, regional identifications were dominated from the very beginning by a series of political events and institutions, not by a common cultural tradition. In the East, on the other hand, large-scale immigration and the transition from an agricultural to an industrial economy transcended the older cultural and economic character of the regions. Virtually every state by the mid-19th century had an ethnic mix in its population. Continual immigration and internal mobility prevented the equation of regional identity with cultural identity. The South was the exception. Here a system of production and an accompanying culture, both built on slavery, resulted in a regional identity that led to civil war.

Thus political structure in the U.S. historically derives from the dynamics of capitalist expansion confronting a precapitalist territory. A definitive history of U.S. regionalism would investigate the complex interplay of the economic, ethnic, cultural, and political events surrounding its evolution. In this section, I have traced only the placement and maintenance of the political boundaries that are the framework for regional identity. But formation of the specific regional boundaries is not of interest to us unless events within those regions lead to conflict. In the next section, I explore the content of contemporary regionalism which, I will also argue, is primarily shaped by the significance of the political realm.

Nevertheless, the importance of political boundaries and membership in a nation-state should not be belittled. The experiences of Hawaii and Puerto Rico, for instance, have been starkly different from other Pacific and West Indian territories, primarily due to their incorporation (in different forms) in the U.S. political structure. When ethnic identities or common economic ties are bisected by political boundaries, the possibilities for alliances may be impeded and the fortunes of those with common cause may vary dramatically across borders. The political strength of the Sioux is diluted by their dispersal over several states; auto workers win better concessions from the state government in

Michigan, where their numbers are largest; ranchers fighting coal stripping fare better in Montana than in neighboring states because of Montana's sympathetic political history.

The Nature of Contemporary U.S. Regional Differentiation

Past historians of U.S. sectionalism believed in its vitality. In a 1907 essay entitled "Is Sectionalism Dying Away?" Frederick Jackson Turner concluded that distance from markets, sectional distribution of crops and other economic activities, and the sectional distribution of ethnic stocks "will always tend to produce sectional diversities and conflicting interests in the vast area of complex geographical provinces which make up the U.S."(9) Similarly, Hesseltine claimed that "the divergent interests of sections have constituted the major problems of America's past and bid fair to be the major issues of the future."(10) His analysis emphasized the struggle for control within regions as well as the fundamentally different economic interests of each section. While both regional scholars acknowledged the increasing economic integration of U.S. regions and the clear movement toward national planning (11) each championed the hardiness and desirability of sectionalism.

Over the past hundred years, political structure and political power, rather than economic or cultural stakes, have increasingly become the causes and targets of regionalism. Increasing cultural and economic homogenization in the United States has broken down the old basis for regional rivalries. Previously, the division of state power between federal and state levels of government resulted in persistent sectional differences based on economic and cultural claims of each section of the national government.(12) For instance, the agrarian and non-industrial sections (Upper Midwest, Plains, and parts of the West) would fight in federal forums for concessions from the industrial Northeast. But the advance of capitalist industrialization has increasingly eliminated such geographic differences in mode of production or sectoral specialization. New regional rivalries appear to be much more an artifact of pure state power struggles than of true economic or cultural differences. Without charting in detail the 20th century diminution of economic and cultural roots, the following argument relies on a consideration of the current significance of these features across U.S. regions. By looking at particular regions and relationships within them, we can decipher the forces that give rise to the consciousness of regionalism and test the contention that political forces dominate.

The cultural roots

While some cultural pockets thrive, strong forces undermine cultural commonality as a regional phenomenon. First, the settlement patterns in the U.S. referred to above, and the continually high rates of migration by members of all classes and many ethnic groups, tend to break down the boundaries between culture and region. Some urban neighborhoods may remain culturally intact, but contemporary regional politics demand transcendence of particular ethnic affinities in order to forge alliances – whether they be corporatist regional policies or indigenous battles against federal domination. Regional cultural identity has eroded in recent decades. Whereas the Communist Party could, in the 1930s, propose a black nation in the cotton belt, today the case for a nationalist, regional potential of a people within the U.S. would be difficult to make.(13) (The single exception is the claim by Native Americans to western land. Yet the reality of the moment is that the Cheyenne must join forces with Montana ranchers to protect their adjacent lands from capital incursion.)

The commercialization of culture has also preempted people's self-determination of their own culture. In place of an indigenous tradition, plastic images of regional culture are packaged by television, novels, and the press. David Whisnant has documented the destruction of Appalachian mountain culture.(14) Economic development funds overseas have been used to encourage craft production, resulting in Taiwan-made replicas of Appalachian arts sold to tourists at highway stands. Likewise, the appropriation of hillbilly music by pop culture insults the indigenous tradition of Appalachian music. The degradation of their culture through such commercialization has destroyed Appalachian pride in it, making it a dying art. Similarly, superficial images of the California beachcomber, the Texas cowboy, and the northern lumberjack pick up on a tiny traditional truth and smear it on billboards, records, movie screens, and restaurant menus. In this way, people's experience with their culture tends to come through the media, not through daily contact with similar people. The overwhelming cultural characteristic of post-World War II America is the homogenization and commercialization of culture through television.

These observations suggest that there is no major cultural content to contemporary U.S. regionalism. While cultural and ethnic ties may be extremely important at the family and neighborhood levels, they have been largely eliminated on the regional level by capitalist mobility and cultural control.

A deep longing for an ethnic or cultural regional identity remains, as evidenced by the popularity of the synthetic, commercially-imposed images. The full understanding of this quest for local identity may be blocked in Marxist analysis by the overemphasis on the material relations of <u>production</u> at the expense of an analysis of the <u>reproduction</u> of labor power under capitalism – that is, the training and upbringing of workers. The community is the sphere of this reproduction, and the assertion of local pride may be a statement by women and children, in particular, of the importance of the reproductive mechanisms such as family, school, and church, and the issues of control over them.

The economic roots

As scholars applied the analysis of imperialism to Appalachia, the Great Lakes, Native American reservations, the South, and the Northeast, the uneven development of capitalism across regions has become evident.(15) Regions that are differentially occupied by capitalist accumulation are classified as "developed" and "underdeveloped," – an unsatisfactory delineation, since underdevelopment can arise from multiple sources. It can refer to incomplete incorporation into the mode of production of a particular people, the result of resistance by a prior mode or the blocking of full development of free wage labor. On the other hand, it can refer to particular features of capitalist dynamics in a fully integrated region, such as the exhaustion of a resource base, or the persistence of racism that prevents certain groups from freely entering the labor market or encourages them to migrate. A body of weak and incomplete analysis of regional economic development by Marxists has produced a legacy of confusing notions, such as the internal colony, core-periphery, dependency, and backwash effects.(16)

Capitalist development is impervious to the needs of people in any particular region and will seek out cheap labor whenever and wherever it is profitable. No region's fortunes under capitalism can be analyzed without an understanding of other regions; and no historical interpretation of empirical regularities of regional features is yet warranted. Regions may reverse their position (e.g., the South and the Northeast, cities versus rural areas) as favored locations for capitalist development. Economic forces are not reducible to regional boundaries or regional qualities.

However, there are two ways in which regional economic differentiation may still feed regionalism. Even though, over the long haul, each region faces the same capitalist dynamics, its experience at any particular time may be problematic and different from other regions. The significance of the law of uneven development is that it describes the experience of temporal (not spatial) aspects of capitalist development. After many years of stagnation one region may be characterized by rapid growth. But rapid growth or decline can be problematic; each is disruptive of existing productive and reproductive structures.

Thus despite ubiquitous incorporation of a region into the industrial and monopoly capitalist mode, the age of the regional capitalist economy and its rate of change may be a source of continued regional economic differentiation. People in such circumstances may view the experience of another region as the cause of their plight. For instance, people opposing rapid growth in the West, with its myriad boomtown problems, might blame the eastern demand for energy and argue that the Northeast should tighten its belt. People in the Northeast, experiencing the pains of job loss, might blame the South and the West for stealing jobs. These perceptions are not accurate since the culprit is capital, which knows no home. But upon such regional anxieties, as I argue below, a politically-inspired regionalism is imposed.

The second source of persistent regional economic differentiation is the immobility of certain sectors within regions whose fortunes are tied to that of the region. These may be of two types. First, even though manufacturing, construction, finance, and transportation have decentralized radically, some degree of sectoral specialization may still exist in certain regions. A current example is energy, which places mineral and fuel rich regions in a potentially antagonistic position as suppliers with respect to energy-consuming regions like the Midwest and Northeast. However, the need for energy makes strange bedfellows, with states such as Alaska, Louisiana, and New Jersey supplying off-shore oil to consumers from California to New England. Thus sectoral specialization as a basis for regionalism is somewhat unpredictable. The second type of local capitalist interest tied to regional futures are those industries whose assets are tied to regional land uses and population centers: banks, real estate, commercial interests, etc. – the constituency of the local chambers of commerce. Their stakes in regionalism have not changed perceptibly over the course of U.S. development. Prominent among these is the local press, which has a virtual monopoly over local regional consciousness and is supported by the chamber of commerce coalition, but whose economic asset (its circulation) is not mobile. This single fact may result in the prevalence of a regional consciousness even when the material conditions for regional differentiation have disappeared.

The political roots

In the U.S. the entire progress of capitalism has been shaped regionally by the not-so-invisible hand of the State. The consolidation of economic power in industrial, monopoly, and multinational corporations has been accompanied by a concomitant growth in national government power and domain. Radical historians have documented the employment of regulation, national government spending and federal land policy in the interests of the capitalist system as a whole, frequently overriding or eliminating more specialized capitalist interests whose behavior stood in the way of the smooth process of capitalist accumulation.(17)

Current regional actors know that the State's activity can vastly affect their region's development prospects. Past federal policies and structures that have affected regional differentiation can be conveniently grouped into five categories: regulatory and commercial policy, land policy, infrastructure and public investment, intergovernmental functional allocations, and explicit regional development policies. I have elsewhere rejected the current sunbelt-frostbelt rhetoric that accuses the federal government of aggregate unfairness, measurable in fiscal flows.(18) The reality is far more complex, and far more profound than fiscal flows analysis suggests.

Regulatory and commercial policy have profoundly affected regional growth rates, but in ways that are frequently hard to gauge conclusively. The Civil War was largely a regional battle over federal commercial policy toward two competing modes of production. The inability of the auto industry after World War II to secure tariff barriers to imports was a result of regional concentration of production (and therefore lack of congressional power). The congressional disinterest helped spur the industry to disperse auto production away from the Michigan axis, while imports made big inroads on U.S. markets, further harming regional growth. Natural gas regulation is purported to have shifted a great deal of industrial production to the South. Regulation of transportation rates (truck, railroad, and air) has shaped regional growth, principally through successive waves of decentralization. Oil quotas for years stimulated the growth of Texas, Oklahoma, and Los Angeles. Such regulatory policies never appear on fiscal flows tallies.

Land policy, including settlement policy, determined basic U.S. settlement and land ownership patterns in the nineteenth century. Particularly significant were the extensive lands given to the railroads, the engendering of petty bourgeois farming by homesteading arrangements, and the retention of vast amounts of forest and arid lands in the public domain. In more recent years, the disposal of these lands (and offshore shelves) through cheap leasing arrangements to energy companies, timber companies, and ranchers has undoubtedly stimulated the growth of coastal and western interior areas. The recent growth of western coal stripping at the expense of Appalachian expansion may be in large part a result of the advantages of cheap federal land in the West.

Infrastructure and public investment programs, especially the location and construction of military bases, have been incalculably important to regional growth rates. Military installations, especially through porkbarreling by southern Congressmen with electoral longevity, favored the South and Southwest. Army Corps of Engineers programs for improving waterways (e.g., Mississippi, St. Lawrence), and building dams for water and power have secured the income of North Dakota wheat farmers and western slope irrigators. Likewise, the construction of the interstate freeway system profoundly rearranged access networks in this country, stimulating a continuing decentralization of industrial production.

The intergovernmental allocation of responsibilities and resources, especially in the areas of tax, welfare, and labor policy, have allowed regional differentiation to flourish in ways that are functional for capital. A labor policy that has left questions like right-to-work, workman's compensation, and health and safety issues up to the states has permitted the more conservative dominated states to prevent unionization in the South and to undercut northern unions by attracting industry away from high wage areas. Similarly, tax and welfare policies left to the discretion of individual states have resulted in competition that tends to discourage high tax and welfare levels, with industrial relocation among the states the disciplining force. On the other hand, where competition among states would hurt capital (e.g., trade policy), banking policy functions are centralized at the federal level.(19) In this way federal decisions regarding the delegation of state power among levels of government have shaped regional growth.

Finally, there have been two sets of explicit regional policies implemented in this century. First, in the 1930s, the Tennessee Valley Authority, the Bonneville Power Administration, and sister proposals for other regional power and water development schemes aimed at stimulating regional economies through outright public construction and subsidy of a basic industrial cost. These explicit regional programs were legitimation devices to ward off radical transformation in regions with broad-based radical coalitions (e.g., communists and black sharecroppers in the South). They succeeded. The TVA was a mainspring of the regional migration of manufacturing activity to the South and capitalist incorporation of wage labor. Bonneville was the key to the aluminum industry's expansion in the Pacific Northwest (the bauxite was imported), which in turn permitted the development of an aircraft industry.

In the post-World War II era, territorially based policies gave way to regional planning that explicitly attempted to force integration of regions into the capitalist mainstream.(20) The postwar policy aimed at destroying isolated communities and existent regional networks by inducing regional migration to "growth poles" – cities organized around wage labor and full integration of the population into capitalist production and consumption structure. The most outstanding example is the Appalachian Regional Commission with its conscious intent to destroy the subsistence economy in the hollows, by encouraging people to migrate to Lexington and Cincinnati, by withdrawing health services and public schools from small locations, by emphasizing education and manpower training, and by encouraging capital to migrate into new growth pole cities.(21) Its major component was a new highway system designed to relocate people and jobs spatially, a project that was also a boon to capital accumulation through the traditional method of stimulating the construction sector. This has succeeded in its task of securing capitalist incorporation, though not in eliminating poverty.

Thus the past records show tremendous regional consequences from federal and state government policies. I have refrained from offering a comprehensive theory of causation or a definitive accounting because I believe that in large part the regional consequences were not the aim of the policy but incidental to the more pressing needs of U.S. capitalism: state underwriting of accumulation, state discipline of labor, state championing of petty bourgeois structure in agriculture, state defense policy, and state distribution of favors to particular industries. But the belated recognition of these regional consequences and of their persistence is a prime force in the ideology and reality of contemporary U.S. regionalism.

POLITICAL ISSUES

The Nature of the New Regionalism

What is the new regionalism? It is the emergence in the early 1970s in the media, in the lobbying world, in regional organizations, and in the state itself (especially Congress) of a strong regional identification and assertion of conflicting interests among such loosely delineated regions as the frostbelt, the sunbelt, the South, the Southwest, the Northeast, etc.(22) While the emergence was concurrent with academic "discoveries" of reversals in central city and regional demographic and economic trends (23) and with state and local government fiscal ills associated with disruption in development paths, the actual popular jargon seems to have begun with several press accounts, namely, Kirkpatrick Sale's Yankee/Cowboy hypothesis and the original National Journal article that announced "Federal Spending: The North's Loss is the Sunbelt's Gain."(24) (Not so ironically, given its charge of sunbelt robbery of the northeast, the latter article uses data from, and seems to have been inspired by, the Dreyfus Fund – New York all the way – study of fiscal flows. Can we conclude that regional capitalists were the inspiration from the beginning?) Subsequent to the press announcement of the "Second War Between the States," congressional caucuses on regional lines were formed and two governors groups emerged: the Conference of North Eastern Governors (CONEG) and the Western Governors' Energy Policy Office.(25) Numerous groups launched studies of regional shifts in economic activity and population, and attempts were made to document federal favoritism toward one region or another.(26)

The rhetoric, of course, obscured the primary culprit of regional hardship: capital mobility. While always an impetus to regional reorganization, capital mobility was particularly fierce in the early 1970s because of the conjunction of a recession and the energy crisis. The recession closed down older industrial plants, located primarily in the more easterly regions, and underscored the significance of state sector inducements such as the interstate freeway system and post-World War II military base locations. The energy crisis, the only stimulus to accumulation during the recessionary period, channeled investment into a sector highly dependent on certain resources, mostly located in the South (the Gulf Coast) and the West (interior gas, oil, coal). Furthermore, the high capital intensiveness of energy production (huge plants, pipelines) required a labor-intensive construction period, encouraging short-term jobs in these areas. During the recession the typical cyclical repression of labor through unemployment and downward pressure on wage rates, and through cutbacks in social services, hit hardest in the northeastern region and in central cities around the country. In response to high energy costs and labor militance, jobs continued to migrate out. (Not all of these jobs went to the South; many went to Taiwan, the Philippines, and Korea, and to rural areas within the originating region. But people who witness jobs leaving their yard only to appear next door are apt to perceive next door as the locus of the problem.)

From the point of view of capital as a whole, only the recession itself is a problem. The regional impacts, unless so severe that they affect the availability of other factors of production or regional markets – are of no consequence. In fact, neoclassical economists would argue that this is simply a hiatus of capitalist development, working toward an interregional equilibrium. The right of capital to pursue cheap labor wherever it exists, i.e., the right to mobility, is guaranteed by the state. (Despite the recommendation to Third World countries that they employ controls of all capital flows, the U.S. has never taken its own advice.)

Current U.S. economic structure produces different regional politics than the 19th-century constellation of eastern industry and commerce versus southern slave cash crops versus western agrarian politics. The hegemony of the capitalist mode of production and the mobility of capital have eliminated the 19th-century economic cleavages between regions. The predictions by Turner and Hesseltine that U.S. sectionalism would persist were based on an assumption of continued divergent economic interests of major proportions, where the dominant classes in each region were based in entirely different and competing economic bases.(27) Capitalist class interests have now become nationalized, even internationalized, so that the leadership of regional coalitions has devolved upon remaining locally tied economic groups such as the financial sector, and their government counterparts. But local financial capitalists, minus their industrial capital counterparts of an earlier era, are less strong as the core of a continued regional politics, so that they have made greater efforts to build cross-class coalitions.

Two sets of economic factors are still important in regional politics. The first set, arising from capitalist "age" and growth experience, produces a bewildering array of coalitions – rural versus urban, Northeast/Midwest versus South and West – that impede the establishment of contemporary "sections." Only the Northeast appears to be at all unified around the issues posed by rapid and persistent manufacturing decline, and even there several states have refused to join the common front.

The second set, the enterprises with regionally fixed assets, are replicated across regions. They engage in competition for resources and privileges from the federal government and their own state and local governments. This competition does not rise from regional differences but from substitutability: each set of bankers and rentiers wants development to take place within its domain. The relationship between the regionally tied business interests and the multinational corporations is not simple. The former may in fact be multinational in outlook – such as New York commercial banks – investing money capital internationally; nevertheless, large numbers of their deposits and fixed assets are dependent on the health of the local economy. They may thus be found in both types of lobbies (for freedom of capital movement and for maintenance of the regional economy). Such interests will oppose capital controls and propose federal impact aid or subsidies for the latter.

Unlike their multinational employers, workers are apt to perceive that they have a stake in regional development. While many are mobile (especially professionals, certain classes of workers such as construction, transportation, and farmworkers, and very poor people), frequently workers <u>want</u> to stay in a particular place for reasons of family, friendship, rearing children, home ownership, and what we might call affection for a particular environment. For workers, the costs of migration are much higher than for capital, so that while they may "choose" to move, given the options, it is not a pleasant prospect. When workers see neighbors and friends unemployed, defaulting on mortgage payments, or drinking heavily, they fear the same consequences for themselves. They become angry and search for the cause of their situation and a target for changing it. Similarly, workers and residents in boomtown communities fear the consequences of rapid growth – unless they benefit from it financially.(28)

Regional leadership – generally the press, state and local government, and the chamber of commerce – steps into this situation with the suggestion that the villains are elsewhere, that the federal government is in cahoots with those regions, and that citizens should join together to fight at the federal level for money to save jobs or to mitigate adverse boomtown effects. The same corporations that are constructing new plants in Taiwan must lobby to save their local plant real estate investments or smooth the way for their intrusion into new areas. Since they cannot direct their demands to capital because they are part of capital, and because they are engaging in precisely the same underlying behavior, they direct their demands at the state. Their hope is that state sector subsidies will slow down local deterioration or ameliorate disruptive boomtown growth so that their particular interests will be secured. The inclusion of labor in regional caucuses (only big labor – not ethnic or community groups) obscures the responsibility of capital mobility, diverts workers' attention from the plight of workers in other regions, and focuses political energy on the federal government, not on capital locating decisions.

Two recent examples of coalitions between progressive groups (unions, environmentalists, church groups, community organizations) and local capitalists reveal the nature of demands on the state that are likely to result from partnerships. In Youngstown, a coalition of local businesses, church groups, and the union has culminated in a lobby for the federal government to provide a capital grant to a worker/investor takeover of the plant as well as a long-term commitment to buy a fixed proportion of its steel procurements from the plant. In Massachusetts, the new state funded Community Development Finance Corporation, supported by a similar coalition, will provide equity capital for low-risk small and medium-sized businesses and community development corporations. Both of these efforts are fruits of regional coalitions; both involve capital subsidies and/or market guarantees; and neither changes the fundamental structure of ownership, production or market environment.

The survival of such coalitions and capital-subsidizing strategies will depend on their ability to produce results, preserve jobs, and stave off regional decline. (The British experience would suggest that such strategies do not work in the long run.) Progressive groups will only remain in such coalitions if they perceive real results. Such results are apt to depend on the level of subsidy, which in turn is constrained by the reticence of national capital to permit the federal government to use revenues unproductively for the benefit of a few local business interests. The failure of the Carter administration to convince Congress to add a 5 percent targeting to high unemployment areas onto the Investment Tax Credit extension suggests that resources for regional bailouts will not be substantial. Thus, regional coalitions may not become powerful, except in cases with very unusual circumstances. Indeed, the Northeast/Midwest coalition may find greatest unity, not in pursuit of its own development, but in opposing federal pro-Western energy development policies.

The fact that the new regionalism is directing its demands toward the state is not surprising given the state's history of regional differentiation. Regional lobbies are the logical outcome of the growth in state expenditure and power, to the point where hardly any sphere of economic activity is free from state influence. In addition to the sheer size of the federal government, two other features of U.S. political structure are important in explaining the new regionalism.

First, regionalism is facilitated by spatial political representation, an ingenious synthetic device of the liberal state in the U.S. democracy. Unlike the first nation-states under capitalism such as England and France, where representation was strictly allotted by class (the House of Lords, the French Estates), U.S. political representation is distributed by place. (The initial representation system was also classist, since it required property ownership, but the peculiar exigencies of colonial revolt required a geographical representation system that has become a powerful framework for democratic ideology.) People identify with government primarily on the basis of where they vote, e.g., as a Coloradan from the 7th District. On election night, filtered through the media, people watch how their city, county, and state voted, rather than how their class or ethnic group voted. The political identification of citizens is individualist; one is a voter, not a Tory or a Socialist or a Communist. One may also be a Democrat or Republican, but this identity is given form almost entirely by the press, television, and the primary election ballot, not by any real organization experience. The Democratic Party may have some vague connotation of class, but its nonclass character dominates.(29)

Second, in the 1960s, demands on the federal government often originated directly from local ethnic or class groups, such as welfare rights organizations, blacks, and poor people, and were responded to by programs like Model Cities and OEO. The Nixon regime replaced these programs with his "new federalism," which strengthened local and state government through revenue sharing and dismantled class and ethnic programs, ostensibly under the rubric of "decentralization." The new federalism makes more explicit the extent of federal government fiscal control over state and local governments (now as high as 40 percent), and sets up a formal competition among levels of government and regions for a share of the federal pie.

It is apparent, then, that the new regionalism is not new but is only a more intense and explicit manifestation of a process that has accompanied the growth of the capitalist state since its inception. This leads me to hypothesize that the vociferousness of the regional charges and the strength of the claims of "newness" are ideological and serve to obscure capital's role and undermine worker solidarity across regions. It is this latter feature that is perhaps its greatest strength for capitalism as a whole. In an era when large-scale immigration is not a primary source of capitalist expansion of production, and ethnic and gender divisions are increasingly under attack, capitalism can exploit regionalism as a means of promoting a new division of the working class under the guise of "placism." Given the virtual disappearance of strong ethnic or experiential differences among working populations in various regions, such exploitation is a credit to the ingenuity of capital. Could it be that capital is superimposing a new regional image and affinity on regional members, packaged in a way that it can easily be discarded by leavers or adopted by newcomers? (Colorado is full of eastern-born cowboys whose "saddle" alternates between a truck and a bar stool.)

The Prospects for the New Regionalism

No social phenomenon of major import is without its contradictions. The new regionalism, which I have presented in its least attractive garb, does speak to people's concerns, even while it diverts attention from the fundamental causes. And, even if the concept is a reified one, the region is where many people feel they can organize and affect change. Therefore, progressive impulses and organizations have also evolved on a regional level, sometimes competing for control of the regional political apparatus, sometimes building alliances across regions to destroy the divisive quality of the new regionalism.

Suppose, for example, that the new regionalism encounters no resistance. Then, in twenty years or so, we will be able to look back on it as a powerful device for bailing out capitalism yet one more time. The new regionalism has multiple advantages for capitalism. On the one hand, it rationalizes the spatial structure of capital deployment at a time when its movement is becoming problematic. Whether this takes the form of impact aid for capital at both ends of the migration process (aid to distressed cities and aid to boomtowns), or the form of regulation of capital movement through locational incentives, it will smooth out the worst effects of mobile capital through restraint or subsidy. (The choice of a direction – subsidy versus regulation – will depend on the relative lobbying strength of industries and regions compared to the constraints on spending by the state.) The result will be consistent with the needs of capitalist accumulation and mobility, either in a partnership in which the federal government stimulates the economy and investment through more infrastructure, or by further tax rebates and concessions that encourage new investment in older areas. Thus a by-product is the use of regional trauma to guarantee a new wave of capitalist accumulation. And as we noted above, such policies will serve <u>regional</u> capital by bolstering the profitability of immobile plants.

Meanwhile, the ideology of regionalism will have served well in disuniting the working class across regions, with workers in declining regions arguing for aid to cities, national development banks, etc., and workers in booming areas arguing for impact aid for themselves and their children. Each will see the demands of the other group as antagonistic to their ends, since the regional debate will focus on who gets what rather than how big the pie is for all. Each group of workers will feel compelled to participate with regional capital in lobbying the federal government. And each may also begrudgingly participate in disciplining their own ranks, since this will be represented as the only way to attract capital and stem further job out-migration. At the state and local level, they will also be compelled to permit public service cutbacks at the same time business tax rebates are extended, and to employ questionable tactics such as Pennsylvania's $50 million subsidy to Volkswagen to locate an assembly plant within its borders.

Admittedly, this scenario is exaggerated. There is no reason to think that working people would, in fact, put up with such manipulation. Furthermore, various manifestations of opposition to the new regionalism have already developed, as I will detail below.

First, there is the commitment of some unions, such as the UAW and the textile workers, to organize those areas of the country currently unorganized and to join with local workers to defeat state right-to-work laws. In the West as well, the United Mine Workers have organized the Navajos and are trying to organize strip miners in the more northern states. This may herald a reversal in the decades-long lack of interest on the part of organized labor to organize the unorganized.

Second, western coalitions of ranchers, environmentalists, Native Americans and workers have formed to fight unrestricted energy development. The most sophisticated is the Northern Plans Resources Council in Montana, which is fighting to maintain the Montana severance tax, to protect and extend the state's progressive industrial siting authority, to oppose local control by the Bonneville Poser Administration, and to control strip mining and air pollution. The council has also stopped construction on the two new units of the Colstrip coal-fired electricity plant.

The Northern Plains Resources Council has spawned several sister groups in Wyoming, North Dakota, and Colorado, and is working closely with the Northern Cheyenne Resource Council. It hopes to unite many groups in the Pacific Northwest to stop or control massive incursions of capital associated with energy extraction, production, and the feared consequent industrialization. It has also contacted groups in Appalachia, including the mine workers, about common interests at the national level regarding coal development and strip mining.

Third, environmental groups concerned with ecological damage, community health and, increasingly, workers' jobs and health, are succeeding in slowing down new capital developments, especially in the energy sphere. New groups are appearing, such as the Appalachian Alliance, a new community and union-oriented umbrella organization to raise issues of development in Appalachia, and the National Citizen Labor Energy Coalition, a group dedicated to forging a strong alliance across those interests. Local- and state-level groups concerned with economic development have demanded controls on capital mobility and have designed their own alternative institutions. The Ohio Public

Interest Campaign, for instance, has proposed a law calling for charging out-migrating capital the costs of its exit and requiring notice of intent to leave. Environmental impact statements are a form of control over capital mobility, as are western states' siting authorities. Alternative institutions such as co-ops, publicly owned and worker owned businesses, community development corporations, and state banks exist, succeed, and challenge the inevitability of capitalist economic structure. These constituent organizations are supported by funds and analysis from various small foundations, technical assistance groups, academics, and the Conference on Alternative State and Local Public Policies.

If such groups succeed, the following, more optimistic prognosis can be sketched. The new regional capital-dominated coalitions will find themselves thwarted by only partial cooperation from labor and other community groups. Such groups will have stronger ties to their kin in other regions and be unwilling to participate in disciplining their own ranks or going along with capital-inspired schemes such as the national development bank. Instead, interregional labor cooperation will succeed in unionizing across regions, preventing wage rate erosion, and standardizing welfare treatment. Interregional environmental and economic development groups will combine arguments about the physical and economic damage of capital mobility and press for severe controls on mobility. Interregional groups will continue to make inroads on the private sector by using public funds and people's labor power to build public and cooperative institutions that form an alternative and a move in the direction of socialism. If private capital becomes less profitable, because it is held responsible for its regional damage, smaller scale, decentralized and locally controlled production will become increasingly possible. Changes in the economic base will be accompanied by changes in the political base and will reintroduce real democracy into the political sphere.

Of course the forces of reaction are strong. The most serious threat to this second scenario is imperialism. Thus a progressive interregional strategy is only a part of an international strategy. In addition, the possibility of repressive deployment of the state to protect the interests of capital against strong interregional coalitions of workers and community interests is also a possibility. At that point, we would be talking revolution or fascism.

However the future cannot be predicted, only created. I have surveyed the elements of the emerging new regionalism in the U.S. by specifying its cultural, economic, and political content. Economic realities will outline the possibilities, but political struggle will determine the outcome.

NOTES

(1) Collective for the Special Regional Issue, "Uneven Regional Development: An Introduction," 1978.

(2) Walker, "Two Sources of Uneven Development," 1978.

(3) Brenner, "The Origins of Capitalist Development," 1977.

(4) Schumpeter, Imperialism and Social Classes, 1955, p. 65.

(5) Collective for the Special Regional Issue, "Uneven Regional Development: an Introduction," 1978.

(6) Castells, The Urban Question, 1977.

(7) Feldmann, "Manuel Castells' The Urban Question," 1978.

(8) A detailed documentation of this political shaping and the subsequent sectionalism that focused on the federal political structure is presented in Turner, 1932, especially Chapters II, XI, and XII.

(9) Turner, The Significance of the Section in American History, 1973.

(10) Hesseltine, "Regions, Classes and Sections in American History," 1944, p. 35.

(11) Hesseltine, "Regions, Classes and Sections in American History," p. 43; Turner, Significance of the Section in American History, p. 311.

(12) Turner, Significance of the Section in American History, pp. 327-328.

(13) Allen, "Racism and the Black Nation Thesis," 1976.

(14) David Whisnant, Talk on the State and the Arts.

(15) See URPE, 1978; Simon, "The Labor Process and Uneven Development," 1978; Markusen, "Regional Political Economy," forthcoming.

(16) Collective for the Special Regional Issue, "Uneven Regional Development: An Introduction," 1978.

(17) Kolko, The Triumph of Conservatism, 1964; Boyer, "National Land Policy," forthcoming.

(18) Markusen and Fastrup, "The Regional War for Federal Aid," 1978.

(19) Friedland, et al., "Political Structure Conflict, Urban Structure and the Fiscal Crisis," 1978.

(20) Friedmann and Weaver, Territory and Function, 1978.

(21) Burlage, "ARC's First Six-Year Plan," 1970.

(22) Markusen and Fastrup, "Regional War for Federal Aid," 1978.

(23) Sternlieb and Hughes, "New Regional and Metropolitan Realities of America," 1977; Weinstein, Regional Growth and Decline in the U.S., 1978.

(24) Sale, "The World Behind Watergate," 1973; Havemann, et al., "Federal Spending," 1976.

(25) Business Week, "The Second War Between the States," May 17, 1976.

(26) Rafuse, "The New Regional Debate," 1977.

(27) Turner, 1932; Hesseltine, 1944.

(28) Markusen, "Class, Rent, and the State," 1978.

(29) Bay Area Kapitalistate Collective, 1977.

4 The Origins and Legacy of Urban Renewal*

Marc A. Weiss

"I just hope that we'll be very careful that you don't use the words 'urban renewal' too often. That has a bad connotation." This was Senator Hubert Humphrey's response in the summer of 1977, to a suggestion that the federal urban renewal program, which had terminated at the end of 1974, should be revived.(1) A decade of riots and protest in ghetto communities, much of it aimed at the unpopular "negro removal" program, had the former vice-president and his colleagues on the defensive. And with good reason. Urban renewal agencies in many cities demolished whole communities inhabited by low income people in order to provide land for the private development of office buildings, sports arenas, hotels, trade centers, and high income luxury dwellings.

The National Commission on Urban Problems, appointed by President Johnson in response to urban disorder and headed by former Senator Paul Douglas, documented the negative impacts of urban renewal on low income neighborhoods. As of June 30, 1967, approximately 400,000 residential units had been demolished in urban renewal areas, while only 10,760 low-rent public housing units had been built on these sites.(2)

*Special thanks to Ann Markusen and Roger Montgomery for extensive, enthusiastic assistance in the research and writing of this paper. Thanks also to Martin Gellen; Michael Teitz; T.J. Kent, Jr.; G. William Domhoff; John Mollenkopf; Amy Glasmeier; Seymour Adler; Madeline Landau; Richard Walker; Peter Marcuse; and the Institute of Urban and Regional Development, University of California, Berkeley, for ideas, assistance, and encouragement. Part of this research was undertaken with financial assistance from Judith de Neufville, and I thank her both for this and for her helpful criticism.

The Douglas Commission argued, however, that the unhappy consequences of urban renewal for low and moderate income city residents were not what Congress had in mind when it created the federal program in 1949. Since the policy goal of the 1949 Housing Act was "a decent home and a suitable living environment for every American family," the Douglas Commission concluded that the urban renewal program was a "failure" because "too many local and Federal officials in it and too many of their allies and supporters either did not understand its major purposes or did not take them seriously."(3)

Given that the 1949 Housing Act was the product of a Democratic president and a Democratic Congress, it is not surprising that the Democratic oriented Douglas Commission should wish to shift the blame elsewhere. During the past 30 years many people have propounded or accepted the view that urban renewal was "a slum clearance program with the avowed purpose of improving living conditions for slum residents," and thus that the program had failed.(4) Nothing could be further from the truth. The fact is that if one traces the history of Title I of the 1949 Housing Act back to its origins in the early 1930s there is a remarkable continuity between the vision of the program's original proponents and the ultimate results.

Urban renewal owes its origins to the downtown merchants, banks, large corporations, newspaper publishers, realtors, and other institutions with substantial business and property interests in the central part of the city. Through the Central Business District Council of the Urban Land Institute and local chambers of commerce, these influential groups and individuals refined, packaged, and sold their proposal. The state and local laws passed in the 1940s and 50s and the federal law passed in 1949 fulfilled the goal that this powerful coalition had set for itself. Most of the actual renewal projects were based directly on plans and priorities that had been thought out many years earlier.

From the beginning city planners were urban renewal allies with downtown businessmen. While their aims for the city were somewhat different, they discovered that their relationship was mutually beneficial and it prospered accordingly. Urban renewal has been an important reason for the growth of the city planning profession, so it is only fitting that city planners today are confronting the many problems left in its wake.

Public housers are a different story altogether. Initially they were on opposite sides of the barricades from the central business district boosters. The key backers of replanning and redevelopment were the staunchest foes of public housing. The housers resented the persistent attacks they received from what they called "the reactionary lobby," but by the mid-1940s the public housers began to view urban renewal as the silver lining to their political cloud. Slums could not be cleared without adequate relocation housing, they reasoned, and in a time of severe shortages public housing would be needed for lower income people. Fortified by this logic, they energetically supported urban renewal and helped lobby it through Congress and state and local legislative bodies. But when it came time for the public housers to claim their reward for "good behavior," the central district businessmen were still firmly in command. The more progressive minded housers were completely shut out of the shaping and operation of urban renewal. They were condemned to watch from the sidelines, their active role confined to writing critical reports.

Poor people and minorities learned that they could not count on the paternalism of the public housers to save them from the bulldozers. Eventually they rioted, organized, and won some rights and benefits that contributed to urban renewal's formal demise in the mid-1970s (only to be reincarnated as Community Development Block Grants and Urban Development Action Grants).

It is hoped that planner/houser-activists of the current generation have learned a lesson from this modern tragedy: if a program has serious conceptual problems, it may be better to oppose it altogether instead of reluctantly supporting it and hoping it will magically transform itself "sometime in the future." At the very least, adopting this opposition strategy gives one the satisfaction of being able to say "I told you so," when failure results. At most, it helps lay the essential groundwork for building powerful coalitions and mass movements that can achieve long-term progressive structural change.

MYTH #1. URBAN RENEWAL WAS DESIGNED TO HELP SLUM RESIDENTS

The Genesis of "District Replanning"

Urban renewal was discussed seriously as a public issue in the early 1930s after the collapse of the urban real estate boom of the 1920s and the onset of the Great Depression. At that time urban renewal, then termed "district replanning," was heralded as the solution to the problem of "blight." A blighted area was not necessarily the same thing as a slum. A "slum" was a social concept; low income people living in generally crowded, unsanitary, and crime-ridden conditions.

Blight, on the other hand, was an economic concept. Basically it meant declining property values. In the 1920s and 30s, the market for developed land in the inner city was shrinking due to the movement of middle income people and industry to peripheral areas.(5) Downtown property owners, including major financial institutions such as banks and insurance companies, industrial corporations with downtown office headquarters, commercial land developers, hotel owners, department store and retail store owners, newspaper publishers, major realtors and realty management companies, and trustees of private hospitals and universities feared that property values would plummet and their businesses would suffer.

This coalition of powerful interests turned to the government for assistance. They wanted to initiate large-scale efforts to replan and rebuild the blighted areas bordering the central business district for profitable commercial use and high-income residential developments surrounded by parks, good transportation access, and attractive public facilities.

District replanning was first spelled out in detail at President Hoover's Conference on Home Building and Home Ownership in 1932. Interestingly enough, the coalition behind district replanning did not include the construction industry.

The Committee on Blighted Areas and Slums defined a blighted area as an "economic liability to the community" and a slum as a "social liability."(6) It also noted that due to extremely high densities slums are often economically profitable and therefore not technically blighted, but argued that slums should be cleared anyway because "they are not infrequently found to exist on highly accessible, and thus potentially very valuable, urban land."(7) Since, in the midst of the Depression, committee members assumed that business could not extend across all blighted areas, they argued that slum clearance "contemplates the use of former slum sites for the housing of higher income groups."(8) This would be accomplished principally through wholesale demolition of the existing structures, followed by large-scale rebuilding operations.

To accomplish such rebuilding, sizable tracts of land had to be assembled within a reasonable amount of time and at a price that would make the subsequent development profitable. Here there were a number of obstacles. Most developers simply did not have the capital necessary for such large-scale operations. The major banks and insurance companies had the capital, but the land developers they financed found it extremely difficult to assemble complete land parcels that would span an area large enough to cordon off the new development from undesirable slum dwellers and from noisy and unsightly commercial and industrial land uses. Two principal problems faced the would-be large-scale operator: 1) the asking price for the land was often more than they wished to pay; 2) they occasionally faced "holdouts," where, for one reason or another, they could not obtain a particular parcel at all. Their solution was for local governments to use eminent domain powers to acquire land and then resell it to private corporations at a discounted price, with accompanying tax abatements.

The first part of this solution, the use of eminent domain, had already been tried in New York City. In the late 1920s a group of area banks promoted a district replanning scheme for Manhattan's Lower East Side.(9) The city used a provision of the state constitution permitting it to take land for public works projects and sell or lease the excess to private developers.(10) The land was taken, the tenants evicted, and the buildings razed. But the effort collapsed because the city was forced by the court condemnation proceedings to pay such high prices for the slum property that "the private builders who had previously expressed interest now expressed only dismay."(11) The area was later turned into a park. From this experience downtown corporate institutions resolved to fight not only for the public sector to use its legal powers to help replan the district, but to use its taxing powers to pay for a substantial portion of the costs.

As to the legality of the district replanning approach, the Committee on Blighted Areas and Slums took the position that "the elimination of slums is a public purpose."(12) It conceded that local governments could also eliminate slums by strictly enforcing housing codes and demolishing slum dwellings as fire or health hazards, but committee members disliked this method because "the land remains in the hands of the original owners."(13) They preferred district replanning, since government would transfer land ownership to new large-scale developers.

While elimination of slums was the public purpose of district replanning, the committee members did not seem concerned that once slum dwellers were cleared from the "potentially very valuable land" they would continue to live in slum housing somewhere else. The President's Conference final report emphatically opposed providing any public assistance or requiring rebuilders to provide private assistance to slum dwellers displaced by district replanning:

> We do not concur in the argument that the slums must be allowed to exist because there are persons dwelling in them who could not afford to dwell in better surroundings. It is our view that the slums must, nevertheless, be removed for the benefit of the community. We are confident that a large portion of the group displaced by slum clearance will be able to find suitable accommodations elsewhere.(14)

Another vital element in the district replanning scheme, was that private enterprise must be provided with "the benefits of up-to-date city planning."(15) In other words, in order for the property values and development opportunities to be upgraded, the local government was expected to pay for the supporting infrastructure that would accompany private rebuilding. This would include new street systems and transportation facilities, schools, parks, playgrounds, public buildings, and utilities such as water and sewer lines. Equally important, the downtown landowners insisted that the local government use its regulatory powers and city planning apparatus to guarantee that undesirable land uses be kept out of the district through zoning ordinances, density and lot coverage restrictions, and building and housing codes, all tied together by a master plan for the area. Thus the public sector was being called upon to protect and enhance the value of the current and future investments of the large-scale rebuilders and their downtown allies. This use of government to rationalize and stabilize corporate expansion, generally on behalf of the larger economic interests at the expense of smaller ones, was already well established by the Progressive Era, of which "up-to-date city planning" was a part.(16)

By 1932 the basic plan for what was later called urban renewal was already clearly spelled out. Very little changed over the years except that the federal government ended up playing a much larger role than anticipated in the early 1930s. In fact, the federal government eventually picked up the tab for two-thirds, three-fourths, or more of the costs to local government of land acquisition, clearance, site preparation, improvements, and city planning. The heavy federal subsidies solved the problem of high land costs by allowing the local government to resell the land to private developers at a considerable discount. This enabled local governments to resuscitate the moribund urban land market by moving in and purchasing large chunks of land for renewal purposes, without passing on the considerable costs to the large-scale rebuilders. The downtown property lobby did not propose this federal solution in 1932 because they did not think that such massive federal expenditures were feasible. The New Deal, of course, changed their perceptions of the political potential of the U.S. Treasury.

The Selling of District Replanning

Planners' efforts to popularize the concept and refine the principles of district replanning in the 1930s, were backed up by the more powerful lobbying efforts of the big urban realtors. This effort was led by the National Association of Real Estate Boards (NAREB).(17) In 1935 NAREB's executive secretary, Herbert U. Nelson, unveiled a plan for neighborhood protection and improvement districts that would enable 75 percent of the property owners in a district to form a public corporation which, if approved by the city council, could condemn land and levy taxes within its district in order to facilitate "improvement."(18) Such an arrangement certainly accorded with Mr. Nelson's own philosophy, as outlined in the letter to the president of NAREB in 1949:

> I do not believe in democracy. I think it stinks. I believe in a republic operated by elected representatives who are permitted to do the job, as the board of directors should. I don't think anybody but direct taxpayers should be allowed to vote. I don't believe women should be allowed to vote at all. Ever since they started our public affairs have been in a worse mess than ever.(19)

The Neighborhood Improvement plan made limited headway in a few state legislatures, and the following year Nelson began to expand NAREB's efforts by setting up the Urban Land Institute (ULI) as a research arm of NAREB. During the next few years NAREB, their colleagues in the United States Savings and Loan League (USSLL), the U.S. Chamber of Commerce, and other builder and business groups, along with their allies in the Federal Housing Administration (FHA), were preoccupied with the battle against public housing. Only after they had successfully blocked any further public housing appropriations in Congress in 1939 did they turn their attention back to district replanning.

In 1940 the Urban Land Institute, reconstituted as "an independent agency for research and education in the field of real estate" and an "advisory service to aid cities in replanning and rebuilding,"(20) and with a Board of Trustees including Herbert U. Nelson and leaders of a number of large corporations, undertook as its first major project a nation-wide study of the problem of decentralization.(21) During the next two years the ULI published studies on Boston, Cincinnati, Detroit, Louisville, Milwaukee, New York City, and Philadelphia, each one recommending some plan whereby the city could condemn land in the blighted areas near the central business district and then sell or lease the land to private developers for replanning and rebuilding.(22) In a major ULI board meeting in January of 1942 the ULI adopted a postwar replanning program.(23) The plan, not too different from what was adopted by Congress seven years later, called for local redevelopment commissions (created under state enabling legislation) to use federal funds to acquire land in blighted areas and then sell or lease the land to private businesses for redevelopment. It also recommended that the federal government provide grants to local planning agencies "for the purpose of preparing master plans for metropolitan areas and replanning blighted areas," a proposal not enacted until 1954. Having promulgated the plan, the ULI, NAREB, and allied parties began a concerted effort to win passage of the program at the federal, state, and local levels.(24)

ULI's model for the proposed federal urban land agency was the FHA. NAREB had been one of the FHA's biggest boosters since its inception in 1934.(25) Its members appreciated the close and mutually supportive relationship between FHA officials and private realtors, lenders, and builders. The FHA field directors, in particular, were extremely close to private sector groups. FHA personnel came mostly from building, lending, and realty businesses.(26) Thus it is not surprising that the FHA produced its own report in 1941, _A Handbook on Urban Redevelopment for Cities in the United States_,(27) or that three years later Sewart Mott who, as Director of the FHA Land Planning Division, had been involved in the preparation of the 1941 _Handbook_, became the Director of the ULI.

By 1943 the ULI had prepared federal legislation for a neighborhood development act sponsored by Senator Robert Wagner of New York. The planners prepared their own bill, the Federal Urban Redevelopment Act, which was introduced by Senator Elbert Thomas of Utah. This bill was the communal brainchild of Alvin Hansen, a New Deal economist then working for the Federal Reserve Board, Alfred Bettman, one of the leading planning and zoning attorneys in the U.S., and Guy Greer, an editor of _Fortune_ magazine. The Hansen-Bettman-Greer proposal grew out of discussions within the National Resources Planning Board, the American Institute of Planners and The National Planning Association.(28) The planners, as Catherine Bauer later recalled, "saw redevelopment as the means toward more rational and efficient organization of central areas, by removing wasteful or inappropriate land uses and facilitating new development in conformance with some kind of plan for the area."(29)

Planners' enthusiasm for large-scale redevelopment envisioned greater public sector powers over future land use. This was the principal difference between the two bills. Under the Thomas bill the local redevelopment agency could only lease the land to private developers, retaining title and therefore control in the agency's hands. Also, the federal subsidy would be in the form of long-term, low-interest loans and annual contributions to help amortize the redevelopment agency debt (similar to the federal public housing program). The annual contributions would give the federal government some continuing control over the redevelopment process. The ULI opposed the leasing only provision and the annual contributions. They wanted the local government to be able to sell the land to private developers. They also wanted the federal government to make large one-time capital grants to the local redevelopment agency and then keep its nose out of the whole business. In Title I of the 1949 Housing Act, ULI beat the planners on both points.

Winning at the State and Local Level

The Wagner and Thomas bills were essentially shelved by Congress until after World War II. ULI, impatient to get on with the job of urban redevelopment, began to focus more of its efforts on state government. Corporate leaders in the various downtowns across the country started hiring planners to draw up plans for postwar redevelopment. Fearful that federal redevelopment efforts might be linked to a revived public housing program after the war, ULI and its lobbying partners decided to exert more leverage on state and local governments as a way of bypassing federal control. They reasoned that if their own program was already firmly in place at the state and local level, it would be easier to exert pressure on Congress, the president, and the federal bureaucracy for ULI-preferred solutions.

When Seward Mott became director of ULI in 1944 he immediately began lobbying aggressively in state legislatures for the ULI redevelopment program. (In 1946 ULI created a special Central Business District Council to work with local business groups promoting urban redevelopment legislation.)(30) This program was spelled out in a document entitled "Principles to be Incorporated in State Redevelopment Enabling Acts,"(31) which grouped the various state laws and bills into three categories: Type 1, which ten states had already passed, Type 2, which had been passed by the Arkansas and Tennessee legislatures, and Type 3, favored by the ULI. Under Type 1, either the private corporation or the municipality assembles the land under eminent domain powers and then the corporation clears the site and redevelops it. ULI disliked these laws because they generally did not allow for reuses other than for housing, and they were not sufficiently comprehensive in their approach to large-scale planning and coordination of transportation and public facilities with the redevelopment project. What ULI liked was the fact that a Type 1 redevelopment corporation law "provides an excellent channel for the investment in housing of the huge sums in the coffers of the insurance companies and similar large financial institutions."(32) The Principles concluded that "This legislation has been fairly easy to pass and is considered by many an opening wedge toward the further consideration of the whole problem."(33)

Type 2 included laws that "make the public housing authority the redevelopment agency. They usually require the rehousing of displaced tenants, and greatly broaden the power of the public housing authority." ULI was unalterably opposed to this approach because: 1) the emphasis was on housing for low-income tenants rather than "for the benefit of the city as a whole"; 2) placing redevelopment in the hands of the public housing authority "would tend to discourage the participation of private enterprise"; 3) a greater role should be given to the local planning commission; and 4) redevelopment "should not be under the control of any special interest" such as public housing officials – rather it should be in the hands of civic leaders and private enterprise redevelopers.(34)

ULI's preferred redevelopment legislation (Type 3) was eventually adopted by the majority of the states, many of them before 1949. Type 3 laws authorized the creation of a local urban redevelopment agency, "a department of the local government composed of representative citizens,"(35) completely separate from the public housing authority, and under local, not federal control. The reuse of the cleared land in the blighted area could be for any purpose "in accordance with a comprehensive plan and with the objective of securing the highest and best use of the area."(36) This meant profitable development of any variety, not necessarily residential.

Two principles that ULI held dear were that "there should be no restrictions on the profits or dividends derived from private redevelopment projects," and "the redevelopment agency should not be required to provide for the rehousing of displaced tenants."(37) The first of these was generally accepted by state legislatures and the federal government. The second principle was violated by the federal statute, which placed a moral if not a financial responsibility on the local redevelopment agency for relocation. As the subsequent history of the program demonstrated, however, federal, state, and local officials honored this requirement more in the breach than in the observance.(38)

That ULI should have typified Type 1 as a law benefiting large insurance companies grew directly out of an experience in New York. The state of New York had passed an Urban Redevelopment Corporation Law in 1941, but no redevelopment took place until 1943, when the Metropolitan Life Insurance Company forced the legislature to change the law by removing restrictions on profits and dividends as well as removing any responsibility on the part of the redeveloper for relocating displaced tenants. In addition, Metropolitan Life was granted a 25-year property tax abatement. This tax abatement ultimately proved so costly to New York City that it would have saved $11 million by simply giving the land to Metropolitan.(39) The net result of this 1943 New York law was Metropolitan Life's Stuyvesant Town, where 10,000 low income people were driven from their homes in an 18-block area of

Manhattan to make way for an expensive apartment complex for 24,000 people. Stuyvesant Town was restricted to whites only and, of the 10,000 people displaced by the project, only 300 could afford to live in the new complex.(40)

ULI objected to the New York law because housing was the only permitted reuse, and because there was no provision for comprehensive planning for streets, parks, schools, and other amenities that would enhance the property values in the surrounding area. ULI wanted open ended reuse combined with significant planning, infrastructure, and financial support from the public sector. Their model was Pennsylvania's Type 3 law and its application in Pittsburgh.

Pennsylvania passed a redevelopment enabling law in 1945 at the urging of Richard King Mellon, head of a corporate empire that included Gulf Oil and Alcoa. Mellon had hired Robert Moses and a number of other planners and lawyers to come up with a comprehensive plan to boost property values in the central business district – the Golden Triangle. With the cooperation of Pittsburgh's Democratic Mayor, David Lawrence, Mellon enlisted the other major corporate leaders behind his strategy. The strategy involved creation of an independent redevelopment agency based on the ULI Principles, the recruiting of Equitable Life Insurance to construct an office complex (the first commercial redevelopment project), the construction of two new parkways, a state park, a convention center, a sports stadium and arena, luxury apartments, and more high-rise office buildings.(41)

The Pittsburgh plan, hailed by the media as a "Renaissance," set the tone for central city redevelopment across the country and became the model for downtown business interests and planners before the 1949 Housing Act ever reached President Truman's desk. This ULI model was the one that prevailed: a federal FHA-type agency to financially assist locally controlled Pittsburgh-style urban renewal in every city in the United States.(42)

Winning at the Federal Level

The story of the passage of the 1949 Housing Act has been recounted in detail elsewhere.(43) Essentially, the Act was a triumph for the ULI. Its one minor setback was an inconvenient but relatively painless provision that required land use in the project area to be "predominantly residential" either before or after redevelopment. The "before" allowed housing to be torn down and replaced by commercial or industrial facilities. Despite this rather large loophole, defenders of Myth #1 insist that the predominantly residential requirement proves that the consensus of Congressional opinion was that urban renewal's primary purpose was to provide more low-income housing. This is simply untrue.

The predominantly residential requirement was included in the 1949 Act mainly at the insistence of conservative Ohio Senator Robert Taft. Taft was the key Republican backer of the Housing Act and it could not have passed without his support. Taft was basically opposed to the ULI-

FHA-Pittsburgh model of publicly-funded urban redevelopment, and argued that the only type of redevelopment program that the federal government should pay for was construction of low income housing. Here are his statements during 1945 hearings on housing and redevelopment:

> But why we should undertake to relieve cities just because they don't look nice and because they don't have the real-estate values that somebody once thought they had, I don't understand that. Some people made plenty of money out of that real estate at one time. What is the justification for our going into that thing beyond the housing question? As long as it is just housing I can understand it.
>
> I like the idea, myself, of tying it up to housing, as compared to the more ambitious plans that are being presented both by the Bettman-Hansen group and the real-estate boards. . .
>
> I think a limited redevelopment in the hands of public housing authorities is a more defensible program than one of having the Federal Government interest itself in rebuilding the whole city.(44)

What is important about Senator Taft's position is that not one single witness supported it, not even the various representatives from the public housing lobby, because of a previous compromise they had made to back the realtor's program in exchange for new public housing authorization. Taft's efforts to block ULI redevelopment failed, and all that survived was the toothless "predominantly residential" language, which did not require construction after clearance to be either residential or for low and moderate income people, nor did it require that low income housing be built elsewhere for displaced slum dwellers.

MYTH #2. URBAN RENEWAL WAS AN OFFSHOOT OF THE PUBLIC HOUSING MOVEMENT

Urban scholars and planning professionals often portray urban renewal as simply an extension of the goals and methods of the public housing movement.(45) However, public housing activists and urban renewal lobbyists were bitter foes in the 1930s, each representing a different constituency and pursuing different interests. Proponents of urban renewal such as ULI and NAREB led the fight against the public housing program. Conversely, public housing advocates such as Catherine Bauer and Nathan Straus strongly opposed ULI's redevelopment proposals.

Public housing's primary supporter was organized labor. During the Depression the building trades' unions were desperate for public works projects. With so many people unemployed and overcrowded into poor housing, construction and industrial unions put their political strength behind the public housing program. Labor, in particular, the building trades, showed great enthusiasm, for obvious reasons. Senator Wagner read into the Congressional Record a resolution of the American Federation of Hosiery Workers that pointedly mentioned labor's "double interest in the construction of low-rent dwellings." Labor was "representative both of the unemployed building and material workers and of low-income families in need of better housing." In the climate of the New Deal, a program aimed at rehousing the "submerged middle class" was seen as politically acceptable.(46)

Downtown property interests, while strongly opposing the federally financed public housing program, fought to assure that, in carrying out the program, local public housing authorities purchased inner-city, blighted land to bail property owners out of the moribund market. "The importance of the public housing program of the 1930s in bolstering blighted area land prices is often overlooked or brushed aside by housing enthusiasts."(47) The prospect of the federal government as a major central-city land purchaser helped whet the appetite of certain business interests for a large-scale redevelopment program. Construction of public housing on cheap vacant land on the periphery of the city was anathema to realtors, home builders, financial institutions, and their chief government ally – the FHA.(48)

Ironically, while most public housers considered themselves distinct rivals of the NAREB and its supporters, the creation of the United States Housing Authority in 1937 ultimately played a vital role in paving the way for the federal urban renewal program by clearing away the legal, political, and institutional roadblocks. By the end of the 1930s nearly every state had passed enabling legislation that was upheld in state courts verifying the constitutionality of the use of eminent domain to clear slums and blighted areas. It is extremely important to note that the public purpose of the rehousing program was considered to be _slum clearance_; in other words, the legal justification for the public housing program was to alleviate the threat to the community's health, safety, morals, aesthetic sensibility, and general welfare caused by the existence of slum housing. The valid public purpose was to _eliminate_ bad housing, not to build good housing or to subsidize disadvantaged people's incomes. How the land was reused and what became of the former residents was incidental to the main goal.

Public housing also created the political infrastructure that made urban renewal possible. Not only was its legality generally established by the late 1930s, but in most large and many smaller cities housing authorities had demonstrated the viability of using federal monies to execute a locally controlled urban development program. Public housing had created employment for contractors, construction suppliers, building trades workers, architects, landscapers, planners, engineers, social welfare workers, and public officials. (This latter group had its own professional organization, the National Association of Housing Officials, later renamed the National Association of Housing and Redevelopment Officials, which demonstrates the relationship.) When appropriations for construction of new public housing were voted down by Congress in 1939,(49) this disparate group focused on redevelopment for a major federally funded urban public works program. The realtors and financial institutions who had fought against public housing began to push for urban redevelopment much more vigorously after 1939, as soon as the threat of an expanded low-rent housing program had been squelched.

Public housing and urban renewal are completely different programs. The former is redistributive to low income people whereas the latter is redistributive to upper income people. The base of support for the two programs in the 1930s and early 40s was extremely different. At the same time, however, public housing blazed the trail for redevelopment in three ways: 1) politically, by popularizing the idea of intergovernmental public action to clear slums; 2) legally, by establishing the public purpose of clearing slums and blighted areas in state legislatures and the courts; and 3) organizationally, by creating a federal-local infrastructure of interest groups and professionals ready and willing to embrace the new program.

MYTH #3. ALL THE PROBLEMS OF URBAN RENEWAL CAN BE BLAMED ON THE REPUBLICAN PARTY

Publication of the Douglas Commission Report in the late 1960s offered Democratic politicians and urban planners a safe haven from the heavy criticism they received about urban renewal. It did this by blaming the evils of urban renewal on the 1954 Housing Act, passed by a Republican Congress under a Republican President, rather than on the original 1949 Act, passed by a Democratic Congress under a Democratic President (50) (the 1954 Act changed "urban redevelopment" to "urban renewal," but this was very little more than a cosmetic name change; for background, see Colean (1953) and President's Advisory Committee, 1953). There is absolutely no basis for this particular brand of partisan, political buckpassing.

The Douglas Commission attacked the Republicans for doing two things: emasculating the public housing program and eroding the predominantly residential requirement. A careful look at the record demonstrates that neither of these charges is true. The emasculation of public housing and the trivialization of the "predominantly residential" rule had taken place in the Truman Administration, much earlier than 1954.

Richard Davies has pointed out about President Truman that "he gave every appearance of staunch liberalism in his housing policies, but in the day-to-day conduct of his housing agency he closely adhered to the real estate lobby's position."(51) The real estate, builder, and financial lobby made a concerted effort throughout the struggle over the 1949 Housing Act to defeat the public housing program and to insure that urban redevelopment would be separated from public housing agency control both nationally and locally. The ULI and colleagues pressed for the new urban redevelopment program to be operated by the FHA, because of FHA's close ties to and supportive relationship with realtors, builders, and lenders. At one point early in 1949, after Truman's come-from-behind reelection and the Democratic Congressional victory, NAREB and other lobbyists supported an abortive effort to separate urban redevelopment from the Housing Act altogether.(52) Such a separation would have made clear the true nature of urban renewal according to the ULI-Pittsburgh model.

Once the Housing Act passed, however, ULI lobbyists were not disappointed by the results. Urban redevelopment was kept entirely separate from the Public Housing Administration and was lodged directly in the Office of the Administrator of the Housing and Home Finance Agency (HHFA), Raymond Foley. Foley, who had served for two years as head of FHA and 11 years as FHA Field Director in Michigan, was well favored by NAREB and friends.(53) Foley's choice to head the new Division of Slum Clearance and Urban Redevelopment (DSCUR), Nathaniel Keith, staffed the division with professionals from FHA and other business-oriented agencies.(54)

No sooner did the DSCUR program get started than Keith, under prompting from Truman and Foley, began issuing regulations and making statements that discouraged redevelopment agencies from using projects for low-rent housing and encouraged redevelopment for high-rent residential, commercial, or industrial purposes.(55) Truman slashed public housing drastically as soon as the Korean War broke out in June 1950.(56) Within less than a year after the passage of the 1949 Act, "the language of the housing reformers" within HHFA was replaced by "the vocabulary of the real estate and mortgage finance industries."(57)

Given that public housing was "emasculated" both at the federal level and in local communities in 1950, the Douglas Commission's complaint against President Eisenhower is relatively groundless. As to their discussion of the "predominantly residential" rule, I have already demonstrated that its origins can be traced to Senator Taft and not to liberal Democrats or housing activists. Furthermore, the rule, aside from helping to give redevelopment some legal and moral legitimacy by linking it to the issue of slum housing, has always been relatively meaningless because it still allowed redevelopers to tear down low-rent dwellings and replace them with high-rise office buildings. The Douglas Commission conceded that this was "technically true" (National Commission, 1969, p. 157), but they claimed that Congress envisioned redevelopment primarily as a low-rent housing program, based on some ambiguous wording in a Senate committee report but <u>not</u> in the 1949 Housing Act. Had the Congress been serious about such matters they would have included strict and enforceable legal safeguards in the legislation itself. According to the Douglas Commission, such an approach was rejected by Congressional urban renewal advocates because "clamping down conditions and requirements. . .would have amounted to a strait jacket on local action or would have killed the program."(58) On this point the Douglas Commission was in complete agreement with the realtor-developer-financier lobby, which had argued from the very beginning for maximum flexibility in the urban renewal program.

Despite this rather large gap between legislative language and political rhetoric, the Douglas Commission still insisted that the so-called "skid-row amendment" to the 1954 Housing Act somehow perverted the original spirit and intent of the 1949 redevelopment program. This amendment exempted 10% of urban renewal funds from the "predominantly residential" requirement and was passed with bipartisan support (Senator Taft had died the year before). The rationale behind the amendment was that there were nonresidential areas around central business districts, universities, hospitals, and other institutional settings that certain city interests wished to clear and redevelop for nonresidential purposes. In 1959, under a Democratic Congress, the exemption was extended to 20 percent plus colleges and universities, and in the New Frontier-Great Society years it was further extended to 35%, plus hospitals, medical schools, nursing schools, and several other special exemptions.

Long before this wave of exemptions advocated principally by liberal Democrats, the Democratic officials who ran HHFA and DSCUR from 1949 to 1953 paid only lip service to their "predominantly residential" requirements. The classic case of abuse was the Columbus Circle Slum Clearance Project in New York City, crafted by Robert Moses and approved by DSCUR during the Truman Administration. Columbus Circle at 57th and Broadway was a valuable commercial site in the early 1950s when Moses induced the New York City Planning Commission and DSCUR to approve it as a Slum Clearance Project. This designation was based on the argument that a small number of aging tenements at the far end of the project's carefully drawn boundaries, constituting less than 1 percent of the total property value of the project area, were "substandard" and "insanitary."(59)

The redevelopment plan for the two-block area called for the construction of a commercial exhibition hall (the New York Coliseum) occupying 53 percent of the site and a luxury high-rise housing development occupying the other 47 percent. Since the "predominantly residential" rule was defined by DSCUR as being at least 50 percent of the total square footage of the project area, Moses needed to tip the balance by 3 percent. He announced that the tenants of the new apartment building could park their cars in the Coliseum's underground garage if their own parking lot was full. The New York City Planning Commission and DSCUR then designated 18,000 square feet of the Coliseum's underground garage as "residential," which made the entire Project "predominantly residential" in its reuse.(60)

The Columbus Circle charade prompted Congressman John Phillips of California, a Republican, to introduce an amendment to the 1954 Housing Act limiting redevelopment funds solely to residential reuse. Big city Democrats generally denounced the measure as limiting the flexibility of the urban renewal program. Business interests such as the owners of the <u>New York Times</u> lobbied heavily against the measure and defeated it in the Senate.

The New York courts had already ruled that under the 1949 Housing Act federal and local government agencies could define "substandard" dwellings and "predominantly residential" any way they wished. One judge's dissenting opinion, however, pointed out that the New York City Planning Commission and HHFA had completely ignored the physical condition of the numerous commercial structures in their determination of the area as blighted and suggested that the sole reason for including the few tenements in the project area may have been "merely to lend color to the acquisition of land for a coliseum under the guise of a slum clearance project."(61)

Such was the record of the early implementation of urban redevelopment under the Democratic Administration. And yet when Charles Abrams criticized HHFA Administrator Foley's handling of the new program, Foley was vigorously defended by none other than Senator Paul Douglas himself. In 1952 Douglas told the National Housing Conference that Foley was "acting in complete accordance with the intent of Congress." So pleased was Douglas with Foley's behavior, in fact, that the Senator proclaimed: "I feel like conferring upon him the Congressional Medal of Honor."(62)

The Role of City Planners in Urban Renewal

Since urban renewal was so clearly harmful to low and moderate income people even in its earlier incarnations as urban redevelopment and district replanning, why did so many planners enthusiastically support and participate in creating, selling, and implementing this program? The obvious answer is that in many ways city planning had its principal base of support among the various business groups that were most actively involved in pushing for urban renewal.

The growth of the city planning profession is inextricably linked to urban renewal. "Up-to-date city planning" was an integral part of the renewal package from the very beginning. The Urban Land Institute and the downtown lobby fought for comprehensive planning as an important element in their efforts to bolster central business district property values. Planners worked hard at ironing out the details of urban redevelopment legislation and at making the program academically, professionally, and politically respectable. It is hardly coincidental that the original name for the program was "district replanning."

Planners participated in these efforts because they saw urban renewal as their best chance to redesign and rebuild the city according to a more rational land use pattern.(63) Many planners, such as Seward Mott or Alfred Bettman, worked closely with the downtown corporate coalition because they shared the same values about what was best for the city. Others worked with the downtown business leaders simply because they were a politically powerful group that supported city planning. Alan Altshuler has documented how in Minneapolis the "planning activity was sustained mainly by the support of the Downtown Council."(64) Leaders of several large corporations wanted urban renewal, and the Minneapolis city planning department expanded to accommodate them. Studies of Pittsburgh (65) and New Haven (66) also detail the role of planners in designing urban renewal strategies at the behest of powerful downtown businessmen. The alliance that city planners made with local business leaders, whether out of shared values or political realism, has been a continuing part of the urban renewal saga. In 1942, for example, the National Resources Planning Board (NRPB) decided to promote a scheme they called "progressive planning." The head of its urban section decided to initiate several demonstration projects, during which an NRPB planner would move into a medium-sized community and, backed by technical assistance from the NRPB and other federal agencies, involve local residents in preparing a comprehensive physical, social, and economic plan. The NRPB wanted to use these demonstration projects to test their model for federal urban redevelopment.(67)

NRPB's approach in Corpus Christi, Texas was to turn to the most powerful elements of the community for support:

> . . . the mayor, the president of the largest bank, the head of Southern Alkali Corporation, representatives of the extractive industries (oil, gas, and fishing), and real estate board, and the Junior Assistance Club, who were interested in redeveloping the central part of the city and preserving land values, each pledged the support of his particular constitutency. The NRPB's agents, in turn, were sensitive to the interests of those whom it relied upon for assistance.(68)

Apparently the NRPB's definition of progressive planning did not include participation by other groups in Corpus Christi. Funigiello points out that "the needs of other segments of the community (Chicanos, blacks, the unorganized and inarticulate) seem to have been ignored with impunity," leading to "the now familiar practice of demolishing inner-city ghettos, uprooting ethnic minorities, and replacing them with high-rent commercial and residential dwellings occupied by well-to-do-whites."(69)

Many city planners' jobs have directly depended on urban renewal activities. When Congress passed the 1949 Housing Act there were only 600 planners in the country.(70) By the 1960s there were thousands of city planners, thanks largely to the federal government's 701 Planning Grants to local government, initiated in 1954 to facilitate workable urban renewal programs. For example, the Douglas Commission notes that "some smaller cities and urban counties have been stimulated by the availability of urban renewal funds to develop a capability for comprehensive urban planning which they previously lacked" (National Commission, 1969, p. 163). This is equally true for larger cities, particularly during the 1950s. While the new generation of planners was being trained to implement renewal techniques, the old-timers, such as Harland Bartholomew and Ladislas Segoe, had more business than they could handle traveling from city to city in the 1940s and 50s consulting on downtown renewal plans.

The planners' only other option for survival would have been to build an alternative coalition for city planning based on different values and different people's needs. The best example of this type of effort was the public housing movement in the mid-1930s.(71) Labor unions and unemployed workers' groups constituted an important part of the coalition supporting this program. A number of planners worked on various aspects of public housing. Had they been able to sustain this alliance, their livelihoods would have been dependent on a different set of interests than those of the large corporations and central city bankers and realtors. But NAREB, ULI, and other corporate lobbyists succeeded in defeating the public housing movement in 1939 and again in 1950, after which the movement dissipated and the program dwindled. Most planners interested in city rebuilding chose to work for corporate expansion – many of them willingly, others more reluctantly. Dissenters turned to community organizing or teaching.

The Role of Public Housers in Urban Renewal

When the ULI, NAREB, and their allies began pushing for urban redevelopment as a better slum clearance program than public housing, many public housing supporters were distinctly hostile to what they saw as an attack on their program.(72) Catherine Bauer, whose Modern Housing (73) had been a manifesto for the public housing movement in the 1930s, denounced the ULI approach in characteristically strong language:

> In the sacred name of "master plans," "bold reconstruction," "saving cities," and whatnot, it is proposed to bail out with Federal subsidy the owners of slum and blighted property – not in order to rehouse their present tenants properly, but to stimulate another wave of speculative overbuilding for the well-to-do and thus, it is naively hoped, to turn the tide of decentralization and preserve downtown property values based on high densities and even higher hopes.(74)

Yet in 1946 Catherine Bauer wrote that she "had no objection to bailing the boys out" provided "we get more workable cities" in return.(75) Bauer remained skeptical of urban renewal because she did not feel that urban decentralization could or should be reversed. But most of the others in the public housing lobby became strong supporters of redevelopment legislation. After 1939, they hoped to strike a deal with the realtors in order to save public housing. "The realtors could have their 'urban land Triple-A' (a reference to Agricultural Adjustment Act, which was interpreted here to be a "bail-out" for farmers) if the low-income segment of the population received public housing."(76)

At the end of World War II the prospects of high unemployment and a severe housing shortage began to worry many Americans. Public housing activists felt that such a situation would force Congress to revive the public housing program. In order to achieve the broadest possible base of political support for their program, it was included in the massive Wagner-Ellender-Taft Housing Bill. Public housers lobbied vigorously for passage of the entire bill. The legislation contained many provisions that were strongly backed by the builder-realtor-financier-FHA lobby and that helped underwrite the great postwar suburban expansion. The bill also included the urban redevelopment title. Public housing activists reasoned that, given the housing shortage, slums and blighted areas could not possibly be rebuilt without new public housing for the residents who would be displaced. Supporting redevelopment, they thought, was one way of getting more support for their own program.(77)

But there were also other reasons that public housers lobbied for urban redevelopment, in addition to the political bargain that was struck over the inclusion of public housing in the overall Wagner-Ellender-Taft Bill. Many hoped that local redevelopment agencies would sell or lease cleared land at cut-rate prices to local housing authorities. They hoped in vain, however, because the HHFA and the local agencies wanted redevelopment for private enterprise, and had no interest in using cleared land for public housing.(78) Had subsidized land costs been the sole aim of the public housers, however, they could just as easily have fought for this subsidy as a direct part of the public housing program rather than pinning their hopes on an entirely separate redevelopment program. Senator Taft suggested such an approach during the 1945 Senate hearings, but the public housers were already committed to their compromise strategy.(79)

Public housers also supported redevelopment because many of them believed in comprehensive city planning and wanted to see public housing interspersed with middle income housing, parks, recreation areas, schools, and retail stores, instead of being isolated in large projects.(80) City planners, however, were more interested in ULI-type concerns than in public housing.(81)

Finally, most housing reformers were middle class people who placed a high value on the elimination of slums as an end in itself. Their concern with tearing down unsightly buildings often took precedence over their concern for the welfare of the people who lived in them.(82) This attitude on the part of many constituent groups in the public housing movement made it possible for them to be pleased with a program that would clear slums, regardless of the ultimate fate of the anonymous slum dwellers.

The paternalistic attitude held by housing reformers led to a serious conflict of interest between the leaders of the public housing movement and the people for whom they were allegedly speaking. Public officials, writers, lawyers, and union leaders were not the ones who would be displaced by the federal bulldozer. While they may have been disturbed by the "relocation problem," many argued in 1949 and even later that urban renewal's contributions to civic welfare outweighed its deficiencies.(83)

As the price for its support of urban redevelopment, the public housing lobby successfully included in the 1949 act a requirement that those displaced by slum clearance be relocated in "decent, safe, and sanitary dwellings" at affordable rents and in convenient locations. The price, however, was never paid, for the provision was never enforced by the HHFA, and local redevelopment agencies simply ignored it.(84) Public housers gave their vital support to urban renewal, and without them the legislation might never have passed.(85) Yet they simply did not have the power to force the federal, state, or local governments to meet their terms. NAREB, ULI, and their allies exerted enough power to block public housing after the passage of the 1949 act.(86) The large downtown corporations also exerted a vast amount of power, ensuring that the urban renewal program they had been fighting for since the early 1930s was implemented to their satisfaction.

Thus the public housers were placed in the position of having helped to pass a program that failed miserably for them. Urban renewal did not build low-rent housing – it destroyed it.(87) It is a sad commentary that public housers and planners, by their active support of urban renewal, lent public legitimacy to this destruction. It was clear too, that the downtown corporate coalition understood the value of this added legitimacy. For example, Richard King Mellon's lawyer asked Pittsburgh's Democratic Mayor to head the new redevelopment agency because "If we condemned people's properties, it was better for the Mayor with his popular following to be responsible, rather than someone with the Mellon or U.S. Steel nameplate."(88)

Even if more relocation housing had been available, however, this still might not have mitigated the effects of urban renewal's destructiveness on people's lives.(89) In most cases the residents of blighted areas wanted to stay where they were. To be rehoused in a public housing project provided little consolation. Besides, politicians and businessmen often deliberately used relocation housing to increase racial segregation.(90)

Since the days of "district replanning" in the 1930s, when the committee on Blighted Areas and Slums recommended that slum dwellers be removed from "potentially very valuable urban land"(91) many public housing advocates have all too willingly agreed with the ULI position that "Slum sites are most often desirable for private housing for higher income families."(92)

LESSON #1: POOR PEOPLE MUST SPEAK FOR THEMSELVES

The lesson of urban renewal is that poor people must be politically well-organized and must speak for themselves. They cannot rely on middle class organizations and individuals who represent different interests to speak for them. Had the slum dwellers been highly organized in the 1940s, they would surely have fought against urban renewal. Such opposition might have forced other elements of the public housing coalition to shift their position. This shift might possibly have defeated urban renewal or brought about some useful reforms. It took another twenty years before the urban riots of the 1960s forced Congress to pass legislation providing modest financial assistance to people who would be displaced by future urban renewal projects. Congress also amended the renewal laws to provide for some degree of citizen participation by community organizations fighting redevelopment. Both of these reforms were hard-earned victories of a mass political movement.

In the case of welfare reform in the late 1960s and early 70s, poor people did defend their own interests rather than relying on other voices to speak for them, with surprisingly good results. President Nixon's proposed Family Assistance Plan (FAP) was supported by many liberal politicians and social work professionals as a "foot-in-the-door." Liberal professionals and the organizations they represented argued that despite its drawbacks, FAP was a positive measure that should be passed and then improved at a later date. This was precisely the position that the public housers took during the urban redevelopment debate in the late 1940s.

However, an organization of welfare recipients – the National Welfare Rights Organization (NWRO) – strongly opposed FAP because it would take away many of their hard-won rights and benefits. The NWRO did not agree with the liberal foot-in-the-door theory. They saw it more as a "foot-in-the-rear." Welfare rights members preferred no reform to the Nixon reform. Many leaders of the social welfare lobby labeled NWRO's position unreasonable and extremist. But the ghetto riots had given poor people some political leverage. NWRO convinced a few key Senate liberals to withdraw support for the FAP, contributing to its defeat.(93)

In San Francisco a plan was prepared in the mid-1940s to redevelop a large area near the downtown. This area – termed the Western Addition – had experienced a rapid influx of blacks during World War II. It was a low-rent district that also contained a large number of Japanese-Americans who had resettled there after their release from the U.S. internment camps. San Francisco's civic leaders wanted to clear the area and rebuild it with middle and upper income housing that would be attractive to suburban commuters.(94) Local residents turned out at a public hearing in 1948 to oppose the designation of their neighborhood as a redevelopment district,(95) but this protest went unheeded and, over the next 25 years, thousands of Western Addition residents were displaced.(96) By the 1960s the community was considerably angrier and better organized – enough to initiate a lawsuit temporarily halting the displacement process. By this action the community gained a substantial amount of publicly assisted housing within the project area.(97)

The experience of massive displacement in the Western Addition, combined with the potential effectiveness of community protest, prompted a group of tenants and property owners in San Francisco's South of Market redevelopment area to launch their own movement against the bulldozers. Retired merchant seamen and longshoremen living in the project area, with their trade union backgrounds to guide them, built a protest organization called Tenants and Owners Opposed to Redevelopment (TOOR) in the late 1960s. TOOR used a lawsuit to block the proposed Yerba Buena project for several years and eventually won their demand for publicly assisted relocation housing located in the South of Market area, with TOOR as the developer.(98)

LESSON #2: A BAD BARGAIN IS WORSE THAN NO BARGAIN

In neither the Western Addition nor the South of Market case, however, were the protesters able to stop the redevelopment agency from taking away their community. This confirms the wisdom of the NWRO strategy to stop potentially regressive measures before they turn into repressive public agencies with large budgets. Whether urban renewal actually could have been stopped is questionable, given its powerful base of support. But at the very least, if the organized poor and housing reformers had banded together and pursued an opposition strategy, the mythological excuses enunciated by the Douglas Commission and its supporters would not have held up for so long. Such opposition would have made clear who was for redevelopment and who was against it.

The emerging progressive coalitions of the 1980s must be based solidly within community and labor organizations. Planners, housers, and other professionals will then be in a better position to choose sides and avoid the compromises of the 1949 Housing Act that (according to Professor Donald Foley) Catherine Bauer later characterized as "a sell-out." We would all do well to heed the advice offered by a black community spokesman at the 1948 San Francisco redevelopment hearings:

> You will recall that during the fight in the State Legislature this association, with these other organizations, asked that certain definite guarantees be written into the law to protect the rights of minority citizens, and to guarantee that public housing would be available so that persons of low income groups could enjoy the privileges enjoyed by others. We lost at this period of the game. Everyone said, "This is not the time to talk about such projects."
>
> We came to the San Francisco City Planning Commission, presented our problems, and once again were told "This is not the time."
>
> Now, the association, as it looks upon the law as written, and as it is to be implemented, feels that the difference between the proponents and the opponents is this: Some people say, "Let's go into this thing and revise it after we take this step." Experience has taught minority peoples that if we don't start out right we might not end up right.(99)

NOTES

(1) U.S. Congress, Joint Economic Committee, Financing Municipal Needs, 1977, p. 77.

(2) National Commission on Urban Problems, Building the American City, 1969, p. 163.

(3) Ibid.

(4) Frieden and Kaplan, 1975, p. 23.

(5) Hoyt, 1933, p. 279-367; Walker, Urban Blight and Slums, 1938; Urban Land Institute, Decentralization, 1940B; National Resources Planning Board, Better Cities, 1942A, p. 19; Ludlow, "Land Values and Density," 1945, p. 5.

(6) President's Conference on Home Building and Home Ownership, Slums, Large Scale Housing and Decentralization, 1932, p. 1.

(7) Ibid., p. 9.

(8) Ibid.

(9) Ibid., p. 4.

(10) Jackson, A Place Called Home, 1976, p. 188.

(11) Caro, Power Broker, 1974, p. 375.

(12) President's Conference, 1932, p. 9.

(13) Ibid., p. 9.

(14) Ibid., p. 10.

(15) Ibid.

(16) Kolko, The Triumph of Conservatism, 1963; Weinstein, The Corporate Ideal, 1968; Scott, American City Planning, 1969; Fitch, "Planning New York," 1976.

(17) Gelfand, A Nation of Cities, 1975, p. 112.

(18) Walker, Urban Blight and Slums, 1938, pp. 227-231; National Resources Committee, Urban Land and Planning Policies, 1939, p. 279.

(19) U.S. House of Representatives, Hearings Part 2, 1950, p. 25.

(20) Urban Land Institute, The Urban Land Institute, 1940A.

(21) In 1940 the ULI released the results of a survey of 512 appraisers from 221 cities entitled Decentralization: What Is It Doing To Our Cities? (ULI, 1940B). At the same time it commissioned detailed studies by local realtors and financiers of the problems of decentralization in 13 American cities. A large portion of the money for these studies came from the Estate of Marshall Field, the largest property owner in downtown Chicago (Business Week, January 18, 1941, p. 61), through its trustee, George Richardson, who was also a ULI Board member, and who had been a member of President Hoover's Committee on Blighted Areas and Slums and Committee on Large-Scale Operations.

(22) Urban Land Institute, Proposals for Downtown Boston, 1940C; Decentralization in New York City, 1941A; Proposals for Downtown Cincinnati, 1941B; Proposals for Downtown Milwaukee, 1941C; Proposals for Downtown Philadelphia, 1941D; Proposals for Downtown Detroit, 1942A; Proposals for Downtown Louisville, 1942B.

(23) Urban Land Institute, "Urban Land Institute Adopts Huge Post-War City Replanning Program," 1942C, p. 1.

(24) Urban Land Institute, Outline for a Legislative Program, 1942D.

(25) U.S. House of Representatives, Hearings, Part 2, 1950, pp. 19-22.

(26) Wheaton, "The Evolution of Federal Housing Programs," 1953, pp. 356-8, 431.

(27) Federal Housing Authority, A Handbook on Urban Redevelopment, 1941.

(28) Greer and Hansen, 1941; National Resources Planning Board, Better Cities, 1942A; National Resources Development, 1942B.

(29) Bauer, "Redevelopment: A Misfit in the Fifties," 1953, p. 9.

(30) Urban Land Institute, The City Fights Back, 1954, pp. 9-15.

(31) Urban Land Institute, Technical Bulletin No. 2, 1945A.

(32) Ibid., p. 2.

(33) Ibid.

(34) Ibid.

(35) Urban Land Institute, Statement by Seward Mott, 1945B, p. 3.

(36) Urban Land Institute, Technical Bulletin, p. 3.

(37) Ibid., p. 4.

(38) Hartman, "The Housing of Relocated Families," 1964.

(39) Abrams, The Future of Housing, 1946, p. 380.

(40) Burdell, "Rehousing Needs," 1945; Strauss, The Seven Myths of Housing, 1944, pp. 179-80; Gelfand, p. 124.

(41) Lubove, Twentieth Century Pittsburgh, 1969, pp. 87-141; Urban Land Institute, City Fights Back, 1954, pp. 185-95; Lowe, Cities in a Race With Time, pp. 110-63.

(42) Domhoff, Who Really Rules?, 1978; Hartman, Yerba Buena, 1974; Mollenkopf, "The Postwar Politics," 1978; Edel, "Urban Renewal," 1971; California State Commission, Blighted! 1946; Urban Land Institute, The City Fights Back, 1954 and Nine Cities, 1969; Mowitz and Wright, Profile of a Metropolis, 1962, pp. 1-140; Caro, Power Broker, Lowe, Cities in a Race with Time, 1967.

(43) Gelfand, A Nation of Cities, 1975; Wheaton, Evolution of Federal Housing Programs, 1953; Keith, Politics and the Housing Crisis, 1973; Davies, Housing Reform, 1966; Feinstein, "Policy Development," 1974; Foard and Fefferman, "Federal Urban Renewal Legislation," 1960.

(44) U.S. Senate, Hearings Pursuant to S. Res. 102, 1945, pp. 1558, 1699, 1792.

(45) Bellush and Hausknecht, Urban Renewal, 1967.

(46) Friedman, Government and Slum Housing, 1968, pp. 99-117; Woodyatt, "The Origin and Evolution," 1968.

(47) Ludlow, "Land Values," 1945, pp. 5-6.

(48) Strauss, Seven Myths of Housing, pp. 47-93.

(49) Woodyatt, "Origin and Evolution," pp. 193-229.

(50) National Commission, Building the American City, 1969, pp. 156-7.

(51) Davies, Housing Reform, 1966, p. 135.

(52) Wheaton, "The Evolution of Federal Housing Programs," 1953, p. 432; Keith, Politics and the Housing Crisis, 1973, pp. 89-90; Gelfand, A Nation of Cities, 1975, pp. 149-50.

(53) Davies, *Housing Reform*, 1966, pp. 60-62.

(54) Feinstein, "Policy Development in a Federal Program," 1974, p. 82.

(55) Feinstein, Ibid., 1974, pp. 81-107.

(56) Davies, op. cit., 1966, pp. 130-131.

(57) Feinstein, op. cit., 1974, p. 89.

(58) National Commission, *Building*, op. cit., 1969, p. 153.

(59) Feinstein, op. cit., 1974, p. 260.

(60) Feinstein, op. cit., 1974, p. 232.

(61) Feinstein, op. cit., 1974, p. 263.

(62) Feinstein, op. cit., 1974, p. 263.

(63) Sanders and Rabuck, *New City Patterns*, 1946.

(64) Altshuler, *The City Planning Process*, 1965, p. 295.

(65) Lubove, *Twentieth Century Pittsburgh*, 1969.

(66) Domhoff, *Who Really Rules?*

(67) National Resources Planning Board, 1943A. *National Resources Development Report, Part 1*, 1943A, pp. 31-6; and *National Resources Development Report, Part 2*, 1943B, pp. 102-5; Funigiello, *The Challenge to Urban Liberalism*, 1978, pp. 163-86.

(68) Funigiello, *Challenge to Urban Liberalism*, p. 182.

(69) Ibid.

(70) Feinstein, "Policy Development," 1974, p. 67.

(71) Woodyatt, "Origin and Evolution," 1968.

(72) Strauss, *Seven Myths of Housing*, 1944, pp. 69-93; Gelfand, *A Nation of Cities*, 1975, pp. 117-8.

(73) Bauer, *Modern Housing*, 1934.

(74) Funigiello, loc. cit. *Challenge to Urban Liberalism*, 1978.

(75) Gelfand, *A Nation of Cities*, 1975, pp. 136, 204-5.

(76) Ibid., p. 128.

(77) Bauer, "Is Urban Redevelopment," 1946 and "Redevelopment and Public Housing," 1950; Vinton, "A New Look," 1949: Meyerson and Banfield, Politics, Planning and the Public Interest, 1955, p. 19.

(78) Feinstein, "Policy Development," 1974, pp. 87-92.

(79) U.S. Senate Hearings on Housing p. 1699.

(80) Ibid., pp. 1738-41; Abrams, The Future of Housing, 1946, pp. 378-9.

(81) Vinton, "A New Look," 1949.

(82) Friedman, Government and Slum Housing, 1968; Meyerson and Banfield, Politics, Planning and the Public Interest, 1955, p. 18.

(83) Keith, Politics and the Housing Crisis since 1930, 1973; Abrams, The City is the Frontier, 1965.

(84) Hartman, "The Housing of Relocated Families," 1964 and Yerba Buena, 1974; Caro, The Power Broker, 1974, pp. 961-83.

(85) Bauer, "Is Urban Redevelopment Possible?" p. 66.

(86) Feinstein, pp. 87-8; Davies, pp. 126-32; Meyerson and Banfield, Politics, Planning and the Public Interest, 1955.

(87) National Commission, Building the American City, 1969, p. 163.

(88) Lowe, Cities in a Race with Time, p. 134.

(89) Gans, "The Human Implications," 1959; Fried, "Grieving for a Lost Home," 1963.

(90) Lowi, The End of Liberalism, 1967, pp. 25-65; Bowly, The Poorhouse, 1978, pp. 111-32.

(91) President's Conference, 1932, p. 9.

(92) Abrams, 1946, p. 379.

(93) The Welfare Fighter, October 1972; Kotz and Kotz, A Passion for Equality, 1977, pp. 261-78; Moynihan, The Politics of Guaranteed Income, pp. 532-3.

(94) San Francisco City Planning Commission, Western Addition District, 1947A and New City, 1947B.

(95) City and County of San Francisco, Public Hearing, 1948.

(96) Hartman, 1974, p. 100.

(97) Mollenkopf, "Community Organizations," 1973.

(98) Hartman, Yerba Buena, 1974.

(99) City and County of San Francisco, p. 27.

5 Housing and the American Economy: A Marxist Analysis*

Michael E. Stone

SHELTER POVERTY AND THE STRUCTURAL BASIS OF THE HOUSING PROBLEM

Under capitalism human labor power is a commodity. That is, most people need to sell their labor power for a wage in order to be able to obtain housing and other necessities, which are, for the most part, commodities as well. In the long run the minimum level of wages must be sufficient for the working class to maintain and reproduce itself at the level of subsistence. It is in the immediate interest of capitalists to have wages at the lowest possible level that will assure them the quantity and quality of workers they wish to employ – a level that may be above or below subsistence. In industrialized capitalist countries like the U.S., a combination of factors – the history of the class struggle, the demand for various kinds of skilled labor, the intensive exploitation of other parts of the world, and the need of capitalists to have buyers for their products – have enabled most people to achieve incomes above the level of subsistence. Nevertheless, the labor market exerts a constant downward pressure on working class incomes, and working class standards.

Under capitalism the price of housing is determined primarily by the structure of the housing market – which includes not only the retail market for homes and apartments but also much of the land market, the construction industry, the materials industry, and finance capital. However, since housing is both a necessity and a commodity, its price is also greatly influenced by people's ability to pay, which interacts with the profit expectations of the various housing capitalists. If the price of existing housing is much lower than the cost of producing new housing, it will not be profitable to produce new housing. Indeed, it may not be profitable to keep some existing housing on the market. The shortage may force some people to double up and may eventually drive the price of existing housing up toward the cost of producing new

*Portions of this chapter appeared in U.S. Capitalism in Crisis (New York, 1978).

housing, but the price is ultimately limited by people's incomes. The labor market can thus restrict the profitability, and hence the quantity and quality of available housing.

While the squeeze between high housing costs and limited incomes has a depressing effect on the housing market, it exerts an upward pressure on wages. Businessmen in the housing market may be indifferent as to whether the price of housing leaves households with enough income to pay for other necessities, but they do want buyers who can pay their price. Workers, in turn, struggle for higher wages to pay the price required for shelter and for their families' other needs. The price of housing thus enters into the determination of the level of wages; the interests of capitalists in the housing market being advanced by higher wages, while the interests of capitalists as employers being served by lower wages.

At first glance, the relationship of housing costs to wages and living conditions appears no different from the cost of food, clothing or other necessities required for reproduction of labor power. It might also seem that there can be no inherent conflict between the requirements of the labor market and the housing market: since housing is itself a product of labor, the level of wages should simultaneously and consistently determine both the cost of producing housing and the level of working class incomes. In fact, housing possesses a number of distinctive characteristics that distinguishes it both socially and economically from other commodities, gives it a fundamental and pivotal role in determining working class living standards, and makes it unusually and inherently problematical for capitalism.

Housing is a bulky, immobile, and durable good that can rarely be purchased in amounts other than whole dwelling units and usually is used over a considerable period of time. These characteristics make it extremely difficult, at least in the short run, for a family to alter the quantity, quality, or amount spent for the housing they consume. Sudden changes in the income of a household, especially downward changes, are generally reflected immediately in other expenditures, including food, but not in the amount spent for shelter. Increases in housing costs usually must be offset by reductions in other expenditures, rather than reductions or substitutions in housing consumption. When the rent or property taxes go up, a family cannot readily give up its living room or switch to a cheaper brand of bathroom to offset the increase.

Obviously in extreme financial emergencies people will normally buy the food they need to survive even if it means not paying the rent. But above this starvation level, food consumption patterns and expenditures of working class families can and do vary from day to day and week to week. They vary because, unlike housing, food products are quickly consumed and must be purchased anew and because each purchase involves a mix of distinct items rather than a single, costly item.

The second way in which the cost of housing affects the overall standard of living of a family is through its determination of where a family can live. This relationship influences the physical quality of the housing people are able to obtain, the amount of dwelling space they have, and the type of community and neighborhood they live in. This influence over locational choice means that the amount a household can pay for housing affects its access to commercial facilities, the quality of schools and other social services, the character of the immediate physical and social environment, and the availability of transportation networks to jobs and other services. No other consumption item is nearly as pervasive in its effects. Together, housing costs and income levels are the most decisive determinants of the material quality of life.

Furthermore, because housing is so durable, in an economy where housing is a commodity (i.e., produced for profit, to be exchanged, and held for its value in exchange rather than only as a useful product), it is generally bought and sold many times during its useful life. This means that at every point subsequent to its initial production and sale, the market value of a residential structure is determined not by its actual cost of production, but rather by its replacement cost adjusted for depreciation. In addition, because housing is tied to the land, its market value includes the "value" of the land, i.e., the rent-generating potential of the particular location. At the time that housing is initially built, the value of the land amounts to a fraction of the total value created in producing the building. (In formal Marxist terms, the land owner appropriates a fraction of the surplus value created by the workers who built the house). Subsequent to the initial production and sale of the housing though, the value of the land can and does change considerably as the rent-producing potential of the location changes.

Finally, the actual shelter costs for a particular housing unit do not involve the direct payment of the sales price or market value to the seller in one lump sum, but rather incremental payment to the investors or financiers over time. On top of this incremental payment system there is, of course, the payment of interest or profit – a form of rent – to the investors. There are also property taxes and operating expenses. Thus the actual cost of shelter, as determined by the structure of the capitalist housing market, bears only a tenuous relationship to the general level of wages – or even to the level of the wages of the workers who produce and service housing.

Because shelter costs generally represent a major claim on a household's income, when we say that people are paying more than they can afford for shelter, we mean that after paying for their shelter they have insufficient resources left to meet their other needs.

Using U.S. Bureau of Labor Statistics (BLS) "lower budget" estimates for 1976 reveals, for example, that a family of four would have needed an income of more than $12,000 to be able to afford to spend the government stipulated maximum of 25 percent of their income for shelter. Indeed, if their income were about $7,500 or less, they could not have afforded to pay anything for shelter if they were to meet their other needs at the minimum level of adequacy. Clearly the conventional 25 percent standard hides the hardship faced even by families paying a lower percent of their income for shelter, but who are still "shelter poor" because the squeeze between housing costs and income leaves them insufficient resources for meeting other needs at even a minimally adequate level.(1)

The extent of shelter poverty, based upon the income-dependent standard just described, has been estimated from Annual Housing Survey and Census data. In 1976 more than 20 million households in the U.S. were shelter poor – nearly 30 percent of all households. This included about 10 million renter households – almost 40 percent of all renters – and more than 11 million homeowner households – about 25 percent of all homeowners. Nearly 90 percent of all shelter poor households in 1976 had incomes below $10,000, and virtually 100 percent had incomes below $15,000. Between 1970 and 1976 the total number of shelter poor households increased by 10 percent.(2)

Shelter poverty in the United States is a persistent, pervasive and growing problem that cannot be eliminated simply through growth in the economy or government subsidies. It could only be eliminated if every household were guaranteed an income sufficient to pay its housing costs, meet its other needs at a minimum level of adequacy, and also pay its taxes. Labor would then take a bigger share of the nation's productive output; profits would decline, leading to reduced investment and cutbacks in production. With the working class no longer manacled to low-wage jobs by the threat of unemployment, capital would lose its power over labor and the working class could no longer be maintained in a subordinate position by job competition and insecurity. This solution would thus lead to the collapse of the labor market – the central institution of capitalism.

On the other hand, if a large proportion of American families continues to have insufficient incomes to pay for shelter, the housing market will collapse, as it already has in many urban neighborhoods where housing has been abandoned. More generally, to eliminate shelter poverty without disturbing the labor market, the price of housing would have to be set at a level the occupants could realistically afford after paying for their other necessities. Housing prices would be driven down, in many cases to zero. Property values would collapse, and private investment in housing would cease. Mortgage payments would stop on many buildings, leading to collapse of the mortgage system, and with it much of the financial structure. While such a collapse would wipe out a portion of real estate values and mortgage debt, as it did in the 1930s for example, it would also bring production to a halt.

Western European experience seems to indicate that these problems are not inherently unsolvable for capitalism, i.e., that the private housing market can be eliminated without undermining basic institutions. Actually, the European situation reveals that the housing problem _is_ deep-seated and that control or elimination of much of the entrepreneurial element in housing does not affect the essence of the capitalist housing market.

After World War II most Western European governments maintained strict control of rents and restrictions on eviction to protect tenants from landlord exploitation amidst a severe housing shortage. Other prices were not similarly controlled, so the costs of operating housing and building new housing rose, with no compensating increase in the price of existing housing. As a result, private housing investment dried up, as landlords, bankers, and developers had predicted. Instead of returning control to the private market though, the state became a major developer and owner of housing; and unlike public housing in this country, what has been produced is at least as desirable as most private housing.

Governments, however, generally buy land in the marketplace and pay private builders to construct the housing. They still raise funds for housing by borrowing from financial institutions and wealthy individuals, and this money must be repaid with interest out of rents and taxes. In other words, housing continues to be very expensive. Bankers, builders, and land speculators continue to profit from it; working class people continue to pay, partly through their direct housing expenditures and partly through their taxes. In a pinch landlords are expendable; their demise would not destroy capitalism, but neither would their disappearance solve the housing problem.

THE 19TH-CENTURY HOUSING QUESTION

The conflict between incomes and housing costs is not new, having emerged with urban industrial capitalism, which transformed housing as well as labor power into commodities. During the 19th century, the dynamics of economic growth led to tremendous population increase in the United States through natural growth plus immigration, and to the concentration of this population in cities. The growth of population in cities generated the need for the construction of more housing and – within the framework of the capitalist labor and housing markets – to conditions of overcrowding and exploitation in housing. That is, the squalid housing conditions in 19th-century cities essentially reflected the attempts of urban landlords to exploit the growing need for housing within the limits imposed by low wages.

These conditions manifested themselves as massive fires and disease, which threatened not only housing investment, but also worker productivity and even the health and well-being of the middle and upper classes in adjacent parts of the cities. In the late 19th century the government began to respond to this contradiction primarily through the enactment of building, housing, and health codes. However, enforcement of these codes in existing working class housing was generally lax because the costs of compliance would have eaten into landlords' profits and/or caused higher rents, which would have put upward pressure on wages. The codes were applied to newly constructed buildings, though, resulting in higher costs, and thus an end to building new housing for the poor.(3) What the system needed at this point was a mechanism to stretch out construction costs over time, so that it would be profitable to build new housing to accommodate the growing urban working class without exerting too much upward pressure on rents and wages.

The evolving structure of housing costs had important political implications. Prior to the late 19th century, operating expenses for urban housing were quite low. Residents provided their own fuel and there were no other utilities. Maintenance was often negligible, there was no insurance, no organized professional management of low income apartment buildings, and property taxes were not high. Thus nearly all of the rental income went to the investors.

Furthermore, most of the investors were risk or "equity" investors. They were not guaranteed a certain return on their investment – their profits went up or down with the market. If the economy went down and unemployment was high, the returns were lower. Landlords would either hold the property for better times or sell out at deflated prices. Working class people could not afford much housing and were in a weak bargaining position vis-a-vis landlords, but housing costs had the capacity to adjust to fluctuations in the overall level of income.

Since rents generally fluctuated with the economy, and since housing investors were relatively unimportant capitalists, the problem of incomes and housing costs posed no serious threat to the system. In fact, this was the situation in most American and European cities at the time Engels wrote The Housing Question in 1872. On the other hand, an indication of the danger that might have been posed had housing costs not been flexible was provided by the Pullman strike of 1894. The Pullman Company owned the workers' housing in the town of Pullman, Illinois and thus had monopoly power over rents. In 1894, the company cut wages but refused to reduce rents. Although the origins of the strike were complex, it was this failure to cut rents in the face of wage cuts that triggered the strike.(4)

The growing rigidity of housing costs in the 20th century poses a similar kind of political threat but in a much more pervasive and profound way. This rigidity grew directly out of the need for a mechanism to stretch out construction costs and the simultaneous need for new sources of capital to finance urban growth.

THE FIRST RISE AND FALL OF INSTITUTIONAL MORTGAGE LENDING (5)

In the late 19th century, the U.S. economy began to pull out of a generation of stagnation and depression following the Civil War. This economic upsurge led not only to a tremendous need for urban housing, but also to a massive increase in the amount of funds in financial institutions – particularly commercial banks, mutual savings banks, savings and loan associations, and life insurance companies. Thus around the turn of the century the financial institutions began to increase their investments in residential real estate, financing both the construction of new housing and the buying, selling, and refinancing of existing housing. They did not generally invest as property owners, but instead made loans to developers and buyers with the real estate itself serving as collateral for the loans – mortgage lending.

Between 1900 and 1929 residential nonfarm mortgage debt increased ten-fold – from $2.9 billion to more than $29 billion. Financial institutions held less than half the housing debt in 1900, but more than 60 percent of it by 1929.(6) The rapid growth of institutional mortgage lending during this period was significant for both the housing sector and the overall economy because it firmly established the power of the lenders and dependence on credit, and because it had certain contradictory results. An awareness of some of the developments of this period is important in understanding the problems of recent years, for these developments set the stage for large-scale government intervention in housing and revealed the persistent danger to capitalism of the discrepancy between low incomes and high housing costs.

It is important to note that, during this period, institutional lenders would generally make loans for no more than 50 percent of the value of a piece of property. In this way, if they had to foreclose on the mortgage, they could be sure of recovering their money by selling the property. The large down payment or "initial equity" needed to obtain a mortgage loan and buy a piece of residential real estate meant that most borrowers were either middle class families with sufficient savings for the down payment or landlords with other sources of equity capital. Thus, the mortgage system, along with the automobile, supported a wave of suburbanization that increased the proportion of nonfarm, owner-occupied units from 37 percent in 1900 to 46 percent by 1930.(7) The vast majority of the urban working class, however, remained tenants without a vested interest in property and without the sobering burden of personal housing debt.

In addition, most mortgage loans were for terms of just three to five years. During the term the borrower made interest payments to the lender, but usually did not repay any of the loan itself. At the end of the term, the entire loan was due for repayment. Normally, the lender would just refinance the loan for another term – perhaps at a higher rate of interest – if he believed that the economic situation of the borrower and the housing market would ensure continued interest payments and maintain the value of the property.

The mortgage system thus came to depend for its survival on continuous economic growth and prosperity. Indeed the rapid expansion of mortgage credit was a way lenders could contribute to the prosperity they needed to protect their investments. But this was also their undoing. Between 1900 and 1929, residential mortgage debt grew more than four times as fast as the economy. In 1900 per capita mortgage debt was equal to about 20 percent of per capita disposable income; by 1930 the ratio had more than doubled to 41 percent.(8) A larger and larger proportion of the nation's income therefore went to mortgage payments. The potential squeeze between incomes and housing costs was developing into an actual tension between incomes and mortgage payments – and between past debts and future prosperity.

When the economy collapsed at the end of the 1920s, the mortgage system collapsed as well, adding significantly to the speed and depth of the country's plunge into the Depression. Because residents were out of work, they no longer had the incomes to sustain their previous level of housing costs. Homeowners could not keep up their mortgage payments; landlords could not collect enough rent to pay their mortgages. People went to the banks to withdraw their savings, but the banks could not give them the money, in part because it had been invested in mortgages.

The banks had foreclosed on about 1.5 million nonfarm properties by the mid-1930s – including more than a million owner-occupied homes, comprising about 10 percent of all owner-occupied housing. Homeownership decreased from a peak of 46 percent of all occupied housing units in 1930 to 41 percent in 1940. New mortgage loans on 1- to 4-family houses, which had amounted to $4-5 billion a year during the 1920s, were less than $3 billion a year throughout the 1930s (including less than $1 billion by nongovernmental lenders in both 1933 and 1934). Loan losses and repayments far exceeded new mortgage loans, so that the total nonfarm residential debt declined from about $30 billion in 1930 to about $24 billion in 1935 and increased very little thereafter until the end of World War II. Deposits in savings accounts decreased in some years and increased only slightly in other years throughout the 1930s and through 1942.(9) With no funds, residential construction practically came to a halt, and the private housing market nearly ceased functioning.

THE NEW MORTGAGE SYSTEM

The collapse of the mortgage and housing markets during the Great Depression was second in significance to the collapse of production and massive unemployment. Indeed, the collapse of residential construction was an important contributor to high unemployment and economic stagnation.(10) Government intervention in housing was an inescapable part of the general response to the Depression. The patterns of this intervention inevitably reflected the prevailing capitalist ideology, as well as the distribution of power within the existing housing sector.

The principal strategy for dealing with the various aspects of the housing problem was the promotion of mortgaged home ownership through long-term, low down payment mortgage loans. This new type of loan was designed to undercut the income/housing cost problem in two ways: 1) economically, by lessening the monthly payments for a given size loan and reducing the personal savings needed to buy; and 2) politically, by promoting the illusion of ownership through the reality of debt. This type of loan was supposed to stimulate the demand for houses and mortgages, which in turn would contribute to overall economic growth as well as benefit the construction and lending industries.

The tremendous insecurity of renting plus the apparent economic and social benefits of ownership have long made homeownership the desired goal of most families in this country. The long-term, low down payment mortgage was designed to make this goal realizable for the majority of people, even as it mitigated the benefits and served the larger interests of capital. Homeownership has long been seen as a device for social control in a capitalist society; and the burden of a mortgage is even more effective than freehold ownership. Engels denounced homeownership schemes a century ago as a trap for the working class. President Hoover's Conference on Home Building and Home Ownership in 1931 considered the promotion of homeownership to be an essential ingredient for increasing social stability. And one of the clearest statements of class interest was voiced by a consultant to the National Commission on Urban Problems following the urban riots of the mid-sixties: "Homeownership encourages social stability and financial responsibility. It gives the homeowners a financial stake in society. . . . It helps eliminate the 'alienated tenant' psychology."(11)

Under capitalism homeownership ostensibly provides the working class with some measure of compensation for their continued exploitation and alienation in the workplace – some control over one's existence. Yet, in the process the interests of the homeowners tend to become tied to the interest of landlords and lenders. Homeowners generally become concerned about property values, hoping they will rise indefinitely and resenting the intrusion of "undesirable" neighbors. They become tied to a location. This loss of mobility means a concomitant loss of power to negotiate their conditions of employment. And because of the burden of mortgage payments they become more reluctant to jeopardize the stability of their incomes through strikes or other militant actions, fearing foreclosure and consequent loss of both their investment and their shelter.

Such a homeownership strategy could never have been implemented without substantial government support. In order to encourage financial institutions to make loans with low down payments and long terms – indeed, to stimulate almost any lending in the 1930s – the federal government had to provide protection and assistance. This included mortgage insurance and guarantees through the Federal Housing Administration (FHA) and later the Veterans Administration (VA) so that the banks could lend money for the construction and sale of owner-occupied housing without having to fear any loss if the borrowers could not pay. It included the Federal Home Loan Bank System (FHLBS), which insures savings accounts and provides back-up funds to lending institutions that specialize in homeownership loans. It included the Federal National Mortgage Association (FNMA), designed to facilitate the free flow of mortgage money throughout the country and attract additional funds to the residential mortgage system. And it also included a plan to make income tax benefits available to owners but not to renters.(12)

Even with all of these devices, the financial institutions could not undertake any lending at all if they did not obtain savings deposits. It thus took World War II to restart the economy and generate the savings needed to set the restructured mortgage system in motion. By 1946 savings deposits were nearly twice their 1940 level.(13) These new funds, along with the need for housing, which had been unmet since the start of the Depression, provided the impetus for the postwar housing and mortgage boom. This was facilitated by the availability of low down payment, long-term, federally backed loans.(14)

For two decades after World War II this strategy was remarkably successful. Along with military spending and imperialism, the suburban/debt economy fueled the postwar prosperity of the U.S. Between 1946 and 1965 more than 29 million new housing units were started, most of them single family suburban homes, representing a construction cost of over $300 billion. Owner-occupied housing increased from about 40 percent of all housing at the end of the war to over 60 percent by the 1960s, as the number of owner-occupied units more than doubled, while the number of renter-occupied units barely increased.(15)

During the same years, total debt in the economy grew from a little less than $400 billion to more than $1,200 billion, of which housing debt was the biggest single element (see table 5.1).

In 1900 mortgage debt was equal to about 20 percent of disposable income; by 1930 the ratio had more than doubled to 41 percent. In 1930 residential mortgage debt was about $30 billion; in 1935 it was about $24 billion. As late as 1946 it was less than $30 billion. But by 1965, the proliferation of suburbs financed primarily by government-insured mortgage loans had increased residential mortgage debt by more than 750 percent to nearly $260 billion. The rapid growth of suburbs and homeownership also generated a vast increase in consumer spending for cars – so residents could get to and from their homes – and furniture and appliances – to put in their homes. At the same time, spreading housing developments generated other large suburban construction projects such as shopping centers, roads, schools, and municipal buildings.(16) This consumer spending and infrastructure was also financed largely through credit, but the amount was far less than the housing debt. The new mortgage system was indispensable for the postwar boom. But it also contained some serious weaknesses that began to surface along with other problems of U.S. capitalism in the late 1960s.

CONTRADICTIONS IN THE NEW MORTGAGE SYSTEM

The structure of the housing and mortgage industries after World War II contained four major contradictory elements.

Mortgage Debt Increases

First, the rapid and massive build-up of residential mortgage debt, which was such an essential contributor to and component of economic growth, was considerably faster than the growth of the economy as a whole. Housing debt thus grew faster than the ability to repay it, just as it had during the 1920s. Between 1946 and 1965 total private debt increased from 73 percent of GNP to 127 percent of GNP; residential debt was the biggest element of the increase, growing from 14 percent of GNP in 1946 to 37 percent of GNP in 1965. In 1950 the per capita

Table 5.1. Debt Outstanding in the U.S. Economy
(in billions of dollars)

	1946	1965	1970	1975	1978**
Total Debt	$396.6	$1,252.5	$1,881.9	$3,028.8	$3,786.9
Federal Government	229.5	266.4	301.1	446.3	622.7
State & Local Governments	13.7	98.3	144.8	222.7	300.9
Total Private Debt	153.4	878.9	1,397.2	2,281.0	2,755.8
Consumer Credit	8.4	89.9	127.2	196.7	275.6
Residential Mortgages	29.2	257.6	358.2	592.1	881.5
Commercial Mortgages	7.7	54.5	85.6	159.3	211.8
Debt of Non-Financial Corporations:					
Long-term bonds	24.4	97.8	167.9	254.2	422.8
Short-term debt	20.4*	71.2	128.9	207.5	
Gross National Product	209.6	688.1	982.4	1,516.3	2,106.9
Disposable Personal Income	158.6	472.2	685.9	1,084.4	1,451.4
Residential Mortgage Debt as a Percent of GNP	13.9%	37.4%	36.5%	39.0%	41.8%
Residential Mortgage Debt as a Percent of Disp. Pers. Income	18.4%	54.5%	52.2%	54.6%	60.7%

*1950
**1978 preliminary

Sources: Federal Reserve Board, Federal Reserve Bulletin, and U.S. Dept. of Commerce, Survey of Current Business, Various issues; and Economic Report of the President: 1978.

housing debt was 23 percent of per capita disposable income (i.e., income minus taxes). By 1960 it had swollen to 46 percent, and by 1965 to 55 percent (see table). Once again, the debt, which was essential to growth in the past and present, was placing an increasingly heavy burden on the future.

The growth of mortgage debt was attributable to the rapid increase in housing construction and home buying in the decades after World War II. The growing debt was also induced by the change in mortgage loan ratios and terms. Lower down payment loans create more debt even if house prices and market activity do not increase, and longer terms mean lower rates of repayment in the early years of the loans. At current interest rates, only 10-12 percent of a twenty-year loan has been repaid after five years and just three to five percent of a thirty-year loan.(17) Thus, lenders have had to place more and more reliance on new funds, instead of being able to finance new loans from repayments on old loans.

Housing Production Fluctuations

Second, while the growth of mortgage credit contributed tremendously to the growth and profitability of the entire housing industry, increasing dependence on credit made the production of new housing and the cost of buying and occupying both new and used housing increasingly sensitive to the supply and cost of mortgage money. Because of high production costs and because the industry has not been dominated by corporate giants with internal sources of funds, about 75 percent of the money used to finance the construction of new housing in the postwar era has been borrowed. Builders and developers have usually obtained short-term construction loans – for several months for single-family homes and up to two to three years for large projects – which have to be repaid when the project is finished and sold or occupied. The major construction lenders for multi-family housing have been commercial banks, while savings and loans associations have been the major lenders for single-family homes.(18)

Lenders have generally been willing to make construction loans only under several conditions. These loans must be as profitable as other types of investment (with adjustments for perceived differences in risk). Savings and loans associations are required by law to put most of their money into housing, but they can adjust the mix between construction loans and long-term mortgages. Commercial banks have no such restrictions; construction loans have been extremely attractive to them when other short-term interest rates are low, but when corporations and the government have increased the competition for the funds of commercial banks, builders and developers have tended to get squeezed out because it is harder for them to pass on higher interest costs. This is partly because their heavy dependence on debt makes the cost of a new house much more dependent on the interest rate than is the price of a manufactured good or the budget of a government. Large corporations and governments can also easily pass on higher interest costs because they have more of a monopoly than housing developers.

Rising interest rates have likewise tended to reduce the willingness of lenders to make construction loans because these loans (and the interest on them) are paid off through the long-term loans that are taken out when the housing is completed and that, in turn, have to be repaid by residents out of their incomes. Until the highly speculative lending booms of the late 1960s and early 1970s, construction lenders generally required developers to have a commitment for long-term financing before they would grant a construction loan. Long-term lenders would only make such a commitment if they were sure there would be residents willing and able to make the monthly payments on long-term loans. Thus rising interest rates for long-term mortgages, as well as for construction loans make it harder for developers to devise economically feasible projects and obtain construction financing.

Ironically the lengthening of mortgage terms, intended to reduce the monthly cost of mortgage payments, has made the payments much more sensitive to interest rates. When interest rates double from five percent to 10 percent, the monthly payments on a ten-year loan increase by only 32 percent, but payments on a 20-year loan go up by 46 percent and on a 30-year loan by 64 percent.

The increased sensitivity of housing to short-term and long-term interest rates has led to ups and downs in housing production; as interest rates have varied, the total supply of credit and housing's share of credit have also varied.(19) Although the business cycle was relatively mild for two decades after World War II, housing production fell an average of 30 percent during each of the three major periods of restricted mortgage credit that have occurred prior to the mid-sixties. Thus while the mortgage system made substantial housing production possible during the postwar period, its year-to-year instability left the construction industry permeated with small, labor-intensive firms that could easily enter and leave but which, for the most part, could never develop factory technology and achieve economies of scale. More significantly was the risk that a downward turn in the business cycle could lead to major economic problems if the inability of buyers to obtain and afford long-term mortgages left developers with houses they could not sell and lenders with uncollectable construction loans.

Financial Vulnerability and Thrift Institutions

The third major contradictory element in the new mortgage system has been the increased vulnerability of those financial institutions that have specialized in long-term mortgages. Savings and loan associations and mutual savings banks – the so-called thrift institutions – have been the mainstays of residential lending since World War II. In 1946 they accounted for about 35 percent of the money outstanding as housing debt; by 1965 their share had increased to 57 percent, where it has remained. Savings and loan associations, as required by law, have consistently had more than 80 percent of their assets in residential mortgages; by 1965 the percentage had reached more than 85 percent. Although mutual savings banks have not been legally required to invest in mortgages, they have become steadily more involved since World War II: in 1945 just 20 percent of their assets were in residential mortgages; by 1965 the ratio had grown to nearly 70 percent, and has since leveled off. Out of their total mortgage portfolios, the thrift institutions have on average had less than 10 percent in short-term construction loans; more than 90 percent have been long-term mortgages.(20)

Long-term, fixed interest rate mortgages provide lenders with the same rate of return year after year regardless of what has happened to interest rates since the loan was made. This is not a problem for diversified lenders, such as commercial banks, which do not have most of their funds tied up in such long-term loans. Nor would it be a problem for thrift institutions if they obtained their funds on a long-term, fixed interest rate basis. The potential difficulty arises because thrift institutions have obtained money almost entirely from savings accounts, which have been attractive investments for many people because they offer liquidity as well as security and geographical convenience. Those who want to be able to withdraw their funds quickly – small savers who must meet unexpected expenditures or emergencies; and wealthier savers in order to shift their money into more profitable investments – benefit from savings accounts.

Thrift institutions cannot easily or quickly raise the interest rates they pay on savings accounts because most of their income is from long-term, fixed interest rate mortgages. Until the mid-1960s interest rates on savings accounts were generally competitive with other investments and were substantially higher than the rate of inflation so this rigidity was not a problem. Thrift institutions were thus fairly successful at sustaining a steady inflow of funds and using them to support their own growth and finance a large fraction of the expansion of mortgage credit. In periods of tight money, housing funds were restricted, but primarily because corporations and the federal government could compete more successfully for the funds of commercial banks and insurance companies as indicated earlier, not because of significant changes in savings deposits and mortgage lending at thrift institutions. As the major suppliers of housing credit, thrift institutions were relatively insulated from the rest of the capital markets, and the risk in "borrowing short and lending long" did not yet manifest itself as a contradiction.(21)

Promotion of Homeownership

The fourth major tension in the new mortgage system has grown out of the promotion of homeownership. The vast and overwhelming majority of Americans have aspired to be homeowners. For many years, the new mortgage system made the dream available to most who pursued it (though certainly not the poorest), even though it saddled people with immense debts. Homeownership became a symbol of status and almost a civil right for anyone who saved up for the down payment. Homeownership was also considered a hedge against inflation and a way to accumulate wealth. Having created the expectation, fostered the hope, and promoted the dream, what would be the consequences if capitalism could no longer deliver the goods?

THE CRISIS OF CAPITALISM AND ITS EFFECTS ON HOUSING

During the 1960s, the postwar prosperity began to crumble. U.S. imperialism was challenged at home and abroad. Resistance of the Third World to U.S. domination, especially in Southeast Asia, forced the government to increase military spending. Urban riots and domestic opposition to the war forced increases in spending for social programs while restricting tax increases. The federal budget thus had a growing deficit in the late 60s, which had to be financed by borrowing in competition with other users of credit.

At the same time that Third World insurgency was beginning to threaten the foreign investments of U.S. firms, growing competition from Europe and Japan posed an additional challenge. These foreign pressures, along with decreasing unemployment and rising wages at home resulted in a sharp decline in corporate profits in the late 60s. In response, the corporations began to borrow more money to finance moveouts and mergers that they hoped would restore profits.

These new demands for credit have come on top of the continuing needs of other sectors of the economy, including housing. This process has increasingly exposed a fundamental contradiction in the whole system of debt financing. On the one hand, if the federal government allows the money supply to increase to meet all of the system's needs for borrowed funds, prices will rise (since the amount of borrowed money being spent will increase faster than the amount of goods and services being produced). Inflation leads to higher interest rates and more borrowing in anticipation of further price increases. Debt accelerates far ahead of the ability to repay it, leading to a financial crisis.

On the other hand, if the government tries to restrict the growth of credit to prevent or limit inflation, some borrowers get squeezed out. Previously accumulated debts eventually have to be paid, and many individuals and businesses are totally dependent on new loans to pay off the old ones. Without continued access to credit to pay their bills, they may go bankrupt. Since the banks and other creditors have also borrowed heavily to expand their lending and stimulate the economy, when they do not get paid a chain of defaults can ensue. Thus a credit squeeze can also bring the financial system to the brink of collapse.

As the corporations and the government have tried with increasing desperation to reverse the decline in profits, the economy has swung more and more violently between the poles of this contradiction. Housing has been at the center of the crisis because of the problems arising from the spread of long-term mortgages and the associated growth of mortgage debt.

Since 1966, increasing competition for loans has caused a steady, long-term rise in the general level of interest rates on top of the short-term fluctuations. Periods of tight money have been increasingly severe, with interest rates soaring higher each time and housing credit being restricted ever more sharply. As interest rates on savings accounts have become less competitive, wealthier depositors have withdrawn savings to invest in more profitable instruments offered by commercial banks, the federal government, and industrial corporations. For example, during the tight money period in 1966, households diverted more than $16 billion of their savings into other types of investments. In 1969, they diverted $27 billion from savings accounts, and in 1973-75 nearly $85 billion. New savings deposits and mortgage repayments barely offset these massive withdrawals from thrift institutions, leaving them with little money for new long-term mortgages and construction loans.(22)

In addition to the problems of the thrift institutions, increased corporate borrowing left commercial banks with less inclination and ability to continue to make construction loans whenever credit was restricted and short-term interest rates rose. Thus, in 1966, housing starts plunged 30 percent in just six months to the lowest level since 1946. As the credit supply was allowed to expand again, housing production recovered in the late sixties, and then declined somewhat less severely in the recession of 1969-70. Housing then led the credit boom of the early 1970s (see table 5.1.), as production reached the highest level in history in 1972. But by 1974, when the economy entered the worst recession since the 1930s, the bottom fell out. In 1975 housing starts were more than 50 percent below the 1972 peak and lower even than in 1966. Half a million new homes stood vacant and thousands of apartment buildings were left unfinished as mortgage credit evaporated. Housing production has traditionally led the economy out of recession, but at the beginning of 1977, nearly a year and a half after the recession supposedly hit bottom, housing starts were still 30 percent below what they had been in 1972. By mid-1977, after three and a half years of depression in the housing industry, a new speculative boom finally brought housing starts back up to an annual rate of about two million units, where production remained until the end of 1978. However, even after this eventual recovery, housing production has remained far short of the official national goal set in 1967 of an average of 2.6 million units a year. Over the 10 years since this goal was established, housing construction has fallen nearly 9 million units short of that 26 million unit target.(23)

In addition to its impact on housing production, the crisis has also had a devastating effect on the cost of housing. Because of the dependence on credit and the sensitivity of housing costs to interest rates, the cost of shelter reflects a piggy-back effect of rising interest rates on top of rising house prices. Thus, between 1970 and 1976, while median family income was rising 47 percent and the overall Consumer Price Index went up 46 percent; median sales prices for new houses rose 90 percent, and the monthly ownership cost for a median-priced new house rose 100 percent, while the monthly ownership cost for a median-priced existing house rose 65 percent. Between 1976 and 1978 median family income rose another 16 percent, but median sales prices for both new and used single-family houses rose about 27 percent, and ownership costs for buyers of such houses rose nearly 40 percent. During the 1950s, about two-thirds of all families could have afforded the typical new house. By 1970 the proportion had declined to one-half, by 1976 to just one-fourth, and by 1978 only 15 percent of all families could afford the typical new house.(24)

Housing has clearly been one of the disaster areas of the past decade. However, the housing sector has not been merely a passive victim of the pervasive crisis. Housing and finance capitalists, with the aid of the government, have made considerable effort to deal with the weakening financial structure of the mortgage industry. These attempts have only exacerbated the inherent instability of the economy and made housing more significant strategically.

HOUSING AS CONTRIBUTOR TO THE CRISIS

Mortgage lending has traditionally been a rather localized and specialized business, involving investors who could directly evaluate and monitor both the properties and the borrowers. Mortgage insurance, plus the gradual standardization of mortgages, was supposed to open up this market by making mortgages more attractive and less risky to investors who might be far away from a property or might not have invested extensively in mortgages before. Local thrift institutions or mortage companies still originate the loans, but they they can sell the mortgages to other investors – life insurance companies, pension funds, banks, or even thrift institutions in other parts of the country. The local lenders act as collectors of the monthly payments and receive a fee for this service.

In this so-called secondary mortgage market – originally created just for FHA and VA loans but extended to include privately-insured loans as well since 1970 – mortgages are traded much like bonds. Sales price discounts or premiums make up the difference between the interest rate paid by the residents of the housing and the rate of profit desired by the investor. In this manner local originators of mortgages are not locked into a loan waiting for the borrower to pay it off and funds are attracted from more sources and directed to local areas with high demand.

The secondary mortgage markets have never worked fully as intended. Large private investors, such as pension funds, have continued to regard mortgages as too risky and unfamiliar. So government-backed agencies have become the principal investors in the secondary mortgage market as the economic crisis struck the traditional mortgage industry. In the tight money period of 1966, the Federal National Mortgage Association went to Wall Street, raised $2.1 billion, and used the money to buy mortgages from thrift institutions and mortgage companies. In

1969-70, FNMA, the newly-created Government National Mortgage Association (GNMA), and Federal Home Loan Mortgage Corporation (FHLMC) raised $9.6 billion in the capital market to buy mortgages. During the massive inflation and depression of 1973-75, these three agencies borrowed $17.5 billion to pump into residential mortgages.(25)

In addition to these secondary mortgage market activities by federal agencies, the Federal Home Loan Bank Board also raised money to prop up thrift institutions that were losing savings deposits. They provided nearly $1 billion in 1966, another $5.3 billion in 1969-70, and $13.7 billion in 1973-74. In 1969 and 1974 more than 40 percent of all the new money for residential mortgages came from federal agencies. This money came not from traditional savings accounts, but from the national capital markets.(26)

State and local finance and development agencies also mushroomed since the late 1960s and raised more money for residential mortgages. By the middle of 1975 they had $10.6 billion in housing loans outstanding, and by the spring of 1978 they had $13.1 billion. These agencies obtain funds by selling tax exempt notes and bonds in the national financial markets. Indeed, the increasing activity by state and local governments in raising mortgage money in this way has led to attempts by the federal government to limit such activity to funding for low income housing because of concern that the U.S. Treasury will lose billions of dollars in taxes because the notes and bonds are tax exempt.(27)

Real Estate Investment Trusts (REITs), which are private companies with special federal tax advantages, also became a new force in the mortgage industry. Their assets grew from almost nothing in the late 1960s to over $21 billion by the mid-1970s. At their peak of success in 1974, about $6.7 billion of their assets were in residential mortgages – primarily construction loans for luxury apartments and condominiums. They obtained money partially by selling shares in the stock market, but mostly by borrowing at high interest rates from large commercial banks. However, they became a victim of the financial crunch of the mid-1970s and never fully recovered – their residential mortgages amounted to only $2.4 billion in the spring of 1978.(28)

The development of these new institutions to raise and allocate mortgage credit has not been entirely successful, as revealed by the 65 percent drop in housing starts during 1973-75. They have, however, had two very significant consequences for the financial stability of capitalism. First, they increased the total demand for credit in the economy. When the supply of credit has been plentiful, the result has been a more rapid growth in the total amount of debt and a relatively larger share allocated to real estate in general and housing in particular. For example, during the late 1960s, before the new mortgage institutions reached their maturity, the growth of mortgage debt slipped relative to that of corporate and government borrowings. From 1946 through 1965 residential mortgages accounted for 27 percent of the total increase in debt; in the following five years housing debt was only 15 percent of the total. However, during the boom of the early

1970s, despite the massive increase in corporate and government borrowing, the new institutions enabled housing debt to increase its share to 21 percent of the total increase in debt. In the late 1970s, as corporate and government borrowing leveled off, residential debt accounted for an astounding 38 percent of the total increase in debt in the economy (see table 5.1), as discussed more fully below.

There was a huge increase in the construction of conventional housing, subsidized housing, condominiums, resort and retirement communities. There was also a large amount of speculation in land and existing buildings, as rents and house prices spiraled upward. The changes in mortgage financing thus gave a substantial boost to the real growth of the economy and also to the unprecedented inflation and the overblown credit "bubble."

On the other hand, when government monetary policy has sought to contain inflation by reducing the supply of credit, the new mortgage institutions, especially the federally backed agencies, have only intensified competition for scarce credit, leading to even higher interest rates throughout the system. Higher interest rates not only added to inflation but also led to further withdrawals of savings deposits, as savers pursued the higher returns available elsewhere. Increased withdrawals from thrift institutions substantially offset the additional housing funds raised through the capital markets and so weakened a number of small local thrifts that they were saved only by being absorbed by large financial institutions. Thus the atempts of mortgage lenders and housing capitalists to compete more effectively for funds during periods of economic contraction have not been fully successful, but they have contributed to higher housing costs, higher interest rates generally, and greater concentration in the mortgage industry.

Second, residential finance is no longer a relatively separate and insulated component of the credit system. Many investors other than thrift institutions and small savers now have tens of billions of dollars tied up with the mortgage system. In particular, large commercial banks – the linchpins of finance capital – became deeply enmeshed in direct construction loans, in loans to REITs, and in securities of federal and state housing credit agencies. The stability of the structure of residential debt is thus increasingly vital for the stability of the entire financial structure of capitalism. But the stability of the housing debt system depends upon continued mortgage payments from people in existing housing and affordable long-term mortgages for new housing being built with short-term construction loans. The ratio of mortgage debt to disposable income, which had climbed from 27 percent in 1950 to 46 percent in 1960 and 48 percent in 1970, soared to 55 percent by 1975 and 61 percent in 1978 (see table 5.1). In the mid-1960s and again in 1975 more than one percent of all homeowners were 60 days or more behind on their mortgage payments. During the 1960s the number of mortgage foreclosures per year doubled from about 50,000 to about 100,000 and by 1975 had increased to over 140,000, which was about one-half of one percent of all mortgaged structures, most of them homes and apartment buildings.(29)

The real estate bubble of the early 1970s burst in 1973. Over the next three years increased mortgage defaults reflected the worst financial disaster since the early 1930s. Overbuilding plus soaring development costs and rising interest rates resulted in a 40 percent drop in housing starts in 1973. With the addition of tight money and rising unemployment, housing construction plunged 40 percent more through 1974 and into 1975. Many developers who had begun projects before the collapse ran out of money before they finished. Lenders refused to provide more money because they now had little money to lend and because they knew that there would be no market for the housing even if the projects were finished.

The collapse of the real estate boom hit the REITs especially hard because of their involvement with some of the most speculative and risky types of projects such as resort and retirement communities and luxury apartments and condominiums. Also, to qualify for the special federal tax loopholes, which made them such an attractive form of investment, REITs had to pay out nearly all of their earnings to investors, leaving no reserves to absorb losses. Confronted, on one hand, with unfinished or unmarketable projects that generated no income, and the need to repay or refinance hundreds of millions of dollars in short-term bank loans at interest rates of 13 percent or more on the other, many REITs simply defaulted on these loans.(30)

In December 1975, for example, Continental Mortgage Investors of Boston, the second biggest REIT in the country, with assets of $600 million, defaulted on over $500 million in short-term loans. Three months later it filed for bankruptcy in federal court. Chase Manhattan, the largest REIT, with assets of $800 million, and a product of the Rockefeller financial empire, was earning no income on 70 percent of its assets in 1976. It reorganized and managed to reduce some of its loans but it never recovered, and it, too, finally filed for bankruptcy early in 1979.(31)

The real estate collapse of 1973-75 also helped to trigger the fiscal crisis of state and municipal governments when the New York State Urban Development Corporation defaulted on $130 million worth of bank loans in February 1975 – the largest government default since the 1930s. UDC was a construction agency set up in 1968 to develop housing and new communities, financed through the sale of tax exempt bonds and notes. Caught in the same vise of rapidly rising construction costs and interest rates, a decreasing credit supply, and a weakening housing market, UDC was unable to pay its bank loans as they came due. Denied new credit to pay off the loans, the agency defaulted. UDC investors were soon bailed out by a $200 million state appropriation to finish projects already underway, but the default called into question the security of state and local debts across the country.(32)

More and more defaults by real estate borrowers, large and small, sent shock waves through the banking system. Not only did the banks suffer losses on their investments; they themselves had built up huge debts that could not be fully repaid. In late 1973, the U.S. National Bank failed, with assets of $800 million. This was followed in 1974 by the collapse of the Franklin National Bank, the 20th largest bank in the U.S., with assets of $1.7 billion. In 1975, 13 U.S. commercial banks folded, along with a number of European banks. In nearly every case, losses on direct real estate loans and loans to other mortgage lenders, such as REITs, were significant elements in the bankruptcies.(33)

The financial system did not, of course, collapse. Many real estate developers went out of business and individual and institutional investors probably absorbed at least a billion dollars in losses from the assorted loan defaults, bankruptcies, and reorganizations. Many of the largest commercial banks offset some of their losses by forcing financially strapped city and state governments to refinance their own outstanding debts at extremely high interest rates. The governments, in turn, had to cut back on public services, thus forcing the mass of people into the position of indirectly paying for many of the losses associated with the financial collapse. The eventual recovery of the economy did restore the profitability of much of the foreclosed real estate and even some of the REITs – such as Continental Mortgage Investors – though in much reduced versions.(34)

HOUSING AND THE CONTINUING CRISIS

From 1975 to 1979 the U.S. economy once again experienced a period of growth. It continued to be a period of crisis though, as inflation again soared to double-digit levels and as credit expanded faster than real growth in the economy. Again, housing was an essential element in the expansion. This time, however, housing inflation and mortgage borrowing were an even bigger part of the economic bubble, so that there is now every reason to expect another financial disaster, with housing as both a major contributor and a major victim.

Between 1975 and 1978, residential mortgage debt increased by nearly $300 billion – an increase of nearly 50 percent in just three years. Housing mortgages accounted for 38 percent of the total increase in public and private debt and more than 60 percent of the total increase in private debt, proportions that far exceed any prior period (see table 5.1).

This debt explosion contributed to and was a consequence of the tremendous inflation in residential property values in the late 1970s and the extraordinary rate at which houses were sold and refinanced. Sales prices, as indicated previously, have, in recent years increased by about 15 percent a year. The volume of new homes sold was about 820,000 a year in 1977 and 1978 – about 100,000 above the previous peak in 1972 and 300,000 above the 1974 trough. On average, about 3.5 million existing homes changed hands each year in 1976, 1977, and 1978 – nearly 50 percent above the peak years of the early 1970s. Finally, many owners of existing, single-family homes have simply refinanced their mortgages in order to extract the rise in property values without selling their homes. For example, in the second quarter of 1977, the mortgage debt on existing single-family homes increased at an annual rate of about $60 billion through refinancing of existing mortgages.(35)

The remarkable amount of buying and borrowing in the housing market in recent years has occurred in spite of – and, in part, because of – the declining affordability of single-family housing. Many of those who have bought homes, and all of those who have refinanced their homes, were already on the escalator of rising property values, although their new mortgages have generally been for larger sums and at higher interest rates so that their housing costs have risen substantially. More significantly, younger, first-time homebuyers have not dominated the housing boom. Those who have jumped onto the escalator to avoid being left out of homeownership altogether have frequently taken on a severe financial burden. For example, in a survey of 2,000 who bought new homes between mid-1977 and mid-1978, only 30 percent were first-time buyers and over 60 percent of these first-time buyers had two incomes in the household. The median income of all the buyers in the survey was nearly $25,000, and in buying the homes their monthly housing expenditures increased, on average, by over 60 percent.(36) Expressed in aggregate terms, residential mortgage debt increased from about 55 percent of disposable personal income in 1975 to nearly 61 percent in 1978 – by far the highest level in history – suggesting the growing danger posed by the conflict between housing costs and incomes (see table 5.1).

As in the past, the boom was fueled by the credit expansion policies of the Federal Reserve Board, plus special government efforts in housing finance, which prop up the housing industry and use housing as a stimulus to the overall economy. This time, all of the previously established institutions – except the REITs – continued to play a major part, along with an important new instrument that helped the thrift institutions to attract and retain deposits as interest rates rose. In June of 1978, the government decided to let thrift institutions issue six-month savings certificates, paying interest up to a quarter of a percent higher than 6-month Treasury bills. With interest rates on these certificates of up to 10 percent, more than $150 billion had gone into these certificates by the spring of 1979 and then into residential mortgages. Of course, mortgage interest rates rose in response, passing 10 percent late in 1978 and, in some parts of the country, reaching nearly 12 percent by mid-1979.(37)

With inflation accelerating out of control, stimulated in part by the continued availability of high-cost credit, the end of the boom was in sight by 1979. Housing starts declined 30 percent in just several months; signs of overbuilding of new housing appeared in parts of the country; and the government was forced to reduce the interest rate on the 6-month certificates. This action triggered a record outflow of $1.5 billion from thrift institutions in April 1979.(38) The expanding housing bubble was clearly beginning to shrink. The crucial question, though, was whether the onset of recession – with reduced credit and rising unemployment – would cause the bubble to deflate gradually or to burst suddenly, wreaking havoc comparable to or even greater than that in 1973-75.

HOUSING AND SOCIALIST POLITICS

Ultimately, there is no way out for capitalism. All that it really has to offer at this juncture is higher-priced houses and more debt. Moreover, rapid expansion of debt on top of existing debt just increases the risk of financial collapse since the next downturn in the economy will leave an incredibly large number of overmortgaged homeowners and developers unable to maintain their mortgage payments.

At the same time, though, the growing dependence of the entire financial system on the ability and willingness of people to continue to pay the mortgage debt costs – directly as homeowners and through rents as tenants – has given housing rather remarkable strategic significance. In the short run it is politically inconceivable that even a small percentage of the population could be organized into a force that would deliberately threaten to use this power as leverage to bring about radical change. Furthermore, any attempts to organize on this basis would surely bring swift and heavy repression and would generate little sympathy from the majority of people who, at this point, still believe that they can benefit from the capitalist housing system.

On the other hand, the strategic importance that housing has acquired does provide the working class with a weapon that a powerful movement might eventually choose to use as part of a revolutionary strategy. There will be and have been situations where fairly sizable groups of well-organized tenants may decide to try to force their buildings into foreclosure and then prevent evictions and resale of the property, in order to wipe out the mortgage payments that are at the heart of most families' housing problems. Such militancy will obviously meet considerable capitalist resistance, even though isolated instances certainly do not threaten the entire financial system.(39)

The fact that tenants do not generally share homeowners' direct interest maintaining mortgage payments leads, finally, to an interesting consideration for socialists. Although most tenants are working class people, the distinctions between tenants and homeowners by no means corresponds to class distinctions, especially since so many working class people have become homeowners. Nonetheless, the growing housing problem in the United States seems to be giving rise to a process of "tenantization," which is reducing the possibility and meaning of homeownership, especially for the working class.

There are, so far, three discernible threads to this tenantization process. First, many young families who, in the past, could have eventually expected to buy a home are now finding it financially impossible. As indicated earlier, only about a quarter of the population can now afford the typical new house. Most first-time homebuyers with incomes under $20,000 a year have little choice other than mobile homes or two- to four-unit houses in neighborhoods where property values are rising little, if at all. Even here the costs are staggering, while the economic benefits are illusory. In many areas and for many young families, these options are not even available. Thus they remain caught in the rental market.

Second, many families who bought homes in the past ten years have lost them (and their investments) through foreclosure and have been forced back into the rental market. As mentioned above, the rate of foreclosures has nearly tripled since the early 1960s. Most of the victims have been working class people and a large proportion have been black, especially in older urban areas where tens of thousands of homes were sold under FHA programs. These new homeowners often discovered that they had acquired unsound houses at inflated prices, which they could not afford to repair and continue to make mortgage payments, particularly in the face of inflation and unemployment.(40)

Third, in many cities there are working class areas where homeowners are unable to sell their houses. "Redlining" practices – the refusal by banks to lend mortgage money and insurance companies to issue fire insurance – declining city services, deterioration, and inadequate incomes have led to the virtual collapse of the housing market in these areas. In some instances, real and imagined dangers have caused people to abandon their homes and move into apartments elsewhere. In most cases, though, residents remain and continue to pay their mortgages and property taxes, even though the market value of their equity (property value minus outstanding mortgages) may be negligible or even negative. They may have a deed, but they are, in effect, tenants.

While one should never underestimate the capacity of capitalism to find imaginative, short-run solutions to its problems, the slow but steady disintegration of the system will surely undermine the myth of homeownership as a mechanism for containing working class consciousness and militancy. The first symptom of this disenchantment will be the growing frustration at being denied the opportunity to realize the American dream of a home of one's own. The second symptom could be a declining commitment to the protection of property values and the payment of debt, especially as the capitalist mortgage and housing system is seen to conflict with the need for adequate shelter, as well as with the need for food, clothing, and medical care.

Consciousness will of course change slowly – the myth of homeownership has been deeply rooted and well cultivated – but changing objective conditions will provide socialists with the opportunity to contribute to the growing realization that capitalism can never meet people's legitimate desires for secure tenure, decent housing, safe and congenial communities, and for an economic cushion, which so much of the myth of homeownership rests upon. Socialists can also contribute to the growing realization that housing struggles can be an important arena in the process of transcending capitalism – not only because these struggles can help to build organization and consciousness, but because they also have the capacity to threaten the most vulnerable part of the capitalist house of cards. And finally, socialists can use housing to begin to project a vision of an alternative society by promoting the revitalization, adaptation, and expansion of public housing – not ugly, isolated, oppressive, welfare ghettos – but attractive, well designed, resident-controlled housing that is free of the burden of mortgage payments and dependence on the private credit market, and is financed through direct government construction grants. The struggle for such a program can contribute immensely to building the kind of movement that will be required for the larger conflict to come.(41)

NOTES

(1) The problem of incomes and shelter costs is more fully discussed, the operational definition of shelter poverty is developed and justified, and detailed results on the extent of the problem are presented in Stone, Shelter Poverty: A New Approach to Defining and Measuring the Housing Cost/Income Problem, 1980.

(2) Ibid.

(3) A fascinating, popular account of history of one New York tenement building, including the late 19th and early 20th century context of housing reforms, is Klein, Let in the Sun, especially Chapters 4 and 5 and the notes to these two chapters, which refer to some of the classic accounts of the period; see also, Marcuse, "Housing in the History of Early City Planning."

(4) Brecher, Strike! 1972, p. 78.

(5) Most of the rest of this chapter has been drawn from Stone, "Gimme Shelter!" 1978, pp. 182-93, with the addition of analysis of developments betwen 1975 and 1979.

(6) U.S. Bureau of Census, Historical Statistics of the United States, Colonial Times to 1970, 1976, p. 648.

(7) U.S. Bureau of Census, Statistical Abstract of the United States: 1976, 1976, p. 743.

(8) U.S. Bureau of Census, Historical Statistics, 1976, p. 224, 648.

(9) Ibid., p. 265, 646-651, 1032.

(10) U.S. President's Committee on Urban Housing, A Decent Home, 1968, p. 54-5.

(11) U.S. Congress, House, Committee on Banking, Currency and Housing, Subcommittee on Housing and Community Development, Evolution of Role of the Federal Government in Housing and Community Development, A Chronology of Legislative and Selective Executive Actions, 1975, p. 1; National Commission on Urban Problems, Building the American City, 1968, p. 401.

(12) For more detailed analyses of federal supports for mortgage lending and homeownership, see the following: Aaron, Shelter and Subsidies, 1972; Harvey, "The Political Economy of Urbanization," 1975, pp. 119-63; Sawers and Wachtel, "The Distributional Impact of Federal Government Subsidies," 1975; Stone, "Federal Housing Policy," 1973, p. 423-33; Stone, "The Housing Crisis," 1975; U.S. Department of Housing and Urban Development, Housing in the Seventies, 1974.

(13) U.S. Bureau of Census, Historical Statistics, 1976, p. 1032.

(14) The modern mortgage loan typically covers 70 to 100 percent of the price of a house or apartment and is for a term of 20 to 40 years. Interest rates are usually fixed for the term of the mortgage, ranging from about 4-6 percent for loans made before the late 1960s and 8-10 percent or more during most of the 1970s. U.S. Bureau of Census, Statistical Abstract, 1976, p. 752; Federal Home Loan Bank Board, Journal, various issues.

Monthly mortgage payments generally are computed so that the loan will be fully paid off by the end of the term and so that payments will be constant from month to month, with a declining proportion of each payment going for interest as the unpaid balance decreases. Although the monthly costs are reduced by the long repayment term, mortgage payments are normally the biggest single element of occupancy costs, accounting for about 30-70 percent of the cost of shelter for both homeowners and tenants. U.S. Bureau of Labor Statistics, Rent or Buy?, Bulletin 1823, 1974, p. 15; John P. Shelton, "The Cost of Renting versus Owning a Home," Land Economics, 1968, p. 65; Stone, People Before Property, 1972, pp. 136-41.

(15) U.S. Bureau of Census, Historical Statistics, p. 639 and Statistical Abstract, p. 743.

(16) The interaction between the housing and mortgage industries, on the one hand, and the auto and related industries, on the other, in the development of the suburbs has been close and complex. This paper focuses on the crucial importance and housing and residential debt, while others have placed greater stress on the automobile; see, for example: Paul M. Sweezy, "Cars and Cities," 1973; Larry Sawers, "Urban Form and the Mode of Production," 1975.

(17) At the interest rates which were common until the late 60s, after five years of amortization 40-45 percent of a ten-year loan had been repaid, but only 15-20 percent of a twenty-year loan, and only 7-9 percent of a thirty-year loan.

(18) Schulkin, Commercial Bank Construction Lending, 1970 and "Construction Lending at Large Commercial Banks," 1970.

(19) For an excellent discussion of the problem, with data through 1970, see Schechter, The Residential Mortgage Financing Problem, 1971; a good source of more recent data and elementary analysis is U.S. League of Savings Associations, Savings and Loan Fact Book, annual.

(20) Historical Statistics, op. cit., 1976, p. 647; Savings and Loan Fact Book: 1977, p. 82; Arnold H. Diamond, The Supply of Mortgage Credit: 1970-74, 1975, pp. 326-45.

(21) Savings and Loan Fact Book: 1977, p. 55.

(22) Ibid., p. 11.

(23) Figures on housing starts are published monthly in U.S. Bureau of Census, Constructions Reports, Series C20; National Housing Goals were established in the Housing and Urban Development Act of 1968, Public Law 90-448, sections 1601-1603; a listing of the goals and actual production over the ten years can be found in Tenth Annual Report on the National Housing Goal, 1978, p. 26.

(24) Frieden and Solomon, The Nation's Housing: 1975 to 1985, 1977, pp. 103-4, 124; U.S. Bureau of Census, telephone communication of 1978 income data unpublished as of this writing; National Association of Home Builders, "Housing Background," January 20, 1979, p. 2; Federal Home Loan Bank Board, Journal, various issues; Hunter, "Realities of the Market-place Forcing Smaller Units on U.S. Home Buyers," 1975; Jay McMullen, "American House-Buying Power Fading Fast," Boston Sunday Globe, May 6, 1979.

(25) Savings and Loan Fact Book: 1977, p. 34.

(26) Ibid.

(27) U.S. Department of Housing and Urban Development, HUD News, HUD-No. 75-361, September 10, 1975, Table 8, and HUD-No. 78-241, July 26, 1978, Table 20; Miller, "Carter to Back Curbs on Tax-Free Housing Bonds," The New York Times, May 13, 1979.

(28) Securities and Exchange Commission, Real Estate Investment Trusts, 1975, pp. 46, 48, 50; HUD News, HUD-No. 78-241, loc. cit.

(29) "More Mortgages Said Delinquent," Boston Sunday Globe, July 20, 1975; Statistical Abstract, p. 751.

(30) The collapse was chronicled thoroughly in the pages of the business press throughout 1975 and 1976, especially in The New York Times financial sections, The Wall Street Journal, and Business Week.

(31) Corcoran, "CMI-A Crisis Among the REITs," Boston Globe, 4 parts, March 28, 1976 - March 31, 1976; Nessen, "The Small Investor Back in Real Estate," The New York Times, March 11, 1979.

(32) The UDC default and its aftermath were chronicled in detail in The New York Times throughout 1975; the official investigation of UDC and related agencies resulted in the publication of Restoring Credit and Confidence: A Reform Program for New York State and Its Public Authorities, A Report to the Governor by the New York State Moreland Act Commission on the Urban Development Corporation and Other State Financing Agencies, March 31, 1976; a detailed analysis of the relationship of housing to the spreading crisis of state and local governments is presented in Michael Stone and Emily Achtenberg, Hostage! Housing and the Massachusetts Fiscal Crisis, 1977.

(33) Ibid.; Lenzer, "New Signs of Vitality in REITs," Boston Sunday Globe, May 13, 1979; Nessen, "The Small Investor."

(34) National Association of Home Builders, "Housing Background," p. 2; Scott-Stokes, "Mortgage Borrowing Soars in U.S.," The New York Times, December 18, 1977.

(36) National Association of Home Builders, "Housing Background," p. 5.

(37) Don de Bat, "Chicago Bank Mortgage Rates Go to All-time High," Boston Globe, May 21, 1979; Powell, "U.S. Home-loan Rates Reach Record 10%," Boston Globe, April 21, 1979; Dorman, "No Matter How High, People Still Buy," Boston Sunday Globe, May 20, 1979; Bennett, "A Harsh Cure for Savings Banks," The New York Times, June 3, 1979.

(38) Ibid.; U.S. Bureau of Census, Construction Reports, series C20; Lindsay, "Will Orange County Housing Lead the Way Down?," The New York Times, March 25, 1979.

(39) For a discussion of the strategy, see Achtenberg and Stone, Tenants First! A Research and Organizing Guide to FHA Housing, 1974, pp. 108-14, and Brodsky, "Tenants First: FHA Tenants Organize in Massachusetts," 1975; for the response, see "Major Conspiracy Suit Threatens Tenants' Right to Organize Union," 1976, and "An Historical Analysis of Tenants First Coalition," 1977.

(40) See, for example, Boyer, Cities Destroyed for Cash, 1973, and Competition in Real Estate and Mortgage Lending, Hearings before the Subcommittee on Antitrust and Monopoly, Committee on the Judiciary, U.S. Senate, 1971.

(41) Such a housing program is worked out in some detail in Hartman and Stone, "A Socialist Housing Program for the United States," in this volume.

II

Progressive Political Responses

Introduction

Basic changes in the economy, including those related to austerity policies and spatial shifts, which were the focus and point of departure for the analyses presented in the chapters of Part I, have their impacts on political forces and on the way we think about political forces. The politics of the postwar period in western countries was, until the middle 1970s, a politics adapted to economic growth. Growth sustained the dominance of moderate coalitions that governed without overt ideological positions by regulating the access of class and economic sector interests to shares of growth and by projecting the image of modernity – consumer goods available on ever easier terms, roads, shopping centers, urban renewal, airports and other spectacular public and private projects. Part of the image involved the trappings, if not the real functioning, of modern public administration: program budgeting, planning, and other technical innovations demonstrated by a corps of, to use David Halberstam's phrase, "the best and the brightest" young people.

The words of politicians reflected the language and models of mainstream public administration and political science of the period. Social scientists had proclaimed the end of ideology; political programs were, supposedly, not ideological. The political machine had given way (superficially) to reform-minded professional administration. Local politics was sustained by coalitions around growth and real estate investment. Class was an important category, but in an economic, not a political sense. All of these images made sense, despite mounting challenges from the Left, so long as economic expansion continued.

The growth phase had consequences for the function of planning. Planning became a featured part of every government program for national economic management. The French invention of "indicative planning," which attempts to predict economic and business conditions so as to aid public guidance of the economy in cooperation with corporations, was adopted in one form or another in many capitalist countries. Moreover, local level planning went through growth and expansion, from a position of rather narrow physical design functions to one of general programming for local and regional economic growth and social services. The numbers of persons who formally identified themselves as planning professionals grew by a large factor, including those formally trained in other fields, such as health, transportation, social services, who claimed to do planning as part of their work. During the period when federal aid to cities for infrastructure programs in such areas as urban renewal and economic development was increasing, city planners were at the center of a political process involving reform coalitions – real estate interests, construction unions, good government groups and others – which held out hope of general improvement while maintaining support of both middle class and minority and working class constituencies. Planners performed something similar to the indicative planning function in this process: they kept track of the paper work involved in the flow of federal grants. They also calculated costs and benefits involved in keeping the various members of the coalition secure in their belief in the special as well as general benefits to be derived from the planned measures.

The basic ideas of planning, however, which involved drawing systematic pictures of what the future might bring, were at odds with the tenets of liberal, special interest group, and growth oriented politics. Planning entailed at least a degree of goal oriented, comprehensive thinking, while liberal politics stressed the virtue of special interest entrepreneurship. Academic observers had pointed this out. Banfield's "neoconservative" attack on interventionist urban programs,(1) a series of treatises by Lindblom,(2) and a number of diatribes by Wildavsky (3) led the way, though none pointed out that these contradictory tendencies derived from the rapidly growing economy.

Aside from these material and ideological obstacles to systematic planning from the private economy, planning programs faced increased pressure as the urban reform coalitions began to crumble after the middle 1960s. This occurred when large central cities became near ghetto constituencies, middle class people moved out and/or lost faith in the urban programs of that period, and politics became increasingly oriented to constituencies with a base in the city service bureaucracies: schools, public safety, hospitals, sanitation and welfare. Elkin described this as a transition from reform regimes to service regimes,(4) while others cited the arrival of "dependency politics,"(5) that is, as populations became increasingly poor, unemployed, black, Chicano, Puerto Rican, and elderly, politics responded to these constituencies and, even more, to those professional and bureaucratic employees brought to deal with these "problem populations." In these circumstances, the political environment of planners was radically altered. Their justifications for their programs became more important both because of the increasing size of the programs and because of their increasing fiscal and administrative relationship to the federal government, which required accounts and plans.(6) At the same time, the clients of these programs increased in number and in their demands for access to agency decision making, thus providing an opening for grass roots contact for agency professionals, including planners.

By the middle of the 1970s the attack on planning became an onslaught. Skepticism found its way into interoffice memoranda and political debate, and as a practical result planning became vulnerable to budget cutting. More precisely, liberal regimes still found planning useful, but they sought to bring planners under political control to keep them from questioning the decisions about structure and allocations that had been made on political (not planning) criteria. This took the form of attacking the goal formulation function of planners while supporting their technical and legitimizing functions.

With the onset of economic crises and budget constraints in the middle 1970s, politicians had to start using planners in a new way. At the national level, economic crises led to the abandonment of national planning in some cases, to ad hoc project emphases in others. Planners came to be used merely to justify projects that had been previously decided on by politicians, rather than as originators of their own projects. Thus they lost legitimacy, as the governments that hired them lost legitimacy.

Politically, what occurred in the cities had two main facets. On the one hand, there developed what many have called a "legitimation crisis" for government and particularly for the service agencies. It was not just that there was a fiscal crisis. There was also a deepening doubt on the part of clients that the programs were really working for their benefit, making the process of administration difficult. Second, there was a fragmentation in political constituencies. The most obvious contrast was between the pole identified with big business and the dependent populations. This raised knotty questions for politicians and government workers: How should the job be done? What clients should be served? How can I obtain support for my policies?

These developments, foreshadowed in the criticism of liberalism that had appeared in the 1960s by Lowi, Mills, and others, began to be articulated in a more positive and immediately programmatic way by Marxist political scientists and economists in the 1970s.(7) Most important of these for its general impact was the argument presented by James O'Connor.(8) O'Connor outlined the involvement of government in supporting and legitimizing monopoly sector capital – a point made earlier by such liberal and conservative analysts as J.K. Galbraith and Daniel Bell – but O'Connor carried the argument forward to the conclusion that this support is breaking the public treasury and exhausting the public patience.(9) Unable to find private markets for its ever expanding and higher priced output, or employment for its redundant managerial as well as unskilled labor, capital increasingly relies on public causes to bail it out: wars and defense gadgetry, public works, high technology innovations in health, public safety and other public and quasi-public services, and the creation of a "social-industrial complex" to provide at least the appearance of effort to satisfy the needs of society's victims. Further, the government legitimizes these activities by spending money and time telling us that they are solving pressing problems and by supporting technical analyses to that effect. Meanwhile, the crisis deepens, and it becomes difficult to find the public funds (from poor and middle income taxpayers) to pay for the financial needs of monopoly capital, just as it becomes more difficult to argue persuasively that these needs are legitimate.

O'Connor argues that this situation presents two opportunities for democratic organizing. First, professionals in the government find it difficult to justify their monopoly support programs to client populations with whom they are in direct contact and they therefore provide these groups with help in their own organizing efforts by offering information, by joining client organizations and movements, and by using discretionary power in their favor whenever possible. Second, with the increasingly obvious pressure that monopoly sector interests exert on low and middle income populations, the appeal of a free enterprise ideology diminishes and the basic impulse to resist deepens.

Both these general themes – the legitimation crisis of liberal governments, and the rise of new kinds of interest groups and coalitions – are dealt with and illustrated in the pieces in Part II. Kennedy and Burlage touch on both topics in the health care sector. They describe the deepening conflicts between government attempts to support the "medical engineering" establishment and its approach to health care, while at the same time satisfying popular demands for high quality and widely distributed care. They then suggest the kinds of popular movements that may be emerging around health issues. Goldstein describes an analagous phenomenon in central city economic development programs. In this case the conflict is between requirements for profitability, that restrict community development corporations and serve the interests of corporate business, and the tendencies toward local participation and neighborhood control that have arisen around many of these programs. Dreier, Gilderbloom and Appelbaum describe a special aspect of a similar conflict that exists in housing as related to rent control and tenant coalitions. They describe and criticize an aspect of corporate ideology – that rent control drives out investment from housing. They also review tenant organizing efforts in several parts of the United States.

The Burton and Murphy chapter is less descriptive, more analytical. Starting from the inherent conflict between a capitalist economy and a democratic polity, they go on to formulate criteria for assessing what makes a movement truly democratic. The chapters by Clavel and Hartman and Stone are also analytical and prescriptive. Clavel suggests a new political environment for planning based on a perception of regional movements in Wales and Appalachia. He lays out prescriptions for political strategy and the role of planners in a new politics. Hartman and Stone formulate a socialist housing program for the United States.

The developments cited in these papers – the progressive developments, at any rate – bespeak a different kind of politics of planning. There are implications in these chapters not only for political practice and for the kinds of plans and strategies that are or may become viable, but also for the way we think about politics and planning. In the long run this may be as important as whatever political and economic gains are or are not made in the next decade.

One of the most crushing legacies of the postwar period has been the dampening effect of liberal political science on the aspirations of those with a more egalitarian vision for society. Progressive movements were seldom studied in this framework, and when they were, the lesson drawn tended to be cynical: special interests will always win, collective goals of any substance are never achieved. What is implied in these pages is the need for a new political theoretical framework that will encourage minute study of the progressive tendencies identified here. This would encourage new sophistication and perceptions of what has theretofore been branded as "the Left" in America: the ability to see in the structure of the economy and the bureaucratic apparatus the steps on which democratic movements can gain footholds; a codification of organizing experience and tactics; ultimately, perhaps, the ability to discriminate among the organizations and movements that arise so that the best of them can be further supported and encouraged.

NOTES

(1) Edward Banfield, The Unheavenly City, 1970.

(2) Charles Lindblom, The Intelligence of Democracy, 1965.

(3) Aaron Wildavsky, "Does Planning Work?" 1971. "If Planning is Everything, Maybe It's Nothing," 1973. "Why Planning Fails in Nepal," 1972.

(4) Stephen Elkin, "Cities Without Power: The Transformation of American Urban Regimes."

(5) Ira Katznelson, "The Crisis of the Capitalist City: Urban Politics and Social Control," 1976.

(6) J. Hayward and M. Watson, eds., Planning, Politics and Public Policy: The British, French and Italian Experience, 1975.

(7) Theodore Lowi, The End of Liberalism 1969; and C. Wright Mills, The Power Elite, 1957.

(8) James O'Connor, The Fiscal Crisis of the State, 1973.

(9) J. K. Galbraith, The New Industrial State, 1967; and Daniel Bell, The Coming of Post Industrial Society, 1973.

6 Repressive versus Reconstructive Forces in Austerity Planning Domains: The Case of Health

Louanne Kennedy
Robb Burlage

The health care sector is an example of the more general problem of state intervention in the midst of fiscal crisis. James O'Connor, in defining the fiscal crisis of the state, argues that the growth of government expenditures is major, inevitable, irreversible, and critical to the maintenance of the political and economic system: that the system requires expenditures that will lead to crisis after crisis; and that the manifestation of those crises will find their fullest expression in urban (sectoral) conflicts.(1)

Health care exhibits these qualities in a variety of ways. A "fiscal crisis" in health service expenditures exists along with a "health crisis" involving social determinants of health status that extend beyond the scope of the medical care industry. Health Systems Agencies (HSAs) created under the Health Planning and Resources Development Act of 1974 are required to engage in austerity planning, while new progressive alliances and a new popular and public health movement also show signs of life. These are in contradiction, and they raise the question of how they might be resolved in a progressive way. Can we identify repressive and reconstructive forces within and around the present health planning environment as the basis for a more progressive research and strategic agenda?

THE UNDERLYING CONTRADICTIONS IN HEALTH CARE

The contradiction between the health care needs of consumers and the current organization of the health care industry is a mirror of the present fiscal crisis. It is the temporary resolution of this contradiction, through the use of a particular pattern of government reimbursement, that has produced the fiscal strain now evident.

The fiscal crisis in health can be seen by examining health expenditures. Between 1974 and 1976, the total amount spent for health rose by 14 percent to $139.3 billion, an average per capita expenditure of $638. Since the growth in health care expenditures coincided with a general slowdown in economic activity, health expenditures represent a larger share of the GNP in 1976 (8.5%) than in 1974 (7.8%). The public share continued to grow to 42 percent of the total spent on health in 1976. The largest portion was spent on hospital services (39.8 percent). Physician services amounted to 18.9 percent. The rise in expenditures had continued.(2) Rapid increases in health care costs cannot be accounted for by changes in population size, characteristics, or utilization patterns.(3) The government has attempted to blunt the effects of the fiscal crisis by encouraging cutbacks in services and relying upon individual responsibility strategies.

This fiscal crisis rests on deeper contradictions. On the one hand, historical forces seek to control the definition of health and the health services system ideology. The medical engineering model of health service, with its emphasis on "cures," has focused attention on the individual rather than the collectivity. Individuals are held accountable for their own health status and are urged to use less services, to engage in self-care health practices to ensure their well-being, or to utilize various professional practitioners to guarantee their continued health. More generally, there are structural constraints that can be observed in all capitalist societies as they attempt to deal with health. Renaud argues that:

> . . .capitalist industrial growth both creates health needs and institutionalizes solutions to these needs that are compatible with capital accumulation. The key mechanism in this institutionalization is the medical engineering model which transfers health needs into commodities for a specific economic market. When the state intervenes, it is bound to act so as to further commodify health needs, thus favoring the unparalleled expansion of a sector of the civilian economy to the profit of those who capitalize on it, and thus further alienating individuals from control over their bodies and minds but without a significant improvement in the available indicators of the health status of the population.(4)

The medical engineering model has prevailed despite evidence of its limitations and producer-oriented bias. Improvements in health status over the past century have come about, not only or even primarily as a result of a proliferation of new technologies housed in high cost institutions, nor from the growth of manpower devoted to specialty practices, but from public health advances in sanitation, housing, clean water, and improved nutrition.(5) In the face of this, health service producers have been able to maintain a restrictive definition of health that helps perpetuate their interests. Berliner and Kelman have elaborated on these definitional issues, showing that measures of health status depend on the <u>definition</u> of health. Struggles over the control of the definition are an aspect of class struggle.(6)

Increasingly, this model of health care has come into conflict with demands for health services. In the 1960s, the interest generated by the "poor people's movement" seemed a potential threat to the existing order, with the health sector a focus of many of their demands. In 1965 new legislation (e.g., Medicare, Medicaid) was enacted to expand access to health services for the poor and the elderly. The model of sciêntific medicine and the institutionalized hegemony of health providers were, nonetheless, maintained intact. These reforms were not structural in nature. Rather, services were rendered without critical examination of the object of health services. The relationship between illness and personal health services was assumed to be a perfect correlation. Hospital oriented payment systems and specialty controlled hospitals reinforced the current technological base of health services delivery and work relations, even as services were rendered to an expanded population. Renaud's comment is again pertinent.

> This is what universal health insurance programs are all about: they maintain or improve the conditions for capital accumulation and they recreate social harmony by slightly redistributing income. Paradoxically, they may be interpreted both as a "victory" for the working class, which "wins" easier access to medical services, and as a "victory" for the medical care producers, because of the benefit they get from increased consumption.(7)

The expansionist model of health service activity in the period 1964-1974 reflects this general tendency. The State, in its attempts to be responsive to both the economic requirements of the health industry and to the organized demands of the public, is forced to serve two masters. The State must endlessly search for legitimizing solutions to ever more extreme contradictions and social tensions. In this situation, planners are subjected to definitional and ideological control implied in the medical engineering model. Explicitly and implicitly, the model shapes the methods and alternative roles for health planners, and also critically influences the possibilities of political alliance with consumers and working communities in the actual planning process.

HEALTH SYSTEMS AGENCIES: STRUCTURAL CONTRADICTIONS

It is within this context that the new health planning legislation of 1974 was born.(8) The Health Planning and Resources Development Act was designed organizationally to combine the expansionary optimism of the 1960s with the cost-containment thrust of the early 1970s by creating a national network of state and local health planning agencies. This set the conditions for austerity planning in health care. The primary goals of the act include the containment of hospital costs, the improvement of health status, and equal access to quality health care. There are clear contradictions for area-wide HSA's created under the act as they attempt to implement these goals. At present some 205 such agencies have been formed,(9) along with 50 two-division state government agencies; State Health Coordinating Councils (SHCC) and State Health Planning and Development Agencies (SHPDA). Ten regional health planning technical assistance centers were originally funded across the nation, then were cut back to four centers in 1979.(10)

The establishment of this multi-tiered system, intertwining local, state and federal entities, was mandated federally as a new state intervention to control existing health expenditures more comprehensively. The rationale behind the move was that such a planning system must be in place before any national health insurance is enacted. The experience in runaway costs accelerated by federal Medicare and federal-state Medicaid left policy makers certain that some network of state and locally based control mechanism be established in advance of any further expansion of publicly subsidized entitlements.

Yet the system was also unveiled with priorities directed toward locally based quality services that would improve the overall health of the population. This is currently at direct variance with attempts at solving the crisis of health care costs, not because the two could not be approached simultaneously, but because to do so would call for a restructuring of current health care institutions and their financing. The demand for improvement of health status would require the assessment of populations at risk and the measurement of their mortality and morbidity with resources arrayed to meet those needs. Instead, cost containment, of growing concern to a post-Proposition 13 Congress and hence necessary for HSA's political survival, has taken a front seat in planning efforts. Planning becomes, then, regulation of the existing health sector.

Most of the determinants of the U.S. health system are excluded from the purview of the HSAs. Physicians and other health professionals continue to function just as autonomously as before, and the system's financing continues unchanged.

Austerity planning becomes a vehicle for "regionalized" retrenchment around the current vested interests, not a model for considering new alternatives. Moreover, alternatives to expensive tertiary care, which offer the only possibility of long-term cost effectiveness, such as primary and preventive care, public health and educational programs will all require short-term investment. In times of contraction they will be eyed as new spending programs, untried experiments and amenities compared with the acute care system. Little constituency exists for new programs, while funds channeled to established programs have helped to build a dependence on those programs by both workers and users, thereby creating a constituency to guard against cost cutting.

The planning process serves the interests of those who are able to direct and focus its use and attention. Behind this process is the assumption that the public good can be served and integrated through a pluralist process. It is further assumed that planning activity has a theoretical and methodological structure that permits the formation of goals, the production of data, and the weighing of evidence by these local agencies so that a rational plan can be divorced from politics.

Planning is attempted by developing a set of goals which, while perhaps exemplary as statements of aims, are clearly unachievable because of the limits of the financial structure and implementation potential of the organizations created to plan the system. In effect the planning system maintains the institutional forces that have dominated health care delivery since the turn of the century. Social, environmental and occupational health issues are kept off the agenda in favor of resource reallocation of existing institutions biased toward a definition of health centered in terms of the absence of disease.

The ability of the market to create a demand for services has been the primary determinant of the spatial distribution of manpower and facilities. Little planning has been based on the health status of the population and their need for various services, except certain marginalized public health programs.(11) Unlike pure market models in the private sector, the major purchasers of health services are not individuals but third party payers (Blue Cross, Blue Shield, federal, state, and local governments through Medicare and Medicaid). Paid in this way, health provider institutions have been insulated from any need to plan or control the expansion of their services.

Individual demand for health services has traditionally been regulated by physicians who have a monopoly control over medical information and judgment. The potential of collectivities to consider alternative social or self-care programs is thus limited and to some extent legally restricted. The cultural beliefs about good health care include visits to a physician and the acceptance of the physician's opinions, prescriptions, and referrals for any further necessary services. Physicians and their institutions (hospitals, medical laboratories, etc.,) are the major determinants of demand; they are encouraged by the guarantee that the costs of these services will be met largely by third parties not involved in the original transaction.

The move toward cost containment can be viewed in part as an attempt to satisfy third party payers and corporations which pay a major portion of insurance costs in lieu of workers' wages. The major purchasers will no longer tolerate unplanned, limitless expansion. Their focus is not on health as a social phenomena. Rather they accept the current organizational and manpower imperatives and look to the elimination of what is defined as wasteful duplication, overbedding, inefficient distribution of technology and insatiable demand. The industry is rationalized along monopoly corporate lines and the planning process is used to achieve this end. Thus solo physicians with small practices, small hospitals and small nursing homes become vulnerable in this conflict between monopoly capital and smaller private interests.

Methodology

Present planning practice utilizes technical methodologies with little examination of the theoretical assumptions in which the methods are embedded.

In the case of health planning it is difficult to counter the dominant ideological paradigm since it is assumed by its users to be a theory verifiable by hypothesis and empirical evidence. The unstated assumptions of the model compound the difficulties, for these assumptions are tied to the interrelationship between health planning, the medical system and the political economy.(12)

In this context planning as technique has gained prominence. Planners concerned solely with technique reduce problems of politics to problems of method. These planners accept the definition of their practice as value-neutral and develop formulas for forecasting bed needs, physician/population ratios and the like on the assumption that such problems are basically technical, and are therefore capable of technical solutions. Thus planners are often unable to see the ideological nature of their practice. They are caught in the tension between their interests as professionals, in which they have their own methodology, unavailable to the lay person, and the demand for community based, local decision making for the system's users.

The health planning law requires that plan development rely on a population-based rather than a resource-based approach. A simultaneous demand is directed at cutbacks in resources. How do the various planning methodologies address these issues? In population based planning, health needs are assessed using epidemiological methods, and resource requirements are based on an assessment of the health status of the population.

> By basing its analysis on the subsets of the population and their risk levels rather than on the resource structure, population based planning facilitates the identification of the social, economic, and environmental problems which predispose a population to high risk of disease. The methodology, therefore is capable of addressing an array of health problems that extends well beyond the medical care system, and more adequately accommodates the growing awareness of the social and environmental determinants of health.(13)

While the health planning legislation requires this model of plan development, there are major obstacles to the use of a population based approach. At the present time, "data on the distribution of demographic, medical and environmental risks for geographic areas small enough to be useful for planning do not exist. What is available is data on hospital and clinic utilization, which is compatible with resource based planning."(14)

There are methods available to perform needs assessments but they require innovative and costly research designs. In most cases where they have been undertaken, needs assessments have rarely attempted to question the object of medical care but instead have estimated needs for physicians, nurses and hospital beds by soliciting expert opinions to determine the relationship between health status and service requirements.(15)

Health planners concede that there are barriers to the measurements of need, yet they adopt the inadequate methods available since financial imperatives of the planning process render other activities difficult. The health planning legislation discourages the use of surveys to assess needs. They do this by allocating no monies for epidemiological studies. Instead planning staffs rely on existing data sources. These data sources suffer from instability of numbers in planning for small areas, and more importantly limit analysis of health to the treatment of disease through utilization of facilities. The continued use of a demand model will ultimately only reflect any misuse currently in the system. This criterion of need reflects what medical science and technology are capable of delivering at a given time, according to the best practice of the day. This normative concept of need is essentially a technological or engineering approach to planning.(16)

The reliability of expert opinions needs to be challenged because the bases on which experts render such opinions are seldom made explicit, and different groups of experts produce different numbers. The criterion of need, single valued and unambiguously quantified, propose priorities that their authors assume to be self-evident and compelling. Individual as well as community characteristics, are often ignored. Various psychological, social, and cultural factors that differentiate perceived health status from expected health are often omitted as well.

Resource based methods are thus not advantageous in assessing or addressing the need for improved health in the population but are deemed useful for cost containment and rationalization of the system. These methods are value laden instruments that implement a particular ideology of medical care under a guise of objectivity. Health advocates working within this structure must constantly struggle against the tide of cost containment priorities to raise progressive concerns about people's health needs.

PLANNING ROLES AND THEIR POTENTIAL AS RECONSTRUCTIVE FORCES WITHIN AGENCY ARENAS

Agency arenas demonstrate the contradictions and attending conflicts between improvement of the health status of their populations (through a restructuring of the health system) and cost containment, in which existing facilities and manpower distribution are examined, only to rationalize and reduce potential competition for scarce resources (patients and monies) among institutions. There is a continuing tension between plan development, which centers on improvement in health status, and regulation, which centers on cost containment. The same planning staffs must carry out both sets of activities in an environment in which cost containment success determines the continued existence of their agency. It must be clearly understood that, given what we have argued in this paper, there are clear structural limitations to what can be accomplished in agencies of the state, especially in an austerity era.

There are at least three areas where planning practice can provide reconstructive potential within HSAs: 1) in the development of accountable, participatory, representative consumer practice; 2) in progressive plan development; and 3) in the regulation of high technology, inpatient care. These areas suggest the marginal limits of HSA actions, but these should not be undervalued.

While the law mandates more than 50 percent consumer-dominated boards, the potential of such members to influence policy making is limited. The general population has less of a stake in determining the health care industry as a result of the very nature of health issues:

> Health concerns, though important, are intermittent for most people. They are not as clearly or regularly salient as the condition of housing or children's schools – situations citizens confront regularly. Consequently, it is far more difficult to establish regular public participation in HSA's than in school districts or renter's associations. Much of the empirical evidence on HSA's supports this view.(17)

Providers, on the other hand, can be expected to invest far more of their scarce resources in trying to influence institutions that regulate their industry.

The cost of citizen participation is extensive.

> . . .participation requires an expenditure of time, effort, and money in order to attend hearings, become involved in planning workshops, respond to questionnaires, be interviewed, write letters to officials, secure information about issues, and take part in advisory committees. As these necessary expenditures of resources increase for any particular public decision, an increasing number of citizens is excluded from participation. They are priced out of the public decision-making process either because they are unable to afford the time, effort or money, or because such expenditures cannot be justified in terms of the benefits they perceive will accrue from the participation.(18)

The HSA staff is one resource that could help consumers in their attempts to balance health planning politics. It is not enough simply to add numbers and assume that accountability and participation will naturally emerge. Various HSA staffs have aligned with consumers in some areas. In Philadelphia, for example, HSA staffs have supported consumer representatives in their efforts to reform long-term care programs away from a concentration on institutionalization and toward community based home care alternatives. In this case the staffs were educated by consumer members of the committee concerned with rehabilitation to move from a resource based orientation, where focus is on the institutions already present in the area, to advocacy planning for maximizing the participation of the aged and their representatives.(19) Significantly, the consumer advocates represented an already organized constituency. Consumer interests do not work in concert with staff planners in all cases. The consumer members are primarily selected to represent a cross section of the population in an area and, depending on the election process, may or may not come armed with knowledge about health issues or with the political savvy to argue effectively for alternative noninstitutional care or quality and accessibility for all groups.

Staff planners have a reconstructive potential in seeing that board membership meets the minimal representative mandate by encouraging widespread information dissemination about HSA activities. The western Massachusetts, Philadelphia, and Los Angeles staffs attempted such a process. Although voter participation was substantially lower than in general elections, these agency arenas at least escaped the situation where board membership was determined only by established political organizations or older preexisting planning bodies.

Even after election, consumer participation must continue to be developed to provide an effective balance against provider interests. Here, planning staffs have additional potential to provide support since few, if any, user/consumers have the organizational backing for data collection, analysis and report preparation equal to the capabilities of provider organizations. These activities assume that planning staffs are not only knowledgeable about alternative forms of health care delivery but that they can locate and align themselves with community organizations to assure their representation.

Several methods are appropriate for assuring broadly based representative boards. These include the development of consumer constituencies by identifying specific issues, i.e., families approaching childbirth, senior citizens, low income groups concerned with access. Community forums can then be held to provide information on important health issues to increase consumer awareness and help build an organization of consumers, particularly where community organization is limited.

On another level of organizing around HSAs, it is important to recognize the role ideologies play in reducing consumer participation. One of the biggest obstacles in mobilizing people to fight hospitals and doctors is the "helping" ideology that tells us that providers are individuals and organizations that sacrifice themselves in a commitment to our health. To the extent to which we use consumer-provider rhetoric, we call attention to the commodification of health care. Identifying health as a commodity in our culture helps people examine medical transactions in the same light that they examine auto, grocery, or loan transactions. Acknowledgment of the commodity relationship is a prerequisite for its transformation.

Staff activities by themselves cannot assure the development of new levels of health consciousness. In fact, there are often extremely severe sanctions against staff involvement in community organizing.(20) Plan development, then must also offer a range of reconstructive potentials for staff. Target goals are developed to identify populations at risk and to determine programs to reduce levels of illness. It is here that the contradictions between population-based and resource-based planning are played out. Given the limitations of the available data for small areas, health status indicators must be gathered from additional sources. Rather than relying on provider interests as the sole basis for expert opinion on need, information from community-based organizations is sought as well. These groups are an important focus for interpreting needs for such unrepresented groups as the elderly, disabled, mentally ill or retarded, and women. Activist groups concerned with the above issues are more likely to have recent information on need as well as an understanding of the appropriateness of current services. In Philadelphia, for example, the plan development committee concerned with rehabilitation was able to mobilize organizations to assess the number of elderly living in substandard housing and those in need of nutritional and home care services. They were able to involve community actors, not only in identifying the scope of the problem but also in identifying the treatment in terms of community support rather than solely in increasing the number of long-term care beds demanded by institutional providers. This effort required combined action of community groups, consumer representatives and planning staffs.

Plan development is a critical area for linking consumers, providers and agency staffs. If a technocratic approach predominates, there is a tendency once again to reduce the social and political process to technical matters, i.e., data collection and analysis geared primarily to cost effectiveness. Nontechnical board members are discouraged from playing an active role by the obscurity of language in reports prepared by providers and/or planning staffs.(21)

In the plan development process, there is a strong pressure for agency staffs to write the plan with limited input from other groups. The plan is then given to providers and consumers for comment. This process occurs largely as a result of the time constraints imposed by regulations, which require a comprehensive plan within a short time frame to achieve legal designation of the HSA by the Department of Health, Education and Welfare. Providers have a greater perceived stake in the plan and the work process encourages provider dominance and consumer passivity.

The staff work demands become excessive in plan development and expectations that they will consistently encourage the education of consumers and their active participation is often to require that the staffs submerge their own professional survival (meeting the deadline for the Health System Plan) to the ideal of a participatory process. Planning tasks and functions are completed more readily when conflict is reduced. Conflict reduction is achieved through ". . .withholding of information, encouragement of passivity, and suppression of legitimate and relevant conflict. . .only issues likely to result in widespread agreement tend to be raised."(22)

Only by moving back and forth between community organizing and agency based activity can reconstructive forces around plan development be achieved. Community representation is easier to achieve in areas where consumer members are already sophisticates in the planning arena. Development of such individuals and constituencies in relatively unorganized communities requires not only staff leadership within the HSA, but the identification of potential community groups.(23)

Regulatory activities, such as the certificate of need process require the most sophisticated technical information and involve the most complex political issues. Planning staffs are required to evaluate the appropriateness of services and the extent to which new construction or changes in services are consistent with the health needs of the area as defined in the Health Systems Plan.

HSAs have a wide range of responsibilities in addition to their primary one of cost control. These responsibilities include improving access to health care services, ensuring that health care resources are equally available to all area residents, and enhancing the quality and comprehensiveness of care. This range of objectives must be achieved through the narrow tool of certificate of need. The reconstructive potential of HSAs can be seen by examining the manner in which certain areas have attached conditions to institutional requests for service changes. So long as these conditions are reasonably related to the purpose of the review (cost, quality, access, acceptability, comprehensiveness), this is permissible for HSAs.(24)

The range of reconstructive activities is suggested by the following cases where conditions were effectively applied:

- Hospital may only expand if it gets another hospital in the area to voluntarily delicense an equal number of beds (Ventura-Santa Barbara, California)
- Hospital must agree to share new equipment with other hospitals (western Massachusetts)
- Hospital may acquire equipment only if it switches from proposed lease to a less expensive purchase and passes the savings on in the form of lower charges. (northern Virginia)
- Hospital must agree to fewer radiology rooms and less equipment. (northern Virginia)
- Hospital must hire Spanish-speaking staff or sufficient number of translators. (Ventura-Santa Barbara, California)
- HMO (Health Maintenance Organization) must hire sufficient number of bilingual translators (West Bay, California)
- Nursing home required to accept Medicaid patients up to 65 percent of its population. (Golden Empire, California)
- Nursing home currently spending less money on food (per patient per day) than is spent by the county jail must increase its food budget by 30 percent. (West Bay, California)
- HMO must agree to sliding scale based on ability to pay. (western Massachusetts)

- Community Health Center must agree to sliding fee scale based on ability to pay. (Western Massachusetts)
- Nursing home must provide 24-hour a day RN coverage. (Golden Empire, California)
- Hospital must take positive steps to increase the number of Spanish-surname personnel. (western Massachusetts)

The above examples are not an exhaustive list of HSA activities; the scope of progressive planning in an austerity era has yet to be fully analyzed. An excellent series of cases involving advocacy and organizing for effective participation can be found in the Health Law Library Bulletin, ranging, for example, from Arkansas, Texas, eastern Kentucky, and Illinois representation victories to Cape Cod health workers union and community alliance to Philadelphia women's and maternal health issue struggles in the HSA arenas.(25)

STRATEGIC QUESTIONS AND PROJECTIONS

How are potentially reconstructive activities within HSAs related to the overall context of critical health planning actions toward progressive alliances?

A major set of questions arises in considering advocacy for broader consumer representation and participation, for local community and worker control, and, in the context of uneven development across the country, planning for and around medical-technological and institutional service area regions. In an interest group framework, for instance, Vladeck comments on the tension between local government and various health care technologies.

> The fragmentation has the advantage of bringing control. . . "close" to the citizenry but the technologies of health care. . .require truly regional planning. . .(there is also) the tension between the extreme size, complexity, and decentralization of sociotechnological systems like that of health and the desire of citizens to exercise some direct control of services intimately affecting their most important personal concerns.(26)

There are significant regional variations across the U.S. in the degrees of unity and intensification of medical institutional empires,(27) of state and areawide (usually multi-county) government commitment to planning and regulation of health, and of potential unity of reconstructive forces toward, and repressive obstacles to, progressive alliances. For example, there are inner city minority community and health worker resistance actions around municipal hospital closings and public health cutbacks; Appalachian coal miners strikes and working community actions around union health fund support of clinics; southern and western metropolitan areas' fights against conservative local political forces, and expansionary professional and proprietary institutional interests.

The uneven political context of state and local health planning and regulatory agency structures and leaderships makes it difficult to formulate general strategic approaches within and around them. Health planning agencies across the country are immersed in day-to-day bureaucratic survival issues. Local provider and political forces attempt to dominate, delimit and even openly sabotage those limited actions attempted by HSAs to expand participation or to regulate institutional investments "according to the law." This contentious organizational environment tends to obscure awareness of larger historic contradictions of fiscal and health crises.

However, the seeds of a popular new public health movement can be observed throughout the country. While HSAs are, in some cases, involved in or leading this new movement, for the reasons noted above, much of this activity is occurring outside traditional planning domains. Progressively inclined planners have been instrumental in forming these new alliances.

Some approaches to critical health planning action contributing to progressive coalition-building have been developed in recent months. The Health Policy Advisory Center (Health-PAC), a New York City advocacy group is but one such example. Areas of action have included the following in New York alone:

1. Critical planning studies – Recent targeted analyses of the impact of fiscal crisis cutbacks on essential community preventive and primary care and public health services have laid a formal groundwork for community planning action. Building on years of monitoring municipal and community hospitals takeovers and closings – including "planned shrinkage" of public investments, medical institutions, and housing abandonment in the city (e.g., in the South Bronx), these studies have utilized current health planning and public health agency information.(28)

2. Alternative community health development – Recent alternative plans and proposals have been developed for publicly supported community preventive and primary care health centers and community based networks of such centers. These are based primarily in federally designated "medically underserved" areas such as the South Bronx, Harlem, the Lower East Side, and North-Central Brooklyn. These advocacy plans are actually being implemented with existing community health center and development groups in cooperation with community planning boards as well as HSA districts, providing living seeds of an alternative plan strategy, political budgeting and institutional organization base.(29)

3. Community-consumer planning actions – Frontal challenges to medical empire institutional plans, including Health Systems Agency and state government project review, has created preconditions for larger medical-regional resource reallocations. For example, a community council and revised facility program plan has been created in the area around Columbia-Presbyterian Medical Center with area and citywide health planning board and staff support covering the Washington Heights-Inwood area and much of the Upper West Side and Harlem.

4. Action-education toward a progressive local plan coalition – At a well-attended city-wide forum held to publicize basic health services cutbacks, to display public and community-oriented alternatives in other cities, and to demonstrate solid political support, including city government and health worker union officials, the newly formed Coalition for a Rational Health Plan was unveiled. Beginning with black community and medical house staff protests of municipal hospital closings, the coalition has attempted to involve all impacted communities and major unions of both city hospitals (District 37 of the American Federation of State, County and Municipal Employees) and private voluntary hospitals (1199/National Health and Hospital Workers Union) in its efforts. United resistance is being sought to cutbacks and closings of public and community-based hospitals and health services affecting the neediest communities and minority areas and for the implementation of more preventive and primary care oriented priorities.

5. Support of Constituency Actions – Women's rights and older people's mutual aid insurgencies in particular have been a basis for support of progressive movements toward inclusive race, class, workplace and working community alliances for health. This has ranged from the local Coalition for Abortion Rights and Against Sterilization Abuse (CARASA) unifying women (including low income people and minorities with concerns about medical genocide), to the New York Committee for Occupational Safety and Health (NYCOSH) conducting educational programs with CARASA and labor unions on reproductive hazards of the workplace. The latter outreach has emphasized the need for federal and state government occupational health and safety coverage and protection of small, unorganized, and public services workplaces where most minorities and women work.

Institutional reviews carried out by planners have included issues of sterilization and other medical experimentation and treatment abuse. With increasing pressure from women's health groups, planners have emphasized home birth and universal, community-convenient abortion services (despite federal funding restrictions), thus going beyond federal-regional high-technology obstetrical/gynecological beds and services guidelines. A special occupational-environmental section of the HSA has taken policy positions stronger than federal protection standards around such issues as the handling of nuclear materials for public service employees. This has become one supportive intersection of health planning with the growing antinuclear movement, which has focused its attention on nuclear power sites dangerously near New York City's metropolitan millions.

Predominantly older people who are involved in tenants' mutual aid groups in integrated working class communities such as Coney Island and the West Bronx have taken action on the appropriateness, control and accessability of primary health services. In this effort, they have received support from agency planners reviewing public medical expenditures.(30)

These vital local health issue groups are mutually supportive of action networks across the nation such as CARASA; COSHes in their "Workers' Right-to-Know" campaign regarding all information on workplace exposures and health implications; and the Grey Panthers' campaign for a national health service.

The apparent keys of a new national popular and public health movement are local actions and coalitions with the support of community and consumer oriented planners. Local public and community health services' demands are related now by some groups to broader policy calls carried, for example, by the Coalition for a National Health Service and endorsed by the American Public Health Association. Expanding labor movement health lobbying and politics nationally toward activist, locally based coalitions, as well as toward national health insurance endorsements, has been a major thrust of new national groups. The AFL-CIO endorsed Consumer Coalition for Health is organizing for consumer controlled health planning. Consumer controlled planning and occupational-environmental prevention are part of the orientation of the health cost control program of the Machinists Union-initiated coalition, Consumers Opposed to Inflation in Necessities (COIN).

In mid-1979, the immediate dangers of pure cooptation in health planning and policy arenas appear far less threatening than the direct assaults of repressive and regressive forces. Nationally, in Congress there were moves to dismantle broad consumer representative provisions and population-needs-oriented mandates, if not to kill the extension of locally based HSAs themselves. This comes at a time when a major Presidential priority is a watered down Hospital Cost Containment Act, which relies more on aggregate federal and state government caps on current institutional resource expenditures amidst voluntary institutional cost cutting campaigns aimed at health workers and marginal community outreach services, and a moratorium on aggregate institutional beds that could hurt the neediest areas. This "resource-based planning" in reverse is no longer for projected expansion but primarily for the consolidation and survival of the economically, professionally, and politically strongest institutions, regardless of basic access needs in underserved communities.

At the same time, locally based planning as a step toward comprehensive public national health insurance has (as of 1978) been supplanted by presidential (and even labor-oppositional) endorsement of the gradual phasing in of national packages of predominantly private insurance coverage with no provisions for local budgeting around population needs.

An alternative health movement, therefore, is also challenging the present fragmented and biased health care system and, along with lobbying for universal and comprehensive national health financing, is helping build alternative minisystems locally. These minisystems, although they tend to remain within the domains of medical care and do not directly challenge systemic social, environmental, and occupational causes of illness, offer bases for national health system change. These positive ingredients include the following:

1. Preventive and primary care-oriented public health and hospitals programs. For example, the city of Newark clinics network that, with federal support and emphasizing prenatal care, has contributed to halving the infant mortality rate from 1970 to 1975; the Stickney Township, Illinois community of 240,000 has had low cost "taxpayer-prepaid" primary medical and dental services in public health centers for more than 20 years; the coalition of hospital workers and community activists in Cape Cod, Massachusetts that swept 16 of 17 seats in the local health planning council election and insisted that the local HSA work to improve access to primary and preventive care.

2. Community health centers – For example, rural clinics in the South and urban neighborhood health centers, once funded by the Office of Economic Opportunity and now funded by Health, Education, and Welfare, have emphasized prevention and paramedical worker outreach to challenge the social causes of illness. National Health Service Corps physicians, (about one-fourth of medical graduates in 1979) received federal scholarships and take federally approved assignments in medically underserved areas, often in community health services.

3. Community-based health maintenance organizations. HMOs are prepaid group practices such as the user controlled Puget Sound Plan in the Seattle area or the labor backed Contra Costa County, California HMO run by the local government.

4. Labor health centers – For example, the coal miners' community clinics in Appalachia, as a result of the 1978 miners strike settlement, now rely more on public funding and less on coal company insurance coverage. Yet these labor health centers provide a possible base for occupation-environmental health advocacy in opposition to corporation-paid "company doctor" obfuscation and repression.

There are, however, difficulties. Only a small percentage of the population is covered by federally certified HMOs (about two percent of Medicaid patients nationally and practically none of the working poor). Most of these are not community or labor based or local government initiated, and federal HMO assistance funds remain restricted.(31)

Municipal hospitals across the country are being closed, turned over to proprietary management corporations, or being reduced in size and scope. Local public health programs remain underfunded and understaffed, a victim of the current fiscal crisis, while federal appropriations for preventive and primary health services are squeezed. The challenges mounted in localities by community and health worker coalitions thus reflect the nation's economic health.

STRATEGIC LIMITS AND LESSONS

How are we to evaluate the role of local health planning actions in relation to the overall possibilities and necessities of a new, popular public health movement?

To the extent that HSAs are successful in challenging elite providers and combating irrational expansions and repressive cutbacks in services, they carry the danger of legitimizing the planning arena as presently organized. If legitimation occurs, only scattered and limited examination of the object of health services planning can result.

The emerging austerity planning domains in health are contradictory and limited. Locally based HSAs are unable either to legitimate and to implement real cost control or to achieve effective reallocation of resources. They are also unable, in and of themselves, to advance progressive service alternatives. Thus, HSAs are incapable of making structural reforms in the health system.

Legislative cutbacks and disentitlements, along with resource shrinkage decisions – not local planning arenas – will likely be the focus of repressive forces amid increasing perceived scarcity for capital as a whole. Such conservative cutbacks thus far seldom refer explicitly to area-wide planning rationality or local participation for legitimation.

The current costs of the health contradiction for the U.S. economic system as a whole is dramatized in a current position paper for COIN by Sander Kelman. An equal amount is now spent treating the maladies caused by the present industrial system and environment – in medical care, disability, and workers' compensation payments as on the expansion of that system – $240 billion for fixed business investment, "while the captains of that same industrial system complain that environmental prevention policies stifle investment."(32)

Explosive general fiscal factors, along with price and cost escalations within the health sector, are calling forth specific new austerity oriented state interventions in health services, in contrast to earlier state legitimation with subsidies for private medicine. The previously referred to medical commodification and high-technology engineering model is facing government cutbacks and an emerging ideological thrust for private and individual responsibility for medical services coverage and health.(33)

The historic voluntary partnership – a contradictory regional institution and uneven reimbursement market model of health planning rationality and feasibility – has not only prevented equitable and universal access and democratic control, it has also heightened the medical-technological and social contradictions that obstruct real health cost-effectiveness. This ineffectiveness could increasingly delegitimate scientific medicine as the overwhelming institutional and professional force of social control, an assessment that can also be used to deny equality of its access. This raises questions about the limits of acute medical interventions and superspecialized caring as compared to preventive interventions against systemic causes of illness, and as contrasted with more generalized community support.

In this fiscal and legitimation crisis atmosphere, progressives should be wary of diversions, dissipations, and cooptations within the austerity planning domains for health. The de-skilling of planners and the segregation and channeling of community-consumer participants toward regional institutional domination and private financial voluntarism drain the critical potential of consumerism and cost containment. Agency participants can become implicit partners with health providers, legitimizing traditional policies of regionalization and reimbursement, while tolerating aggregate cutbacks and settling for reorganizational experiments only at the margins.

Elitist provider and socially unrepresentative political domination must be confronted directly in form and content. Politically disabling workers-consumer divisions in local working communities should be overcome – of community users, of self-health active and services-involved citizens, of environmentally active citizens and occupationally active workers, of consumer-oriented health practitioners, and of health workers – while maintaining unified consumer insurgency on those issues of industry exploitation that must be confronted from this adversary base.

The strategic challenges to critical health planning action are:

1) To shift the health cost control question from simply "containing" the government fueled reimbursement market sphere to the question of alternative public planning, budgeting and organization for health prevention and caring in communities as the most cost-effective base; and 2) To shift the health question from the private, individual sphere of medical services coverage and personal behavior to the specific imperatives of collective public intervention against the systemic and production-related causes of illness. The politicizing of the health planner as critical urban and regional community planner is a vital aspect of this arena and the object of the political struggle for health.

To be effective, planners must challenge, displace, and, broaden their definitions, goals and processes. Strategically, community-based national public budgeting for health services and worker-community action for environmental, occupational, and social health are the reasonable models of planning action for health. Planning for health operationally would thus become the epidemiologically-oriented pursuit of a population-based process toward the development of comprehensive well-being and health protection in affected target working communities. This necessarily requires, for example, a detailed critical analysis of the regional and national corporate economic environment behind specific disease causation and confronting effective prevention.(34)

Community-based, comprehensive local government planning and budgeting arenas are, therefore, important for health protection and promotion beyond area, regional and state cost-containment review domains focused only on medical services institutions. But nothing short of a new popular and public health alliance agenda is required. Such a plan must recognize the structural limits and uses of HSA's and all austerity planning domains for health in relation to basic fiscal crisis and health crisis contradictions.

Parallel questions must be raised about the uneven composition and necessarily decentralized action and program emphasis of any effective national alliances to which planning action relates. This is true, for example, compared to the call for a National Health Service specifying community-worker-based local planning, budgeting and organizational control such as is contained in the Dellums Bill. There are obvious lessons in the health movement experiences for the direction of any nonreformist and relevant appeals for national progressive program alternatives in the austerity era across many areas, including full employment and public housing.

Political action alliances toward a population-based model of planning for collective definitions of needs are related to more general historical forces of political class struggle. O'Connor describes this challenge as follows:

> The democratic movement is groping for ways to redefine social life in terms of direct social and material needs. Capital and the state measure irrationality in terms of dollars and cents; the democratic movement measures irrationality in terms of human neglect and suffering and unmet and irrational needs.
>
> State planning of social life. . .creates a fundamental division between conceptions of systemic needs of capital accumulation on the one side and popular conceptions of social and community needs on the other. . . .Essential to this work is the elaboration of a concept of needs as socially determined and fulfilled, i.e., the rejection of need definitions as individually determined and satisfied in the commodity form. Important is the struggle to redefine the results of social planning and policy.(35)

The need for broader political forces and objects in health than even the few organized consumers and activist planners of traditional private medical resources reaches beyond the specific planning arenas themselves and into the heart of general national political priorities and processes. Indeed, this goes to the heart of the political economic system itself. The general mobilization of popoulation-needs-based forces to redefine and to redirect the objects of work and of state intervention, from working communities upward, is the political imperative if we are to move beyond narrow and repressive uses of planning in the present austerity era.

NOTES

(1) O'Connor, The Fiscal Crisis of the State, 1973.

(2) Health, United States, 1976-1977, U.S. Department of Health, Education, and Welfare.

(3) Klarman, Rice, Cooper, and Stettler, III, "Sources of Increase in Selected Medical Care Expenditures, 1929-1969." 1970.

(4) Renaud, "On the Structural Constraints to State Intervention in Health," 1975.

(5) See Powles, "On the Limitations of Modern Medicine," 1973 and Dubos, Man, Medicine and Environment, 1968. For a recent interpretation and array of evidence regarding inner city and minority health problems, see Ellen Hall, Inner City Health in America, 1979.

(6) See Berliner, "The Emerging Ideologies in Medicine," 1977; and Kelman, "The Social Nature of the Definition Problem in Health," 1975.

(7) Renaud, p. 566.

(8) Previous federal interventions include the 1946 Hill-Burton Act, the 1965 Regional Medical Program and the Partnership for Health Act of 1966. Hill-Burton was primarily concerned with facilities construction, the latter two acts provided funding for both planning and operating, and the local participation including consumers was incorporated in the legislation. For further elaboration of the history of federal interventions in health care see for example: Shonick, Elements of Planning for Area-Wide Personal Health Services, 1976; Hyman, Regulating Health Facilities Construction. 1977.

(9) Of the local HSA's formed, about three-fourths have final designation by HEW and most of the rest are at least conditionally designated. Elaborate rules govern the composition of HSA boards to assure that they reflect a broad representative nature. Consumers comprise 53 percent of all HSA board members. Boards vary in size from a low of 15 to a high of 137. Subarea advisory councils, covering the community or local area of planning vary in number from Arizona Area I with a single council composed of 15 members to New York Area VII in New York City having 33 councils. Total board membership across the country numbers 15,000. This is the grassroots base of health planning participation although specific planning and project review committees and general HSA and State boards are the source of operating and legal power.

(10) Twenty-six of these agencies (SHPDA) are located in state health departments; 20 are in state health and welfare departments; six are in governor's offices and three are located elsewhere. Federal SHPDA appropriations have risen from $19 million in 1976 to $29.5 million in 1978. For further discussion of The National Health Planning and Resources Development Act of 1974 (Public Law 93-641) see for example, Sieverts, Health Planning Issues and Public Law 93-641, 1977. See also Lander, "HSA's: If you Don't First Succeed," 1976; Krause, "Health Planning as a Managerial Ideology," 1973.

(11) Public health historically has defined its mission toward categorical contagious diseases and sanitation with limited financial support from public sources.

(12) See Tannen, "Health Planning as a Regulatory Strategy: A Discussion of History and Current Uses," International Journal of Health Services, (forthcoming); See also Navarro, "Political Power, The State and Their Implications in Medicine," Spring 1977; Kotelchuck, "The Depression and the AMA," 1976; Ehrenreich and Ehrenreich, "Hospital Workers: Class Conflict in the Making," International Journal of`Health Services, 1975.

(13) Tannen, "Health Planning."

(14) Ibid.

(15) For an example the Lee-Jones method described in Lee and Jones, "The Fundamentals of Good Medical Care, Publications of the Committee on Costs of Medical Care, No. 22, 1933.

(16) Klarman, "Planning for Facilities" in Regionalization and Health Policy, Ginzberg, ed., 1977. Also Klarman, "Health Planning: Progress, Prospects, and Issues," 1978.

(17) Marmor, and Marone, "HSAs and the Representation of Consumer Interests: Conceptual Issues and Litigation Problems," 1979. See also Vladeck, "Interest-Group Representation and the HSAs: Health Planning and Political Theory," 1977. Cf. Judd and McEwen, "A Handbook for Consumer Participation in Health Care Planning," Blue Cross, 1975. Also see USGPO, DHEW, PHS, Health Resources Administration, "Consumer Participation in Health Planning: An Annotated Bibliography," 1976. Also see position papers from the Consumer Coalition for Health, 1511 K Street, Suite 220, Washington, D.C. 20005 and the Coalition for a National Health Service, P.O. Box 6586, T Street Station, Washington, D.C. 20009. For a historical perspective on the new popular and holistic health movements see Berliner and Salmon, "The Holistic Health Movement and Scientific Medicine: The Naked and The Dead," 1979.

(18) Cooper, "The Hidden Price Tags: Participation Costs and Health Planning," 1979.

(19) Granger-Jaffe, "The Social Planning Imperative: An HSA Experience" (Paper for the 1978 Annual Conference of the American Institute of Planners, New Orleans, September 29-October 1, 1978). Also paper presented at Health Planners Network, Health/PAC, March, 1979.

(20) Personal correspondence with Mark Kleiman, Executive Director, Consumer Coalition for Health, Washington, D.C.

(21) Bradley, "Volunteer Education: Key to Building an Effective Planning Process," 1979.

(22) Ibid.

(23) Checkoway, Barry and Michael Doyle, "Community Organizing Lessons for Health Care Consumers," unpublished manuscript.

(24) The range of certificate of needs experiences is drawn from personal correspondence with Mark Kleiman, Consumer Coalition for Health, Washington, D.C. The range of experiences around CON was summarized by Mr. Kleiman for use by congressional staff.

(25) For further information on reconstructive forces and perspectives, see Milton, "An Ecological Approach to Health Planning for Illness Prevention," 1977; Source Catalog Collective, Organizing for Health Care: A Tool for Change, 1974.

(26) Vladeck, "Health Planning and its Discontents," 1979.

(27) On uneven development of "medical empires," see Health Policy Advisory Center, Health-PAC Bulletins and books, including: Burlage, New York City's Municipal Hospitals, 1967; Ehrenreich and Ehrenreich, eds., American Health Empire, 1969; Kotelchuck, ed., Prognosis Negative: Crisis in the Health Care System, 1976; on the planning and regulation of "medical empires," see, e.g., Kotelchuck, "Government Cost Control Strategies: Futile Monitors," 1977.

(28) Clark et al., Report on the Impact of Fiscal Crisis on Preventive and Primary Health Care in New York City, 1974-78, Health Policy Advisory Center, March 1979.

(29) Also see Plan and Proposal for a Preventive and Primary Health Care Center in Community District #6, South Bronx, May 1978, and Plan for a Community-Based Network of Health Centers in the South Bronx, May 1979, prepared as Studio Projects, Division of Urban Planning, Graduate School of Architecture and Planning, Columbia University, in cooperation with Division of the Community, Community Service Society, New York.

(30) Also see Coney Island Project Report and Guide for Older People, Mutual Aid Project for Older People, 17 Murray Street, New York 10007.

(31) Also see Davis and Schoen, Health and the War on Poverty, 1978, for a review of rural and neighborhood health centers and the Medicaid and Medicare experience in relation to, e.g., HMO's.

(32) Available from Sander Kelman, Department of City and Regional Planning, Cornell University, Ithaca.

(33) A projection of the potential convergence of "holism" in health beyond individual responses, an anticorporation "popholism" and a new popular and public health movement is outlined in Burlage, "New Health Alliance," 1979.

(34) For a beginning framework, see a report on corporate power in the chemical industry and links to area occupational-environmental illness causation in the Kanawha Valley of West Virginia for National Science Foundation citizens educational-action hearings, by Joyce Goldstein et al., Public Resource Center, 1747 Connecticut Avenue NW, Washington, D.C. 20009, June, 1979.

(35) O'Connor, "The Democratic Movement in the United States," 1979.

7 The Limits of Community Economic Development

Harvey A. Goldstein

The New York Times Magazine cover story of January 14, 1979 officially announced an "urban renaissance" taking place in many of the large cities of the Northeast. Neighborhoods were being economically revitalized, the middle-class was returning in the "gentrification" wave, and even new or relocating businesses were seeking out central city locations. This announcement, though, has been accompanied by less dramatic but more frequent announcements of public service cutbacks and the continued physical and social decay of communities caused by private and public disinvestment.

The shaping of community economic development programs and activities is seen as a key element in this superficially paradoxical, but structurally contradictory process of overlaid neighborhood revitalization and decline now taking place. Community-based organizations (CBOs) have taken a strong interest in community development and in developing strategies to successfully intervene in that process, as have banks and other capital investors, private businesses, local chambers of commerce, and local governments. Needless to say, the interests of these groups do not generally coincide, and the possibilities for conflict in this area are strong. This paper attempts to identify how the focus and interests of community economic development have shifted qualitatively in response to the changes in the perceived requirements of capital accumulation. It also outlines the principal issues and areas of conflict that have recently been informing and shaping community economic development taking place in the larger, older central cities of the U.S. Finally, some prognoses for future strategy building in the domain of community economic development are conditionally made, and the likely contradictory tendencies in the urban political economy, which might provide new opportunities for objective gains to distressed communities and for political strategies for the Left, are tentatively identified.

THE SHAPE AND INTERESTS OF COMMUNITY ECONOMIC DEVELOPMENT

Community economic development in the U.S. is generally concerned with directing and stimulating flows of capital toward particular geographic areas or communities within local economies. Community, urban, and municipal economic development differ not only by their spatial concerns but, correlatively, by concern for different constituencies and political and economic interests. Urban economic development has been principally concerned with the overall level of economic activity in the local economy, while municipal economic development has been principally concerned with the level of tax-assessible economic activity within the corporate boundaries of a city. This should not necessarily imply that class struggle is drawn between community economic development versus municipal or urban economic development, or that community economic development is that mode of development that most benefits the poor and working class. Urban economic development often results in increased demands for labor, a higher wage structure, and more stable employment, all of which affect the local economy even though the full impact is diminished by segmented labor markets. Moreover, municipal economic development can result in improved services for the poor by increasing tax revenues, or can improve the wage bargaining position of municipal workers. Finally, the phenomenon of gentrification and displacement on the one hand, and labor-saving plant modernization on the other, corroborate the belief that, in a capitalist system, capital is not necessarily diverted to a particular community to benefit the residents or workers in that community but because it is perceived to be profitable for investors.

Activists on the Left prefer adopting a community economic development strategy for improving the economic and physical conditions of the poor because it seems to offer greater possibilities for gaining community control of the development process through such organizations as community development corporations, cooperative associations, self-help organizations, etc. In this paper, I will argue that this is not always true – that the economic and investment conditions in local economies at a given time strongly determine the amount of control community based organizations have over the community's economic development. In particular, the state, at both the federal level, through enactment of legislative programs related to urban development, and at the local level, through its own degree of economic development capacity and the discretion given by federal program regulations, acts to weaken community based control of community economic development when the needs of capital accumulation dictate it. This idea, and the role that community economic development plays in the capital accumulation process can, perhaps, best be understood by outlining the phases of economic development as well as the derivative characteristic stages of community economic development activity in the large, older U.S. cities in the postwar period.

CYCLES OF EMPLOYMENT CHANGE

The economic vitality of the large northern central cities, as measured in employment levels, has displayed a cyclical trend. Between 1948 and 1954 employment levels in central cities barely held their own; from 1954 to 1963 there were significant job losses; 1963 to 1969 was a period of modest job growth; and 1970 to 1976 has been a period of serious job decline.(1) Since 1976, some of the large northeastern central cities have started experiencing the above mentioned urban renaissance. Not only have the central cities experienced new residential growth, but many have once again become attractive places for manufacturing plant location and expansion.

STAGES OF MACROECONOMIC CONDITIONS AND THE FUNCTIONAL ROLES OF COMMUNITY ECONOMIC DEVELOPMENT

Having generally defined community economic development as an intervention activity concerned with directing capital flows toward particular geographic paths or communities within local economies, we can identify its four characteristic phases (which define different interests, institutional forms, loci of control, etc.) during the thirty-year postwar period.

From the passage of the Federal Housing Act of 1949 to around 1962, the only community economic development activity of significance was urban renewal. Generally urban renewal programs were not controlled by community based organizations. Instead, urban renewal frequently motivated the creation of such organizations to resist it, and the interests served were not generally those of community residents and workers. The underlying function of urban renewal was to create the conditions for private capital to invest in high tax-assessible facilities. They could be consumption-related (e.g., luxury housing), production-related (e.g., office buildings), or both (e.g., shopping centers or mixed-use facilities). For this strategy to work in a period of stagnant or declining economic vitality of central cities and a high rate of suburbanization of its population, however, the urban renewal areas had to be those with existing adjacent anchors (e.g., the downtown business district or large well-endowed institutions such as universities, research hospitals, and government facilities). The areas also had to be relatively inexpensive, which usually, but not always, meant areas in physical decline. Community economic development as urban renewal took the form of the targeting of public capital to strategically designated communities in order to induce private capital investment with local mechanisms (redevelopment authority, right of eminent domain, and, in some cases, financial assistance for interested private investors). The strategy as a whole did not work, largely because the conditions for investment in central cities, even with the publicly provided financial incentives, were not strong enough to divert private capital from investing in the highly lucrative suburbanization process.

Table 7.1. NonGovernment Employment Covering Major Industry Groups for Selected Central Cities: 1947-1972 (a)

	1947-48(b)	1954	1958	1963	1967	1972
Baltimore	227,400	231,000	237,000	212,600	216,400	202,200
Boston	236,700	235,800	227,600	203,700	209,400	190,000
Buffalo	153,400	160,700	136,600	113,800	125,400	110,600
Cleveland	333,100	335,000	311,800	275,900	283,100	237,000
Detroit	531,000	496,800	404,800	364,100	382,100	328,600
Milwaukee	211,800	204,600	214,400	198,900	205,400	190,300
New York	1,839,900	1,904,300	2,021,100	1,954,900	1,956,300	1,779,200
Philadelphia	547,300	534,800	524,100	479,500	482,600	414,700
Pittsburgh	188,100	169,100	195,000	167,600	176,200	142,400
9 Cities	4,268,700	4,272,100	4,272,400	3,971,000	4,037,400	3,595,000
% Change	+0.1	--	-9.1	+1.7	-11.0	

(a) Industry groups are those included in the economic census: Manufacturing, Retail and Wholesale Trade, and Selected Services; does not include government employment. 1977 employment figures for cities have not yet been published.

(b) The manufacturing employees are for 1947; all others were counted in 1948.

Sources: U.S. Bureau of the Census, County and City Data Book, 1952, 1956, 1962, 1967, 1972, 1977.

1963-1968

Although the federal urban renewal program extended beyond 1963, the principal function and thrust of community economic development shifted thereafter to one of community based social services for the poor, concentrated in designated urban and rural poverty areas.(2) Starting with the Community Mental Health Centers Act of 1963, through the Community Action Program of 1964, and the Model Cities Program of 1966, federal programs carved out a new level of service areas. In each of these programs newly created community centers served as the foci for a limited amount of community control over the direct delivery of federally funded social services. Since the federal programs were designed to by-pass local government, major conflicts in community economic development arose between the local government and community leaders over the control of antipoverty funds.(3) This form of community economic development, in a period almost coterminous with that of economic recovery in the older central cities, fueled by the Vietnam War, represents a shift from the use of public capital to stimulate private capital flows into the formation of fixed capital in these cities to a modest, and relatively cheap infusion of capital for social investment and social expenditures. From an overall view of the capital accumulation process, the strategy was rational because it attempted to balance the increased level of capital flows in immediate production and consumption activities in the central cities (as indicated by the employment gains and a relatively high demand for labor) with a more productive labor force.(4) It was also a rational strategy because it did not, as urban renewal had tried and generally failed to do, compete for capital flowing into suburban geographic paths by subsidizing capital's costs in an attempt to divert it to central city locations. Of course, the taxes used to fund the antipoverty programs were a drain on profits to capital and thus a diversion from other, more profitable investments (i.e., in the suburbanization process or in foreign investment), but this was a modest drain compared to the positive political functions that were served.

1969-1975

The approach to community economic development again shifted in the late 1960s. This shift coincided with the end of the period of employment growth and of relative economic gains for minorities in the central cities. The systematic dismantling of the federal antipoverty programs initiated by the Nixon administration left the community centers with very little money with which to deliver services. Instead, largely brought about by the creation of the Special Impact Program (SIP) in 1967, community economic development shifted its focus to minority business development, under the umbrella of SIP-funded community development corporations.(5) Although this new approach was much more ideologically consistent with the broader social program of the new administration, it retained the prior institutional structure. Indeed new CDC facilities were often located in the old CAP and Model Cities centers, and there tended to be a strong continuity in leadership. Local government was still not generally involved in CDC activities, nor in community economic development of any sort. This may have been disadvantageous to the program because, in these earlier days, CDCs were frequently denied access to the local power structure, including lending institutions, city planning and zoning commissioners, and city hall.

The principal funding institutions – the Office of Economic Opportunity in the federal government and the Ford Foundation – were effectively able to force the shift in focus from community service to business development through legislative restrictions, funding stipulations, and threats to cut funds when such a shift was resisted by community leaders. A number of different evaluations and audits of CDCs were conducted within the first four or five years of their funding. In general these audits were not motivated by concern for the impact on the communities themselves.(6) The consensus of those most familiar with the program was that CDCs were more successful in their social development efforts than in nurturing successful business ventures. By traditional cost-benefit criteria, CDCs would have been judged inefficient users of public capital. Michelson has argued that if a cost-benefit framework is to be used for judging the performance of, and by implication, the funding for, CDCs, then there are relevant nonmarket (social) costs and benefits that must also be included in the calculation, which would tip the balance in favor of the CDCs.(7) Regardless, since the state was now consciously moving away from social development unless it came as a by-product of successful minority entrepreneurship, the only relevant criterion was whether the community based organization could spin off market-viable ventures and whether the CDCs or other sponsoring groups could run self-sufficient programs.

The intervening variable, not usually taken into account in the evaluation of the self-sufficiency of community economic development activities but particularly relevant here, is that from 1969 to 1975 the national economy, with two major recessions, two devaluations of the dollar, and extraordinarily high rates of inflation, performed dismally. Profit rates in the domestic industrial sector had been falling and private capital was even more sharply diverted from production-related activity in the primary and secondary circuits to speculation in real estate and consumption related construction (e.g., condominiums, shopping centers, hotels), but <u>not</u> in the large central cities. The shift in the focus of community economic development to minority business development primarily in ghetto areas was not intended to be a strategy for inducing significant amounts of private capital investment in any form (housing or factories) to these areas or even to adjacent areas: any ghetto gilding strategy of this sort, combined with inadequate amounts of total CDC funding, could not possibly work under the prevailing economic (business investment) conditions. Instead the shift can be interpreted as the beginning of the state's effort to unburden itself of a possibly open-ended fiscal responsibility for social services to the poor, which it could no longer afford economically or politically.

In short, the shift in focus to minority business development was the essential first step toward self-help in the trajectory of community economic development under the control of community-based organizations. Ironically, the state's response in this successful push was to threaten to cut off the already meager federal allocation if community based organizations did not concentrate on promoting self-sufficient business ventures. The self-help approach assured, at best, the continued marginality of community economic development in the areas of the central cities in the worst social, economic and physical condition, as well as the consumption of a great deal of valuable human energy. Meanwhile, the state waited for improved investment conditions to return and, with minimal political resistance, diverted precious public seed funds to more attractive areas of the city in an attempt to induce substantially large amounts of private capital investment.

THE PRESENT SITUATION: DIMENSIONS, ISSUES, AND CONFLICT ARENAS

Two series of events have been principally responsible for passing the control of community economic development back into the hands of local states for the first time since the urban renewal days. First, the recession of 1974-75 and the economic damage it caused, along with the realization that we had finally come to an end of an era of long-term economic prosperity, made central city governments and the dominant downtown business interests understand the necessity for developing strong local economic development capacities in order to compete for shares in a shrinking economy. Second, the federal government's consolidation of categorical programs channeled various funds formerly allocated to distressed urban areas for housing, urban renewal, manpower training, job creation, etc., into large block grant programs (primarily the Community Development Block Grant Program, created by the Housing and Community Development Act of 1974, and the CETA programs created by the Comprehensive Employment and Training Act of 1973). The block grants were designed to give local government "the authority to determine local community development (and employment and training) needs, establish priorities, and allocate resources."(8) By virtue of the sheer amount of resources available, these programs gave local government effective control of community economic development. The level of resources easily dwarfed those available to community-based organizations, and with the newly acquired economic development capacity, local government could compete successfully against community based organizations for any outside private capital investment. The caveats were that the block grants did have some stipulations on the eligible activities and also on the directing of funds toward low and moderate income communities, as

Table 7.2. Major Federal Community Economic Development-Related Programs Funding Levels, FY 79 (in millions)

Agency	Grant Program	Level	Loan Program	Level
Economic Development Administration	Title I	$228.5	Title II	$182.5
	Title III	90.8		
	Title IX	88.5		
			Trade Adjustment	225.0
Small Business Administration	---		501 & 502	95.0
Housing and Urban Development	UDAG	400.0		
	CDBG	3,500.0		
	Neighborhood Strategy Area Program	80.0		
Community Services Administration	Community Economic Development Program	46.2		
	Community Food & Nutrition Program	26.0		
Employment and Training Administration	CETA	12,000.0		
Proposed National Development Bank	Grants	550.0		

Sources: The CCED Review, Spring 1979 and Roberts, Jr. (1979), pp. 138-140.

well as toward those groups experiencing the most difficulty in the labor market. Meanwhile, federal programs specifically aimed for city-wide economic development activities, such as EDA's grant and loan programs, were still rather small compared to the number and size of the projects that the central cities' economic development agencies considered necessary for their economic revival.

Under these conditions the strategy that the central cities adopted (i.e., those cities that had generated some economic development capacity), and the strategy that now dominates the practice of community economic development, was to combine and package readily available public seed capital from various funding sources and divert it to those areas of the central cities that would maximize the leveraging of private capital. In some cases, the package of public funds is used to match funds for larger publicly provided grants and loans.(9) The areas to which the federal community economic development funds are being diverted include downtown business districts, on the one hand, and areas already undergoing economic revitalization through the "normal" market process, on the other (through gentrification and displacement). The buzzwords "coordination" and "public/private partnerships" lend a tone of legitimacy to the new strategy, while its theoretical justification rests on usual grounds of economic efficiency, i.e., public community economic development funds generate a greater aggregate of personal income and new jobs if diverted to areas other than those in the worst condition. Usually attached to this argument is the implicit assumption that the differential economic benefits gained by pursuing this strategy can and do get filtered and otherwise redistributed to the poor and working class. There is little evidence thus far that this has been the case. Even Chinitz recognizes that there are tradeoffs between the goals of business development (private sector job creation) and the reduction of unemployment.

In order to gain some positive roles, community based organizations involved in economic development have been forced to a position where they must depend upon the good will, cooperation, and the development of policies by local government.(10) Most of the development tools currently available are institutionally or statutorially within the domain of the state (e.g., tax incentives, industrial and commercial revenue bonds, land banking, etc.). Thus, while community based organizations are free to enter into cooperative arrangements with private business to initiate development projects within their own communities, they are at a competitive disadvantage with the local government for attracting either the investment capital or the enterprises considering central city locations. CBOs often must become partners in projects that have minimal multiplier effects and considerably lower chances of success.

CONTRADICTORY TENDENCIES AND PROGNOSES FOR STRATEGY BUILDING

The analysis above would suggest that under <u>existing political and economic conditions</u> in the large, older, northern central cities, community economic development via community based organizations such as CDCs is not likely to produce social and economic gains for the residents in the most distressed areas of those cities on a scale commensurate with their needs; nor is it likely to lead to mass political movement on the Left. Current struggles around housing and health have more possibilities for building mass movements among the working class and the nonworking poor because these conflict areas tend not to be as widely fragmented along intraclass lines or as spatially isolated.(11)

This pessimistic prognosis is qualified, however, by the continuation of the political and economic conditions characterizing the large central cities since the end of the 1974-75 recession. Indeed, the sine qua non of the success of city-wide economic development efforts in the same large central cities during this period has been the return of favorable central city economic conditions. However, these favorable conditions have been, on the whole, independent of the local state's intervention and stimulation efforts.

The recession left the large central cities, particularly those hardest hit with losses in population and employment from out-migration, plant shrinkages or plant closings, with many bargains for 1) potential investors in real estate (industrial, office and residential) caused by large forced "write-downs"; and 2) for prospective and existing firms in labor costs caused by the unusually slack labor markets. The loss of real wages by nonmanagerial workers was also abetted by a strong ideological shift to the right. In New York City, for instance, where the municipal labor unions have a singularly important role in the setting of the entire local wage structure in the entire city, a sufficiently large public acceptance of the myth that the greed of the municipal labor unions was the principal cause of the city being forced into de facto bankruptcy helped to force the unions to accept declines in real wages and thus to make New York City's wage structure a positive attribute in the city's subsequent promotional campaign to attract new firms. There is now fragmentary evidence that in some key labor intensive manufacturing industries, wage rates in certain sunbelt cities are higher than those in some large northeastern central cities. It is well-known that hundreds of sweatshops have sprouted literally overnight in areas like the South Bronx to take advantage of the large supply of unskilled labor willing to work for well below the legal minimum wage.(12) Moreover, the more favorable investment conditions have led an increasing number of officials to question the rationality of offering customized packages of locational incentives to prospective firms when there are indications that these firms might be sufficiently attracted to locate in the central cities anyway.

The point is that the favorable macroeconomic conditions giving rise to the recent attractiveness of doing business in the large, older central cities is unlikely to continue through the 1980s. When the national economic downturn does occur, the same general economic development strategy employed by local governments since around 1975-76 will no longer be a viable one, and the rationale for diverting public capital away from progressive community based institutions will not be as convincing. Still, a general economic downturn, with new waves of mass unemployment, is more likely to assist CBOs' efforts in the political and organizing arena than in the economic arena. The demand for a more rational economy, capable of providing full employment could potentially unite the working class and poor into political coalitions with community organizations serving as the institutional bases for these coalitions.

A different prospectus for the success of community based economic development emerges if one looks to the smaller industrial cities of the Northeast and Midwest, and, to some degree, the South.(13) Here the possibility that the interests of city and/or regional economic development will coincide with the interests of community based economic development (from the perspective of progressive community based organizations) is a stronger one. Recent major plant closings, and the likelihood of many more in the 1980s, pose a set of crisis conditions that existing institutional structures are unequipped to handle. Bergman has proposed a list of propositions for a new practice of local economic planning with worker- and community-ownership of productive enterprises as its principal goal.(14) The relevant question here is whether this strategy can go byond a merely different form of self-help. The ideology of "economic democracy" for instance, is gaining acceptance and gives a negative answer to the above, but its inherent weakness as a progressive political strategy seems to be based in part on the assumption that people can be "fooled into socialism."

The questions arise of whether community economic development can: 1) successfully produce qualitative improvements in the objective economic conditions of the working class and the poor; 2) produce "nonreformist" reforms in the road toward socialism; and 3) if it can, under what conditions? These questions are unanswerable in the abstract, although theoretical and historical analyses provide important insights. We need to know how changes in the larger macroeconomic and political conditions serve to bring underlying contradictions to the surface in the concrete settings of local economies. We need to know more about the possibilities of how the various fragmented class interests might line up in the face of local economic distress induced by exogenous forces of the flight of externally owned productive capital. We also need to explore ways for the individual states to perceive citywide economic development interests as overlapping with the interests of a coalition of progressive community based organizations engaged in the economic development process. The historical sketch of the development of community economic development provided in this paper underscores the notion that local and even federal initiatives in local economic development are still based upon poor analyses of how city economic development proceeds. The limits and the legitimacy of a state's ability to manage and stimulate local economies will likely be severely tested in the 1980s, and the contradictions that will flow from such conditions may spawn a whole new set of opportunities for progressive local economic planning in the United States.

NOTES

(1) Harrison, Urban Economic Development, 1974. The periodization is only approximate because employment figures are not generally available on an annual basis.

(2) Some might argue that service delivery is not a development activity, since it does not generally result in any net capital formation, and thus this is not a phase of community economic development at all. There are at least two important arguments against this view. The first is historical: the institutional and leadership roots of many community development corporations were in CAP and Model Cities centers, and so there is a direct legacy of one phase from the other. The second argument, a theoretical one, is stronger, and is developed in the text: these federal funds were used for social development and represented a flow of capital in the tertiary circuit targeted in low-income communities. From the point of view of the circuits of capital, education, manpower, and health are all social capital investments which (theoretically) to some degree are necessary to the long-term continuation of the capital accumulation process.

(3) See Piven, "The New Urban Programs," 1975, for greater descriptive detail and an interpretation of the political motivations for the Kennedy and Johnson administrations' antipoverty programs. Alternative views are given, for example, in Kramer, Participation of the Poor, 1969; Pressman, Federal Programs and City Politics, 1975; Warren, The Structure of Urban Reform, 1974; and Frieden and Kaplan, The Politics of Neglect, 1975.

(4) There has been an unfortunate tendency for some writing in the Marxian tradition to use the categories "legitimation" and "accumulation" as two distinct categories, to describe the roles of the modern capitalist state, with the implication that the former can be analyzed independently of the dynamics and forces of the capital accumulation process. In this chapter, the role of the legitimation function in the state's community development politicies is recognized, but I wish to emphasize the legitimation aspects of the policies as elements of the overall capital accumulation process (i.e., as purposive shifts of public capital among circuits and among specific geographic paths to legitimate some of the "irrational" systemic effects of flows of private capital).

(5) See, for example: Garn, Tevis, and Snead, Evaluating Community Development Corporations, 1976; Center for Community Economic Development, A Review of the Abt Associates, 1977; and Harrison, Urban Economic Development, 1974, for a review of the history of community development corporations in general and the Special Impact Program in particular.

(6) See Center for Community Economic Development, A Review of the Abt Associates, 1977, and Goldstein, "Special Impact Program," 1978, for reviews of the evaluations of the SIP, and Garn, Tevis, and Snead, Evaluating Community Development Corporations, 1976, for the constructed evaluation for the Ford Foundation of three of its funded CDCs. The CCED document is a very critical review of the ABT Associates SIP evaluation conducted for the Nixon administration.

(7) Michelson, "Community-Based Development in Urban Cities," 1979.

(8) Economic Development Law Project, "Coordinating CDC and Block Grant Community Development Programs," 1977.

(9) See CUED's set of case study analyses (National Council for Urban Economic Development, Coordinated Urban Economic Development, 1978) for descriptions of examples of this strategy in practice, written by the organization which has done the most development and promotion of it. Also the Community Economic Development Demonstration Program is an excellent example of how the federal state is being responsive to the central cities' economic development leaders' wishes for "greater flexibility" in the use of federal community development and manpower training funds for stimulating private capital investment. (See National Council for Urban Economic Development, Community Economic Development, 1978, and a forthcoming evaluation of that program by Abt Associates, Inc., Cambridge, Massachusetts). Also, the new federal Urban Development Action Grant program (UDAG) supplies local governments with funds for initiating large development projects which maximize private capital investment, and represent a further strengthening of the local state in diverting economic development funds away from the most distressed areas of the central cities.

(10) Butler, "Strategies for Neighborhood Economic Revitalization," 1976, has compiled a list of strategies for CDCs to adopt which he feels are crucial for successful neighborhood economic revitalization and community economic development. Seven of the eight strategies are directed to urging local government to adopt local economic development policies that involve CDCs in certain ways or to design and implement certain institutional mechanisms that make it easier for CDCs to put together development projects.

(11) See, for instance, Kennedy and Burlage, "Repressive vs. Reconstructive Forces," 1979, in this volume for a view of the potential conflict arenas in health care.

(12) See, for example, Koeppel, "The New Sweatshops," 1978.

(13) See, for example, Carlisle, Redmond, et al., "Community Participation in Selecting Worker Ownership," 1978; and Luebke, McMahon, and Risberg, "Selective Recruitment in North Carolina," 1979, for examples

of efforts toward community- and worker-ownership of plants in the South.

(14) Bergman, "Local Economic Planning: Propositions for Practice," 1978 (Paper presented at the 20th Annual Conference of the American Collegiate Schools of Planning, New Orleans, La.).

8 Rising Rents and Rent Control: Issues in Urban Reform

Peter Dreier
John Ingram Gilderbloom
Richard P. Appelbaum

The rising cost of rental housing has become a serious problem throughout the United States. The Department of Housing and Urban Development recommends that no more than 25 percent of family income go into housing. But according to the 1977 Annual Housing Survey by the Bureau of the Census (the latest figures available) more than two-fifths (42 percent) of the nation's renter households pay greater than that amount on rent; 28 percent of renter households pay over 35 percent of family income on housing. Over 80 percent of the inner city residents pay more than the recommended 25 percent. As rising rents continue to outstrip wage increases, tenants have less and less money to spend on essentials such as health care, food, transportation, and clothing. For some, even the 25 percent guideline may be too high – urban economist Michael Stone, employing Bureau of Labor Statistics standards, has found that a family of four earning under $7,500 needs that amount alone to cover all nonhousing necessities.(1) For a family of four earning $8,000, only eight percent remains for housing if other basic necessities such as food, health care, transportation and clothing are to be met first. For many low income people the high cost of housing can contribute significantly to their impoverishment.

Slightly more than one-third of all Americans now live in rented housing – a figure that has changed little over the past decade.(2) A Census Bureau study in 1977 found that, on average, tenants' income is only 60 percent that of homeowners. Minority groups and senior citizens, both because they are poorer and because they frequently face discrimination in the housing market, are more likely to rent than to own a home.

The rising cost of home ownership has all but priced low and moderate income persons out of the housing market. For example, with homes currently averaging over $63,000 nationally it is extremely difficult for young working people, the elderly, and members of traditionally disadvantaged minorities in that area to gain access to the private housing market. According to the California Department of Housing and Community Development, as far back as 1973, 86 percent of all renters could not afford to buy their own homes. And the situation in California is not atypical.

As a result of these conditions, the past decade has witnessed the creation of a potentially significant category of tenants – "lifers" – those individuals who failed to acquire a home prior to the current inflationary period, and who therefore can reasonably expect to spend their lives as renters. Their condition has been adversely affected by the removal of a proportion of rental housing from the market in the past few years, through condominium conversion and gentrification. For example, it is estimated that fully one-seventh of Washington's population will be displaced by these processes over the next four years. In California the State Department of Housing and Community Development estimates a shortage of 536,000 housing units for low and moderate income persons at rents they can afford.

As a response to these pressures, close to 120 municipalities have enacted some form of rent control during the past decade – most of them in New Jersey.(3) Rent control laws are also on the books in Massachusetts, New York, Virginia, Maryland, Alaska, Connecticut and the Virgin Islands. These municipalities have adopted a form of rent control generally known as "moderate" rent control.(4) It differs from more restrictive forms of rent control (e.g., World War I and II controls), which virtually froze rents, making it almost impossible for landlords to increase rents to meet rising costs. Moderate rent control generally provides a formula for annual adjustments, allowing landlords to "pass through" to tenants any cost increases (taxes, maintenance, utilities), and guaranteeing a "fair and reasonable return on investment." Moderate controls are usually administered by an appointed board. These laws require landlords to maintain their buildings and protect tenants from arbitrary evictions.(5) The main thrust of this legislation is to provide protections against extreme rent increases or "rent gouging"; in general it does not significantly lower rents.

THE EFFECTS OF RENT CONTROL

There are a number of criticisms of rent control commonly made, both in academic studies and in the popular press. First, it is argued that rent control frightens off potential builders and mortgage lenders, thereby stifling new construction; this in turn exacerbates the housing shortage, particularly for the poor. Second, rent control is alleged to inhibit a "fair return" on landlord investment on the grounds that expenses inevitably outpace allowable rent increases; this discourages maintenance, contributes to deterioration, and in extreme cases causes outright abandonment. Both of these consequences – a diminished housing supply and declining property values – are held to erode a city's tax base.

Most studies of the adverse consequences of moderate rent control rely on the work of George Sternlieb, an urban economist.(6) Sternlieb's studies of moderate rent control in Massachusetts and New Jersey have received wide acclaim from economists, lawyers, housing officials and real estate organizations. Moreover, the popular press reflects his view that moderate rent control is a "disaster" and "unworkable." For example, the Los Angeles Times (August 16, 1976) states that:

> . . . rent controls generally contribute to urban decay by discouraging new construction and, eventually, by reducing the landlords' incentive to keep their buildings in good condition. It's true, also, that rent controls tend to erode the property tax base by reducing the value of income properties. They increase the burden borne by ordinary homeowners.

The Wall Street Journal similarly holds that:

> . . . rent control makes no sense economically or socially. Holding return on investment below market levels lowers the value of property investment, and therefore reduces assessed valuation . . . rent control and even the threat of rent controls dries up investment. Keeping rents artificially low also contributes to housing decay by discouraging reinvestment and ordinary maintenance.(7)

Finally, Forbes Magazine (September 15, 1967) asserts:

> . . . that rent controls deter construction of new rental dwellings is no longer a question. Mortgage bankers shy away from lending on rent controlled structures. . .owners are beginning to demolish property.

A close examination of Sternlieb's studies, however, reveals serious shortcomings that serve to bias their results, calling into question the conclusions of the many technical and popular reports that are based on his findings.(8) Principal among these defects is the failure to examine systematically a comparable set of rent- and non rent-controlled cities, and – in those few studies that attempt such comparisons – the failure to control adequately for potentially confounding effects.

One systematic study has been undertaken to attempt to assess the short-term impact of moderate rent control. In a report prepared for the California Department of Housing and Community Development, Gilderbloom examined a matched set of rent-controlled and non rent-controlled cities in New Jersey, in terms of the effect of rent control on construction, abandonment, and valuation of property. Gilderbloom looked at all cities with 1973 populations greater than 13,000 in which at least 14 percent of the housing stock was available for rent. For cities with rent control, he limited his sample to those that had enacted their ordinances during the eight-month period beginning September

1972 and ending April 1973. On this basis, 26 rent-controlled cities (out of a possible 102) and 37 non rent-controlled cities were selected for study.(9) Gilderbloom employed a standard ordinary least-squares regression analysis to control for the potentially confounding effects of a number of variables which, along with rent control, might conceivably be expected to influence construction, demolitions, and taxes. These variables included population, urban growth, tax rate, median rent, percentage of housing units available for rent, racial composition of population, type of city (urban, urban-suburban, suburban), and construction activity and demolitions prior to rent control (i.e., the period 1970-1972). Rent control was treated as a dummy variable in the analysis.

First, Gilderbloom found that rent control has not hindered the amount of multifamily construction, at least in the short run. In an earlier study, he found that there was actually more construction in rent-controlled communities: comparing the immediate pre- and post-rent control periods (1970-1972 with 1973-1975), for example, indicated a 65 percent decline in apartment construction in non rent-controlled cities, compared with a 19 percent decline in rent-controlled cities. In fact, Gilderbloom found that at a time of a nationwide decline in housing construction because of the increased cost of mortgage financing, 11 of the 26 rent-controlled cities he looked at actually had an increase in construction after controls were enacted in 1973.(10) In Gilderbloom's 1979 analysis, which controlled for related variables, rent control was not found to be significantly associated with total construction during the three-year period following the enactment of rent control (1973-1975, $p \leq .10$); only total construction during the three years preceding rent control (1970-1972) and municipal population size were found to be (positively) associated.

A study by Emily Achtenberg of Urban Planning Aid further supports these findings.(11) Achtenberg found that construction in rent-controlled cities in Massachusetts was outpacing construction activity in nearby noncontrolled cities. How much new housing is built depends much more on other factors – the availability of land, government housing programs, zoning laws, and the general health of the economy. That rent control is not a factor should come as no surprise – since moderate rent control typically exempts newly constructed buildings and guarantees a fair and reasonable return on investment comparable to other investments with similar risks.

Second, Gilderbloom offers evidence to dispute the claim that controlled rent increases fail to keep pace with rising costs and that, as a result, landlords lower maintenance standards, leading to the abandonment and eventual demolition of the housing stock.(12) The number of demolitions during the three-year period following rent control (1973-1975) was not significantly associated with rent control ($p \leq .10$) when other variables were taken into account; only the number of units demolished prior to rent control (1970-1972), and municipal population, were found to be (positively) associated.(13) Gilderbloom's findings parallel those of the National Urban League, which – in a study of abandonment – ranked New York City fifth behind St. Louis, Cleveland, Chicago, and Hoboken (cities without rent control and with newer housing stock). According to the New York State Commission of Living Costs and the Economy:

> The abandonment process is a social and economic process which is both cumulative and self-generating, spreading through many low income and ghetto neighborhoods. Rent control, however, can have little effect for it is clear that it is the oldest, least desirable tenement housing which is abandoned – housing which is unable to produce substantially more income in a free market.(14)

Marcuse, in an extensive study on New York City rental housing undertaken for the city's Division of Rent Control, drew similar conclusions. Based on an analysis of data from the 1978 Special Census of Housing and Vacancy, Marcuse concluded that losses from the housing inventory were a function of the age of the structure and general neighborhood deterioration, rather than rent control; statistically, the incidence of removal during the period 1975-1978 was no higher among rent-controlled units than decontrolled ones.(15) It is clear that abandonment has less to do with rent control than with other causes – redlining, vandalism, arson for insurance purposes, neighborhood decline, and the exhaustion of accelerated depreciation and other tax benefits.

The reason that moderate rent control does not encourage deterioration and abandonment is simply that in most controlled cities landlords cannot receive rent increases unless they keep the building well maintained and comply with local housing codes. Rent control thereby provides an incentive for landlords to keep buildings in good repair. Moreover, the landlord is allowed to pass along all increases in costs to tenants. Economist Joseph Eckert examined the audited income and operating statements of rent-controlled properties in Brookline, Massachusetts, and found that the percentage of the average rent dollar going to maintenance increased from 4.2 percent in 1970 (the year rent control was adopted) to 5 percent in 1974. Achtenberg's study of four Boston area communities (Cambridge, Somerville, Brookline, and Lynn) showed that permits for alterations, additions, and repairs increased in all four cities – from 22 percent in Somerville to 69 percent in Lynn – after rent control was introduced.(16) The widespread view that rent control leads to deterioration and abandonment customarily rests on Sternlieb's findings that, under rent control, costs outpace rent increases in controlled areas.(17) But Gilderbloom contends that Sternlieb used misleading figures in his computations to demonstrate that landlords' costs rise faster than rents.(18) When calculating "total increase in expenses," Sternlieb included maintenance, utilities, and taxes, which have all increased substantially. But he left out mortgage payments, which remain fixed and account for one-third to two-thirds of a landlord's total expenses. By recalculating the figures to include mortgage payments, Gilderbloom found that Sternlieb had seriously overestimated cost increases. He also found that landlords in Sternlieb's study underreported the rents they collected. Gilderbloom's research showed, too, that for similar cities and similar buildings without rent control, rent increases far outstrip increases in landlords' actual costs. Sternlieb's own data also contradict his statements on rent control which show that the percentage of the rent dollar going into maintenance increased after the enactment of rent control in the cities Sternlieb studied.

Gilderbloom also took issue with a third argument against rent control: that it erodes a city's tax base by shrinking and further devaluing the housing stock. In his early work, Gilderbloom found that comparable New Jersey cities with and without rent control had identical average increases of 25 percent in their tax bases. Of the more than 100 rent-controlled cities in the state, only seven experienced a decline in the total tax base after rent control was enacted. None of the tax assessors in those cities blamed rent control for the decline. In the regression analysis, Gilderbloom found that the percentage increase in total taxable output of apartments during the post rent control period 1973-1976 was not significantly associated with rent control ($p \leq .10$); the only variables that appeared to be associated with such increases were demolitions of multifamily housing during the post rent control period, tax rate increases during the same period, the total taxable output of multifamily housing in 1973 (a proxy for unmeasured factors affecting output both before and after enactment of rent controls), post rent control multifamily construction and whether or not the city was classified as suburban.(19) Gilderbloom reasoned that rent controls exerted a negligible effect on taxable output because of their moderate nature. While the enactment of controls might have reduced the value of apartments in which high profits were being made through rent gouging, this was possibly offset by the decision by apartment owners who were formerly charging below-market rents to raise their rents to the maximum permitted by the rent control board. Achtenberg's studies of rent control in the Boston area offer support for Gilderbloom's conclusions. She found that in Lynn, Cambridge, and Somerville – which did experience a tax erosion – the slide began before rent control, while in nearby Boston and Brookline the tax base increased steadily after controls were introduced. A community's tax base was, it appeared, influenced more by other factors: departing industry, redlining, tax concessions for business and large property owners, changes in zoning laws, and the acquisition of property by tax-exempt organizations such as colleges, the government, redevelopment authorities, and charitable groups.(20)

Despite Gilderbloom's findings – which bear the imprimature of the California Department of Housing and Community Development – the news media continue to echo the housing industry's point of view on rent control. In opposing June 1978's rent control initiatives (and arguing for voluntary rent relief in the wake of the Proposition 13 property tax cut) the Los Angeles Times as well as local dailies in both

Santa Monica and Santa Barbara echoed the kind of arguments made by Sternlieb. Business Week interviewed Gilderbloom for a story on the "groundswell" of rent control activity around the country. But when the story appeared in the October 24, 1977 issue, it repeated the standard criticism of rent control – even quoting Sternlieb directly – and ignored Gilderbloom's counterevidence. The editor of Business Week, in a personal interview with one of the authors of this paper, stated: "I made up my mind about rent control twenty-five years ago and I don't care what any college kid says."

Time (April 30, 1979) and Newsweek (June 4, 1979) magazines featured long articles on the growing interest in rent control. Both articles quoted Sternlieb approvingly and repeated the myths about rent control's alleged negative effects. Both, in particular, linked New York City's housing problems to its long-term rent control program. Time even titled its story, "Catching the New York Disease."

THE POLITICAL IMPLICATIONS OF RENT CONTROL

Whatever the evidence concerning the effects of rent control, the issue is primarily political, and is perceived as such by both tenants' groups and the housing industry. Its success or failure depends on the extent to which organized tenants' movements can neutralize the obvious economic and political strength of their more powerful opponents. Rent control has worked best where well-organized tenants' groups have exerted a steady pressure on elected officials, landlords, and rent control boards. In Washington, D.C. – where 70 percent of the population are renters – the Rental Accommodations Office (RAO – the rent control agency) was understaffed and intimidated by the housing industry throughout its first four years; only during the past year has it been able to efficiently and effectively administer the city's five-year-old rent control law. This is due in part to pressures put on the RAO by Washington tenants' groups, and in part to internal reorganization of the agency itself, in which the director and top staff were recruited from citizens' and tenants' associations. The RAO now sees itself in an advocacy role, actively involved in outreach and public education. But none of this would have occurred – nor would the agency's level of funding have increased – had not the City Wide Housing Coalition exerted political pressure.

Similarly, in East Orange, New Jersey, a strong rent control law reflects the influence of a strong tenants' group, the East Orange Tenants' Association (EOTA). Two of EOTA's members sit on the five-person rent control board. With a full-time staff of seven (funded in part with CETA and community block grant money), EOTA has organized tenants in as many as 100 buildings and set up an "abandonment alert" to monitor landlords who fail to comply with local regulations. Where landlords have been found delinquent, tenants have been allowed to name a receiver, who is then authorized by the court to collect rents and manage the building. Moderate rent control gives EOTA leverage in organizing tenants and enables it to educate tenants concerning the economics of income property as well. EOTA is affiliated with the New Jersey Tenants' Organization (NJTO), the largest and most powerful tenants' group in the country. Created in 1969, the NJTO can take credit for the fact that over 100 New Jersey municipalities have rent control laws. The group has also lobbied the state legislature to pass some of the toughest landlord-tenant laws in the country. State law now prohibits eviction of tenants who complain about housing conditions, bars landlords from refusing to renew a lease without "just cause," permits courts (with tenant approval) to collect rents until repairs are made, and requires that landlords pay interest on security deposits.

During the past few years, the reaction to rent control on the part of the housing and business communities has been strong and, in many instances, effective in reversing earlier gains made by tenants and their organizations. In Boston, for example, property owners considerably undermined the city's rent control law by prevailing on the city council to pass "vacancy decontrol" – a measure that permanently removes an apartment from controls whenever a tenant moves out. When the vacancy decontrol law took effect in January 1976 there were 95,000 units under rent control. In the next two-and-a-half years, nearly 30,000 units were removed from control as they became vacant. In the fall of 1977, a report by Andrew Olins, housing adviser to Boston Mayor Kevin White, recommended ending rent control altogether (except for apartments occupied by senior citizens on fixed incomes). But White was facing a tough reelection campaign. When the Boston Committee for Rent Control and Massachusetts Fair Share (a citizen action group that includes more homeowners than renters) mobilized to dispute Olins's conclusions – that rent control hurt the city's tax base and housing stock – the mayor backed away from repeal. Boston's rent control ordinance expires on December 31, 1979. As of the summer of 1979, tenant groups are again facing an uphill battle to strengthen the law and to protect tenants from a wave of condominium conversions.

In Lynn, Massachusetts (1974), Miami Beach, Florida (1976), and Somerville, Massachusetts (1978), the local business community did convince the city council to end controls. In Somerville, a working class community of 80,000, the repeal of rent control after seven years was hastened by the poor administration of the ordinance. A prolandlord mayor appointed opponents of rent control to a majority of the seats on the rent control board, and underfunded and understaffed the agency. Tenants and landlords alike complained of excessive delays in processing petitions, which eroded the credibility of rent control and support for it.

In California in 1976, landlord groups pushed a bill through the state legislature that would have prohibited municipalities from imposing rent control, but Governor Brown vetoed the measure. In New Jersey, landlord groups have brought suits in state courts challenging local formulas for granting rent increases.

Real estate groups have succeeded in keeping rent control out of Philadelphia, Minneapolis, Madison, New Orleans, Chicago, Seattle, and other cities. Most recently the battle has focused on California, where both landlord and tenant groups are well organized. When the two sides faced off in three city-wide referenda in Berkeley (April 1977), Santa Monica, and Santa Barbara (June 1978), rent control was defeated all three times.

Rent control advocates in Berkeley made a number of strategic mistakes – their proposal, for example, extended controls to small "mom and pop" landlords as well as larger property owners – but they were also badly outspent. The Berkeley Housing Coalitions operated on about $5,000. The Berkeley Committee Against Rent Control raised $150,000 – or about $8 a vote – 80 percent of which came from out of town. The money financed direct mail, billboard, radio and newspaper ads, and 15,000 phone calls to voters.

Chastened by the Berkeley defeat, rent control activists in Santa Monica and Santa Barbara started early and mounted precinct-by-precinct campaigns. Both towns seemed ripe for controls. They are medium-sized coastal communities that have experienced enormous land speculation in recent years, and both have been strongholds of progressive political activity. Tenants make up 80 percent of the population in Santa Monica and 60 percent in Santa Barbara. In both cities, the rent control proposals were of the moderate form discussed earlier: they exempted newly constructed building – both to avoid the hostility of the building trades unions and to counter the charge that rent control discourages new construction. But unlike most rent control ordinances, the Santa Monica and Santa Barbara measures called for elected boards, in hopes of short-circuiting an unfriendly mayor or city council.

The pro rent control forces managed to raise about $10,000 in Santa Monica and $21,000 in Santa Barbara. Two groups, the Santa Monica Residents and Taxpayers Committee and the Santa Barbara Housing Council, were set up by local real estate interests specifically for the rent control fight. The money they raised – $257,000 in Santa Monica and $160,000 in Santa Barbara – was more than had ever been spent for a referendum or election campaign in either city. Part of that money came from the newly formed California Housing Council (CHC), a statewide organization of the state's 200 largest landlords, which raised half a million dollars by levying members $2.50 per apartment. The anti-rent control organizations hired professional consultants who drew on previous successes and ran a slick advertising campaign. In Santa Monica, pamphlets with a photograph of a burned-out tenement in New York warned that "rent control will turn Santa Monica into a slum." Eight separate mailings went out to every voter in the city, followed up by phone calls from "opinion researchers" asking questions like, "Did you know that New York-style rent control is being proposed for Santa Monica?" In Santa Barbara, special mailings were tailored to Democrats, Republicans, Spanish-speaking citizens, homeowners, and senior citizens. Voters received copies of a Reader's Digest article by liberal senator Thomas Eagleton (D-Mo.), entitled "Why Rent Controls Don't Work." The mailings were reinforced by ads in the local media. And in an unusual move, almost the entire department of economics at the University of California's Santa Barbara campus spoke out publicly against the rent control initiative.

The money spent by anti rent control forces had a dramatic effect. Polls showed that only a few months before the initiative, a majority of voters in both cities favored rent control. On election day, though, it was defeated by a 55-45 margin in Santa Monica and by a 64-36 margin in Santa Barbara. Money was not the only reason for the loss, however. The timing of the elections was also disadvantageous to supporters of rent control. The rent control issue went to the voters the same day as the Proposition 13 tax cut, which triggered a strong voter turnout among homeowners and conservatives and focused a general feeling against any forms of additional governmental bureaucracy.

Groups attempting to introduce rent control in a city for the first time have been forced to reconsider the referendum strategy in light of the growing list of defeats. The disparities in campaign spending can be expected to reappear whenever rent control is on the ballot. Viewing Madison, Berkeley, Santa Barbara, and Santa Monica as initial skirmishes, The National Association of Realtors, The National Association of Home Builders, and other groups are now preparing a campaign against controls to be coordinated by a new organization, the National Rental Housing Council (NRHC). An article in Multi-Family News, a trade journal, reports that NRHC plans to create a national lobby to provide local anti rent control groups with research, legal assistance, and campaign advice, and to improve media coverage. The NRHC has been pressuring bond-rating services such as Moody's to include rent control as a reason for lowering a city's credit rating. It also hopes to make repeal of rent control a precondition for federal aid to cities – a formula endorsed by former Treasury Secretary William Simon. Public officials in cities that have or are considering rent control are being supplied with a six-inch thick looseleaf notebook filled with news clips from around the country, academic studies, and statements by politicians, all with the same message: rent control doesn't work. Although each notebook bears the imprint of a local real estate group, it comes compliments of NRHC. Solem and Associates of San Francisco, the campaign management firm that orchestrated successful anti rent control efforts in Madison, Berkeley, and Santa Monica, has published a how-to manual that sells for $90.

On the other front, the recent tax revolt has given new impetus to the rent control movement in those areas where tax limitation measures such as Proposition 13 have been enacted. In California, renters were chagrined to find that the significant tax cuts – in many cases amounting to hundreds of thousands of dollars for large apartment complexes – did not produce rent rebates. In fact, many of California's 3.5 million tenants received notices of rent increases shortly after Proposition 13 passed. Ironically, the tax cut measure, which had contributed to the defeat of rent control in Santa Monica and Santa

Barbara by bringing out the "antigovernment" vote, also set the stage for a significant tenant backlash in the weeks following the election. As a result, tenant leaders in California are calling Howard Jarvis the author of Proposition 13, the "Father of rent control."

Throughout California, tenants who had been hit by increases organized meetings to demand that landlords share the property tax bonanza. Newspapers were filled with stories of outraged renters, embarrassed landlords, and politicians jumping on the bandwagon. For example, Los Angeles Mayor Thomas Bradley, who had earlier lent his name to the anti rent control campaign in Santa Monica and Santa Barbara called for a city-wide rent freeze ordinance.

Amid the public clamor, Governor Brown and Howard Jarvis appeared at a joint press conference last July 18 to "jawbone" landlords into sharing their $1.2-billion windfall – or risk mandatory rent rollbacks and freezes. As the pressure mounted, many landlords did agree to voluntary action in order to avoid controls; they announced that they would reduce rents to May 31 levels and freeze them for six months.

But tenant pressure did not subside. Oakland Assemblyman Tom Bates introduced a bill in the California legislature that would have required all landlords to pass on Proposition 13 savings in reduced rents. The measure was defeated 21 to 12 in late August after heavy lobbying by real estate groups. The battle then shifted to the local level, and temporary rent freezes were passed by the city councils of San Francisco, Beverly Hills, Los Angeles, El Monte, and Cotati. Similar local ballot measures were narrowly defeated in November in San Francisco and Santa Cruz, overwhelmingly defeated in Palo Alto, and victorious in Berkeley and Davis. And lastly, Santa Monica voters went back to the polls this past spring and overwhelmingly passed the most restrictive rent control currently on the books in the United States.

Tenants groups across the state reported a flurry of interest in their activities, and have added full-time organizers to their staffs. Rent strikes by angry tenants have provided impetus to the movement. Tenants' groups in such California cities as San Diego, Santa Barbara, Napa, Hayward, Salinas, Burlingame, Arcata, San Jose, Milpitas, Mountain View and Santa Cruz are renewing their efforts and plan future rent control campaigns. All across California, it seems, the aftermath of Proposition 13 is creating a new consciousness.

Elsewhere around the country, rent control initiatives are gaining momentum even without the impetus of a Jarvis-Gann backlash. The issue is being actively debated by tenant groups, city councils and state legislatures in New Mexico, Nevada, Oregon, Washington, Illinois, Wisconsin, Louisiana, Ohio, Florida, Colorado, Texas, Michigan, Georgia, Pennsylvania, Iowa, Minnesota, and Hawaii.

At best, rent control can only be a stop-gap measure. It cannot build more housing. Nor can it affect the utility costs, property taxes, and mortgage interest rates that force up rents. But it does give some protection to those who suffer most from the absence of a national commitment to ensure a supply of moderately priced housing. Rent control gives people a degree of control over their housing and reveals how the housing system works, thereby providing a useful basis for organizing by focusing attention on the imbalance of power between landlords and tenants. The fight for stronger housing codes, more equitable leases, and greater public scrutiny of the movement of capital in the housing market is of obvious value. Rent control advocates have natural allies among other groups fighting urban decay – citizens who have organized around property tax and utility rate reform, opponents of redlining, groups who are trying to halt the flight of industry from older urban areas, and those who oppose condominium conversion and the destructive aspects of gentrification.(21)

WHY RENTS RISE: A RECONSIDERATION

Any viable strategy aimed at containing rents must at some point consider the reasons why rents have risen so rapidly in recent years. Unfortunately, there is a great deal of confusion on this question, reflecting the "conventional wisdom" held by renters and owners alike. This view holds, quite simply, that the current housing crisis is largely a result of an inadequate supply of housing. For example, tenant activist Myron Moskovitz, states that "the heart of the problem is with the supply of housing."(22) Similar views are propounded by government officials (23) and a host of real estate organizations.(24) The latter typically blames "growth controls" for the inadequate supply. To the extent that this view is incorrect, it misdirects attention away from the real causes of the rising costs of housing in general, and rent gouging in particular. It also divides tenants' groups and advocates of low income housing against those who would otherwise be their natural allies – individuals and groups who oppose untrammeled development and unlimited urban growth.

In a preliminary attempt to explore the influence of scarcity on rental levels in light of other possible influences, we sampled different size categories of California cities.(25) Table 8.1 compares the effects of city size and vacancy (our measure of scarcity) on median rent levels in 1970.(26) Several features of this table are worth nothing. First, across all categories of cities, size effects are clearly more pronounced than scarcity effects: the difference between the smallest and largest places amounts to 56 percent, while the difference between high vacancy and low vacancy places is only 12 percent. Second, when one controls for size, the effects of vacancy appear to be most pronounced among medium-sized places: neither small nor large cities show significant rental differences by vacancy category. Third, the principal rent difference is between the very smallest places and larger ones: medium-size cities have 43 percent higher rents than small cities, while the difference between medium and large cities is only 9 percent. This suggests that the smallest places are experiencing a different housing dynamic than other cities.(27) If we examine only medium and large cities, an interesting pattern emerges: rents are comparable in three of the four size/vacancy categories, showing a significant difference only

Table 8.1. Effects of City Size and Rental Vacancy Rate 1970 on Median Rent Levels: California Cities, 1970, U.S. Census

Size of City:	Scarcity: vacancy rate		
	low vacancy rate (under 5%)	high vacancy rate (over 5%)	means*
Small (2500-10,000) (n=50)	$78	$82	$81
Medium (10,000-50,000) (n=50)	$124	$103	$116
Large (over 50,000) (n=50)	$125	$126	$126
Means*	$111	$99	$105

*Means are weighted averages that correct for the effects of sampling within city-size categories.

in medium-sized high vacancy cities, where rents are close to one-fifth lower ($103 versus $124). The effect of scarcity on rents, then, is not as straightforward as it might otherwise appear: size effects are in general more pronounced, while the interaction of size and scarcity seems to be a determinant for all but the smallest places.

This is not meant to suggest that housing scarcity has no effect on rental levels in a given locale – obviously a tight rental housing market can be exploited more easily than a slack one – but it does suggest that there are other factors that intervene in determining rents whose relative importance is presently unknown. While such obvious supply-related costs as land, labor, materials, fuel, and maintenance expenditures are generally understood by consumers of rental housing, other determinants of rent may not be so obvious. Principal among these are the following:

1. Locational advantages that accrue to rental property, including access to facilities, area amenities, and other externalities.(28)

This is perhaps one reason for the pronounced size effect on rental levels noted in table 8.1, particularly in slack housing markets.(29)

Larger places may confer a higher aggregate level of such positive externalities than smaller ones. The same may also be true of faster growing places, as Appelbaum's recent work suggests.(30) Looking at all medium sized urban areas in the United States that were geographically self-contained, it was found that size and growth rate accounted for almost two-fifths of the variance in median monthly rent in 1979.(31) Even when the effects of associated factors were taken into account, size and growth continued to be significant, with the difference between slower-growing places (under 10 percent decenially) and rapidly-growing places (over 25 percent decenially) amounting to about 10 percent.(32) This suggests that, contrary to the claims of the housing industry, urban growth may not solve the housing crisis through new construction, but rather may exacerbate it through creating a boom-town atmosphere, an increase in locational advantages that result from larger size and such growth-related factors as redevelopment, and possibly also from the price-leading effects of a large volume of new construction. The most profitable housing to build is not low cost housing, but rather construction tied in with other forms of urban redevelopment that may price low and moderate income persons out of an area completely, as the data on table 8.2 suggest. This table divides cities into two categories: those with a high intercensal increase in the number of rental units (over 60 percent), and those with a low increase (under 60 percent). Three size categories are used as a control, as in the previous table. Interestingly, rents are greater in high increase cities than in low increase cities, amounting to a 27 percent increase in the smallest and largest places, and a 9 percent increase in medium sized ones. Furthermore, comparing only medium and large cities, we see that there is no significant difference in median rents for those places that experienced a low volume of intercensal increase in the number of rental units. This is not what we would expect under the scarcity hypothesis, which predicts rising rents in places that experienced the smallest increase in rental housing supply. If we assume that the increase in the number of units is an index of the volume of new construction during the decade, these data indicate that the possibility of a price-leading effect (newly built apartments priced higher than existing units) may be pushing overall rent levels up in places where the relative volume of new construction is high. Moreover, it is plausible that these newly constructed units, which are generally priced for high income tenants are replacing housing units that were occupied by low income persons.(33) Unfortunately, no firm conclusions are possible on the basis of these data alone, but the above hypotheses are worthy of being tested on data gathered for that explicit purpose.

2. The absence of laws designed to inhibit the rapid turnover of properties has caused rents to increase substantially. According to interviews with brokers and realtors, both federal tax policies (for example, accelerated depreciation allowances as enacted between 1954 and 1976) and the logic of pyramiding one's property holdings (also known as speculation) makes it optimal to sell one's property every five to nine years.(34)

Table 8.2. Effects of City Size and Increase in Rental Housing Stock 1960-1970 on Median Rent Levels: California Cities, 1970, U.S. Census

Size of City:	% increase in number of rental units, 1960-1970 low (under 60%)	high (over 60%)	means*
Small (2500-10,000) (n=50)	$75	$95	$81
Medium (10,000-50,000) (n=50)	$111	$121	$116
Large (over 50,000) (n=50)	$107	$136	$126
means*	$93	$119	$105

*Means are weighted averages that correct for the effects of sampling within city-size categories.

As a result, when resale is coupled with rapidly rising interest rates, the cost of refinancing can drive rents up astronomically. Mortgage payments have increased more than any other landlord costs during the ten-year period from 1965-1975,(35) as average interest rates rose from 5.62 percent to 9.75 percent – an increase of almost 75 percent.(36) This is especially significant since mortgages typically constitute between one-third and two-thirds of a landlord's total expenses. For example, a $40,000 thirty-year mortgage at 5 percent entails monthly payments of $215; at 10 percent, the same mortgage would cost $350, an increase of two-thirds. If payments on such a mortgage were to comprise one-half of a landlord's total costs, a "reasonable" rental increase of one-third would be necessary merely to cover the higher interest payments on the loan. In some areas, including many cities in southern California, the combined effects of general inflation, favorable tax laws, and rising interest rates have played havoc with the housing market, producing rapid property turnover and, consequently, routine rent increases of substantial proportions. The solutions to these problems are clearly nonlocal, although antispeculation taxes might provide a stopgap measure.(37) In the long run, however, a combination of tax reform and alternative methods of low cost financing are necessary, along with municipal land-banking and other innovations that remove rental housing from the marketplace altogether. It is highly unlikely, in the absence of a strong national tenants' movement, that the necessary policies and programs would even be seriously considered as viable options.

3. Landlord cartels and other forms of association may play a major role in rent increases and one that is scarcely recognized by tenants and public officials. Landlords are organized both statewide and locally. In California, for example, there are the major statewide apartment associations – the Apartment Owners' Association of California (AOAC) and the California Housing Council (CHC). These groups have successfully lobbied for legislation in their interest, and two years ago nearly succeeded in getting the state to prohibit cities from enacting rent controls. As previously indicated, the California Housing Council has played a leading role in defeating local rent control measures and underwriting expensive and highly effective advertising campaigns; it is further tied in at the national level with organizations such as the National Renting Housing Council. This permits a degree of coordination among landlords presently unknown among tenants. Both the AOAC and the CHC have recently proposed to their memberships "moderate rent increase policies" where landlords hold themselves to annual increases pegged to the consumer price index or some other formula as a form of "self restraint." An annual rent increase is thereby guaranteed. Such policies are promulgated in statewide meetings and in real estate house organs. For example, in the 1978 issue of Real Estate Review, Richard Garrigon discussed the necessity for raising rents an annual 15 percent through the year 1982.(38)

While statewide organizations may provide guidance for rent increases, it is the local real estate associations that are ultimately responsible for implementation. This is accomplished through their association newspapers and local apartment owners' meetings. A December 3, 1978, article in the Santa Barbara News Press, for example, states that landlords at such a meeting were told "when, where, how and by what dollar amount to raise rents." The coordinating efforts of such associations are greatly facilitated by income property management companies, which often operate apartments on behalf of landlords who do not wish to be involved in the daily problems of landlording. A suit brought by a Boston tenants' group against several large realty management firms contends that several of the city's largest firms routinely set rents in collusion rather than compete with each other in the market. The pattern of rents and rent increase suggests that, even in the absence of a formal organization, collusion is not unusual. As with apartment owners' associations, the larger the percentage of rental housing stock controlled by management companies in a city, the greater the opportunity for setting "bottom line rent increases." Since management companies have far closer contact with the realities of income property, their role in determining rents can be critical; often landlords do not tell the companies how much rent to charge; rather the companies tell landlords how much they can get. The companies have a direct stake in increasing rents, since they customarily take from six to ten percent off the gross rent receipts as their fee. For example, in Isla Vista, California – a predominately student and youth community of some 15,000 adjacent to the University of California (Santa Barbara) – five management firms control fully three-quarters of all apartment buildings have 10 or more units. These firms make an annual listing of all their rentals, suggesting proposed rent increases for each. The lists are then calculated to enable all the companies to coordinate their annual rent increases. A recent study by the Center for Housing Research, reported in Nexus, the student newspaper on March 8, 1979 found that despite considerable Proposition 13 tax savings in Isla Vista, 98 percent of the rental units controlled by the management companies showed a rent increase. In the period following the passage of the tax cut measure, property taxes in the community dropped by almost three-quarters of a million dollars but rental income on nine-month leases during the same period rose by about one-half million dollars.

The significance of efforts by landlords to set rents cannot be underestimated; to the extent that landlords are successful in such efforts, it is clear that eliminating scarcity through new construction will hardly serve to offset rising rents. Moreover, the existence of collusion is extremely difficult to document, impeding tenants' strategies aimed at breaking up monopoly control over the rental housing market. Nor is it clear how one might effectively research the extent and effect of such collusion, although one project is currently underway in connection with the Attorney General's office for the State of California. The lesson, however, is clear: rising rents are subject to political as well as economic forces, and must be combatted through political means.

Landlord and real estate groups have recognized that action at the national level can affect the outcome of local initiatives. The housing movement for the most part remains locally based (only seven states have a statewide organization), though a number of progressive federal measures would aid local activists – lower interest rates, more funds for housing rehabilitation and housing cooperatives, and perhaps even an agency to protect the rights of tenants' unions. A federally supported job program to build and rehabilitate energy-efficient, affordable housing would also help to alleviate the housing crisis. But such programs require a well-organized and well-informed constituency to challenge private interests in the housing field.

The authors of this paper do not claim that rent control itself will solve the housing crisis.(39) On the contrary, we recognize that rent control – particularly in its moderate form, which pegs rents to a reasonable return formula rather than to renters' abilities to pay – may instead have the consequence of rationalizing the housing market, reducing disparities in rent levels while diverting attention away from the key issue of affordable housing. Rent control does not question the legitimacy of the private market as a means to providing a basic necessity, at a time when the market appears most ill-equipped to provide that necessity at a price most people can afford. In Marcuse's words "it assumes the existence of that private market. It simply tries to smoothen out that market, to make it function more effectively, to make it more 'orderly.'"(40)

Rent control does, however, have substantial potential as an organizing issue. It deals with an issue that is vital and immediate to large numbers of people – and one that is likely to become of central concern to growing numbers of renters. It has the potential for building bridges between low and moderate income tenants who share a common interest as market economics drive the price of housing out of reach for all but the wealthiest. And, most importantly, it focuses attention on the market itself, creating a forum for exposing its limitations and raising the issue of nonmarket alternatives.

Like any reformist issue, the significance of rent control as an organizing strategy will depend on the political savvy of its proponents – on their ability to link it with a wider analysis in the minds of tenants, and on their ability to forge coalitions that cross-cut divisions of class, race, sex, and age. Because renters themselves cross-cut such divisions, the potential is there. The immediate task lies in creating tenants' organizations that go beyond purely local issues: the need is for the creation of statewide and even a national tenants' movement to counter the growing organization of the housing industry.

Apart from fighting for rent controls, tenants' organizations should pursue legislation at the state level that would provide a more secure context for organizing. Possible avenues would include "just cause" legislation aimed at curbing arbitrary and sometimes retaliatory evictions and controls over condominium conversions. The major effort, then, must be directed toward creating a strong and widespread tenants' movement. The conditions are ripe: the phenomenon of "lifers," coupled with the highly revealing failure of property tax cut measures to produce tax relief, has angered tenants and given new life to their organizations. Nor are conditions likely to improve in the near future. It remains to be seen whether the issues can be removed from the narrow arena of economic debate, where they have so far been confined, to the larger political arena where the sources of the housing crisis are in reality to be found.

NOTES

(1) Although the cost of homeownership has escalated in the past decade, the stable percentage of tenants to homeowners is not surprising. It appears that homeowners are locking themselves into greater long-term debt in order to purchase a home. The New York Times reported on December 18, 1977 that mortgage debt tripled in magnitude in less than three years as owners renegotiated and extended

mortgages, took out second mortgages, and shouldered a larger portion of the purchase price at higher interest rates. It is doubtful, however, that this owner-renter ration can continue much longer if for no other reason than that the population and household growth is outpacing the construction of homes available for purchase.

(2) Stone, "The Housing Crisis," 1975.

(3) Rent control was enacted nationally during both World Wars, but continued only in New York after World War II. In Europe, national governments took the lead in housing following the widespread destruction of housing stock during World War II. Now both government and quasi-public such as cooperatives finance, build, and manage much of the housing. Rent controls in West European countries operate as part of a national housing policy. Even though for-profit housing is a shrinking proportion of the total housing stock in these countries, rent controls have such widespread support that no governments want to take the political risk of abolishing them. In the U.S., by contrast, housing is primarily a local, and a private, concern. The federal government has continued to rely on private initiative with voluntary local participation in public subsidy programs (for the poor and elderly). As a result of this set-up, rent control is a local option available to municipalities, but is stiffly resisted by powerful local propertied interests who tend to control local government (Molotch, "The City as a Growth Machine," 1976). Rent controls challenge the ideological climate that opposes state regulation of prices, particularly at the local level.

(4) Blumberg, et al., "The Emergence of Second Generation Rent Controls," 1974; Gilderbloom, The Impact of Moderate Rent Control in the U.S., 1978, pp. 1-33.

(5) It has been argued that restrictive rent controls, enacted during World War I and II and in New York, have caused a slowdown or halt in construction, a decline in maintenance and erosion of the tax base (Friedman and Stigler, "Roofs or Ceilings?" 1946; DeJouvenal, No Vacancies, 1948; Parish, "The Economics of Rent Restriction," 1950; Willis, "Short History of Rent Control Laws," 1959; Keating, Rent and Eviction Controls, 1976; Pennance, "Introduction," 1972). The intent of moderate rent control is to avoid these problems. To confront the problem of a decline in construction, moderate rent controls exempt housing units newly constructed or substantially rehabilitated, or buildings with fewer than four units. In Washington and in most New Jersey cities, the landlord is allowed to determine the initial rent of all newly constructed housing, but all subsequent increases are subject to controls. In Massachusetts new construction is given an absolute exemption (Blumberg, "The Emergence of Second Generation Rent Controls," 1974; Lett, Rent Control, 1976.) To prevent falling maintenance and eventual abandonment, moderate rent control allows the landlord to pass on all

"justifiable" increases in operating expenses to tenants as rent increases. Landlords are allowed to raise rents annually based on increases in expenses (Blumberg, "The Emergence of Second Generation Rent Controls," 1974.) If these increases do not meet the mortgage and maintenance costs, the landlord may appeal for an increase in rents based on hardship (Lett, Rent Control, 1976.) While the landlord is allowed to pass on any increase in costs, he or she is forbidden from decreasing the amount of money going into services or maintenance. If this occurs, the rent control board can deny a rent increase or lower the amount of rent until the deficiency in maintenance or services has been corrected. Moreover, the courts mandate that moderate rent controls must provide for a "fair and reasonable return on investment" (Lett, Rent Control, 1976). In general, the courts have ruled that a "just and reasonable return" must be similar to returns in other enterprises having similar risks. For example, in Hoboken, New Jersey, a fair return on the equity investment in real property has been legally determined to be six percent above the maximum passbook demand deposit savings account interest rate available in that city. For an excellent analysis and critique of the various forms of rent control, see Marcuse, "The Political Economy of Rent Control," 1978.

(6) Kain, Testimony, Rent Control (March 21), Local Affairs Committee, Massachusetts State House; California Housing Council, 1977; Phillips, Analysis and Impact of the Rent Control Program in Lynn, Lynn, Mass.; Laverty, "Assessor from East Coast Slams Rent Control," Evening Outlook, Santa Monica, California, May 4, 1978; Coalition for Housing, 1977; Elmstrom, Rent Control, 1977; Lett, Rent Control, 1976.

(7) Shelterforce, Winter 1977.

(8) Gilderbloom, Impact of Modern Rent Control, 1978; Achtenberg, Critique of the Rental Housing Association Rent Control Study, 1975.

(9) Of the 102 cities that enacted rent control, 76 of these municipalities passed controls in 1972 and 1973. It was crucial to choose cities that enacted controls as close to January 1, 1973 as possible since two of the dependent variables (construction and demolition) are based on records for the period January 1, 1973 through December 31, 1975. Gilderbloom acknowledges the limitations imposed on his analysis by the reduced time period under consideration, and particularly by the fact that potential long-term effects would not be evident in his data. He is currently planning to extend his New Jersey study over a longer period of time.

(10) Gilderbloom, Impact of Modern Rent Control, 1978.

(11) Achtenberg, Critique, 1975.

(12) Gilderbloom, "Impact of Moderate Rent Control in New Jersey," 1979.

(13) The argument that demolitions are an indication of abandonment is in any case suspect, since many if not most demolitions are done to pave the way for new construction.

(14) New York State Commission on Living Costs and the Economy, 1974:82.

(15) Marcuse, Rental Housing in the City of New York, 1979, pp. 275-8.

(16) Achtenberg, Critique, 1975.

(17) Steinlieb, Rent Control in the Greater Boston Area, 1974, 1975.

(18) Gilderbloom, Impact of Modern Rent Control, 1978; idem, Impact of Modern Rent Control in New Jersey, 1979.

(19) Ibid.

(20) Achtenberg, Critique, 1975.

(21) In many cities, with and without rent control, landlords are turning rental apartments into expensive condominiums, forcing out moderate income tenants, shrinking an already-tight rental market, and changing the social composition (and stability) of the neighborhoods. The U.S. Conference of Mayors has urged a Senate subcommittee on housing to take steps against the spread of condominiums. Senator Harrison Williams (D.-N.J.) chair of the subcommittee, estimates that 130,000 to 250,000 apartments will be converted to condominiums in 1979 alone. A number of cities, Brookline, Mass., Santa Monica, Calif., Washington, D.C., New York City, and Evanston, Ill., among them, have passed regulations to halt or restrict "condo conversion." Although it is not clear whether rent control encourages this process, most rent control advocates now favor some restriction of condominium conversions as part of any rent control ordinance. Some laws, for example, ban conversions when the vacancy rate falls below a certain level. Others require that a set ratio of tenants in a building approve before rental units can be converted to owner-occupied condominiums.

(22) Moskovitz et al., Reapportion Housing and Rents, 1974.

(23) California Department of Housing and Community Development, 1977, Congressional Research Service, The Theory of Rent Control, 1978.

(24) California Housing Council, Inc., The Case Against Rent Control, 1977; Gruen and Gruen, Rent Control in New Jersey, 1977.

(25) Cities were divided into three size categories: small (2500-10,000 persons), medium (10,000-50,000), and large (over 50,000). Within each category, a random sample of 50 cities was selected to assure adequate representation of size. The analysis which follows must be regarded as purely suggestive of hypotheses; given the sampling procedures (e.g., no attempt was made to isolate cities which lie within larger metropolitan areas from those which are relatively isolated; nor cities which lie within the same metropolitan area and therefore presumably share similar housing characteristics), stronger inference is not warranted by the data.

(26) The difficulty with using vacancy as a measure of scarcity is treated in Marcuse, Rental Housing in the City of New York (1979, 103-11). Following conventional treatment, we regard low-vacancy cities as those with lower than 5 percent, and high vacancy cities as those with higher rates. Presumably, market dynamics differ between these two conditions, the former reflecting a tight housing market and the latter a relatively competitive one. As we have previously noted, most contemporary rent control ordinances are written so as to go into effect only when vacancy rates drop below 5 percent.

(27) For the most part, these cities are located in rural areas.

(28) Harvey, Social Justice and the City, 1973, pp. 57-60.

(29) See also Appelbaum, Size, Growth and U.S. Cities, 1973, pp. 34-7.

(30) Op. cit. The analysis looked at all urbanized areas in the contiguous 48 states that (a) contain only one central city of from 50,000 to 400,000 inhabitants and (b) are at least 20 miles from the closest neighboring urbanized area. These criteria effectively exclude suburbs and cities that are part of large metropolitan agglomerations, thereby standardizing the cities studied.

(31) A multivariate analysis was performed in which the effects of region, central-city age, percentage of housing in single-family dwellings and median family income were controlled.

(32) Rates at the time of this writing (June 1979) are running as high as 11.75%.

(33) Gilderbloom, Impact of Modern Rent Control in New Jersey, 1979.

(34) Jacob, Understanding Landlording, 1978, pp. 11-15.

(35) Stone, "The Housing Crisis," 1975.

(36) The voters in Santa Cruz, California recently approved such a measure; it was quickly overturned by the courts on the grounds that it

was confiscatory of private property. The decision is currently under appeal.

(37) The study found that while total operating costs for apartments fell an average of 8 percent because of Proposition 13, rents increased approximately 12 percent.

(38) Richard Garrigon, "The Case for Rising Residential Rents," 1978.

(39) For a far more extended treatment of this issue, which analyzes contemporary rent control both theoretically and historically cross-nationally, see Marcuse, Rental Housing in the City of New York, 1979.

(40) Ibid.

9 Democratic Planning in Austerity: Practices and Theory

Dudley J. Burton
M. Brian Murphy

The democratic potentials within planning emerge in the variety of struggles being carried on within the state and around public policy. As the state increasingly becomes an arena for social struggle – over the allocation of public goods, the definition of social goals, the justice of both bureaucratic procedures and planning decisions, and the level and quality of transfer payments – planners find themselves increasingly in an explicitly political context. This is more than a context of competing claims; it is a context of struggle over what constitutes a valid demand and what counts as a constituency.(1)

This struggle may be seen as a democratic trend in itself, representing the repoliticization of private control of market allocations or bureaucratized decisions. Although this view is oversimplified, the context provides the opportunity to explore what is democratic about these struggles. Such an exploration can inform both political organizing and the response of planners to that organizing. In this land of democratic ideologies and democratic cliches, we want to identify the practices and institutions that constitute a meaningful democracy. This will require us to speak of our visions and our practices; we seek in "democracy" a social order worthy of our allegiance and conviction, a political order worth fighting for.

THE DEMOCRATIC DILEMMA WITHIN CAPITALISM

The present epoch marks a growing contradiction between the structures and institutions of advanced industrial capitalism and those of democracy. For the apologists and strategists of capitalism, "democracy" has increasingly become a problem for capitalism. This problem emerges in two forms: first, in the increase of the number of claims upon the system; second, in the character of those claims. Groups are demanding both more goods and services and a voice in the formation of social policy affecting these goods and services. Furthermore, many claims imply a substantial criticism of centralized and bureaucratized institutions that presently exclude large groups. Anxiety about these developments emerges most vividly in the writings of Trilateral theorists like Samuel Huntington.(2,3) When Huntington refers to the "democratic distemper" that infects the modern period, he is speaking about both the sheer increase in claims upon the managers of state policy, and the anticentralist tenor of many of the claims. Thus he criticizes "bureaucratic pluralism and interests, congressional and interest group politics. . .and. . .a pervasive ideology that sanctifies the independence, rather than the subordination, of economic power to government."(4)

When Huntington proposes the expansion of executive power over credits and trade policy, and the centralization of foreign economic policy under the National Security Council, he is not simply speaking of removing policy determination from annoying, clamoring constituencies.(5) He is also attempting to challenge the very legitimacy of constituent advocacy itself. Put briefly, the clamor of competing interests is too distracting, and the substance of many of the claims are obstacles to the effective centralized planning required for the new alliances among capitalist states. The contradictions he sees are two. First, advanced industrial states must now coordinate internal policies within an international capitalist context (and domestic claims are irrational from the perspective of this new task). Second, at precisely the moment when capitalist economies need more rigid controls, more centralized steering mechanisms, more coordinated fiscal and industrial policies, diverse groups are demanding decentralization, participation, and access.

Huntington reveals the continued unraveling of Western society's ambivalence about democracy. It has often been seen primarily as the formal institutions of democratic representation, the procedural protection of minority rights, and the stability of governmental order. This structure was ideally set within the context of a supposed democratic culture, with liberal commitments and values. But this culture was, in the end, less important than the formalities of democratic institutions. If democracy required anything beyond the formal institutions of mass rule it was only a powerfully productive economy that could satisfy mass needs. In this regard, modern political science celebrates political democracy not so much for its effective and direct representation of diverse claims as for the stability of political institutions that proffer abstract popular sovereignty while providing effective elite control.

The apotheosis of this position is found in the early work of Herbert McClosky in which he discards even democratic values in his theoretical reconstruction of democracy.(6) Finding that most Americans do not agree with the liberal ideals of equality or liberty, that they fear for their security and are enraged by minorities and radicals, McClosky concludes that a society can be democratic despite the fact that its people are not. The necessary condition for this seen contradiction is that these citizens have no real power. As long as the politically literate run things, there is no danger from the misinformed people.(7) Democracy thus becomes simply a question of formal institutions and ideological claims. If it becomes more, then democracy threatens itself. People who believe in democratic processes and have real power are capable of tyranny and misbehavior. They will act out their selfish desires, oppress the minorities and maybe the rich, and drown out the sonorous tones of the politically articulate with their cacophonous chants.

The danger, in short, is that people who live in a so-called democratic state might believe that democratic institutions should be effective for them.(8) This is Huntington's fear. Between 1962 and 1979 the nation has gone through a frenzy of democratic jousting, and now we are faced with the possibility that citizens who believe democratic ideology are about to undermine the pure symbolism of the institutions.

This fear reveals the secret knowledge held by the pluralists: that even bourgeois democracy has always meant more than formal institutions. The claim of representative government is the implicit recognition that the society includes diverse and opposed interests that may demand expression in a contractually free society. Both federalism and the party system were institutions built upon the recognition of regional and special interests along with at least an abstract commitment to mass representation. The Federalists of 1787 sought to legitimize government by popular sovereignty and at the same time insulate government from direct popular rule. They were suspicious of democracy and yet recognized its necessity. But the fear of democracy defines democracy for the Trilateral theorists and their political science brethren. They recognize that there is a tension in the capitalist state between capital's need, both for mobilization for the democratic legitimation of the State. While the State has historically seemed to facilitate capital accumulation, there is the lurking possibility of popular sovereignty. If the State were truly representative of the multiple constituencies in the political economy, then it would be capital's enemy – not its servant.

What are the themes of this formalist democracy? They are those of a traditional democratic theory, translated into political structures. Democracy means stable institutions of mass access; it means legal protection for both grievances and rights; it means the abstract representation of diverse claims; it means legally enforced universal suffrage and the protection of political organizing; it means legal equality and procedural justice under general law.

This notion of democracy is not simple; it is a complex mix of institutions and commitments, values and practices. More important, insofar as this conception of democracy is linked to capitalism, it is self-contradictory. On the one hand, it is ideological and manipulative; on the other, it does embody commitments to abstract liberty, equality, opportunity, and universalization. These commitments imply popular sovereignty and mass participation and as such they are potentially in conflict with a capitalist order that enforces class rule and mass exclusion. This situation creates the ambivalence of bourgeois democracy, of which planning is a part.(9)

NEOCLASSICAL ECONOMICS AND THE PUBLIC INTEREST

The history of planning in the United States represents, in both theory and practice, the embodiment as well as the distortion of democratic ideas. On one hand, this history leads to the frustrating conclusion that democratic societies cannot plan. On the other hand, this history represents an accommodation to both capitalism and bourgeois democracy. To identify and connect these threads and patterns requires some historical account.

The Progressive Era, from about 1895 to 1920, can be understood as the ideological foundation for contemporary American planning. It can be seen as an attack on the willful misuse of economic and political power by the Robber Barons – Rockefellers, Vanderbilts, Goulds, Morgans. At the same time it was an attack on the bosses and political machines that controlled big city politics. Finally, it was an effort to provide some measure of social welfare for poor, uneducated immigrants. The ideology of reform, regulation, conservation, and democratic improvement came from philosophers like John Dewey, sociologists like Benjamin Ward, bureaucrats like Gifford Pinchot, and settlement house workers like Jane Addams. There had to be "good government"; politics had to be taken out of the hands of corrupt politicians and bosses; the management of both industry and society had to be "scientific."

Progressive goals seemed democratic; the reformers spoke of the public good, liberating the people from party machines and corruption, increasing the opportunities of the most oppressed through the initiation of social welfare programs, protecting public resources through conservation, reorganizing government so that it more effectively and efficiently serviced the general welfare. But this version of democratic reform linked the public good to the bureaucratization and scientization of politics, the creation of a professional political caste (including planners), and the "management" of political struggle. In practice this meant the centralization of public power in organizations less subject to popular control, protecting government from the influence of working class constituencies and creating greater opportunities for the centralization and concentration of capital.

Planning was an integral part of the progressive program and bore its peculiar ambivalence. It emerged in the search for a more scientific management of both industry and government. Its private embodiment was Taylorism; its public form was bureaucratic organization and the rationalization of politics. What this meant was a separation of politics and administration. Planning represented the coherent and rational management of resources and policy, separated from the unpredictable and disparate voices of actual popular constituencies. Its claim to being a democratic institution rested in its pretensions of embodying public rationality and efficiency. In serving growth and development more effectively, planning would serve the people.

Two developments in economic and political analysis were central to the democratic legitimation of planning. First, the generally accepted framework of neoclassical economics provided for public goods, from which individuals cannot be excluded even if they do not wish to pay for them, for example, national defense, and merit goods, like education, in order to provide more than individuals would purchase themselves. In short, however much the economy might be organized around private goods and market transactions, there is an inescapable realm of collective goods for which public allocation decisions must be self-consciously made.(10) The realms of analysis, argument, and implementation associated with the provision of these collective goods – whether in regulations, in information, programs, protection, or amelioration – can be understood as the domain of planning according to neoclassical economic theory.

This theory of collective goods has an implicit and sometimes an explicit democratic basis. There is a nominal concern for the public, for the welfare of the people as a whole. This concern expands the notions of rationality to policy areas in which the market processes are not applicable. A technology of welfare economics, cost-benefit analysis, program evaluation, etc., has arisen to aid these collective choices. At the same time, the genuine democratic political foundations of such enterprises are often lost when democracy is interpreted in an economic way. That is, votes and voices are treated like coinage in the expression of preferences for political market baskets. There is often insufficient attention to citizen education and participation, which are most fundamental to the definition and provision of collective goods.

The second important analytic development was the political theory of the public interest.(11) This notion emerged as a progressive criticism of the language of self-interest and competing factions found in the Constitution. The basic idea is that there are genuine shared problems that are above immediate or self-interest, and that require some fully collective choices. The problem has been whether the public interest is to be discovered, or whether it is to be constructed. In either case, the question remains: who determines it? Planners often represent themselves as repositories and spokespersons for the public interest: they presume to listen sympathetically and critically to all the competing and allied claims; they are not elected representatives and hence have no direct obligations to particular groups; their success is judged in the long term rather than by the results of the next elections. Planners therefore have felt themselves to be sufficiently nonpartisan and well-informed enough to define and pursue the public interest. And from this point of view, planners believe themselves to be genuinely democratic, for they try to determine what is the collective welfare and the implications of specific choices for it.(12)

The public interest argument assumes that there exist both a unified public and a coherence of interests. The theory requires that every relevant position or group have a voice; the planner must define and advocate a position for those who have not articulated their own. The theory recognizes that some claims are backed by more money and power and thus can be presented more forcefully than others, whatever their merit. The planner is presumed to be aware of this imbalance and to compensate for it.

Within a capitalist society, the public interest argument is inherently flawed. It has an inadequate conception of public or collective matters and fails to recognize (and indeed obscures) the existence of fundamentally contradictory interests. As a result, when planners presume to speak for the public interest they speak ideologically even if they do not intend to. Planning most often integrates or dissipates legitimate popular demands through processes of rationalization and organization, all in the name of the public. This process tends to support the existing structure of wealth and power.

Planning is therefore an embodiment of the contradiction between democracy and capital, rather than its resolution. While it sounds populist and public spirited, its practices and language are a functional part of the capitalist order. Its practices are rooted in the State's functional relationship to capital. Planning has been an important part of the State's role in reducing investment uncertainty, creating specific investment opportunities, and furnishing part of the costs of the accumulation of private property. Through its regulation of social investments and social expenses, and through both allocative programs and constitutive policies, planning has aided and oriented private capital investment. Its language of technocratic expertise, rationality, and efficiency has intensified the commodification of social life and culture. Its use of cost-benefit accounting, systems analysis, and management sciences have reduced qualitative questions of public concern to formulas and abstract calculations. This language has obscured the conflict-filled, tension-ridden contradictions implied in capital's growth, and thus it has served to further alienate popular constituencies from the political decisions affecting their social and economic lives.

The current setting of austerity, fiscal crisis, and unrest threatens to undermine the functional relationship between planning the state and capital. This threat appears at both the structural and ideological level. Structurally, the increased reliance of capital on state planning, coupled with an increase in demands from the bottom, thrusts planning into a newly politicized position. Austerity may force new confrontations about planning's democratic pretensions. If struggles intensify, the ideology of democratic service and the public interest may become an avenue for truly democratic organizing. That is the focus of our analysis. Planning may be an interesting example of the State's crisis of legitimacy, because its rhetoric of legitimation may make it vulnerable to an assault on its role in capital accumulation. Planners may be in a more pivotal and important place than their current frustrations allow them to recognize.

AUSTERITY

The phenomenon of austerity is part of a complex process involving the creation of prosperity as well as poverty. In this historical period, austerity emerges as one part of the heritage of the 1960s. It is an era of lean economy, the product of lavish spending to finance the Vietnam War and domestic social programs. The combined effects of these different patterns of spending have been inflation and recession, work speedups and unemployment, and an apparent scarcity of resources for most of the population.

The social investment that capital benefited from during the 1960s took the form of military spending, research and technology, incentives to create international markets, and the establishment of programs to absorb excess production. The effect of this investment has been to further centralize the control of capital, to decrease employment opportunities, and to create a crisis of profitability. To resolve the crisis, business has been willing to use inflation and unemployment to encourage labor discipline and to diminish labor's share of production. In this context, State workers and clients find themselves in an even more vulnerable position, ravaged by inflation and attacked as part of the State or as dependents of it. Yet, the rhetoric accompanying the crisis of profitability makes it appear that the State is insignificant in the creation and enhancement of private investment opportunities. As a result of these paradoxes, workers, State employees, and State clients find themselves powerless to confront the imperatives of investment and accumulation. They know they depend upon them; but they also do not want to bear alone the brunt of investment decisions that are likely to further exacerbate the maldistribution of wages and profits.(13)

The political implications of this situation are already emerging in a number of separate struggles and conflicts. The State will become increasingly a locus of confrontation about both the creation and distribution of public goods. As more people depend directly upon the State and find their allocation skimpy in relation to inflation, they will move against this increased dependency by demanding either increased benefits or changes in the whole social service system. As groups not directly dependent upon the State become increasingly hurt by inflation and labor's loss of real income, they will turn to the State in anger or in despair to see either redress from their current burdens or political guarantees against further loss. Instances of this complex and contradictory politicization of what once were market decisions are various demands for wage and price controls and the search for coherent national health, employment, and energy policies. While the historic pattern of both wage and price controls and economic planning has been to subsidize capital, the era of austerity makes it unavoidable that the critical attention of both labor and client groups, as well as others on the bottom will be focused on these issues.

In brief, more groups will appeal to the State when they despair of their ability to solve their economic or social problems by private action. As a result, planners will find themselves barraged by contradictory demands that directly and indirectly relate to the definition and production of public goods. The class character of these demands will not always be clear. Organized labor may seek accommodation with capital in certain areas, at the expense of the unorganized. Wage earning homeowners may indirectly strike out at social welfare in their attempt to save themselves from regressive taxation. Diverse groups of the disadvantaged may fight each other and the State over scarce resources. But even if the class character of many demands were clearer, is this a context in which planners can fulfill a truly democratic potential? Is this politicized environment an opportunity for planners to engage in fundamentally critical and transformational democratic political organizing? The fear we all have is that this emerging context will serve as the occasion for a more centralized and authoritarian formulation of policy, increased technocratic control over social planning, and an extended management of social conflict by the State in the further service of capital. In the face of the possible right wing and fascistic trends, can planners retain the ideological tradition of democratic responsiveness and transform that ideology into a practice of democratic expression?

In answer to this question, we suggest that there are democratic possibilities in the current situation, but that planners and political organizers must think more critically about what these possibilities are – structurally, institutionally, and culturally. We will argue that the emergence of movements and claims contradictory to capital is the necessary ground for any contemporary democracy, and that planners will have to forsake their traditional litany of "the public interest" in the name of a more explicit class analysis. This analysis will have to lay bare the structures of power and organization that have historically blocked any serious realization of democracy – save through the formulations of bourgeois democracy. But such an analysis must go beyond a critique of these forces opposing capital and beyond a critique of the structures blocking mass participation and rule. It must articulate a substantial democratic vision, be realistic in its understanding of the dilemmas of the democratic prospect, but imaginative in its recognition of those social and cultural forms that deserve to be called democratic.

CRITIQUE OF THE RADICAL CRITIQUE

To say these things is to suggest that many current radical critics do not go far enough. Much of the current work being done in Marxist political economy moves in two general directions. The first is toward an appreciation of the new roles and structures of the nation state, that have been made necessary by "the growing internationalization of capital, the intensification of the world-wide division of labor, and the process of disaccumulation in the core."(14) This critique is reminiscent of Huntington's: the State may have to sacrifice democratic pretensions – even formalities – in order to play its new role in this new capitalist order. In the various works of O'Connor, Habermas, Offe, and Wolfe, this is sketched as the deepening contradiction between the accumulation and legitimation functions of the state. That is, the national capitalist state has two simultaneous tasks: "maintain or create the conditions in which profitable capital accumulation is possible," and "maintain or create the conditions for social harmony."(15) The first task leads to increased centralization, bureaucratic and administrative institution of allocation and social investment, and to a removal of popular access to the increasingly sophisticated technical steering mechanisms. The second task demands that the State allow symbolic participation and formal legal equality in order to generate the mass loyalty that enables it to aid accumulation and to maintain domestic peace in noncoercive ways.

This critique leads O'Connor and Habermas to view democracy in a strange double light of ideology and political power. Its ideological character is revealed through the practical weakness of the power won in democratic politics, but the potential for mass participation is more than an illusion. In this view democracy emerges as the slight, necessary concession by the ruling class to the other classes in society. Democracy is characterized by the same formal institutions and beliefs lauded by the social scientists, yet it could become the ideological basis for popular movements that rebel against the State because they believe in the equality promised by the ideology.

The second direction of Marxist criticism is toward an analysis of the connection between democracy and working class struggles for equality or liberation. In this critique democracy is the traditional claim of the working class for participation and equality. The formal institution of universal suffrage or legal equality is the result of victories won through struggles in which the working class seeks their freedom. Locked in conflict with the ideology of market liberalism, which allows capital's domination of the State, democracy seeks popular sovereignty. This view agrees with the political-economic one in that it sees all moves toward egalitarian democracy as simultaneously legitimating and undermining capital, but it focuses more on the social-political origins of the legitimation crisis than on the State's handling of that crisis.

Both lines of argument share a common view of democracy. They find their common ground in Marx's own professed commitment to democracy as "the resolved mystery of all constitutions. . .the essence of every political constitution." This was true because any political constitution "becomes a political illusion the moment it ceases to be a true expression of the people's will."(16) Democracy is, in principle, the political expression of community, of our participatory engagement in the self-creation of history, of the truly active making of common concerns. In this critique political democracy is abstractly understood to express the social community of the proletariat insofar as the proletariat expresses the general condition of the society. Democracy is the appropriate form of politics for the working class insofar as it seeks, as its historic mission, the destruction of all forms of domination and exploitation.

In this, as Wolfe correctly points out, Marx goes back to Rousseau, and democracy becomes both political form and moral content.(17) But many modern Marxists have moved away from both. The political forms that Marx himself so applauded in his own time are now regarded as ideological falsehoods; the moral content implied by Rousseau's Sovereign Community and Marx's true community is replaced by the class struggle itself. Democracy, then, comes to represent – at best and where it is not simply dismissed as functional "politics" – all those struggles of the working class to present their claims to the State. O'Connor characterizes democratic movements as popular movements that seek to define and control a public good or a public policy.(18) To move "from the bottom" to the State is to be democratic. At its extreme, the critique claims that virtually any challenge to centralization and accumulation is, ipso facto, democratic.

This critique focuses, then, on the actual political struggles of dominated peoples to have their real and practical needs met. Marxism thus identifies democracy with the working class, with the political demand for control over production and distribution, and with the fact of struggle itself. Participation is mistakenly equated with struggle. To struggle is to participate, and thus democracy is associated with the actual popular forms of struggle: unions, neighborhood organizations, state-client groups.

The heart of the democratic claim in this perspective is the complex of social economic claims that emerges from the exploitation of people and the revolutionary practice of overcoming that exploitation. In the end political economy speaks less of virtue (as Rousseau did) than of needs. It speaks less of community than of class. In this view the democratic claim is the proletariat, because they are in movement against capital. Thus O'Connor is content to lump together as "democratic" diverse movements of State workers, State clients, citizen action groups, and even special interest groups because they are organizing publicly to demand things that they could not get through the market.

In Marxist political economy, then, democracy connotes more than the formal rights and institutions of bourgeois democracy – suffrage, civil rights, legal equality, and protection of the right to organize. These only become truly democratic when they are the avenues of popular claims for participatory power and equal access to State policy. This is evident anywhere one sees men and women organizing to make demands.

The power of this notion of democracy as "popular demand" is that it focuses on the conflicts that occur when people come to demand things that capital would deny them. It identifies democracy with public claims, not private passivity, and it connects the public character of various struggles to implicit demands for power and sovereignty. Whether this connection is justified is debatable, but the socialist analysis is that virtually any public claim suggests popular sovereignty insofar as it turns what otherwise would be a secure bureaucratic order into a realm of constant struggle over policy issues and State power.

Many political economists are strangely silent, however, about any analysis of the interior of the democratic impulse, a detailed account of the substantive relations among people inside democratic movements. Put another way, political economy has not yet developed a substantive account of either the forms by which equality is expressed or the life of virtue that democratic theorists traditionally demanded. There is, of course, one area in which this is absolutely untrue – in the multiple critiques of party structure – democratic centralism, Leninism, and organizing that have marked recent Left criticisms of political strategy.(19) But these inner debates about the substantive meaning of democracy have not penetrated into the broader accounts of the democratic context in which any party will organize. Thus while O'Connor might argue against abstract Leninism in favor of a more pluralist party, his own recent discussion of the democratic movement nowhere identifies what it is in the organization of these movements, in the substantive relation between movements, or in the daily lives of these movements that makes them democratic.

Similarly, Wolfe's critique of the democratic question leaves unanswered a major part of the question: Are all "demands for participation by ordinary people in the affairs of the entire community" necessarily democratic?(20) From the macroscopic perspective of capital's domination of the State, these demands are disequilibriating and oppositional. But, are they therefore democratic? How are we to differentiate between the demands of the antiabortion movement and the feminist movement, between the tax revolt and the organizing of teachers? Surely there are differences, and the crucial ones may be the presence or absence of democratic commitments and relations.(21)

THE SUBSTANTIVE MEANING OF DEMOCRACY

We have argued that radical analyses often pose the contradiction between capital and democracy in somewhat formal terms. Within these terms, the democratic impulse is expressed by popular claims against capital, often (but not exclusively) through the institutions of bourgeois democracy. Democracy, as both substantive popular claim and formal process, is part of liberation. It is also identified with the kind of society we seek, where democracy means mass participation and the elevation of the needs of the many over the interests of the few. But in both its liberating aspect and visionary importance, our conception of democracy must be more substantive than this. For both our appreciation of what we aim to create and our conception of what we are engaged in organizing, democracy must mean more than the fact of mass engagement.

We must understand democracy as a culture and as a practice of ethical community. If democracy is popular rule, it implies a substantive culture of values and commitments among the people who rule. If it means a sovereignty of popular needs, it requires a conception of action in which the people constitute their own needs. If it is a regime of freedom, it demands a vision of citizenship and equality to animate that freedom.(22) The radical critiques of democracy and its potential political applications must make people aware of these substantive (if initially abstract) visions of human relations, which are traditionally associated with any meaningful democracy.

Regimes or movements are democratic when the people within them rule, and in doing so constitute themselves as a community of active citizens. In such a community, citizens understand themselves to be both equal (socially and politically) and interdependent; citizenship is rooted in the recognition of reciprocal need and the necessity of collective action. Truly democratic citizenship is more than a fact of formal residency or legal standing; it is the expression of a substantive understanding of everyone's fragile dependency on the community, which everyone actively creates. The democratic community is free – and its makers are free – insofar as the community determines what its common life is to be. This means not only that the people have effective power over social and economic resources, but that the institutions and structures of society are themselves the creation of the men and women who live within it. Democracy is thus the regime of action, in which people constitute their own community, its organization, and its social agenda. It is simultaneously a culture of conviction, a sociology of equality and reciprocity, and a politics of participation and creativity.

If democracy has this meaning of community and action, then it is also associated with a conception of plurality and diversity. Democratic regimes and movements have been those that acknowledge the multiplicity of claims and visions, and that protect the unique and the individual. The fact that bourgeois democracy has abstracted these acknowledgments into interest group politics and civil rights laws should not obscure the more fundamental vision – that there will be diversity within any community and that diversity can be the source of great strength and richness. But it creates the tension that always marks democracy: the communitarian claim is seldom neatly reconciled with the diversity of the community. There are two political implications of this tension: that political education is necessary and that participatory structures must be instituted.

The latter idea defines democratic politics and is at the heart of any vision of a community that reproduces and defines itself. But the condition of participation is that there be civic commitments and convictions among diverse people. Political education – teaching about the dialectical relationship of individual and community, makes this possible. Such teaching does not balance the individual and the community as opposites but relates them through a substantive understanding of the self and its relationship to the community. In a larger context, this dialectical relationship takes the form of a federated reciprocity among groups, which speaks through their diversity for common needs. According to democratic theory, political education is the practice of participatory engagement; it is less taught than learned and is rooted in the process of a community or movement setting its own agenda and defining its own problems and dilemmas.

THE THEMES OF DEMOCRACY

What are the themes of this view of democracy, and what do they add to our discussion of planning?

1. The first is the relationship between popular demands and popular rule. Socialists have traditionally understood that popular demands are implicitly democratic because they are popular, that working class claims imply more than their specific content (wages, working conditions, etc.). Within the contradictory structure of bourgeois society such claims can imply a critique of power and hierarchy.

But there are two problems with this position. The first is the substance of every cliche about reformism and revisionism since Lenin – that mass claims may be accommodated within capitalism unless they include a radical demand for the restructuring of society or the state. Demands for access to state resources or more egalitarian policies by state agencies are not always demands for popular power. Democratic claims must be more than an expression of mass or popular demand; they must also raise the question of "who rules?" This involves a critique of hierarchy, and a critique of those elites and structures that exclude the majority from political power. This critique must also raise questions about the legitimacy of organization and authority. This is not a rejection of authority and organization, per se, but rather a questioning of its current form.

The second problem is somewhat the obverse of the first. Popular demands for mass rule, or participatory action, or public involvement in bureaucratic organizations can often be only formally democratic. It has long been a standard critique of bourgeois democracy that its forms of mass access only ratify elite control. This critique can move well beyond parliamentary questions, and focuses our attention on the real issue: the relation between formal power and effective power. If a movement demands access to a state decision process, or moves to democratize a bureaucratic structure through ensuring mass participation, we must recognize that this only becomes substantially democratic when this power means something in concrete ways – when investment decisions or planning results are removed from corporate or elite interests. Demands for access to planning decisions, for example, can be democratic if they are for effective participation in decisions rather than for adequate representation before officials who will finally make the decision.

2. The second theme of this democracy is moral and requires that a connection exist between the democratic process and a democratic culture. When democrats speak of community (as we have) and of a citizenship that recognizes interdependency and reciprocity, they seek to develop a delicate relationship between personal values and institutions. This has been a critical focus of every theory of democracy; it is especially evident in Aristotle, Rousseau, and Marx. What is at stake is the substantive difference between a regime of interests and a regime of virtue. When Rousseau argues that the sovereign community is free

because it obeys only the laws that it has made for itself, he is describing more than a formal process of participatory engagement. He suggests that such an engagement requires – and reciprocally teaches or creates – a kind of citizen, one who self-consciously takes up the concerns of the community as his own because he sees that there is a connection between the needs of the self and the needs of others. Rousseau, like Tocqueville, identifies the "habits" of mind and sensibility that make self-governing more than a formality but a kind of generosity and humanity – a willingness to engage in debate and refutation, an aversion to the suffering of others.

The moral interior of a democratic sensibility is characterized by this self-description: In my appreciation of my own dependency upon other people I am humbled and elevated. I recognize my need for these others and their need for me. Insofar as this need is reciprocal, it gives me no special power, but empowers us together. My generosity to others is not gratuitously moral; it is grounded in my recognition of the mutual fragility we share. I can demand respect for my participation and my unique contribution, as I grant respect to those upon whom I depend or from whom I learn. This understanding and attitude, however reduced to moralism, is sought by radicals everywhere. It is false to reject it as utopian or antiquarian, for it is part of virtually every distinction we make between an oppressive society and one of liberation. It demands an appreciation of the relationship between institutions and values. Democratic values can only develop during the process of democratic participation, but they are not guaranteed by it.

The implications for our own time are many. We seek to describe a democracy that is more than a balancing of interests because the people in it are virtuously seeking a common good. But in the current context of domination, the oppressed might properly dismiss the rhetoric of the "common good" as ideological and stand firmly for their interests. For those of the working class, local communities, or the excluded poor, these interests are in most senses democratic ones. But we must be critical in our involvement with even those movements we support and encourage them to move beyond interest to solidarity and even generosity. We all know that in the current system the immediate interests of the unionized working class, the welfare poor, and of nonunionized Third World workers are often opposed, and that the interests of domestic workers often conflict with those of foreign workers. Determining what constitutes a democratic claim is a complex question, but critical assessments are possible. The ILWU's refusal to load bomb parts headed for Chile was more than anticapital; it was truly democratic because it transcended immediate interest. Conversely, the demands by unionized teachers to control their workplace can be antidemocratic if these demands ignore the claims of local communities to influence what their children learn.

3. The third theme of this democratic claim is more subtle, connecting participation with action, involvement with education. Democracy has traditionally meant more than the formalities of mass rule because the process of participation has demanded a kind of action

from citizens – informed, constructive and creative action. It must be balanced between the equality of participation and the substantive forms of leadership and authority that emerge from debate and engagement. From this perspective, democratic movements are those that engage their members in the broadest possible range of tasks and debates, that seek many kinds of public action, that teach their membership in ways that empower men and women to successfully appropriate decisions affecting their lives. One of our quarrels with bureaucracy is the effective isolation of its dependents through its enforcement of ignorance. We must demand more of popular movements than that they formally oppose this exclusion. We must seek movements that have agendas of education and participation; we must encourage mass action that empowers men and women to think and act beyond the action itself. This implies that one of the central aspects of the democratic impulse will be the taking over of institutions by men and women who will seek to undo the isolation and dependency that has been enforced by most state agencies. As Marcuse pointed out, institutions become dominated and antidemocratic when people lose the sense that these institutions are created by people and can be changed.(23) This view reinforces an ignorance that further solidifies the institutional world. This cycle cannot be broken by groups that participate in these institutions without a knowledge of the history of the institution or a sense of how they might change the structure. Planners must seek to aid and organize movements that attempt to alter the structure of the State through the involvement of their members in decisions affecting their lives.

4. All of this leads to one of the oldest democratic themes: freedom. The democratic possibility is rooted in opposition to capital, and freedom surely consists partly in the process of liberating ourselves from the oppression and alienation of the bourgeois world. The search for freedom also requires a substantive vision of what we hope to create. If we want freedom to live in the vision of participatory community, we must know that not all liberating movements will take the form of such a community. Put briefly, the premise of all democracy is the liberation from capital; but not all liberation is democratic. Yet those movements that truly seek a democratic form of freedom and engagement for their constituencies will inevitably come into opposition with capital. They will also be in the process of creating and determining the practical meaning of any future democracy.

A DEMOCRATIC CRITIQUE OF PLANNING DILEMMAS

There are a number of classic formulations of the problems of democracy as they emerge in critical planning literature. The litany is familiar: there are tensions between centralization and decentralization, representation and participation, efficiency and equity. The democratic claim is always a call for participatory decentralization.

In the following discussion, we attempt to distinguish ideological and nonideological uses of the language of democracy in the formation and evaluation of planning strategy. Our discussions are divided into two main parts. The first section outlines structural oppositions in the conduct of democratic process. The second examines more fully the dilemmas of democratic process.

Structural Oppositions in Democratic Process

Centralization/decentralization

The important questions for democratically oriented planners to ask about centralization are the following: Who is doing it? Against what opposition? What is achieved by it? For whom?

While there has been a pervasive romanticism about decentralization in terms of its implications for participation and direct access to power, planners must know that there are also important rationales for centralization. Many of the groups moving against the structurally embedded forces of capital are themselves small and decentralized. Their democratic demands may not be for decentralization or localism at all. They may be for greater income, access, or goods. Politically, such groups may need centralization in order to gain their objectives, so any analysis of such situations must take account of the social location of, and forms of struggle being employed by, a given group.(24)

On the other hand, when clients demand the decentralization of established powers and bureaucracies, e.g., welfare, the schools, police, energy production, they are using very powerful strategies. They can expand the opportunity for oppositional and visionary ideas to be expressed and they can improve the way the bureaucracies respond. Such initiatives establish cracks in the solid wall of elite, bureaucratic, self-interested decision making processes and thereby expand the range and importance of the issues that can be addressed. Environmentalists and energy critics have used such strategies to effect changes in the composition of regulatory boards and to make capital more accountable.

Although the term may be unattractive to many democratic critics, the general model proposed here is essentially *federalism*. We seek to provide an explicit democratic rationale for decisions about the level, national or local, for which it is appropriate to organize opposition and envision new social forms. In our society, single-minded arguments for localism will play into the hands of globally organized economic and political interests. Also, the necessary conditions for industrial organization cannot be overlooked. Yet the concrete forms of economic production, labor relations, and local control can provide an oppositional force that starts from the bottom. Still, utopian socialist proposals are inadequate to confront the large-scale forces at work to prevent or limit democracy.

Participation/representation

Participation can become confused with centralization/decentralization in the sense that we would probably assume that more effective democratic engagement happens in decentralized settings. Two problems arise, however. First, decentralization alone has little relation to the forms of participation that local government involves. Furthermore, local governments are generally far more rigid and unresponsive to redistributive demands from the lower classes than are large-scale governments. Second, whether participation is an ethical good that ought to be increased in any circumstance still depends on what kinds of social conditions exist. Single-minded demands for face-to-face participation are utopian unless there is massive decentralization in the economy. While a democratic movement might want to be aware of participatory prospects, it must still ask itself about the conditions it faces and the projects it must undertake. Since only some of these will be radically decentralized, a democratic movement must find ways to organize itself to meet the scale of its challenges, both oppositional and visionary. In this regard, it is senseless to imagine fighting energy companies merely with backyard solar collectors, or to assume there can be local democratic and communitarian efforts that can succeed in the absence of a more pervasive attack on the current socioeconomic and political system. Such an analysis suggests that representative forms of decision making may, in many cases, be unavoidable.

While representation is the backbone of bourgeois democratic theory, it can be articulated more powerfully still. The problem for democratic representation is to imagine ways in which representatives can actually reflect their democratic constituencies, rather than being merely mechanisms for the concentration of power. Single issue representation is one way; formalizing the requirement that representatives keep in close touch with their democratic constituencies is another.(25) Until such forces control the power that representatives are able to concentrate and exercise, the appropriate strategies for representation will be tension ridden, as constituencies seek both power and accountability.

Diversity/homogeneity

Whereas tensions between diversity and homogeneity are treated socially, centralization-decentralization conflicts are treated organizationally. The issue is the conception of relations between diverse groups. Their internal composition must be a social movement or visionary analysis, as well as a political-economic oppositional analysis.

For example, there is a genuine tension between trying to honor diverse claims through balancing them and trying to bring them together against an opposition fundamental to all. The problem for an organizer in such circumstances is to honor social diversity in dimensions other than those where a solid front is needed. In order to unite around particular issues, one does not have to give up differences.

Unionists and environmentalists have begun to find common ground in their opposition to developments that degrade both the human and the natural environment.

The Dilemmas of Democratic Process

In addition to the structural dilemmas posed above, democratically oriented planners must pay attention to other issues in democratic process. We shall characterize these as efficiency/equity, organization/equality, expertise/amateurism and public/private dilemmas.

Efficiency/equity

The language of efficiency and equity is itself a rather technocratic formalism used to cover up the essential issue of democratic engagement. Decisions and policies can only be understood as efficient in the context of a social definition. This definition itself implies standards that need to be publicly examined in the process of democratic decision making.

The familiar critique is that social justice and redistributional concerns are inefficient, wasteful, and unproductive activities. Conversely, inequality and hierarchy supposedly contribute to efficiency by distributing tasks and rewards efficiently and providing a structure of authority. But such conclusions imply economic definitions of efficiency and waste, hence accepting the standards of capitalism itself. Those programs that may be extremely inefficient from a quantitative or monetary point of view may be profoundly efficient in terms of human welfare, satisfaction, or fair play. These are the standards that democratic politics and planning bring to bear on the critical evaluation of policies. Without such radical reformulation of the issues, democratic advocates will find themselves back-pedaling against apparently legitimate demands for rationality in political choices, even though such demands may be highly abstract and manipulative.

Bringing the concerns of social justice to bear on efficiency calculations renders the latter more complex and multifaceted, just as it attacks the single-mindedness of capital. We can thus connect moral, welfare, and economic decisions in nontechnocratic ways and can formulate democratic definitions of efficiency by basing our calculations on standards appropriate for the people affected by those calculations. This ideal, though difficult to achieve, is essential. In Mao's China, for example, there were explicit commitments to avoid paths and programs of development that would undermine already hard-won political gains, or sacrifice rural development for urban development, or stifle agricultural for industrial development. These decisions may have been inefficient from the perspective of rapid capital accumulation, but in human and in long-run economic terms, they were more efficient than their alternatives.

Organization/equality

Bureaucracy and democracy have often been thought of as incompatible. Yet there is a strong argument that bureaucracy and democracy were necessarily intertwined in the modern era. The decline of federal and aristocratic rule made the establishment of other arrangements necessary to insure that society's routine tasks would be performed. Bureaucracy, as a formalized, rationalized administrative apparatus arose in the context of presumed equality in liberal, bourgeois democracies. The formal equalities of rights and law associated with democracy may themselves enhance formal bureaucratic structure.

Still, given the tendencies for bureaucracies under capitalism to centralize power, democratic efforts must always struggle within and against such tendencies. Democratic planning must encourage popular access, the decentralization of the service bureaucracies, and the redefinition of bureaucratic missions and resources. Such a strategy does not, of course, imply the denial of all bureaucratic authority.

These strategies become especially important where close bureaucratic associations connect private capital and the State, as in regulatory, scientific, technological, and taxation agencies. These are arenas for the mobilization of challenges to bureaucratic power and resources. In cases where democratic tendencies are not actually weakened by the demise of bureaucracies, as they are now in the deregulation of energy and environmental decisions, we can encourage legislation to require the redesign and reorganization of bureaucratic functions. While such maneuvers are never in themselves sufficient, they can provide the occasion for critical evaluations, organizing, and a redefinition of bureaucratic missions in more democratic directions.

Expertise/amateurism

Planners are typically part of a priest-like elite that uses its arcane knowledge, language, and access to the mysteries of scientific analysis to dominate and manipulate others. As a result, the development of scientific and organizational expertise has enabled planners access to centers of power. It has also separated them from popular constituencies. Planners' expertise presently reflects the kinds of antidemocratic tendencies toward organization and centralization described elsewhere in this section. The concept of expertise legitimizes the creation of a narrow, elite control that is antithetical to democratic access and engagement.

The real issue is of leadership and authority. Appropriate mechanisms for the control of expertise range from the ideological to the institutional. If experts are made to recognize that they are fallible, then they will pay more attention to conflict and alternative opinions. Direct institutional control of experts by amateurs can exert subtle pressures on the language used in public debate, in the content of arguments, and on what choices are eventually made.

Public/private

Planners constantly face debates about public versus private good. They are expected to juggle private claims in the name of public good. But the public good is a tangle of fundamentally contradictory interests. Moreover, the nominal division between public and private obscures the way in which private power determines public policy. The defense of private prerogatives against the State is a truism within democratic thought. But it obscures the difference between different kinds of prerogatives. A private, personal prerogative is one thing – different from the defense of a private, economic power. In a democratic society it is possible to protect a realm of private personal concern and still legitimately attack private (or corporate) economic and social power.

PLANNING AND THE TASKS OF ORGANIZING

Having reexamined problems of democratic movements and organization, what is a planner to do? The obvious implication of these analyses is that planning activists should cease to think of themselves as mediators and rather engage themselves in political organizing.(26) To speak of the planner as organizer is to draw upon some very particular meanings of that durable political concept. If the planner is employed by a state, or a university, his or her task will be quite different from that of the grassroots leader or union organizer. Whether an organizer/member of a local movement or an active supporter, the planner will draw upon the skills and techniques traditionally associated with leadership: the creation of persuasive analysis, the mobilization of sentiment and support, the assessment of social forces and resources, the practical education of constituencies.

These tasks emerge in the practice of planners who see their vocation in a context of conflict and opposition. Seeking democracy and a democratic form of organizing will inevitably lead to a focus on the development and emergence of grassroots movements. In those structures with strong and coherent political constituencies, we must actively support those groups that speak for concerns that oppose capital. In policy arenas presently defined so narrowly or technocratically that their affected constituencies may not yet be mobilized, the planning activist must seek out popular engagement, persuade people of the relevance of policy decisions, and crack open the bureaucratic facade that covers so many decisions.

Arenas for Democratic Organizing

Planners find a variety of democratically oriented movements and activities that offer possibilities for democratic organizing. Some of these are worthy of more detailed discussion, both for their critical possibilities and, occasionally, for their democratic failures.(27) The following list is suggestive in both respects.

1. Impact Assessments Processes. The development of environmental impact assessments has made possible public review and comment on development projects where previously there was none. Proponents of the process have extended it to force explicit consideration of the social as well as natural impact of projects. Vermont even has a state land-use law requiring explicit consideration of the economic impact of project decisions. It is essential for planners to insure that these assessment activities are not captured by local capital, especially real estate interests.

2. Community Development Corporations. In areas where public or private investment has been inadequate to prevent further decay, as in many urban ghettoes, community groups have themselves banded together to form development corporations. These groups have acted as organizing units as well as centers for concentrating public and private financing. There is a national Center for Community Economic Development (639 Mass. Ave., Suite 316, Cambridge, MA 02139) which provides information, analysis, assistance, and evaluations of community development theories and activities around the country. Planners can assist these groups in developing proposals and organizing projects.

3. Cooperatives. Producer and consumer cooperatives in agriculture and food, housing, and education have become part of the American institutional landscape. Now there are also cooperatives that provide credit, health care, legal services, and even funeral services. These coops have long had an implicit and often explicit democratic and radical orientation, which has become more relevant in the midst of our current austerity, the phenomenon that led to their creation in the Depression era. More specific information about types, activities, successes, and failures of coops is available from the Cooperative League USA, 1828 L St., N.W., Washington, DC 20036. Again, planners can aid local cooperatives by providing information and organizational advice, especially concerning the question of broad constituency representation in the cooperative movement.

4. State Banks and Businesses. The fiscal crisis shared by almost every public agency has led to widespread demands for more public control over the investment of public funds. As the Bank of North Dakota, now the nation's only public bank, has shown, such institutions can provide both new revenues and new investments for local development. Proposals for such banks are now being considered in at least eight states. All the proposals consider the use of public money for public needs and the democratic control of public investment funds. Rowan provides a summary of recent literature and legislative activity in this area.(28) But there is a necessity for democratic organizers to make sure that such banks do not simply become public versions of private banks. There must be mobilization to determine the selection of bank officials and the setting of loan and investment policies to insure

support for neighborhood based efforts, workers' cooperatives, and other forms of popular organizing.

5. Worker-Controlled Enterprises. Through the apparatus of Employee Stock Ownership Plans (ESOPs), which have been encouraged by tax and securities policies in order to promote expanding ownership of property, some workers have been able to have a voice in the management of their workplaces. In many cases where business would have otherwise closed or moved out, employees have been able to take over the management of firms. A recent report on employee ownership concluded that there is a direct relationship between productivity and the percentage of company equity owned by nonmanagerial employees.(29) Furthermore, workers reported greater job satisfaction and productivity. For example, a worker in one such enterprise noted,

> You have everyone more united . . . and you have a better outlook on coming to work. It seems as if you're working for yourself. You just don't come in and put in your eight hours. It's kind of a psychological thing. You work like any other job, but it's a psychological thing where you are working for yourself like you're in business for yourself.(30)

Others say things like, "I feel it's more of a family now, more homey. It's a pleasure to work here." Nearly three-fourths of the managers and about one-half of the workers in such enterprises feel that morale has improved; about the same proportions feel that attitudes on the job have improved.

It is important for planners involved in ESOP projects to recognize that morale and productivity are not the same as power. ESOP projects are subject to corporate takeover, for workers' shares do not immediately mean the institution of worker control. ESOP plans are important however, for organizing to demand such control. It should be noted that the idea of worker control can apply to nonownership participation in work-related decisions as well as to employee ownership. Strongforce and Rifkin provide detailed information about recent developments and strategies for worker control.(31)

6. Appropriate Technology. Many of the concerns about appropriate technology have been romantic Luddism. But others have derived from quite specific tensions between democratic needs and corporate imperatives. In energy, resource-extraction, agriculture, transportation, military and other technology-intensive processes, critics have been able to raise questions about jobs, profits, working conditions, and collective or long-term impacts. These questions provide a variety of locations where analysis, struggle, and the formulation of alternative societal visions about the desirable forms and uses of technology can take place.(32)

7. Public Employees and State/Client Union Organizing. The conditions of austerity and fiscal crisis outlined above make it imperative that state employees (teachers, police, service workers) and clients of the state (the poor, the old, the young) be able to organize. They

must not be used as sacrificial lambs in a crisis period. In virtually every public agency there are twin movements toward employee unionization and the direct mobilization of clients. Very often these movements are at odds with one another over prerogatives and power, but the result is a highly politicized environment for those who work in any of these areas.

The most notable of these movements is the broad-based welfare rights movement, with chapters and organizations scattered throughout the nation. There are also fledgling unions of the unemployed, student unions seeking representation in educational decisions, and organizations of the disabled seeking power to influence the decisions that determine their lives. Among employee unions, the American Federation of Teachers, the American Federation of State, County, and Municipal Employees, and the Service Employees International Union are joined by a myriad of other local and state employee organizations, all intent upon participating – if only through collective bargaining – in those issues hitherto decided by civil service codes and bureaucratic hierarchy.

8. Local Groups. The broadest grassroots possibilities are opened by the many local movements that are emerging in the current period of cut-backs and centralization. Ranging from citizen action leagues protesting jail conditions to antigrowth groups, from neighborhood organizations seeking access to public funds and the decentralization of services to city-wide electoral movements, from communities uniting against urban renewal to groups seeking representation on planning commissions, utility boards, and rapid transit governing bodies – this wide and diverse range of political movements is everywhere in evidence. And it may be here that the deepest conflicts develop over decentralization, demands in public resources, and alternative strategies for the creation of new forms of the social good.

Progressive Planning Roles

A progressive planner can aid democratic movements in a variety of specific and concrete ways.(33)

1. The first task is that of analysis and criticism. We can make much more accessible our analysis of the macroeconomic relations of which all struggles are a part. We can assess the impact of local demands on these relations. We can assess the emerging forms of dependency and domination created by the activities of the corporations and the state. This analysis is partly historical, partly structural. It is an attempt to shift the very grounds of critique and argument to educate constituencies about the broader implications of any struggle. In this the planner plays a demystifying role. The planner demystifies the State itself, its relationship to capital, and the significance of marginal reforms. We require a self-conscious attention, then, to analysis which focuses on specific struggles and broadens the meaning of these struggles. While not the basis for practical alliance between diverse popular

groups, such analysis can provide a forum for political arguments about alliances and their necessity.

The planner who makes this kind of analysis available to constituencies breaks through two mystifying veils. The first is analytic itself, and is the veil of ideological misunderstanding and confusion that may obscure the deeper meaning of any struggle. The second is the veil of bureaucratic and technical language. To destroy this abstract commitment to expertise and technology, the democratic planner is forced to engage in what we call "radical translations." All critiques and analyses must be made accessible to constituencies which may lack the ability to understand the State's language of expertise. This is an exceptionally difficult and problematic issue, and one to which organizers must devote a great deal of attention to be both precise and accessible.

It is a project that must be undertaken with some humility. Planners must realize that no analytic critique – however correct – can result in immediate progressive practice. This insight about the relationship between theory and practice has special implication for radical planners. Accustomed to the elegance of formal theory and trained by both education and bureaucracy to be impatient with the conflicting cries and claims of disparate groups, the planner is almost instinctively arrogant. Less a personal trait than a style of work, this arrogance must be overcome through the acknowledgment that nothing progressive will come from the State unless popular forces are actively engaged in conflict. In this active engagement men and women learn their own strengths and limits. They will seek what matters from our analysis and demand that our analysis speak to their needs. To be a political organizer in this context is to inform those needs while remaining responsive to voices initially new to the planner.

This humility teaches the planner to listen to constituencies, to try to learn the many things of which we know so little – the recognition that analysis alone is never enough.

2. Another important progressive project is political education, which has two key aspects. First, we must develop a broader historical and comparative knowledge of practical democratic experience and opportunities to inform our specific concerns. Second, we need to develop a positive vision of a democratic order and attempt to organize and structure the movements in which we work accordingly.

With regard to the first task, radical planners need to draw upon a variety of literatures. These include historic treatments of the emergence of democratic and popular struggles and structurally informed case studies (of a variety of planning problems and arenas) which pay attention to the mobilization (or nonmobilization) of democratic forces. The latter includes comparative analyses of analogous struggles encountered in different countries and regions of the United States. For example, radical city planners who can provide accounts of both their country's history of urban planning and comparative accounts of planning conflicts in Western Europe and the socialist nations would greatly benefit their constituencies. Regional development planners concerned about western resource development can benefit from careful critiques of the experience and strategies of Appalachian mining communities and unions in their effort to organize regionally. Activists engaged in struggles over growth management can build on the careful, critical work done for Santa Barbara's no-growth movement. Advocates of worker control and self-management can learn from the successes and failures of the Yugoslavian experience. In all these instances, comparative analysis can inform a number of straightforward yet radical questions about any particular bureaucracy or agency's goals and strategies.

The second task, the creation of positive visions of the democratic order, has several components. We must avoid making democracy synonymous with the direct, uncritical pursuit of interests and demands from below. Planners can have an important role in clarifying the implications of various strategies for the future of democracy as well as for the vision of society as a whole. The process of critique and opposition can suggest new creations, new construction, new designs, new visionary insights. We can understand freedom by experiencing it. While there is much to criticize in models of society based upon the assumptions of face-to-face conversations or models of utopian communities, we can draw upon such conceptions to inform our daily, practical work. Political organizing is always rooted in the harsh realities of conflict and opposition; successful organizing requires an imaginative, even fanciful, grasp of what we can create.

3. The overriding concern for planners should be the fracturing of the boundaries between the State and its constituencies. In every way imaginable, public movements should be organized into participatory action. For example, in energy planning, activists can aggressively urge union representatives and neighborhood groups to participate in discussions and decisions. In city planning areas, planning activists can seek new ways to democratize meetings, hearings, and review procedures.(34)

Unless a popular constituency is demanding access, such organizing can be suicidal. This suggests a strategy in which the radical planner must seek a group to support and to which he or she may be accountable before he can <u>act</u> progressively. There should be no Lone Rangers in democratic organizing. This means assuming – for want of a less romantic title – the stance of a "guerilla planner." Know your enemies, do not trust your supervisors, unionize every work relationship, and always seek a way of bringing your knowledge to those outside the planning context so as to overcome their exclusion and dependency. In the end, this is the task of a planner to provide an arena for movement.

NOTES

(1) The difficulty and sensitivity of this task is more than evident to us. Almost everyone uses the language of democracy for what is desired and accuses opponents of being elitist or fascistic. As we proceed, it will be apparent that we recognize Schaar's (<u>Power and Community</u>,

1970) warning: "Democracy is the most prostituted word of our age, and any man who employs it in reference to any modern state should be suspect either of ignorance or of bad motives."

(2) Huntington, "The United States," 1975.

(3) The Trilateral Commission was formed by political leaders in the United States, Western Europe, and Japan in response to the OPEC oil embargo of 1973. The Commission has sponsored a variety of studies concerned with the technical and political problems affecting the "industrial democracies." See Huntington, loc. cit., 1975.

(4) Wolfe, "The Capitalist Distemper," 1979.

(5) Ibid.

(6) McClosky, "Ideology and Consensus in American Politics," 1964.

(7) In a conversation about this position, our friend Jeffrey Lustig remarked that McClosky has coined a remarkable new syllogism:

> The ancients believed democracy required a committed consensus around democratic values and beliefs.
> Americans do not share a committed consensus around democratic values.
> Therefore, the ancients were wrong.

(8) McClosky and others of his ilk (See Finley, Democracy, 1972) argue that the fact that voters are apathetic and subject to "working class authoritarianism" itself justifies elite control. But to democrats, this condition suggests the need for political education. As Manicas (The Death of the State, 1974) puts it, "To the extent that persons are saturated with beliefs and feelings induced by their condition, they are both more easily tied, rationally and emotionally, to the existing order *and* when it seems that it is threatened, they become more easy prey *for* quick, simple-minded and *even more* authoritarian 'solutions' to their felt difficulties." Planners can help by clarifying the issues involved in such situations, and by explaining the implications of authoritarian solutions.

(9) See Wolin, Politics and Vision, 1960.

(10) Of course, liberal economists have argued that this realm is not large enough or sufficiently well-funded; conservatives have argued that markets can be constructed and made to operate for more of these goods than we can imagine. But neither view resolves the problem, for some levels of both constitutive and allocative planning are necessary in both cases.

(11) Meyerson and Banfield, Politics, Planning and the Public Interest, 1955.

(12) Friedmann, "The Public Interest and Community Participation," 1973.

(13) Mermelstein, "Austerity, Planning and the Socialist Alternatives," 1977.

(14) Wolfe, "The Capitalist Distemper," 1979.

(15) O'Connor, The Fiscal Crisis of the State, 1973.

(16) O'Malley, Karl Marx, 1970.

(17) Wolfe, The Limits of Legitimacy, 1977.

(18) O'Connor, "The Democratic Movement in the United States," 1979.

(19) Lustig, "On Organization," 1977.

(20) Wolfe, "The Capitalist Distemper," 1979.

(21) The reason for claiming that democratic relations and commitments "may be" the appropriate grounds for differentiating progressive from non-progressive movements is the problem of Leninism. It is always possible, and Leninists would argue always necessary, for a vanguard party to mobilize non-democratically and to create the conditions under which democracy then becomes possible. See Lustig, loc. cit., 1977, for elaboration of this problem.

(22) When Plato and Aristotle speak of a "regime" they are speaking of far more than the government or the ruling class (as in "the present Chilean *regime*"). By "regime" the classics identified the central and important values of a political culture, as they were expressed in and through the institutions of that culture. Thus Plato speaks of the Aristocratic regime as being that political system "ruled by the few," where the few rule according to the values of public-spirited commitment and a love of the city. On these substantive grounds an Aristocracy can be distinguished from an Oligarchy, in which the few rule in their own narrow interest. We use "regime" to identify a set of values as well as practices; a "regime of freedom" is a political system marked by belief in – and commitment to – freedom. In our critique, "regime" signifies the critical and subtle intersections between practices and commitments, institutions and culture.

(23) Marcuse, One Dimensional Man, 1964.

(24) Critics of the Left political economic literature claim there is an inconsistency between its democratic and socialist pretensions, the one implying radical decentralization, the other requiring centralized coordination and controls (Lindbeck, The Political Economy of the New Left, 1977). Our discussion indicates that careful distinctions based upon democratic arguments are necessary to make productive the inevitable tensions here.

(25) Marx, in his comments to the Paris Commune (1933), believed in the implementation of democratic representation. He discussed delegate systems based upon conditional mandates, the immediate recall of delegates, the informational duty of delegates vis-a-vis their immediate organizations, and the rotation of mandates. It is mechanisms like these which Abrahamsson (Bureaucracy of Participation, 1977) argues can provide the substantive democratic content to avoid Michel's "iron law of oligarchy." Since these mechanisms are dependent upon participation, they both limit the exercise of elite power and forestall oligarchy through explicit accountability.

(26) See especially Forester, "Planning as Organizing," unpublished.

(27) More specific information about issues, organizations, case studies, bibliography, and progressive stances on the movement and activities listed here is available from the Conference on Alternative State and Local Public Policy, 1901 Q Street, N.W., Washington, D.C. 20009.

(28) Rowen, "Public Capital," 1977.

(29) Economic Development Administration, "Employee Ownership," 1977.

(30) Ibid.

(31) Strongforce, "Democracy in the Workplace," 1977.

(32) Boyle and Harper, Radical Technology, 1976; Rainbook, Resources for Appropriate Technology, 1977; Burton, The Governance of Energy, 1979.

(33) While this discussion has a strong populist tone, the requirement for detailed structural analysis generates a realistic rather than a romantic populism. While the populist impulse is democratically valid, it cannot rest merely on the "will of the people." As a result, we cannot avoid the problems of organization and authority, but neither can we allow their determination by capitalist imperatives.

(34) Efforts to show, teach, and encourage this are underway. For example, the New School for Democratic Management (256 Sutter Street, San Francisco, CA 94108) sponsors workshops and research for

planners, administrators, and advocacy groups on topics like the following: (1) Democratic Management of Public Agencies, (2) Alternative Financing Strategies for State and local governments, (3) Community economic development strategies, and (4) labor-management relations in the public sector. It holds employee seminars in cities across the country and will soon publish a reader on democratic management.

10 Opposition Planning*

Pierre Clavel

This chapter addresses the question: under what conditions might the general evening-out of political and economic opportunity occur? In particular, it looks at the way equality is suppressed within peripheral regions; even more particularly the role that planning plays in this suppression and might play in lifting this suppression. Thus, I am concerned both with a general theory of the suppression of equality, and with the special role of the institutions of planning in it.

THEORY

The general theory is that those in power and in control of resources are motivated to control political and economic institutions so that the access of other persons and groups to economic and political power is limited. The means for this include force, particularly through the agency of the State, but also the construction of ideology to justify inequality, control of schools and other socializing agencies, and the creation of a dependent population in need of the patronage of the State or of private sector employers.(1) The most important intellectual traditions in Western thought, which I take to be liberalism and Marxism, deal with this proposition in different ways. But they are alike in ignoring the role of regions in maintaining inequalities. Classical liberals saw equality resulting from the development of markets and market-like institutions. They saw poor, backward regions as enclaves both of poverty and local inequalities whose problems would be solved by the diffusion of markets.(2) Marxists and socialists generally saw the

*A version of this chapter appeared in Harvey A. Goldstein and Sara A. Rosenberry, eds., The Structural Crisis of the 1970's and Beyond: The Need for a New Planning Theory, 1978.

problem of inequality in terms of classes, and the suggestion that regional factors be a focus of attention was seen as a diversion from the class struggle, posed in national or international terms.(3)

In Western countries, liberal approaches emphasizing market development and market-like institutions have predominated, with the main variation being the extent to which governments have used government intervention to make markets work. Classical liberalism suggests very little government intervention, and it has influenced the liberal democracies in their regional policies intermittently – during the Eisenhower administrations in the United States, and under Conservative governments in Britain, for example. But the dominant trend has been toward an interventionist market oriented policy.(4) This policy – also called "liberal" – has been accompanied by a set of propositions that can be identified as the dominant or orthodox model for regional development:

1. First, the institutional changes that comprise regional development are regarded, fundamentally, as a shift in the criteria of participation from status to more objectively determined qualifications. Thus, entry into entrepreneurship, universities, industrial labor markets, politics and public sector jobs is broadened, and various kinds of new institutions are created and encouraged: labor unions, savings banks, various business and public services, regulatory agencies and planning bureaus. All increase the level of communication and mobility among institutions and among segments of the population. Barriers of community boundaries, tribalism, ethnicity, and family background are broken down.

2. Second, the way all this is brought about is through the introduction of modernizing influences to the region from somewhere more central in the nation: for example, the introduction of large-scale public and private sector employers who, because of their size or for other reasons, recruit labor on performance criteria rather than status. This eventually causes change and development of institutions throughout the area and in other industrial sectors. When applied spatially to a set of regions, this amounts to a kind of diffusion theory. Modernization starts in one region (called the "center") and is introduced by interregional extensions such as branch plants and offices and government programs, into poor or "peripheral" regions.(5)

These propositions support numerous corollaries and common policy positions. Thus, increases in communication and mobility, and the introduction of modernizing, central influences are said to be factors in 1) the development of market economies;(6) 2) increases in national integration;(7) 3) reductions in income inequality, both within and among regions;(8) and 4) increases in political participation and competitiveness.(9)

3. Another corollary with particular impact in regional development is the growth center policy.(10) As developed in policy, the idea is to concentrate investment and institutions in a limited number of places within regions so as to maximize urbanization economies. In addition, the following rationale exists for growth centers: if there is to be a

demonstration effect from new institutions, concentration will enhance the effect for those who come in contact with it; if funds for national policy are very limited, spreading them around will make them nearly invisible.

4. Finally, the liberal policy attempts to introduce an element of rationalism within the region, and some accountability, through the encouragement and subsidy of regional planning agencies. These are characterized by their supralocal scale, the introduction of highly trained professional staff people, and, typically, a very limited political mandate. The planning they do is advisory only; final authority is retained in the hands of local or national (in the United States, state) governments.(11)

Socialists have differed from liberals in that they have placed less emphasis on the creation of markets and have attempted to use the State to serve the interests of a working class. They have done this through the creation of mass parties, often based on labor unions. But in Western countries the resulting policy toward regions has been different only in degree. This is partly because socialists have accommodated to a situation where most wealth and productive apparatus is controlled by nonsocialists. What results is the mixed economy, where the state regulates the private sector and the nationalized industries, but does not subject them to thoroughgoing popular control. Even in state-owned enterprises, a managerial class dominates – not much different from the private sector counterpart.

A second reason that prevents socialists from developing regional policies much different from those of the liberal model, is the doctrine favoring class based political support, which regards regional political movements as a diversion. The key part of this argument is an adaptation to the belief that the working class is a minority political force that can function best when it operates at the largest possible scale. Thus, where resources are to be allocated by a social democratic party, they go first to build up staffing and political machinery at the national level, and are allocated to regional offices only as a second priority and for temporary purposes, such as electoral campaigns. This generalization is true of almost all those institutions that might be thought part of a social democratic political coalition in countries such as the United States and Great Britain and include national labor unions, political parties, and lobbies. In all of these bureaucratic apparatus develops as a resource for the coalition, but it is a highly centralized resource.

DATA

These comparisons could be laid out in more detail, and a general set of speculations on an alternative policy could be suggested. My objective here, though, is to focus on planning. I have spent parts of the last three years interviewing persons involved in planning, and in local reactions to planning, in Wales and Appalachia. These interviews, together with a review of what has been written on regional policy and planning in Britain and the United States and for Wales and Appalachia in particular, suggest at least four alternative bases for policy and planning that neither liberal nor social democratic policy has adopted.

Official Regional Planning is Not Serious

In both Wales and Appalachia, planning is better developed outside of the official agencies than inside. In Wales, regional planning has been the responsibility of a separate ministry – the Welsh Office – since 1964, but the only formal planning effort, a report completed in 1967 and soon discredited by all factions outside the Welsh Office, has never been revised. No official planning position exists for Wales, though there have been numerous special studies. A Welsh Office economist told me that there is a good deal of informal monitoring of the economy.

In Appalachia, the official regional planning body since 1965 has been the Appalachian Regional Commission. Appalachia does not have the official status Wales does, consisting only of parts of several states, and its power base the governors of those states. Hence, the Commission has taken a rather passive role as planner. Its own planning has largely been in response to that of the states. It has been able to prod the states to draw up plans, but has had little control over the result. But staff planners at the Commission say that it plays a largely informal role in influencing the work of the states.

In both Wales and Appalachia, however, their respective agencies have had cumulative effects and have promoted policies. Both have adopted a public works emphasis, mainly road construction justified by a belief in increasing accessibility of the region to more central parts of the state. Both have supported growth center development, and both have played a role in the creation of local level administrative structure.

Planning Has Stimulated Opposition

In both Wales and Appalachia, the efforts of the official planning agencies have stimulated opposition. In Wales there has been opposition to specific projects, notably against new towns that the Welsh Office supported, and "advocacy research" against these projects. The basis of the attacks was the argument that the new developments would disturb the social structure by bringing in English-speaking migrants and by too rapid growth, causing social pathologies and the destruction of local institutions; or that they would depopulate existing communities. In Appalachia there has been similar opposition. Examples include the efforts of planners to program new investments in growth centers, and clumsy federal flood recovery plans.

In both countries, there is as much opposition to what the regional planning agencies do not do as to what they do. In Wales there is much concern about the lack of an official regional plan; in Appalachia there is concern that the Commission fails to deal with the institutional pattern of absentee ownership of resources, or with the causes of floods, including the destruction of the land through strip mining.

Opposition Planning

In both places, there have been efforts to go beyond localized advocacy, opposition, and specialized research to attack regional policy and planning in a fundamental way. In Wales, this has been spearheaded by the Plaid Cymru, the separatist political party, which created a well-researched plan challenging growth centers, migration policy and the public works emphasis of official planning. This document, written in 1969, served to put the party ahead of the government and, to some extent, structured the agenda for debate of projects. In Appalachia, a diffuse opposition to the Commission exists on similar issues, but no overall plan has been produced.

A New Political Coalition

In Wales, and to some extent in Appalachia, a territorially based political coalition has developed which runs counter to the major parties. These coalitions seem to fuse class and territorial consciousness and provide a context within which opposition planning can occur.

THEORETICAL IMPLICATIONS

These observations are difficult to fit within most theoretical frameworks. Making sense of them requires that one question the usual ways of thinking in several respects: the effects of territorial politics, the conditions of inequality in different kinds of regions, and the general conceptualization of planning under these different conditions.

Territorial Politics

Liberal or pluralist theories of politics see people as more or less rational actors who join groups whose political activities help them get what they want. Pluralist models of politics would have these groups operate in national arenas, and the most developed politics are seen as those with the most complex arenas, with many channels of relatively civilized accommodation among interests. Further, it is argued that the larger the scale at which their interest groups can cast about for coalitions, the more successfully will individuals pursue their ends.

Thus, a nationally integrated political system is seen in both descriptive and normative terms.

The same logic applies for those who define interests as aggregating more in class groupings than along industrial sector or individually idiosyncratic clusters. For them, elites form nationally linked aggregations concerned with maintaining position and the present distribution of rewards, while the masses also organize nationally, along class lines.

In addition to class and special interests, coalitions might include groups with territorial interests as their major concerns, but these would be ancillary to the coalition. The farm lobby, for example, might include groups whose main concern is the preservation of a way of life in a place, but this would be subordinated to the narrower interests of farmers generally, vis a vis other interests (e.g., consumers, railroads, manufacturers).

Abstractly, it makes as much sense that political coalitions would form around the principle of territorial preservation while also appealing to specialized, functional economic and class interests, as that they would be dominated by economic or class interests while also appealing to territorial interests. There have been a few attempts to suggest this. Grant McConnell referred to this concept obliquely in writing about the environmental movement: it behaved differently from other interest groups, he said, because it elevated the aim of preservation of the environment to a moral principle, which any compromise destroyed. Thus, land became an indivisible resource. Either one had territorial (environmental) integrity, or not.(12) In a different way, Harvey Molotch emphasized territory as a basis for political interest. He seemed to summarize all interests in terms of their relationship to their role in dominating territory. Thus, newspapers, realtors, contractors and insurance brokers have an interest in making the economic base of a region grow, and this provides a rationale for supporting local projects and for defusing potential conflicts among them. Expectation of growth thus integrates diverse interests. In contrast, groups whose welfare does not depend on local resources can afford to take a preservationist approach to territory. But both kinds of groups are territorially defined, in contrast to class or special interest groups.(13) Finally, there is Michael Hechter's suggestion that indigenous populations in peripheral regions form an opposition to central cities of any national party and support protest causes against these elites. These also can be thought of as territorial groups, with the most developed form being separatist political parties, as in Wales.(14)

Territorial groups can be hypothesized to behave differently from special interests or class interests in that they are less easy to buy off and/or they may become attached to wholistic views stressing the interrelatedness of many factors bearing on the preservation of territory.

The Differences Among Regions

Why should territorial politics occur? When one encounters it, as in the case of the Plaid Cymru in Wales and in some of the opposition groups in Appalachia, one also encounters a set of ad hoc explanations. The most prevalent explanation, that of common culture and national background as in the case of the Welsh, seems partly correct and explains the relative weakness of territorial coalitions in Appalachia. I would suggest some additional factors: 1) a common local reaction to state and federal bureaucracies; 2) the rapid development of a new class of persons disaffected from the central culture, ready to adopt and help recreate a more authentic regional culture; 3) the inability of the economic structure to absorb an increasingly sophisticated and well-traveled set of young adults in interesting and powerful jobs; and 4) the traditional Marxist explanation of class mobilization – the development of class consciousness resulting from expropriation of the means of production.

Rather than elaborate on these explanations here, I will merely note that their common characteristic is that they do not fit in with the pluralist model of local politics. It seems appropriate to recognize that to incorporate them as explanations requires some relatively general reformulation of theory. They reflect a two-dimensional gap in our thinking about politics in localities and regions: internal cultural differentiation and the power disparities between local and national institutions.

These two main characteristics seem to typify Wales and Appalachia. On the one hand, both places have apparent and relatively marked differentiation between indigenous and nationally linked populations to the point where one can suggest cultural differentiation. In Wales it is most apparent: one population with Welsh roots and one with English roots and connections. There are associated differences in language, religion, and social network.

In Appalachia there is a similar differentiation in roots. An indigenous Appalachian does many things and gets access to things impossible for one with outside roots. The reverse is also true: outsiders may have some access not open to insiders. There is perhaps a corollary to all this. That is, with time, some outsiders may get some of the access of insiders, and vice versa, both in Wales and in Appalachia. But this access is not offered readily. It requires a lot of time – measured in years and decades.

Second, it is useful to focus on the phenomenon of domination by externally controlled institutions over those rooted in the region. This exists both in Wales and in Appalachia. As regions, both are subject to domination as extreme as exists in their respective countries. In Wales, the mechanism of domination includes both English-owned private corporations and nationalized industries, parliament centered political parties, and the state civil service operating through the ministries. In Appalachia, the role of largely absentee-owned coal companies is a prime factor, coupled with federal and state agencies subject to many private sector pressure groups not rooted in the region. The workings of external domination are complex and sometimes domination itself is debated, but the existence of domination cannot be denied.

Cultural differentiation and external domination, together, introduce factors not taken into account as variables in pluralist theories of politics. Cultural differences are usually regarded as temporary phenomena, to be dispensed with as groups are assimilated. Political institutions are described as civilizing the differences between groups which agree on the rules of conflict. This agreement is basic to the pluralist model. External domination is also omitted from the model. For local politics, it is either ignored or seen as a benign, unbiased force which simply makes it easier for all organized groups to compete with each other.

The Wales and Appalachia cases, where these two factors intrude in an extreme way, force us to reformulate our picture of politics generally. Heuristically, four kinds of regions are suggested, which I will refer to as follows:

	Cultural Differentiation	
External Domination	Low	High
High	Hierarchy	Hegemony
Low	Polyarchy	Conflict

1. Hegemony. The cases we have been describing have external domination coupled with insider-outsider cultural differentiation. This seems to be a highly stable, mutually reinforcing combination, which I will refer to as hegemony. By this I mean to emphasize the kind of domination possible in this situation: the outsiders dominate the insiders within the region. Yet the insiders have a basis for cohesion and territorial coalitions may appear.

2. Hierarchy and polyarchy. With internal cultural differentiation relatively low, the possibilities of external domination are more limited. Hierarchy means a case where there is a disadvantage for the region in terms of resource inequalities vis a vis other regions, but insider outsider cultural differences are not a factor. Thus, it is relatively easy for insiders to move into outside positions, and vice versa. Under these circumstances the basic legitimacy of rule is less likely to be questioned, there is likely to be agreement on the goals of regional development, and politics is apt to be relatively uncontentious. But the region is generally poor and lacks control of its major institutions. These are oriented outside the area and local politics generally has to defer to them. Thus, the word "hierarchy."

Another situation is that where neither external domination nor cultural differentiation is particularly high. The lack of domination suggests the word "autonomy" for this case, but in the absence of cultural differences, I am inclined to define this as the situation the pluralist writers had in mind: Dahl's New Haven, perhaps, and call it "polyarchy." (Why not hierarchy? Possibly, but I think this is the case where polyarchy is most likely to appear, if anywhere, and I will retain the name to remind us of that.)

3. Conflict. The case where insider-outsider cultural differentiation persists but external domination is low, produces a situation of conflict more intense and antagonistic than in the polyarchy case. Conflicts are seen in win-lose terms, mutual blocking of the other's objectives occur as group tactics even though no direct gain results. "Immobilism" might be a good term to describe the politics of this case, to distinguish this more intense level of conflict from that entailed in polyarchy. In the interest of brevity, I have not discussed one of the assumptions implied in this typology: that external domination is so highly associated with internal domination that the two can be treated as equals.

PLANNING

Various hypotheses develop from this typology, but my main purpose is to describe how planning relates to these various types of political systems, in particular, how it relates to the hegemony of Wales and Appalachia. Several different descriptions of planning have appeared in the literature, and it seems that they apply with varying degrees of accuracy, depending on the relative amounts of domination and cultural differentiation. That is, the description of planning is different for each type of region, though aspects of each description may appear in any type.

The most familiar descriptions apply to the hierarchy and polyarchy cases.(15) The technical or classical models of planning that assume that goals are provided by a political body best apply to the hierarchy case. This point has been made, often as a criticism of the model, by such researchers as Rabinowitz, Rondinelli, and Banfield, and is perhaps the best-known insight contributed by political science to the study of planning.(16) There have also been several reformulations of planning as an indicative model which does not require goals to be supplied ahead of the process and in which planners provide research data and forecasts that improve the planning of private firms and other governments. This model, which has been pointed out as adapted to the polyarchy situation, has been elaborated on by such writers as Shonfield, Rondinelli, and Meyerson.(17)

Several characteristics of planning in Wales and Appalachia fit neither model, and I attribute these to the hegemonic nature of politics and economics in these places. First, there was a dualism in planning in both places: official planning performed cooperatively with other governments in an approximation of the technical or indicative style, and a much less public, ad hoc bargaining procedure on specific major projects. This is not to belittle major differences between Welsh Office and Appalachian Regional Commission planning. The facade of rationalist planning under central government authority, constructed by the Welsh Office, differs from the facade of gentle prodding by the Commission. But both are facades, and both include cooperative use of data. Also, in both cases, ad hoc planning activities outside the formal process go on.

Second, the real output of planning, in both places, was its effect on political agendas: what projects would be brought up and debated, what topics would be avoided. This effect of planning tends to be obscured. Technical planning within a hierarchical framework is supposed to be a means of programming the detailed steps toward a goal, and people measure the effectiveness of this kind of planning by the speed with which the actions proposed, take place. Indicative planning is thought of as more passive, and is said to work well when it helps other planners get their proposals implemented more quickly. The plans of the Welsh Office and the Appalachian Regional Commission may have done this, but what is more apparent is that they affected agendas within their constituencies. Their plans occupied press attention and the attention of other public officials. By suggesting a project in any location, the planners could make it difficult for alternative actions to be thoroughly aired. By suggesting projects such as new towns and roads (in Wales) or highways and hospitals (in Appalachia) they ensured that these, and not other topics (such as the ownership structure of natural resources or manufacturing plants) would receive most public and official attention.

Finally, Wales and Appalachia both developed a wide-ranging opposition to official planning. This was more developed in Wales, where the Plaid Cymru plan was more detailed and comprehensive than the official government plan, and where a general ideology of opposition developed within which specific arguments were made against specific projects. In Appalachia the opposition was less developed, but a general opposition ideology was also identifiable. These opposition plans and statements can be viewed, like their official counterparts, as efforts to control the agenda of debate rather than as technical plans. As such, they had some success.

All of these characteristics of planning in Wales and Appalachia make more sense in the context of hegemony, than in either hierarchy or polyarchy. Under hegemony, there is a potential opposition to keep under control, and official planning can help in this by manufacturing the agenda for public attention by performing indicative planning to service those interested in industrial development, and by keeping some plans under wraps to forestall opposition. Opposition groups, on the other hand, can organize on the basis of their insider-cultural ties. The existence of official planning (along with other actions of the outsider-controlled bureaucracies and economic structure) provides a comprehensive target around which opposition planning positions can develop.

Some of these characteristics might apply within systems that have been described as hierarchical or polyarchical, for example, the black ghettoes in U.S. metropolitan areas. While the idea of polyarchy has been applied to such areas, and with more justification than would be possible for Wales and Appalachia, even here the hegemony model may be at least partly applicable.

POLICY

The main effect of planning in both Wales and Appalachia has been to maintain hegemony and inequality. But if planning is important for stabilizing hegemony, it might, under some circumstances, be important in effecting a shift from hegemony to another type. Opposition groups might adopt the following policies in using planning to encourage a move away from hegemony.

First, opposition groups ought to consider, within the resources they have, moving from advocacy planning and research on a case-by-case basis to what I have described as opposition planning: a thoroughgoing region-scale program based on an opposition ideology. The purpose would be to combat and challenge the official agenda. In the United States this is made difficult partly by a prevailing pragmatism that rules out plans without an achievable end in view. But this gives away the agenda-setting function, as well as conceding the legitimacy of the overall regional planning machinery. Thus, local activists oppose development-minded regional elites point by point with no overarching challenge.

There is something to be said for pragmatism. Cloward and Piven recently argued that poor peoples' movements ought to avoid becoming organized because they achieved more in the way of tangible benefits by remaining unorganized and thus, more potentially disruptive.(18) The same logic might be turned against the idea of opposition planning. It is my belief, however, that any opposition, to succeed in the long run, must confront official planning in a fundamental way and connect specific with more general issues. This means going beyond issues to challenge agendas.

Second, opposition groups in hegemonic regions should adopt, as either a temporary or a permanent strategy, a goal of broadening the opposition, linking up the poor, the working class, and parts of the middle class in a territorially based coalition. Thus, workplace organizing can be consciously linked to community organizing, as happened in parts of the Appalachian coal fields.

Third, opposition groups might think of their objectives in terms of the typology of political systems outlined earlier. In this typology, it makes as much sense to move from hegemony to conflict situation, as to either hierarchy or polyarchy. The latter would involve the erasing of insider-outsider cultural distinctions, similar to the assimilation doctrine propounded by liberals. The principal objection to this is that it has seemed to operate mainly as an ideological cover for the perpetuation of interest group liberalism, where some groups participate in polyarchy, and others do not. From the point of view of the insider culture, a better objective would be to move toward the conflict situation. The development of opposition planning and territorial coalitions would be instrumental for such a move.

NOTES

(1) Piven and Cloward, Regulating the Poor, 1971; O'Connor, The Fiscal Crisis of the State, 1973; Spring, Education and the Rise of the Corporate State, 1972.

(2) For a general reference on this point, see Hechter, "The Persistence of Regionalism in the British Isles, 1885-1966," 1973. On the adaptation of regionalist doctrine to the market model, see Friedmann and Weaver, Territory and Function: The Evolution of Regional Planning Doctrine, 1978.

(3) For a recent review of this issue, see Hobsbawm, "Some Reflections on 'The Break-up of Britain,'" 1977; and Davis, Toward a Marxist Theory of Nationalism, 1978.

(4) In addition to Friedmann and Weaver, see Sundquist, Dispersing Population, 1975.

(5) The functionalist, diffusion perspective on modernization has no characterized social theory and policy in the West that it is difficult to cite one particular source. One early formulation was that of Smelser, Social Change in the Industrial Revolution, 1969. Tarrow cites Shils, "Centre and Periphery," in The Logic of Personal Knowledge: Essays Presented to Michael Polanyi, 1961. See Tarrow's review in his Between Center and Periphery, 1977.

(6) Hoselitz, "The Market Matrix," in Moore and Feldman, Labor Commitment and Social Change in Developing Areas, 1960.

(7) Deutsch, Nationalism and Social Communication, 1966.

(8) Williamson, "Regional Inequality and the Process of National Development: A Description of the Patterns," 1965.

(9) Walton, "The Vertical Axis of Community Organization and the Structure of Power," 1968.

(10) Friedmann and Weaver, Territory and Function, 1978.

(11) On U.S. multicounty regionalism see Sundquist and Davis, Making Federalism Work, 1969; on Britain see Mackintosh, The Devolution of Power, 1968.

(12) McConnell, "The Environmental Movement: Ambiguities and Meanings," Natural Resources Journal, 1971.

(13) Molotch, "The City as a Growth Machine: Toward a Political Economy of Place," 1976.

(14) Hechter, The Persistence of Regionalism, 1973.

(15) For a summary of various models of planning, see Friedmann, Retracking America, chapter 3, 1973.

(16) Rabinowitz, City Politics and Planning, 1969; Rondinelli, Urban and Regional Development Planning, 1975; Banfield, "Means and Ends in Planning," in Mailick and VanNess, Concepts and Issues in Administrative Behavior, 1962.

(17) Shonfield, Modern Capitalism (New York: Oxford University Press, 1965); Rondinelli, Urban and Regional Development Planning, 1975; Meyerson, "Building the Middle-Range Bridge for Comprehensive Planning," 1956.

(18) Piven and Cloward, Poor People's Movements, 1977.

11 A Socialist Housing Program for the United States*

Chester Hartman
Michael E. Stone

PUBLIC HOUSING: SOME ECONOMIC LESSONS AND IDEAS

The great exception to the commodity character of housing in the United States is public housing.

Following its initial creation as an employment program in the 1930s, public housing has actually served in the postwar years as an important device for regulating the poor, often in close conjunction with the welfare system. Large, isolated, and depressing projects, patronizing and authoritarian management practices, and the fear of eviction into the costly private housing market have made public housing an effective tool for social control. Moreover, the design and operation of public housing in many cities and the stigma attached to public housing socially and physically have been perpetuated quite deliberately to discredit the concept of publicly developed and owned housing. Nonetheless, there are now a great many examples of attractive, appealing, sensitively designed public housing – not huge, ugly projects that stand out from their surroundings, but apartment buildings indistinguishable from unsubsidized buildings, garden apartments, rehabilitated and recycled structures, scattered-site new and rebuilt developments, townhouses, and even single-family units.

Economically, what distinguishes public housing, first of all, is that it is not repeatedly resold and refinanced, with a succession of owners paying ever higher prices and doing so by borrowing larger sums at higher interest rates. The initial development costs are paid off once, and thereafter the only expenses are for operations and periodic modernization. That is, public housing is not a commodity.

*This article has been reprinted, with revisions, from The Federal Budget and Social Reconstruction, Marcus G. Raskin, ed. (Washington, D.C.: Institute for Policy Studies, 1979). We are grateful to Michael Tanzer for his helpful commentary on an earlier draft and to Barbara Philips for her editorial suggestions.

The second important economic feature of public housing is that the residents of the housing do not have to pay off the initial development costs and subsequent modernization costs as part of their rents. The maximum people have to pay is determined by the operating costs for their unit (utilities, maintenance, management, insurance), and where this amount exceeds their ability to pay, they are charged an even smaller amount.

On the other hand, public housing is still dependent on the private credit market for construction and modernization funds. Even though public housing is owned by local housing authorities and subsidized by the federal government (some states and New York City also have their own public housing programs), the money to build it in the first place is borrowed from private credit markets, just as it is for private housing. The money is raised by selling tax-exempt housing authority bonds to financial institutions and individual investors. Each year the government makes an "annual contribution" or subsidy payment to the housing authority to cover the cost of the principal and interest payments due. Thus the government pays for the development costs, but it does so with interest over a period of 40 years. Once the bonds are paid off, though, there are no more debt costs.

In short, despite its dependence on credit – and hence its vulnerability to the private credit market (1) – public housing offers a useful contrast to the dominant housing system in this country.

AN ALTERNATIVE SYSTEM

We are proposing that the economic concept underlying public housing be revitalized and expanded in order to steadily transform a growing portion of the housing stock from a commodity into a social good that people have the right to use and occupy pretty much as they wish for as long as they wish, but that cannot be owned, bought, or sold for a profit. We are also proposing that the dependence of housing on the credit market be steadily reduced by financing a growing proportion of new construction and housing rehabilitation through direct public grants. Together these two proposals would lead automatically to declining dependence on credit for transferring existing housing from one occupant to another. And they would cut roughly in half current housing expenditures required by individual consumers by eliminating debt service as an element in ongoing housing costs.

The basic elements of the program we are advancing are as follows:

1. A substantial and growing proportion of new and rehabilitated housing would be financed through direct construction grants to various local and regional public and private developers. All multifamily and a considerable proportion of single-family and townhouse units would be financed in this way. Private developers and individuals could continue to develop conventionally mortgaged units for occupancy in the private market as long as there were people with the inclination and the means to demand such housing.

2. All new and rehabilitated housing financed publicly would be mixed income, with a minimum proportion guaranteed for low and moderate income households and the rest open to households of any income.

3. Publicly financed housing would have no debt costs to be repaid by the residents or the government and could not be transferred to the private market.

4. Maximum shelter costs for residents of publicly financed housing would be determined by actual operating expenses, with operating subsidies provided for residents unable to afford full operating costs.

5. Existing private rental housing would be converted gradually to public or condominium ownership, with reasonable compensation over time for present owners. Outstanding mortgages would be paid off over their remaining terms. Prior to full conversion to public ownership, rents would be controlled and would be determined by actual operating expenses, mortgage payments, and fixed dollar profit levels. Subsidies would be provided for residents unable to afford full rents. Luxury surcharges would be levied on units with amenities above the standard for publicly financed new and rehabilitated units.

6. The private home ownership sector would continue, with mortgage payments and the right to resell. Owners facing foreclosure due to financial inability to keep up mortgage payments or seeking to lower their housing costs could convert to public ownership and give up their right to resell, in return for which they would be relieved of mortgage payments and compensated for their equity and have the right to remain in the house.

In short, we are proposing that a large-scale commitment be made to a public alternative to the private housing market. We believe, and will try to show, that this alternative will not only be of great benefit to low income people, but would also offer economic and social benefits for middle income people at least as great as present homeownership benefits.

We are proposing that the existing home ownership market continue so that people can be attracted rather than forced into a socialist alternative. Indeed, it would be politically unwise, socially undesirable, and economically unfeasible to propose the complete elimination of private housing outside of a massive revolutionary upheaval. The proposals we are offering do not in themselves require such an upheaval.

FINANCING HOUSING CONSTRUCTION

A growing proportion of new housing construction and old housing rehabilitation should be financed through direct government construction grants, just as the federal government now pays in whole or part for highway construction, dams, bridges, penitentiaries, pipelines, and military facilities. Housing development could be undertaken by private developers, local housing authorities, nonprofit housing development corporations, labor unions, community organizations, and perhaps even by individual families for their own use.

Individuals could still choose to have houses built on their own land by making arrangements through the local housing agency. If the design, site, etc., fell within the basic standards and limits set under the program, such units would merely be incorporated into a local housing agency's overall plan, and funds would be provided for construction. If such homes were above basic standards, funds would still be made available but a surcharge would be levied to cover the additional space or quality.

Funds would be allocated geographically according to housing and community development plans devised by local communities, metropolitan areas, states, and regions, taking into account the expected amount of private, conventionally financed development, and based upon long-range growth and development plans and the condition of the existing housing stock.

Under this scheme, agencies such as state housing finance agencies, which have been quite successful, sensitive, and efficient in a number of states, could play the same role they now do in accepting proposals, approving plans and costs, and disbursing funds as the work proceeds. The major change would be that agencies would obtain funds as grants from the federal government rather than through the sale of notes and bonds in the capital markets. The money paid out to developers would therefore not have to be repaid, there would be no construction financing costs, and no long-term mortgage would be needed to pay off construction loans. Upon completion of the housing, title would be conveyed to the local or state housing authority, as under the existing "turnkey" development program for public housing. The developer would continue to be involved only if it also had a contract to manage the housing.

Is a system of direct grants economically feasible and how much would it cost? The United States is wealthy enough to finance the construction of all new housing and rehabilitation of old housing through direct government spending rather than a debt system which mortgages the future. In mid-1977 private residential construction in the United States was at an annual rate of about $80 billion, which was only about four percent of GNP. It included about $65 billion for new construction and the remainder for additions and alterations to existing buildings. In dollar terms this is the highest level in history. This rate of spending represents an annual addition of about 2.0 million new units – well below the peak of 2.3 million units started in 1972, and well below the national goal of an average of 2.6 million per year, but still much higher than the 1.4 million unit annual average of the past four years.(2) It represents an average construction cost (excluding land) of about $33,000 per unit, including both single-family and multifamily buildings.

Assuming a somewhat higher proportion of multifamily construction and a somewhat lower proportion of luxury units, the rate of new construction could be increased by more than 50 percent and the rate of rehabilitation could be more than tripled. This would produce a total rate of private and public spending for housing construction of about $120 billion a year (in 1977 dollars), which would be about six percent of GNP.

While the figure for the present rate of construction spending does not include the cost of acquiring land for new construction, which would amount to an additional 15 percent or so, it does include the cost of interest and fees on construction loans, which presently amounts to about 10 percent of total development cost including land (see table 5.3, chap. 5 of this volume). Existing methods of construction and the fragmented character of the industry resulting from the unstable and unpredictable market add considerably to per unit costs as well. In addition, about 75 percent of new housing is now single-family units,(3) and many of these are luxury units costing $80,000 to $100,000 and more.

We propose that direct public grants for housing construction be instituted and increased year by year until total public and private spending reaches this target level. If public spending were to increase incrementally by about $10 billion a year (in 1977 dollars), the construction and materials industry could respond without having to cut back on private construction. On the other hand, some, but by no means all, of the effective demand for new private housing would be absorbed by the public sector, so some decline in private construction would occur. On this basis, the target level of $120 billion might be reached in about six to eight years, with public spending at about $60-80 billion and private at $40-60 billion (in 1977 dollars).

If population growth continues to slow and if considerably more effort were put into rehabilitating and maintaining existing housing than is done at present, the $120 billion figure would gradually decline, once the most serious shortages and substandard units were eliminated. And if the market for new private housing for owner occupancy steadily slacks off with the success of the public alternative, public spending would probably remain fairly constant or grow slowly as private construction spending falls. It should be noted that a public expenditure of $60 billion is only about half the military budget and less than half the amount of revenue lost by the Treasury through various tax loopholes.(4)

Under our proposed system, the residents of publicly financed housing would only have to pay for the operating expenses for their housing (assuming property taxes were also eliminated – see section below on operating subsidies). Without mortgage payments, occupancy costs for this housing would be only about half as much as for comparable conventionally financed housing.

AN ALTERNATIVE TO HOMEOWNERSHIP

The existing attractions of home ownership cannot be ignored. Everyone wants security against the threat of eviction. Tenants in this society have a permanent and inescapable anxiety about being so dislocated, even if they have adequate incomes. Homeowners have security against arbitrary eviction, but ironically, the very mortgage system that has enabled them to "buy" their home prevents their security from being absolute, for there is the danger of foreclosure – with the loss of investment as well as shelter. There is also the danger of tax foreclosure for unpaid property taxes, as well as the possibility of condemnation. With the elimination of mortgage payments and private ownership, we are proposing that all residents be guaranteed security of tenure that far exceeds that enjoyed even by homeowners under the existing system.

The relative freedom from control by others of one's personal living space should be not only retained but strengthened and applied to everyone, most notably to renters who now have no such protections and rights. All occupants of public housing should have the right of continued occupancy and control over their living space. They should not be required to move as long as they wish to remain (save those few situations where eminent domain takings are truly unavoidable and in the public interest).

How to deal with some of the traditional grounds for eviction – nonpayment, destruction of property, "antisocial" behavior – is not a question that can be answered easily. (Given the subsidy system outlined below, nonpayment cases would always be willful, not due to inability to meet payments.) One approach to the problem might be as follows: Given the assumption that people have to live someplace, no matter what their behavior, attempts to deal with antisocial behavior should be independent of eviction. Eviction would merely relocate such behavior and inflict it on other neighbors and properties, not eliminate it. (An exception would be poor relationships with specific neighbors not based on any pattern of such difficulties.) If, with housing payments set according to ability to pay, a household refuses to make its payments, then those managing the housing could take independent steps to recover these amounts through court action, possibly wage garnishment. If a tenant's behavior is injurious to property or legitimately offensive to neighbors, a step other than eviction – injunctive court action, damages, counseling, separating feuding neighbors, etc. – should be the attempted remedy.

Another highly valued and positive aspect of the current home ownership system is the freedom of occupants to modify the property, make repairs and renovations, use it in ways that personalize it, give it meaning, adapt it to their changing needs. Secure tenure for all would doubtless increase this kind of informal, voluntary property caretaking and improvement. At present, renters get little benefit from this kind of upkeep and space adaptation because they have no security of tenure and feel their own improvements may, ironically, produce a demand for higher rents. They are also deterred by the injustice of investing time and money on property that someone else is holding and operating for current and future profit. The personal-social benefits from secure tenure would have a complementary value in terms of property maintenance.

The new form of tenure proposed here would also eliminate some of the more conservative, negative impulses produced by the present ownership system. Concern about the protection of property values – either existing equity or an assumed potential for future value increases – is responsible for much of the exclusionary behavior homeowners currently exhibit against racial minorities, people with low incomes, "incompatible" building types and land uses. Absence of anxiety about protecting one's investment (anxiety that often is based on misperception or agitation by realtors and others) may produce less resistance to neighborhood change and socially beneficial construction programs. Reduction of the locked-in feeling that home ownership now tends to produce – again, out of concern for protecting one's investment or reluctance to incur heavy turnover costs such as closing fees – may produce a greater freedom to move in order to take advantage of employment opportunities or otherwise improve one's life.

But the strongest attractions of homeownership are economic – especially the possibility of accumulating some wealth through mortgage retirement and rising property values. Any viable alternative has to confront the strength of this appeal.

Homeownership appears to offer three economic advantages over renting under the existing housing system. First, for an identical house, a homeowner will have slightly lower monthly costs than a renter because there is no payment for the landlord's cash flow profit and overhead costs. Typically, the saving is less than five percent, since the bulk of the rent dollar goes for operating expenses, property taxes, and mortgage payments – expenses that the homeowner also has. Under our proposal, without ownership for profit and without mortgage payments (and with no property taxes either), shelter costs would be no greater than about 50 percent of what a new homebuyer now pays.

The second economic advantage of ownership is the income tax benefit of being able to deduct mortgage interest payments and property taxes from taxable income. The elimination of mortgage payments – and property taxes as well – would save residents far more than existing tax benefits. The supposed benefits are exaggerated anyway – at least for the majority of homeowners. Most taxpayers with incomes under $20,000 do not itemize their deductions, and those who do are in fairly low tax brackets where the deductions are not worth much. More than half the $10 billion in annual tax benefits flow to the 15 percent of taxpayers with incomes above $20,000.(5)

The third and most significant advantage is being able to build up an equity through homeownership. The initial equity is established by a downpayment which is then increased through mortgage principal payments and rising property values. This wealth is seen as a hedge against inflation, since residential property values have, on the average, risen faster than inflation. It is seen as a way of building up wealth either to acquire a bigger, more desirable house, or to be used for retirement by selling and then renting another unit, or to be passed on to one's heirs.

Under the present system the benefits are real, though overstated. First, when homeowners sell their homes and realize a gain from rising property values, they generally have to plunge right back into the housing market and spend the money for another house which has also gone up in price. If the money received from selling the old house is not spent on another house within a year, it is subject to a capital gains tax (except for people over 65). This tax provides a strong incentive not to keep the cash. Also, the new house generally is mortgaged, and at a higher interest rate (old mortgages frequently are at less than six percent, while new mortgages are generally 10-11 percent and higher).

As long as the choice is between rental in its present form and homeownership in its present form, there are real economic advantages to owning. But under a system where a home could be acquired with no downpayment and no mortgage payments, the money saved would more than compensate for the inability to sell and make a profit from a home. (And a more rational housing system would eliminate the unequal benefits the income tax system offers to homeowners as opposed to tenants.)

For example, suppose a family had bought a $40,000 house in 1975 with a $10,000 downpayment and a $30,000 mortgage for twenty-five years at nine percent interest. Monthly mortgage payments would be $252. Suppose the family decided to sell after 15 years. By this time they would have paid out a total of more than $55,000 – the $10,000 downpayment and $45,000 in mortgage payments – $55,000 that they would not have had to pay out under our proposal. They would still owe about $20,000 of their $30,000 mortgage. That is, of their $45,000 in mortgage payments, only $10,000 would have been applied to principal payments that built up their equity. The rest was paid in interest.

Let's suppose that property values continue to soar, so that by the time they sell in 1990, the house they bought for $40,000 is worth $80,000. They sell for $80,000, pay the $20,000 mortgage balance, plus brokerage and other closing costs of at least $5,000, and are left with no more than about $55,000 in cash. With their total outlay of $55,000, they have just broken even. They have recovered their initial downpayment, they have recovered the equity built up through mortgage payments, and their profit has just compensated them for all their interest costs.

By contrast, if this family had acquired the same house under our model – with no downpayment and no mortgage payments – and had put the $10,000, plus $252 a month into a savings account paying five percent interest compounded monthly, by 1990 they would find themselves with over $88,000 – they would have recovered their $55,000 outlay and have a profit of over $33,000. Even if they put that money into a safe deposit box and earned no interest, they would be in essentially the same position as the homeowner after fifteen years of payments and a doubling of property values.

We have made a series of calculations assuming that property values will, on average, increase at an even faster rate – nearly doubling in ten years. We have even allowed for the possibility that mortgage interest rates could go down to eight percent or even seven percent, thereby enhancing the benefits of the existing system still further. Even in these cases it turns out that over a period of 10, 15, 20, or 25 years, a person would do at least as well, and in many cases better, if he or she had the option of putting the same funds into an ordinary savings account (see table 11.1).

We are proposing that people be given this option. The existing homeownership market would still be available for those who were interested in gambling and could afford to gamble. In some locations property values may go up more than an average rate of seven percent per year for the next 10-25 years, in which case the gamblers would do very well. Those who do not wish to take the chance could choose to cut their housing costs by about half and eliminate the need to invest their personal savings in a downpayment. Our system makes available an option that would, on the average, yield at least the same financial benefits as homeownership but with less risk and greater liquidity for a household's investment – since a savings account is safe and easily converted to cash. We think our alternative would be increasingly attractive, but we would not force people to take it.

Of course, under our alternative people might not choose to save the money. They might spend it. And obviously people who could not afford the conventional option would not even have as much money to invest. But this does not alter the economic argument. If for some reason policy makers decide that it would be desirable for people to invest the money saved by eliminating mortgage payments, all that would be necessary would be to defer income taxes on money thus set aside – much as is done now for individual retirement accounts.

THE EXISTING HOMEOWNERSHIP MARKET

As we have indicated, a considerable fraction of new housing would continue to be developed and financed conventionally for individual owner occupancy. There would be single-family homes, townhouses, and even condominiums in multiunit buildings. In addition to newly developed private units for occupancy, most of the existing owner-occupied units would remain in the private sector for some time to come. In both the new and existing units the owners would continue to have mortgage payments and would be free to sell in the private market.

It might be concluded that with a growing proportion of public housing and an economically attractive alternative to homeownership, the private homeownership market would collapse and owners would have their equity wiped out. This is very unlikely for a number of reasons. First, even though public housing would be physically desirable and cheap and would offer residents a high degree of control and secure tenure, the appeal of conventional ownership will not fade quickly. Second, relatively high income people will undoubtedly continue to desire fancier and more individually tailored homes than would be produced publicly. Third, while publicly financed housing would be mixed-income and thus quite unlike conventional public housing and

Table 11.1. Comparison of Economic Benefits: Mortgaged Homeowners versus Public Tenant-Saver (a)

Sales Price

	After 10 years	After 15 years	After 20 years	After 25 years
Sales Price of $40,000 Home, @ 7% annual value increase,(b) compounded	$78,700	$110,400	$154,800	$217,100
Sales Price net of 7% Closing Costs	73,200	102,600	144,000	201,900

Net Gain (c)

Mortgage Interest Rate	Form of Tenure	After 10 years	After 15 years	After 20 years	After 25 years
7%	homeowner	$14,200	$36,200	$72,400	$128,300
	tenant-saver	15,700	33,700	61,400	101,900
8%	homeowner	11,200	31,900	67,000	122,400
	tenant-saver	16,600	35,600	65,300	108,600
9%	homeowner	8,200	27,500	61,700	116,400
	tenant-saver	17,300	37,600	69,200	115,500

(a) Homeowner: $40,000 home, acquired with $10,000 downpayment and $30,000 mortgage with 25 year term. Tenant-saver: initial deposit of $10,000 plus monthly deposit exactly equal to homeowner's mortgage payment into a savings account which pays 5-1/2% annum, compounded monthly.

(b) Over the past few years residential property values have, on average, increased at a rate about 2-3% above the rate of inflation. Assuming that consumer income will be unable to support continuation of such house price inflation, or that the overall inflation rate will average no more than about 5-6% over the next 10-25 years, a 7% per year value increase is a generous assumption. If the present higher rates of inflation are assumed to persist and value increases of 10-12% per year are assumed, the tenant-saver could deposit the money into a money-market fund paying 9-10% per year, thereby remaining competitive.

(c) Before-tax gain, equal to total return minus total outlay over the entire period of the investment. Assumes favorable income tax benefits for home owners that might be eliminated under a more rational housing system.

subsidized housing, most of it would be occupied by households with incomes under $20,000, most of whom are already closed out of the private mortgaged homeownership market.

Existing homeowners with inadequate incomes to support the full costs of occupying their present homes would require special attention. In cases where homeowners face mortgage foreclosure because of their economic inability to continue to afford mortgage payments, they would have the option of having their home converted to public ownership and being relieved of further mortgage payments. The residents could remain in their homes, but they would no longer have the right to sell in the private market. The government would assume the mortgage debt and make monthly payments to the lending institution until the debt was paid off.

This bail-out scheme is obviously far superior to the existing foreclosure situation where the homeowner is forced to move and also generally loses most or all the equity in the property. An even more generous program would not only relieve the residents of mortgage payments and permit them to stay in their homes but would also compensate them for their equity. They might simply be compensated for their original downpayment or for the downpayment plus accumulated principal payments. But certainly there would be no justification for giving them any of the speculative increase in value or any other return on the equity. Persons needing or wishing to turn their homes over to public sector ownership in exchange for relief from mortgage payments would also be eligible for the universal operating subsidies outlined below if their incomes fell below the point where they could afford ongoing operating costs.

How much would such a program for low income homeowners cost? In 1977, total mortgage payments for owner-occupants of single-family units amounted to about $34 billion.(6) With the majority of low income homeowners being long-term owners with no outstanding mortgages, only about 20 percent of mortgage owner-occupied units belong to households with incomes of less than $10,000 a year.(7) Since these homes tend to be older and smaller with less debt, these low income owners probably pay less than 10 percent of the $34 billion in mortgage payments. If the government had to assume this entire burden, the cost would be just $3.4 billion a year. If the owners were also compensated over time for some of their equity, the total cost might be twice as great. As the debt was paid off and most of the housing owned by low income people came into the public sector, the cost would steadily drop off.

Some low income homeowners live in substandard housing, which would be acquired and rehabilitated under the direct grant program. Part of the cost estimated here would thus be covered under the direct grant program instead of being an additional public expense.

Finally, even though the private homeownership market supported by the system of mortgage credit would continue to be significant and substantial for a long time, the other changes in the housing system would reduce the bloated mortgage system and relieve some of the pressure on the debt system. As a large proportion of private rental housing is converted to public ownership and its mortgage debt retired, no new debt would ever be incurred on these units. As a growing proportion of new housing is financed by direct grants, no new mortgage debt would be created for a large proportion of new housing. And, of course, as some existing owner-occupied units come into the public sector, their mortgage debt would eventually be retired once and for all.

ELIMINATING PRIVATE RENTAL HOUSING

The development of publicly financed and owned housing that is physically attractive, mixed-income, and free of the burden of mortgage payments and landlord profits would, of course, steadily undermine the private rental market. Unlike private homeownership, which could continue to be economically attractive to many people, private rental housing would offer little incentive to residents except perhaps for luxury buildings with a level of amenities far above the public standard. Although the stock of appealing and available public housing would increase only gradually, and many people would continue to occupy existing rental housing, tenants in such housing would probably face two kinds of problems if private ownership persisted. First, as property values were eroded by public competition, landlords would try to extract their return by cutting back on maintenance and services and in some cases might even burn down the buildings for the insurance money. Second, the rents would generally be higher than for public units, since even with operating subsidies the rents would still have to pay the landlord's mortgage payments and profit.

On the other hand, there would be no practical way of fully buying out all the rental property at its current market value. In 1975, the total value of all private rental residential real estate – including the value of owner-occupied multifamily buildings – was about $680 billion. About $250 billion of the total was represented by outstanding mortgages, and the balance was the market value of the owners' equity.(8) The total sum is about twice the entire federal budget and more than 40 percent of the GNP in 1975. Even if the compensation were stretched out over an extended period of several decades, reliance on the existing tax system to raise the funds would only make the rich richer, as about 85 percent of investment real estate is owned by the wealthiest 20 percent of the population.(9)

In order to reduce the net public costs and avoid a complete bail-out of private landlords, while avoiding "milking" of the rental housing stock by landlords, we are proposing a strategy with several elements. First, in all rental buildings that are in good physical condition (well maintained and free of code violations), residents would be given the option of buying their units as condominiums. The value of the entire property and each unit would be determined by independent appraisals, and the owner would be entitled to receive part but not all of the value of the equity in the property at the time of sale. The balance of the equity would belong to the resident, serving to reduce the purchase price and providing an incentive to buy.

The equity could be divided in a fair manner as follows: during the time the resident rented the unit, part of the rent went toward mortgage principal payments. The resident's share of the equity should be equal to that unit's share of mortgage principal payments accumulated during tenancy plus the increase in value during the term of tenancy. The landlord would get the original downpayment, plus accumulated principal payments made prior to the present tenant's residency.

For example, in a unit now worth $25,000 with a mortgage balance of $10,000, the total equity would be worth $15,000. If the resident had paid $2,000 of the mortgage principal and the property rose $6,000 in value during the term of the tenancy, the resident's share of the equity would be $8,000, leaving the owner with $7,000. That is, the resident could buy the unit at an $8,000 discount for $17,000; the resident could raise the $17,000 through a combination of savings and mortgage loans. The landlord would get $7,000 in cash and the other $10,000 would pay off the balance of the old mortgage.

The attractions of condominium ownership are of course similar to conventional homeownership, although the units are in multifamily structures and are generally somewhat cheaper than single-family homes. Nonetheless, some residents probably would not want to buy and others could not afford to buy. Once a building was slated to undergo conversion, those who chose not to stay could seek housing elsewhere, and those too poor to afford it would have their units converted to public ownership. The landlord would not receive any greater or lesser compensation for units the residents leave, lest there be an incentive to pressure existing residents. However, the departing residents might not receive the full amount of their share of the equity, since it might be desirable to have an incentive to stay and an incentive for someone else to buy if they depart. That is, a new buyer might be given a discount of, say, half the gain in value or half the resident's equity, with the departing resident receiving the rest of the sales price.

Units converted to condominiums would be like any other owner-occupied housing. Residents could sell in the private market. If they became financially unable or unwilling to continue mortgage payments, they could convert to public ownership with relief from mortgage payments but would no longer have any right to resell in the private market.

We suspect that a large fraction of the residents of physically sound rental housing would make the choice for conversion to condominium ownership in this way. First of all, for some time to come the amount of alternative public housing would be limited, especially for people with the means to remain in the private market. Second, many people would like to stay in their present units. Third, some people would be attracted by the discount, especially where they have been in the building for a long time so that their share of the equity would be substantial. Most luxury rental buildings would probably be converted easily since living conditions would be maintained and residents could afford and benefit from conversion. A substantial proportion of rental units in owner-occupied multifamily buildings might also be converted, since the units would usually be relatively inexpensive compared with single-family homes. Tenants in such buildings are frequently long-term residents, and present owners would receive financial compensation and be eligible in many cases for operating subsidies. Indeed, in some cases low income owners might even convert to public ownership rather than continue to own their own units if they were unable or unwilling to continue mortgage payments. In any event, the existing owner-occupants could remain in their units and would be able to receive operating subsidies if eligible (see next section). The loss of rental income would thus impose no hardship on former owner-occupant landlords who have depended on the rent to make ends meet.

Before considering the problem of rental units that residents might be unable or unwilling to convert to condominium ownership, let us look at the problem of substandard rental housing. Over six million households still live in physically inadequate units, and roughly half this group are tenants. For the most part, the residents have relatively low incomes and thus cannot afford to acquire and rehabilitate the units as private homes or condominiums. Therefore such housing should be acquired and rehabilitated for public ownership under the direct construction grant program. While the units in the worst condition might be acquired quite cheaply (in some cases just for back property taxes the landlord has not paid), these units would need the most work. The average per unit acquisition and rehabilitation cost would probably be about $25,000-$30,000. The total cost for three million rental units at $30,000 each would be $90 billion, and the inclusion of substandard owner-occupied units would double the cost. Under a direct grant program that began with $10 billion in the first year and increased by $10 billion a year up to $60-80 billion, it would take about a decade to acquire and rehabilitate all the substandard units if about one-third of the grants were earmarked for this purpose.

These roughly three million substandard rental units represent about 10 percent of the total stock of rental housing. In addition, perhaps about half the total rental stock might be converted to condominiums. Thus the rest of the rental stock – almost half of all rental units – would have to be dealt with in a different manner to ensure the residents of adequate maintenance, reasonable rents and eviction protection. We propose that this housing be converted to public ownership, with gradual repayment of the outstanding mortgages and compensation to owners over the same period of time as the outstanding mortgages. Landlords would be issued bonds for the amount of equity they would be entitled to receive. This equity would be computed on the same basis as for condominium conversions, leaving landlords in essentially the same financial position regardless of which option their ex-tenants take.

Although the bonds and interest on them would come out of rent, they would be fully guaranteed by the government, so the interest rate need be no higher than the prevailing interest rate on long-term treasury bonds, presently around eight percent.

During the transition period the units would be publicly owned, but the total rental income would be equal to the sum of operating expenses, mortgage payments, and interest on the former landlords' bonds. Tax shelters for rental property would no longer exist;(10) the former landlords would simply report their interest income as ordinary income for tax purposes. Mortgage payments and bond interest would be paid out of rents until all the mortgages had been paid off. At this point the government would give the former landlords (or whoever else held the bonds, since they could be sold privately, just as other bonds are traded) the principal amount of the bonds. There would then be no more mortgage payments or ownership profits.

All mortgages would be paid off over the next 40 years (most would be paid off sooner, but new privately owned subsidized developments have 40-year mortgages), so the compensation to landlords would be stretched out over this period. Assuming that about half the rental stock would come under such a program, the market value of the equity is currently about $200 billion.(11) But as the market value includes both accumulated principal payments and speculative increases in value since the present tenants moved in, neither of which is part of the equity the landlords would receive, the total sum to be paid would probably be no more than about $100-120 billion. Over 40 years this would represent an average of less than $3 billion a year.

Although mortgage payments and some level of landlord profits would continue for a while as the transition proceeded, tenants would not necessarily have to pay the full rents needed to support these costs. Tenants' payments should be computed on the basis of ability to pay, using the same formula as for the universal operating subsidy (see next section). Unlike the alternative public housing sector we are proposing, tenants with sufficiently high incomes to pay operating expenses would pay more, up to the full rent of their unit. Eligible tenants would be included under the universal subsidy for operating expenses, and in addition there would be a special subsidy of the extra expenses of such housing until the mortgages and landlords were paid off. The special subsidy would be similar to the mortgage subsidies in existing Section 236 housing, but based upon the more rational standard of how much of the rent the tenant could afford to pay. The initial cost to tenants and the government of mortgage payments and landlord profits would be about $22 billion a year. The landlords' eight percent on $100-$120 billion would be $8-10 billion, mortgage payments on $125 billion (half the total debt on rental housing) at an average interest rate of eight percent for an average term of twenty years would be $12.5 billion. Assuming the special subsidy program would pay about half this cost, the public would have to lay out about $11 billion the first year and decreasing sums thereafter.

Under the type of program we have described, landlord control of private rental housing would effectively cease as soon as the program begins. Landlords would essentially become bondholders assured of a steady income and eventual return of their share of the equity, but with no opportunity for speculative profits through selling the property and with no hold over tenants. Of course their bondholder interest might become marketable, but this would have no effect on tenants and the government, as cash outlays would remain unchanged regardless of who owned the bonds.

The period just prior to implementation of such a program would be a very dangerous time, though, unless there is a provision making the effective date for determining the ownership and financial status sometime earlier. The rental housing market will not be converted without a fight; a careful and well-developed strategy will be necessary to avoid undue social and economic costs.

UNIVERSAL OPERATING SUBSIDIES

We are proposing that the federal government provide subsidies to all residents of public and private housing who are unable to afford the operating expenses – maintenance and repairs, utilities, insurance, and management – for their dwellings. These subsidies would not pay for mortgage payments, since mortgage payments would exist only for private, owner-occupied units, and since low income owners unable to afford mortgage payments could convert to public ownership with relief from such payments.

Operating subsidies would not pay for the cost of capital improvements and renovations. For publicly owned housing, such costs would be covered directly out of the construction grant program. For private units, such costs represent protection or enhancement of the investment, and should be financed by the owner out of personal savings, a home improvement loan, or a refinanced mortgage. Again, though, an owner who had incurred such debts but no longer had the ability or willingness to pay might be permitted to convert to public ownership and be relieved of the debt and also relinquish the right to sell. Some controls would have to be imposed on the extent and kinds of improvements the public would assume in such cases, lest some owners transform their homes into palaces at great expense and then sell out to the public while continuing to live in splendor.

The operating subsidies we are proposing would not subsidize property taxes, either. We assume that the housing program we envision could only become a reality within a context of progressive tax reform, which would provide substantial relief from or replacement of the property tax – as well as generating revenues to finance direct housing construction grants, a universal operating subsidy, and the transfer of a considerable fraction of existing privately owned housing to the public sector.

The amount of operating subsidy a household would be entitled to receive would be equal to the difference between the operating expenses for their unit and the amount they could afford. There would have to be some standard for determining reasonable operating expenses based upon the size of the unit, the age and type of construction of the building, the type of heating system, and the region of the country. A great deal of information of this sort is already collected regularly for private multifamily housing by the industry trade association, and for subsidized multifamily housing by state and federal regulatory agencies. The HUD-Census Bureau Annual Housing Survey is also beginning to obtain such data for single-family, owner-occupied housing.

The standard of affordability should not be the conventional 25 percent of income, but instead should reflect the amount of resources a household would have left after meeting its nonshelter needs at some minimum adequate level. That is, a standard such as that suggested by Michael Stone (see chap. 5) should be developed, based upon the Bureau of Labor Statistics' lower standard budget. The BLS budgets make it possible to derive such a standard each year for various parts of the country, for various size households, and for households of various compositions.

We have developed an estimate of the cost of such a universal operating subsidy based upon national averages for 1975, the most recent year for which operating cost and household income data are available. Average operating costs per room per month were about $25 in 1975.(12) The modal number of rooms occupied by households of various sizes and tenure in 1975, obtained from the Annual Housing Survey, was then used to determine average monthly operating costs for households of various sizes and tenures. Affordability standards similar to those in table 5.1, chapter 5, for households of various sizes and incomes were then used to compute the average operating subsidy for households of various incomes, sizes, and tenure. The average subsidy for each type of household was then multiplied by the number of households of that type given in the Annual Housing Survey for 1975.

PROGRAM COST SUMMARY

The initial cost of the program we are proposing would be about $58 billion a year. After about a decade the cost would have increased to about $100 billion a year (in 1977 dollars), after which the cost would slowly decline as the transfer to public ownership was completed and the rate of new construction and rehabilitation diminished. The $58 billion cost is only about three percent of the GNP and less than half the present military budget. The program is thus entirely feasible economically, although it certainly would not be feasible under present policies which maintain economic stagnation, increase military spending, and seek to balance the federal budget through constricted social spending. Nor would it be feasible without serious progress toward a more equitable tax system, including replacement of the property tax with more progressive broad-based taxes or state and federal takeover of municipal costs.

The initial $58 billion cost would include about $10 billion to start the program of direct construction grants for new and rehabilitated housing. At an average cost of $40,000 per unit this program would provide about 250,000 new and rehabilitated units, and generate about 500,000 direct and indirect jobs. Another $30 billion would be for the universal operating subsidy program, although it would certainly take several years to make it operational, so the initial rate of spending would be lower. About $3 billion would be for buying out low income homeowners unable to keep up mortgage payments; some additional cost would be incurred for buying out other homeowners who choose to leave the private market. About $14 billion would be for the special subsidies and equity compensation for private rental housing not converted to condominiums or bought under the direct grant rehabilitation program. Another $1 billion might be needed for administration.

Over the years we would expect the direct construction grant program to expand steadily to about $60-80 billion, the universal operating subsidy to remain at about $30 billion, and the buy-out costs to steadily decline. The total cost would thus never go much above six percent of GNP. Some offset to these costs would be provided by eliminating present homeowner income tax benefits, which, as noted above, go largely to upper income housing consumers and cause a loss to the Treasury of approximately $10 billion a year in foregone tax revenues.

On this basis, we have estimated that a universal operating subsidy would cost about $24 billion in 1975 – $14.8 billion for homeowners and $8.8 billion for tenants. About 20 million households would have been eligible for such subsidies in 1975: 11.2 million homeowner households and 8.8 million renter households. By 1977, the number of eligible households would probably have increased about five percent, based on trends from 1973 to 1975. The cost in 1977 would be about 20 percent higher, based upon the increased number of eligible households and a 15 percent increase in operating costs. That is, in 1977 dollars the cost of such a program would be close to $30 billion.

To get some perspective on the cost of such a program, in 1973, just before enactment of the Section 8 Housing Assistance Program, the Department of Housing and Urban Development estimated that if all eligible renters were served, the program would cost $8-11 billion per year.(13) If the Section 8 program were to include owners as well as renters, the annual cost in 1973 dollars would have been at least $20-24 billion. Our proposal clearly differs from the Section 8 program in that it would include homeowners, it uses a more realistic standard for how much a household can afford, and it would not subsidize mortgage payments, landlords' profits, and property taxes. Thus, while our proposal would cost about the same amount, the benefits would flow to the residents and the housing stock, not to the landlords and lenders.

As a final point regarding the cost of our proposal, it should be noted that nearly a quarter of the entire $24 billion cost in 1975 would be for one-person and two-person homeowner households with incomes under $6,000. Such persons typically live in homes with at least five rooms and are thus grossly overhoused, resulting in inefficient use of subsidy money. If such households could be encouraged, but not forced, to move into smaller units, the subsidy cost of these homes might be substantially reduced.

MANAGEMENT AND MAINTENANCE OF THE PUBLIC HOUSING STOCK

Ongoing operation of the publicly owned housing stock would be under the overall supervision of local housing authorities. Multifamily housing might be managed by neighborhood organizations, by user associations, or by the authority itself. Judicious, creative use should be made of the talents and experience of private building managers who presently carry out such tasks on a fee basis. Many such managers are extremely competent in a field where experience and know-how matter a great deal. They could be employed to carry out necessary management functions, such as collection of housing payments and arranging for repairs. Owner-occupants of multifamily buildings should be retained to carry out the management function wherever they are willing to do so and have demonstrated past ability. With respect to single-family homes, the same type of management arrangements are possible. Or the occupants might choose to be responsible for making repairs themselves (except for major items), in the tradition of homeowners and do-it-yourselfers, in exchange for a reduction in housing payments.

Maintenance and routine repairs would be covered via allocation of a portion of housing payments. Disincentives to use such services unnecessarily could be built in by imposing a small charge for each repair visit. Extraordinary repairs and improvements requiring capital expenditures would be made through capital grants from the local housing authority. Capital would also be made available for discretionary improvements and additions. The occupants would pay the costs of providing this capital as a surcharge on their housing payments, in the same way that households could build new housing to their own, higher standards.

Movement from one home to another might be somewhat easier under our proposed alternative system. Elimination of housing ownership obviates the need to sell one's home upon moving, with the expenditure of time and wasteful transfer costs (broker's fees, mortgage origination fees, title search and transfer fees, etc.) this entails. Persons planning to move out of public-sector housing would notify the local housing authority that their unit was becoming available; vacant units in the public sector would be located via centralized housing authority files. Persons wishing to move to another area would contact the relevant local housing authority. Moves within the private sector would be handled as they are now, via real estate offices, newspapers and other public listings.

OTHER ELEMENTS

We have not attempted to address every aspect of the housing problem in the United States. Given our analytical and political perspective, along with practical space limitations, it has seemed most appropriate to focus upon the need to replace the mortgage credit system of housing finance and the commodity character of housing, as these are surely the most important institutional bases of the housing problem. Nevertheless, we do recognize the significance of other factors. For example, although we have not provided any analysis of the impact of property tax on the housing problem, we have implicitly acknowledged its relevance when we propose that it be eliminated as a housing cost and be made part of a reformed tax system.

Complete replacement of the property tax would have required about $50 billion in revenue from other sources in 1975.(14) Although a substantial part of this sum is generated by nonresidential property, most is from housing. Thus a housing program that would entirely eliminate the property tax as a housing cost would add $30-$40 billion to the price tag of the program.

Finally, our proposals do not address many of the elements that contribute to the high cost of producing housing. The demise of debt financing for a large fraction of new housing production would wipe out the cost of construction financing, which amounts to about 10 percent of the cost of a new house. We have said nothing, though, about land costs and the so-called hard costs – labor and materials. Although publicly owned housing will gradually remove some land from the private market, land for new housing will still have to be acquired in this market. Obviously work needs to be done on developing an overall land reform program, which would go far beyond housing and would confront both the existing land tenure system and the fragmented and parochial land-use control system.

As for housing construction costs and techniques, restrictive labor practices and small, labor-intensive firms represent a rational response to the unstable, unpredictable, and inadequate supply of funds for housing construction. By providing a high and stable flow of funds, our financing proposal would assure construction workers of much more secure employment and would make production economies much more feasible. Within such a framework, we certainly would advocate that unions and construction worker cooperatives directly undertake housing development without being hired by entrepreneurs. But any transitional program should also recognize and utilize the practical skills and expertise possessed by many existing private homebuilders. Such involvement should of course occur within a framework of careful but flexible public supervision, which should provide carrots as well as sticks to ensure high quality construction.

Housing is an extremely complex element of our economy and society, and many necessary and desirable changes in the existing system can be envisioned. Yet it is important strategically to identify and focus upon the most decisive flaws and weaknesses. The time has come to move beyond proposals for mere tinkering with an unworkable system; and the time has come to move beyond the limits of local and defensive housing struggles to advance a vision and a strategy for reconstructing American housing as we reconstruct American society.

SOME POLITICAL CAVEATS

In this paper we have tried to show that it would be economically feasible to develop a socialist housing program that would compete with and steadily replace the private housing and mortgage markets. It is important to recognize, though, that the political barriers to successfully realizing this program would be more than just the obvious resistance from landlords and lenders immediately threatened and from general business interests fearing "creeping socialism."

First of all, achievement of such a program would require a broad-based and powerful political force, which undoubtedly would not want to limit itself to housing when there are other fundamental and pressing issues, such as jobs, food, and health. Furthermore, even though the housing program would not necessarily require basic changes in these other areas, it would require substantial tax reform to replace the property tax and generate the needed revenues in a progressive way. Large-scale tax reform would not just threaten housing capitalists; to the extent that it is achieved there will be many claims on the additional revenues.

Second, achievement of this program would not only require a strong political movement, but would also further undermine the existing economic system. Substantial tax reform and massive housing subsidies that did not flow back to wealthy institutions and individuals would probably lead to lower profits, flight of capital, and reduced investment generally. Public spending for housing would not fully compensate for this tendency, and thus the broader issues of public enterprise, economic planning, and control of the economy inevitably would have to be confronted.

Third, a program that would provide people with secure tenure, no mortgage debt, and decent housing at a cost based on their real ability to pay would substantially reduce the anxiety caused by low wages and job insecurity in the labor market. That is, workers' bargaining power would be increased, and greater militancy undoubtedly would follow. The success of the housing program would thus tend to undermine the social control wielded through the labor market. Business certainly would not be happy about such a prospect.

Finally, there are dangers associated with the possibility of actually implementing the program. Although the political barriers to its realization are substantial, the present situation also poses considerable problems for the capitalist system. Declining home ownership opportunities may lead to social unrest, and the unstable debt structure may lead to financial collapse. It is thus conceivable that some elements of the program we have suggested might be picked up and adapted to help rationalize the system, ease some social pressures, prop up the construction industry, bail out mortgage lenders and stave off financial collapse.

Any demands for reform that do not occur as part of a total transformation of the society always have this contradictory quality. There is always the possibility of cooptation. There is also the possibility of bureaucratic inefficiency, corruption, and mediocrity. This does not mean the demands should not be made; it does mean that such reforms should not be seen as an end in themselves, but rather as part of a clear and conscious political strategy. That is, the type of program we are suggesting should not merely be injected into high-level policy debates among a small number of people; it should be part of a political program, a part of the process of broad-based organizing. Then struggles to enact such a program and to control it will be successful – even if the program is distorted or only partially achieved. It will be successful in the sense that it will help to build political organization and consciousness, without illusions about the possibilities of reform and the need for an ongoing struggle for more fundamental change.

NOTES

(1) See Stone and Achtenberg, Hostage! Housing and the Massachusetts Fiscal Crisis, 1977, for a description of how financial institutions used their control over the state's public housing debt to force the state to cut back social services and raise taxes.

(2) U.S. Bureau of the Census, "September 1977 Construction at $173.7 Billion Annual Rate," 1977, "Housing Starts and Building Permits in September 1977," 1977, The Ninth Annual Report on the National Housing Goal, U.S. House Document 95-53, 1977, p. 11.

(3) U.S. Bureau of the Census, "Housing Starts," 1977.

(4) Special Analyses: Budget of the United States Government, Fiscal Year 1978, 1977, Part 1.F.

(5) Data on tax returns are published in U.S. Internal Revenue Service, Statistics of Income, annual. Data on total tax benefits are from Special Analyses, loc. cit. Distribution of benefits by income class is from "Mondale Says 'Tax Expenditures' Benefit Wealthy Most." Study prepared by the Treasury Department for Senator Walter Mondale, May 1975.

(6) Of the $656 billion in residential mortgage debt outstanding at the end of 1976, $554 billion was on 1-4 family homes; Savings and Loan Fact Book, 1977, p. 26. About two-thirds of all the units in 1-4 family

homes are in single-family owner-occupied homes. Assuming a proportional allocation of the mortgage debt, the debt on such owner-occupied homes would be $365 billion. Since single-family homes tend to have higher value per unit and higher debt per unit than 2-4 unit homes, we have raised the estimate to $400 billion. Assuming an average interest rate of seven percent and term of 25 years, mortgage payments come to about $34 billion for the year.

(7) Annual Housing Survey: 1975, Current Housing Reports, 1977.

(8) The most recent figures on the value of residential real estate are for 1974; Statistical Abstract, 1976, p. 736. These figures were first extrapolated to 1975, based on the amount of residential construction in 1975 and the rate of increase in value in previous years. The total value of units in 1-4 unit buildings was $1,550 billion and in five-or-more unit buildings $250 billion. Based on the number of units in 1-4 unit buildings in 1975, the per-unit value was determined to be about $25,000. Multiplied by the number of units in 1-4 unit buildings exclusive of single-family, owner-occupied homes, the value was $430 billion. This figure was then added to the $250 billion in five-or-more unit buildings, yielding $680 billion. The $250 billion mortgage figure follows note 6 about $650 billion in total debt minus about $400 billion for single-family, owner-occupied homes.

(9) Upton and Lyons, Basic Facts, n.d.

(10) Tax shelters for rental housing have provided an incentive for private investment in rental housing, an incentive which certainly would no longer be needed under our proposal. Also the benefits are highly regressive. More than two-thirds of the benefits flowed to less than 15 percent of the population with adjusted gross incomes of $20,000 or more in 1974; "Mondale Says."

(11) In note 8, the total market value was estimated at $680 billion for all rental real estate. Subtracting the mortgage debt of about $250 billion leaves a total equity of about $430 billion. Assuming that luxury units are worth more than the average and that they would be converted to condominiums, the half of the rental housing stock in question would have a total equity worth less than half of $430 billion. Hence the estimate of $200 billion.

(12) Institute of Real Estate Management, Income/Expense Analysis, 1975 edition, p. 7.

(13) Department of Housing and Urban Development – Independent Agencies Appropriations for 1976, 1975, p. 70.

(14) U.S. Bureau of the Census, "Property Subject to Local Taxation," Census Bureau Reports, 1976.

III

Opportunities for Planners

Introduction

Faced with budget cutbacks, what roles can planners play in the struggle to meet social needs? Can planners do anything but serve to justify such cutbacks and streamline programs forced to do more with even less? To understand what planners may and may not be able to do, we need to study the organizations in which they work, the processes by which their work has effects, the political possibilities apparently open or forbidden to them, and finally, the implications of such analysis for the training and education of planners. In the papers that follow in this last section, the authors confront these same questions from different angles and with different approaches.

Friedman, Kossy, and Regan provide an insider's view of the U.S. Department of Housing and Urban Development. Beginning with an analysis of the role of the State in a capitalist political economy, they go on to examine a range of HUD programs as they provide the specific contexts for progressive planning. Using a structural analysis, they point to a number of possible roles for progressive planners: educative and organizing roles, in which the management of and access to information is crucial, as is the attention to coalitions with other progressive professionals and class-based or local community organizations. Thus they develop threads of arguments treated in the papers by Markusen, Clavel, and Burton and Murphy above as they point to the connections between planning insiders and regional movements or community-based progressive organizations. Making it clear through a concrete analysis of HUD programs that the State is anything but monolithic, they lead quite naturally to more specific questions about our understanding of the political organizational contexts and the roles of planners in public agencies.

Baum's paper addresses these questions, not by examining programs, but rather through extensive interviews, by examining the degree to which planners at the present time are sensitive to the political and organizational processes shaping the very agencies in which they work.

As Friedman, Kossy and Regan are concerned with the possibility of planners' supporting and strengthening progressive community and working class coalitions, Baum investigates the ways in which the present consciousness and attitudes of planners seem to prevent or obstruct the possibilities of achieving a more truly democratic planning process, one less dominated by private interests or the structure of the State itself. By exposing the demoralization of planners who soon discover how little power they have, Baum not only calls attention to the ways planning staff come to "make do" with their frustration and powerlessness but he also focuses on a major strategic issue for planners. He stresses that until planners recognize how the political and organizational environments context of their work influences their results, they will be doomed to being ineffective. Thus, through an analysis of the sources of the present blind spots and frustrations of planners, Baum shows what types of knowledge and analysis are necessary if planners are to do more than live with powerlessness. He points to a number of practical strategies and areas of needed competence and training, including interpersonal and organizing skills, sensitivity to informal as well as formal channels of agency influence, and experience in the face of adversarial power.

Anticipating the discussion of Bergman and Sarbib, Baum suggests the implications for planning education of the politically crucial "sensitizing planners to organizations" which he has analyzed. Reading his interview data leads one to share the practical frustrations of the planners with whom he talked. It becomes clear that the present conditions of planning agencies are experienced almost as a betrayal in practice of any democratic vision initially held by planning staff. Under the present conditions of planning education and the lack of planners' own political organizing, planners' sensitivity to organizational and political forces shaping their own influence will most likely remain low, and agency staff will remain "planners who can't plan." Thus, while Friedman et al. assess the structural context of planning and point to progressive roles, Baum focuses more concretely on the politics of planning organizations and the planning staff's own peculiar insensitivities to the politics of planning.

Beauregard's essay examines the concept of "progressive planning practice." For example, is planning progressive because it means well or has noble purposes? Or should we look to the particular consequences of planning practice? If we agree, as Beauregard suggests, that consequences are essential to our evaluation of progressive practices, then we must ask a further set of questions: Which sort of consequences matter? Are there differences between material consequences and ideological consequences? Consider, for example, if it is helpful or misleading to limit progressive practices to those producing exclusively material consequences – those resulting, say, in the actual construction of low income housing for people in need. Beauregard makes the important argument that such material consequences, however crucial they may be, should not obscure another set of consequences of planning practice that might center upon information or consciousness –

for example, a planner's working with a community organization and supplying it with technical and political information so that it is more able to act for itself and with other progressive organizations or class-based groups. The argument that ideological consequences ought to be considered as one dimension of progressive planning practice is especially important in the contemporary political environment, which often treats all ideological consequences of State actions indiscriminately as necessarily "legitimation" of the interests of the private sector or of State domination. In addition, Beauregard suggests that as planning has ideological consequences either reinforcing or weakening the political views and attitudes of those with whom planners work, so it is important that we recognize the content of such ideological changes. Progressive practice may become "praxis" when it not only reflects but also spreads to others a structural and critical analysis of the concrete practical context in which planning issues arise.

Forester's essay examines the character of everyday action in planning agencies to address the practical political questions raised by these essays for planning practice: How is the "educative and organizing" (Friedman et al.), "democratizing" (Baum) or "progressive" (Beauregard) role possible? By focusing upon the particular political impacts of planners' communications with other staff or with citizens, Forester's essay shows how it is that the best of technical intentions, for example, may lead to counterproductive political consequences. Taking a supposedly neutral technical position, a planner may not only obscure the political nature of a given problem and the political process through which the problem may be addressed, but worse, the planner may engender false trust, passivity, and dependency in the community organization member or neighborhood resident. The way in which the planner communicates to other planners, developers, or citizens has significant political (and often "depoliticizing") consequences. By applying the recent critical theory of Jurgen Habermas – the footnotes provide a guide – Forester's chapter argues that if we are to recognize the detailed possibilities of planners to work as educators and organizers, to shape ideological consequences that are not simply legitimations for austerity measures, then we need to understand the particular practical, organizing or disorganizing effects of the communicative actions performed not only by planners, but also by the actors in other organizations and class positions as well. If corporate developers, for example, can be expected to distort information systematically in their meetings with and communications to local residents and community organizations, then the planner's organizing role, in anticipation, may be predominantly an information-based, communicative role: making sure that the community organization has accurate information, that they're not "snowed" by a developer's technical consultant, that they have adequate notice of relevant meetings, and that they know whom to contact and how to influence the decisions and procedures that may affect the proposed project in their neighborhoods. Forester provides an analysis of the practical results of ordinary communications in planning: 1) planners themselves may distort information or raise expectations counterproductively; 2) planners and community members both face politically distorted communications at face-to-face, organizational, and structural levels; and 3) planners and citizens may organize and work together to respond to these disabling distortions at each of these levels. Finally, this paper suggests a number of strategies available to planners who seek to perform progressive organizing roles. Where Friedman et al. are structural in focus, Baum and Beauregard examine the organizational context of planning; Forester examines more how a planner's practice works as a practical and political communication, either to keep affected citizens dependent, trusting, bureaucratically ignorant, and politically uninvolved, or to educate and organize, to spread both technical and political information, to cultivate informal networks, to form progressive coalitions, to develop informed and realistic (rather than co-opted) participation, to enable citizens to act for themselves, democratize the planning process, and support progressive movements more generally.

The threads running through these papers, then, are these: 1) planning practice must be understood as located within agencies of the state. These agencies, however, are not monolithic, and they provide a range of opportunities for progressive, organizing practices by critical planners; and 2) an organizing or democratizing planning practice is sensible only if planners themselves become self-critical about the organizational and political contexts in which they work, consequences that may result in these contexts, and the particular political and organizing actions, informational and communicative practices that make them effective at all. While the previous sections of this volume set the context for the particular roles and practices of planners, each of the papers in this third section points to a significant dimension of the progressive organizing practices that planners may carry out. These analyses are neither gloomy, suggesting that planning is inevitably ineffectual nor are they utopian, pretending that the organizing practices of planners will soon lead to a great new way out of the darkness of the present austerity era. Rather, while they nevertheless affirm a progressive vision of planning practice, each of the analyses clarifies the obstacles to and the opportunities for such educative and organizing planning practices. All the authors recognize as a starting point the truism that planning is a political activity, and each attempts to show what this means specifically for public rather than private, professional, or state-serving ends. Thus, these analyses lead quite naturally to questions about the restructuring of planning education and to questions about the ability of planning schools as presently constituted to provide the education and training necessary for educative and organizing planning practices.

Bergman and Sarbib report on the experiences of the faculty at one of the major planning schools in the U.S. – the University of North Carolina at Chapel Hill. They provide a glimpse not only at the expected problems of introducing explicity political content into university curricula, but also at the complex reactions of students seeking planning careers. Distinguishing a number of possible faculty roles – from the "radical scholar," to the "academic-practitioner collaborator," to the faculty member self-critically assessing the roles of planning schools – in the larger political economy, their essay highlights a number of contradictory tensions that may arise when a faculty attempts to come to grips with the teaching of radical planning. While Bergman and Sarbib do not have definitive answers that clearly resolve the problems they address, they make a number of practical suggestions for initial steps to be taken; their analysis is helpful not only for these suggestions, but more so for the questions they raise – questions pertinent for any planning student or faculty member concerned with the themes and problems addressed in this volume.

12 Working Within the State: The Role of the Progressive Planner*

Joel Friedman
Judith Kossy
Mitt Regan

STATE ROLES AND ACTIVITIES

Necessary for any analysis of the role of the progressive planner working in the state (the "state" refers to the range of governmental and quasi-governmental agencies) is a conception of the state's role in capitalist society. Certain basic elements enter into this conception. First, the capitalist state is not politically neutral but is responsive to many differing and at times conflicting class interests. Second, in the long run the state generally acts in the interests of capital, specific factions within the capitalist class and, in the short term, to the various interests of both capital and the working class. Thus state expenditures fulfill a variety of roles and differentially affect class relations. Finally, particularly relevant to this paper is the notion of state as product, determinant, and especially object of class struggle.(1) Such a theory of the state acknowledges both the functional role of government programs in preserving the basic structure of capitalist relations (private property and accumulation, wage labor, underlying class differences, etc.), and historically specific class struggles that may influence the nature and content of state intervention. The state thus deals with the needs of capital in the context of working class demands and attempts to channel these demands to maintain the existing political system.

A recent paper by Esping-Andersen, Friedland, and Wright, which suggests a way of classifying state activities, may be used to identify possible strategies for progressive planners working within the state.(2) Following this formulation, a given program is classified within a three-dimentional framework based upon the level, form and structural consequences of the program's operation. Level indicates whether a

*This essay reflects the views of its authors, not those of the U.S. Department of Housing and Urban Development or the city of Alexandria, Va.

program enters the society in the sphere of production of circulation. Programs that deal with questions of what and how goods are produced – for example, the construction of physical infrastructures – are production level expenditures. On the other hand, programs involved in the distribution of what is produced, such as tax programs, operate at the level of circulation.

The form of an expenditure refers to the means through which the program operates. A commodified form refers to programs that reinforce production of goods for exchange in the market, such as state subsidies to private industry to produce a given service. By contrast, noncommodified forms, such as production of specific services, produce for direct use, such as public schools, libraries, or national health service.

Finally, the structural consequences of state expenditures refers to the extent to which the program is either reproductive or destructive of capitalist social relations, serving to reinforce and stabilize the status quo, or threatening the system.

Ultimately, the structural consequences of a given expenditure are linked both to the level and form of the program. Assuming that capitalism is based upon the production and exchange of commodities, and that a class system defined by the relations of production exists, programs that reinforce those factors are the most reproductive of existing social relations. Thus, in abstract and oversimplified terms, a noncommodified-production program, which presents a challenge to the commodification and exchange of goods and which focuses directly on class interests, presents the greatest potential threat to the system.

The relationship of the form and level of state intervention to its structural consequences is helpful in the progressive planner's attempts to develop a role within the state. It allows the concept of "progressive" to be developed in a more concrete way. As noncommodified production activities by the state represent intervention inconsistent with the bases of capitalist social relations, a progressive role for the planner would be to influence state programs in a noncommodified direction. Such a direction would increase class conflict and reduce or at least expose the capitalist class's domination of the working class.

Thus, an analysis of state activities and political strategies appropriate to them begins with an identification of form and level and of the relationship of each to the reproduction of capitalist relations. Elements of programs that are commodified and/or operate at the level of circulation would require the most extensive modification and challenge. Characteristics that are noncommodified and/or operate at the level of production should be reinforced and accentuated.

Moreover, the extent to which elements of programs may be considered reproductive or unreproductive should be determined in their historical context. Although commodified circulation activities are generally consistent with the basis of capitalism while uncommodified production programs are not, characterization of a program simply does not sufficiently determine its reproductive or unreproductive consequences.

Table 12.1. The Content of Political Class Demands

REPRODUCTIVE OF CAPITALIST SOCIAL RELATIONS

	FORM of state intervention implied by political demands	
	COMMODIFIED FORM	NON-COMMODIFIED FORM
CIRCULATION LEVEL	Tax-cuts; price supports and other government subsidies; unemployment payments; cash forms of welfare.	Libraries; free goods and services provided by the state; welfare in the form of free goods.
PRODUCTION LEVEL	Government contracting with private capital to build economic infrastructures; Nationalized profit-making industries (e.g. Renault).	National health services; free public education.

UNREPRODUCTIVE OF CAPITALIST SOCIAL RELATIONS

	FORM of state intervention implied by political demands	
	COMMODIFIED FORM	NON-COMMODIFIED FORM
CIRCULATION LEVEL	Adequate guaranteed income (not restricted to retired workers) sufficient to undermine the commodity status of labor power; wage demands combined with profit and price controls.	Community control of public services; community controlled rent boards.
PRODUCTION LEVEL	Demands for infrastructure construction under conditions of the fiscal crisis of the state.	Workers' takeovers of factories which restructured the labor process in ways which increase worker control within production; tenant control of public housing construction.

Source: Esping-Andersen, Friedland, and Wright, "Modes of Class Struggle And The Capitalist State," 1976.

PROGRESSIVE PLANNING FUNCTIONS WITHIN THE STATE

Using the typology introduced above, we will examine the functional roles of six of HUD's programs. Our dual purpose is to identify aspects that can be developed in more progressive directions and to determine how we can use our positions in the state to support and strengthen actions that bring about social transformation.

The analysis demonstrates that HUD's existing policies and activities fall predominantly in the commodified circulation category, thus reinforcing the status quo. It also points out three basic conditions that provide a dynamic for organizing class struggle more progressively: 1) the weakening of these (commodified circulation) policies because of accumulation crises in major economic sectors; 2) the state's diminished capacity to pay; and 3) deepening economic problems that make such policies inadequate even from the point of view of capital. The progressive planner can use these conditions either to justify progressive changes toward uncommodified production policies or to expose basic problems that should be thwarted, eventually leading to different forms of state intervention. Thus, in various programs, one overall strategy may be to accelerate demands on the strained fiscal capacity of the state in order to force the development of more progressive state programs.

More specifically, four general strategies are suggested by this program analysis. First, it is essential to support community action with information and material about state action, policy and resources and about the objective conditions of the community. Information that illuminates the particular effect of the capitalist mode of production on housing and its distribution and exposes the role of the state in mediating the conflicts between consumers of housing and capital is useful in formulating consumption demands or in protesting state action. The planner, as educator, can identify potential uses or applications of programs to achieve progressive objectives in the context of community development. Strong alliances with the community provide the legitimacy and power necessary for effective action within the state. It is difficult for the state to ignore or repress alternatives that represent the view of a vocal and active constituency.

The second function builds on the educator's role to encourage community organization around specific production issues. Planners can show how the state supports the class structure. They can use their positions to support action along specific class lines, to encourage networks of different community groups, and to promote coalitions between consumers of housing and community services and labor, both in public bureaucracies and in construction. Answers to very simple and immediate questions, such as who benefits and who pays, powerfully demonstrate the commonalities of mutual class concerns and emphasize the implications of state proposals.

The third function is to educate other planners in an effort to form a progressive network within the agency. Supportive networks inside the agency are necessary to overcome the obstacles imposed by bureaucratic structure and political ideology. Unless there is coordination and support, progressive recommendations will be isolated and ineffective. In building a network, the planner should show the direct implications of policies designed to reproduce capitalist relations and how this may be transformed. This is especially important for planners at the federal level who have little regular contact with the community.

Finally, planners in the state can aid progressive movements by promoting programs that build relations between producers and consumers and by exploring ways of charging existing programs to noncommodified forms of production. Documentation of the weakness of programs operating through the market, particularly in a period of inflation, can validate the need to explore alternatives.

Development of progressive roles for planners in the state must, however, recognize the limitations of both that role and the potential for class-based policies. The division of labor and power hierarchy divorces progressive planners from their constituency and from the products of their labor: planners do not make final decisions regarding the use of a particular policy or evaluation, nor do they implement the programs that are adopted. The political nature of HUD, for example, and its close relationship with the housing industry and finance capital, hardly creates a climate for developing progressive programs. The planner in the state, like any other political activist, must calculate how far to push, on what issues, and when. A transformation of the relations of housing production undoubtedly will not originate inside the state, with the planners as the vanguard. However, planners can challenge the prevailing political economy of urban development and housing production and support working class struggles in the community. To the extent that planners strengthen and support community-based movements, they will perform some progressive functions.

ROLE AND FUNCTIONS OF HUD

In the context of the arguments set forth above, the U.S. Department of Housing and Urban Development may be seen as a specific agency of the state, established to mediate the contradictions that arise within the housing sectors and in the nation's cities in general. The sections that follow will examine the nature of the specific needs of the capitalist system in housing and urban development, and will analyze particular HUD programs formulated to meet these needs and address their contradictory aspects. Because the topical areas of housing and development are clearly interrelated, consideration of specific programs under one or the other heading represents conceptual, rather than actual, distinctions.

Housing

Housing as shelter, rather than as an aspect of the built environment, will be the focus of the following discussion. From the standpoint of overall production, shelter is an important element in the cost of living. Because wage rates paid by the capitalist employer must take into account the price of housing for the worker, holding down housing costs is in the long-term interest of the entire capitalist system.

Land, finance, and construction interests, however, seeking profitable investments in housing, extract the maximum possible price from owners and renters. Thus labor is in conflict with various elements of capital over the price of housing. Rather than simply allowing the relative strength of these parties to determine the outcome of the conflict, the state has intervened to further the system as a whole.

HUD has developed a variety of responses that attempt to resolve and control the contradictions of the housing market so that the price of housing does not become prohibitive. One prominent effort, because of the key position of financial institutions, has been the reduction of risks for lenders. Loan guarantees, such as the 203(b) mortgage insurance program, and the development of the secondary mortgage market, through the establishment of the Federal National Mortgage Association (FNMA) and the Government National Mortgage Association (GNMA), have shifted the bulk of risk determination and absorption from private finance to the government.

Another general state strategy has been the granting of subsidies to reduce construction costs, such as the Section 235 and 236 programs. Interest rate subsidies have resulted in lower developer debt service, which in turn is reflected in lower housing prices. Finance capital receives its asking price for the use of capital, construction interests are able to use that capital without bearing the full burden of its cost, and the state funds the difference.

The state has also subsidized some housing consumers under such programs as the Section 8 rental subsidy program, where direct payments in effect increase the real income of a household. Such arrangements assure both finance and construction interests guaranteed returns while limiting the burden on the renter.

Finally, in some instances the state has intervened through the public housing program in the actual production of housing. Such intervention has assisted those with incomes inadequate to afford even the subsidized housing provided by the private sector. Such action has generally been aimed at averting social unrest while posing no threat to the hegemony of the market as the principal means of obtaining shelter.

The following sections will examine how HUD's major national housing programs respond to the contradictions of the housing market. Our analysis will suggest elements of these programs useful to the progressive planner in organizing political action.

Section 203(b) Mortgage Insurance

The HUD single-family mortgage insurance program, Sec. 203(b), an essential component of the National Housing Act of 1934, was the piece of legislation that initiated state intervention into a previously autonomous housing market. The basic approach of the program to the problems of housing has remained constant, although certain operational adaptations have been instituted in response to changing economic conditions. Sec. 203(b) insures first mortgages on one- to four-unit houses (predominantly single-family units) against default by the borrower and thus removes all considerations of risk for the institution making the loan. In the event of a default by the borrower, the lending institution is paid the remaining balance of principal and interest by the federal government, specifically the Federal Housing Administration (FHA), an office of HUD. The Sec. 203(b) program finances all payments to lending institutions from receipts from the 'points' (an additional sum charged the borrower for the privilege of receiving FHA insurance).

Sec. 203(b) was the state's response, at the federal level, to the generalized crisis condition of the private housing market during the Depression. The problems of the housing sector during the Depression – widespread unemployment, massive defaults and foreclosures by homeowners (which triggered bank failures in several instances), a fragmented and weakened mortgage system, an underhoused population, and a depressed construction industry were the stimuli behind the development of what has become known as the FHA mortgage insurance program. Viewed as an immediate attempt to solve these problems, the program has served its purpose well. Sec. 203(b) has strengthened and restructured the contemporary housing sector in several ways. First, by transferring the risk associated with mortgage loans from the lending institutions to the state, the program effectively eliminates the danger of bank failures due to catastrophic losses attributable to homeowner defaults and foreclosures, and results in an overall increase in the profit rates of the lending institutions. By shifting the risk, the program has been a major force in the expansion of the housing sector: since 1934 insurance has been written on 10.2 million housing units, approximately 11 percent of all units constructed since that date.(3) Also, by encouraging increased housing production, Sec. 203(b) has extended the possibility of homeownership to members of the working class previously unable to afford it. Such an expansion in homeownership has directly increased the role that mortgage debt plays in the economy: in 1950 the ratio of per capita mortgage debt to per capita disposable income stood at 27 percent, by 1973 that figure had risen to 53 percent.(4)

Due to stringent underwriting standards that favor new housing, a second important impact of Sec. 203(b) has been to encourage suburban development while ignoring developed areas in the central cities. For example, in 1977 over one half of all Sec. 203(b) new construction was characterized as suburban, with an additional 40 percent outside the core city, presumably in the newer and underdeveloped areas near the city's outer limits.(5)

Finally, the program has served to strengthen a severely weakened mortgage system by instituting standardized procedures with uniform rates and terms. The uniformity of the system assures timely repayments on loans and, more importantly, creates a national mortgage market in which mortgage credit can flow across state lines.(6) Such changes cause increasingly large amounts of power to concentrate in relatively few institutions.

The typology developed by Esping-Andersen et al. shows that Sec. 203(b) operates at the level of circulation relationships by dealing with consumers of a commodity – housing – in their role as consumers, and that it does not deal with their role as workers laboring to produce a commodity. Operating at this level, Sec. 203(b) serves that portion of the working class able to purchase housing, an attribute dependent on income differentials within the working class, and systematically ignores others.

The program has fostered homeownership among the moderate income population and has failed to meet the housing needs of the poorest segments. Thus, in 1960 the median family income of Sec. 203(b) participants was $8,252 while the national median income was $5,620; in 1976 the figures stood at $18,821 and $14,958, respectively.(7) In 1977 86 percent of all homeowners who received Sec. 203(b) insurance were white.(8) By thus serving only a segment of the working class, the Sec. 203(b) program has fragmented the class into divisive factions – homeowners and tenants, whites and blacks – and restricted the degree of class consciousness that could develop over issues surrounding the provision of housing.

Section 203(b) takes the form of a commodified program since it accepts the operation of a private market for housing in which homes are commodities produced for their exchange value, and it serves to supplement and expand that market. By validating the concept of private property, and by convincing people that "the system works," the program indirectly reduces threats to the ideological basis of capitalist social relations. The illusion that working class homeowners have complete ownership and control of their homes (even though they are in debt to the lending institution for the length of the mortgage) prevents them from questioning the basis of the system that has "given" them this property.(9) Similarly, homeowners will react negatively to any social changes that appear to threaten their stake in their property: battles over the location of low income housing projects or opposition to increased taxes to pay for needed social services are defensive reactions to the practical implications of homeownership.

An approach that obscures class relations and operates within a commodified market system is strongly reproductive of class relations. By serving only a segment of the working class and by concerning itself with individualized consumption of single units of housing, the program established a system in which members of the working class "compete" for housing and thus are fragmented into intraclass groupings. By simultaneously increasing the profits of lending institutions, developers, construction companies and landowners are legitimating existing class relations through the development of ideological support for the concept of private property. In this way, the Sec. 203(b) program serves an important function in American capitalist society.

On the other hand, the dysfunctional consequences of the program – the urban fiscal crisis, threats to investments in the central city, urban sprawl and the disenfranchisement and heightened alienation of those unable to purchase a home – have come back to haunt the state. The increased indebtedness of the population and our current period of rampant inflation can largely be attributed to the expansion of home-ownership and to the role that Sec. 203(b) has played in that process. Any action toward progressive social change must begin with the recognition of the long-term contradictions of the program and from there proceed to develop the structural causes of the contemporary urban crisis.

The operational approach of Sec. 203(b) is almost perfect from the perspective of the lending institutions and precludes most attempts to modify the program. Its acceptance of the commodity nature of housing and its operation in the circulation sphere sets strict limits to the progressive potential of the program. Ameliorative changes in the underwriting standards of loan terms to allow a greater portion of the working class to purchase housing, will also serve to draw the poor into the ideology of private property.

Since a major result of the program has been the fragmentation of the working class into homeowners and tenants, activists must attempt to organize group coalitions around issues that had previously separated them. Educative programs on the true nature of mortgage finance and the implications of ownership in a capitalist society will show working class homeowners that they are exploited at the workplace in the same way as tenants are.

Because such approaches must, by definition, occur outside the state, the role of progressive planners within HUD is limited. These planners must lead a dual life – cognizant of their weak position within the bureaucracy yet constantly striving to organize the working class outside the state. Unfortunately, such efforts are weak in comparison to the powerful operation of the Sec. 203(b) program. Until the commodified nature of housing is challenged, very little radical action can take place vis a vis the Sec. 203(b) program. The clarification of the functioning of the program and the development of networks of housing consumers must be tied to activities that challenge the commodified, market exchange nature of housing.

An unintended consequence of the program – the fiscal crisis – may move the state away from the commodified-circulation nature of the Sec. 203(b) program. Esping-Andersen et al. noted that the state, in an attempt to forestall the destructive consequences of circulation level programs and to expand its revenues, has increased its direct production level programs. It is thus possible that the deepening crisis may pressure the state toward direct production of housing in an attempt to rationalize the housing sector and recapture the profits now accrued by the private housing industry. Progressives must be aware of this possibility and take actions that would force the state to absorb more of the costs of the Sec. 203(b) program in a crisis situation. Such steps might include reducing the number of "points" thereby exacerbating the contradictory nature of the program and, possibly, moving the state toward more progressive housing programs.

Public Housing

The HUD low rent public housing program represents two basic approaches to the provision of housing. The first approach, supporting conventional public housing, allows local housing authorities (LHA) to finance construction of projects through the sale of tax-exempt (low interest rate) bonds with forty-year terms. Through HUD the federal government enters into an agreement with the LHA to repay the principal and interest on the bonds. This approach was the sole means of funding until the institution of the turnkey program in 1966. In this approach, presently preferred by HUD, the LHA continues to finance project costs through bond sales but, prior to construction, enters into a contract with a developer. The developer secures construction financing and eventually turns over the completed project to the LHA for an agreed-upon price. Significantly, the developer is allowed a margin of profit.

Public housing was originally intended to house the "working poor" (not the destitute) and LHAs were required to meet operating expenses through rental collection. However, because of increase in impoverishment among the urban population, changes in the focus of the program from "working poor" to "housing of the last resort," many LHAs were unable to meet their operating expenses. In 1969, Congress enacted a supplemental program that stipulated that rents should not be more than 25 percent of a tenant's income and allocated operating subsidies to assure the continued financial solvency of public housing.

The low rent public housing program (The Housing Act of 1937), like the Sec. 203(b) mortgage insurance program, evolved during the Depression in response to continued unemployment in the construction industry and the inability of the private market to provide adequate housing for the nation's poor. Although the Public Works Administration had built some housing between 1934 and 1937, the 1937 Act was the first time the state had directly constructed and owned a substantial number of housing units. Except for the turnkey program and the provision of operating subsidies, the basic approach of the program has remained unchanged.

Unlike Sec. 203(b), public housing has not functioned as a major source for the accumulation of capital by the housing industry. The stringest cost limits imposed by HUD, the high costs of construction and the relatively small number of units cut into profits. In comparison to the Sec. 203(b) program, the overall level of activity has been small: approximately 1.3 million units house about 3 million residents.(10) And despite a larger urban poverty population, recent construction of public housing has diminished drastically: 109,000 units in 1969; 33,000 in 1973; and 3,000 in 1977.(11) In contrast to Sec. 203(b), public housing operates at the level of production: the government builds dwellings. As noted earlier, public housing has evolved to the point where it now fulfills the role of producing housing for those unable to purchase or rent on the private market. It complements private capital and does not, at present, pose a threat to "for-profit" housing. Thus median income in 1977 of all public housing tenants was $3,651, well below the national median income figure of $14,958. Approximately 59 percent of public housing tenants are minorities (substantially more in large urban areas), and 73 percent are receiving public assistance.(12)

The unattractiveness of most public housing projects and their general reputation as locations for crime and various other forms of antisocial behavior (conditions somewhat attributable to the way in which the state has conducted the program), have made direct state production of housing socially undesirable except for the portion of the population in dire need of assistance.

Public housing allows the state to exercise a certain amount of social control over the people who live there. Isolated in large, physically deteriorated and inadequate projects, tenants are further demoralized by the encouragement of the negative stigma attached to public housing projects, the use of authoritarian management techniques, and the ever present threat of eviction. The manipulation of benefits encourages complacent behavior and forestalls any challenges to the system that might arise from the most alienated segment of the working class. Also, using public housing only for the poor serves to fragment the working class. Public housing creates the illusion that the poorest segment of the working class is being adequately housed, albeit in the worst conditions.

The turnkey program operates through the market system and thus represents a commodified form, while conventional public housing represents, at least potentially, a noncommodified form. By establishing an upper rental limit of 25 percent of one's income, the program begins to divorce consumption of housing from the ability to pay principle, a basic precept of private market operation. However, since the program is based upon rental of a produced good, it must be conceptualized as a commodified program.

In this respect the public housing program thus becomes strongly reproductive of existing class relations. By establishing a mechanism that allows the state to control a potentially volatile population and fragments the working class into consumer groups based upon income levels, the program effectively prevents any successful challenges to the present means of providing housing or to the capitalist system in general.

In contrast to the Sec. 203(b) program, whose structural approach to the provision of housing negates most possibilities for progressive change, the reproductive character of public housing is a result of the program's actual operation. Because public housing is a potentially noncommodified production level program, the type of program characterized as most unreproductive by our classification scheme, a number of internal changes could be instituted that would develop and strengthen its progressive potential.

First, planners within HUD can push certain operational aspects to insure that the public housing program meets the needs of its residents. They can: 1) organize to raise the cost limits on public housing construction so that the basic necessities of adequate housing are provided; 2) demand that ancillary services, such as day-care centers, medical facilities or job-training centers be included; 3) support efforts to lower the percentage of income figure used to determine rents; 4) attempt to remove restrictions that require turnkey financing and encourage movement toward direct state production of units; and 5) support programs that strive to abolish concentrated public housing (such as the infamous Pruit-Igoe project) and encourage dispersed housing in areas closer to employment.

Second, various interim efforts, such as direct funding of progressive examples of public housing, technical assistance, and personal organizing efforts, should be supported within HUD. Movements that seek to place the control of public housing operations in the hands of tenants should be supported. Coalitions between public housing tenants and residents of other forms of housing, Sec. 8 or private rental housing, should be developed. Further, organizing efforts that link the tenants of public housing as workers to the workers who run the projects should be increased.

Lobbying efforts aimed at Congress and the building of internal HUD coalitions at the policy level should begin to pressure HUD to increase funding and expand unit construction. Such expansion would meet the immediate housing needs of the large number of poor families on public housing waiting lists and would extend state-provided housing services to other segments of the working class. Expansion would begin to present a challenge, both ideologically and economically, to the private housing market. Alternative public housing approaches, such as that proposed by Hartman and Stone (see chapter 11), could be explored as viable alternatives to the present private, profit-oriented approach. The example of Great Britain, in which close to 25 percent of all housing is publicly owned, should also be closely scrutinized.(13) Because public housing, unlike all other programs, does not accept the commodification of housing, the possibility of state-provided housing based upon human need exists. As always, the realization of this potential remains problematic. Ultimately, radical action must confront the social relations inherent in the production, circulation and exchange of value in a capitalist society. To do so requires a multifaceted organizing effort.

Section 8 Rental Assistance Program

The Section 8 program became the major government lower income rental housing program as a result of the Housing and Community

Development Act of 1974. The Housing and Community Development Reporter states:

> (The Act) radically altered national housing policy by effectively curtailing the traditional public housing program, as well as the various subsidized mortgage insurance programs. In their place, Congress thrust forward a heretofore relatively minor part of the national housing scene: public housing in private accommodations, or leased housing.(14)

Although Section 8 deals with new construction, and substantial and moderate rehabilitation, the main element of this program is the provision of rent subsidies to lower income renters (those earning 80 percent or less of the area median income). Successful applicants receive a certificate that enables them to obtain rental housing (within established price limits) for which they pay 25 percent of their total income and the program pays the balance.

The program originally was designed to meet the needs of those whose incomes were too high for public housing, but who could not qualify for homeownership status. However, the virtual cessation of public housing construction, as well as reductions in private production of rental units, have made Section 8 the only housing resource for large numbers of low income households. The mean family income of Section 8's nonelderly recipients is $3,720, approximately the same as that of public housing residents.

The Section 8 program, established in the midst of the severe dislocations in the lower income rental market of the early 1970s, began to make lower income multifamily project investment an undesirable proposition. As the situation became riskier, a drastic curtailment of construction resulted. The direct accumulation potential of multifamily investment had been severely diminished. The juxtaposition of a drastic fall in multifamily construction in the midst of still extensive low income housing needs began to raise the prospect that rental housing prices would escalate beyond the means of working class tenants.

Our typology suggests that Section 8 takes the form of commodified intervention, since rental payments within certain limits reinforce the principle of production for exchange, rather than use. The rental payment constitutes one of the elements that contribute to the profitability of rental investment. The Section 8 subsidy operates to stabilize this factor, and, in the process, acknowledges market value considerations as the appropriate determinant of production. With rental payments the basis for continued occupation of a unit by the tenant, the rent collection process is itself rationalized.

Because Section 8 reinforces the market system in the housing sector, it represents intervention on the level of circulation. The essential thrust of the program is to stabilize effective demand, with the housing consumer the focal point of state expenditure. Through its payment of the difference between actual rent and a percentage of tenant income, the program enhances the competitive position of consumers in the marketplace. Such a form of intervention supports the legitimacy of the market as arbiter of production and confines itself to concerns over more rational or equitable distribution of goods within that structure.

The use of fair market rent figures in an area to determine subsidy limits also strengthens the price system. Regardless of what distortions are influencing area-wide prices, such rents are taken as reasonable indicators of prevailing market conditions. Through reliance on market prices, the program indirectly funds such costs as increased interest from repeated resale of buildings, exploitative rents in areas with low vacancy rates, construction cost overruns, and exorbitant land profits.

State action in the form of commodified intervention and on the level of circulation is the most consistent with capitalist social relations. It is clear that the strong support of the Section 8 program for the structure of the rental housing market makes the program highly reproductive of capitalism. The program's reliance on the market through its subsidies legitimates private appropriation in this sector and assures that investment decisions relate to accumulation, rather than need. The absence of any significant production supports in multifamily rental housing policy reflects the diminished prospects for profits and, therefore, sanctions the flow of capital to more profitable investments.

Commodified responses on the level of circulation also tend to reinforce divisions within the working class. Members are dealt with as consumers and are thus placed in competition for consumption opportunities within the market. Interests defined in this manner tend to be fragmented by labor markets, income, sex, race, etc., and thus inhibit the development of class consciousness based on location within production.

The Section 8 program is also reproductive by virtue of its contribution to the rate of profit enjoyed by the private sector. By holding shelter expenses for program recipients to a certain percentage of income, the program reduces the cost of living. Studies to date indicate that the average family in the program has reduced the percentage of income devoted to shelter from 39 to 22 percent. Since wage rates roughly reflect the cost of living, such reductions hold down wages, thus maintaining or increasing profits. But this, of course, is true of any housing subsidy program, including public housing (see chapter 5). Section 8 subsidies also contribute to profits by making a certain level of consumption possible for those who otherwise could not have afforded it. This insures that the price of housing is eventually paid through rental of the property.

The identification of roles for the progressive planner must focus on the particular ways in which the contradictions of commodified circulation intervention emerge in the context of this program. Current trends tend to accentuate the contradictions of this form of intervention, and such developments represent possibilities for transformation of commodified circulation activity into uncommodified production intervention.

One aspect of the Section 8 program that reflects these developments is the contribution of the program's cost to the fiscal crisis of the state. The various distortions affecting the price system during a period of low rental housing production necessitate increasing state expenditures to make such housing affordable to the working class. Such rising expenditures create a strain on state fiscal capacity, particularly in times of slow economic growth. Thus, one prospect for using the program for progressive purposes may be to push for greater amounts of subsidies available to local government. Based on the large numbers of households on Section 8 waiting lists, such allocations have been inadequate. If state expenditures must expand to meet the housing needs of working class families, the implications of operating exclusively through the private market should become apparent. The expense of public support of this increasingly irrational mode of allocation may eventually provoke direct state intervention in production. See Piven & Cloward, (15) for a similar analysis applied to the welfare system.

The movement for increased allocations would have even greater unreproductive potential through the organization of persons on Section 8 and public housing waiting lists. Given the different income limits of the two programs, such action may begin the process of organizing around housing issues along class lines, and it may be useful in overcoming the fragmentation of the working class on the basis of income.

A similar approach is to reduce the percentage of income to be spent on shelter by program participants. This could be in the form of a lower required percentage or may involve the use of a standard that takes into account all other costs of living, with shelter costs as a residual.(16)

The contradictions engendered by the Section 8 program, however, are less likely to emerge from characteristics of the program itself than from the general policy that it represents. Rental vacancy rates in many cities are dropping below two percent, indicating extremely difficult prospects for obtaining rental housing for lower income people. Condominium conversions in some cities are further reducing the supply of housing in this sector. Such conditions have the potential for social control problems, as resistance to monopoly rent prices mounts and fewer members of the working class are able to find decent shelter.

With exacerbation of the shortage and its attendant problems for the system, pressures mount for a more extensive response by the state. One mode of intervention may be a return to a commodified production orientation through the creation of incentives for private sector reentry into this market. Such efforts, however, would necessitate large expenditures if investment is to be made as profitable as other ventures. The amount of state subsidy would be dependent upon private market conditions, especially on spiraling interest rates, which constitute such a large portion of housing costs. Such efforts would, in effect, be subsidizing inflation, with the likelihood of serious ramifications for state fiscal capacity and the economy as a whole. Finance capital would be the largest beneficiary of such a policy, and has the power to influence the state in this direction unless challenged by working class opposition. The enormous subsidies necessary for such intervention would likely be made possible by further cuts in social welfare programs now benefiting low income people.

The current situation has the alternative potential for a diminution of the role of the private market, along with an increase in public production of working class housing. Should this be the direction of policy, expansion of the existing public housing program may be the most likely response, as state intervention moves to a somewhat more progressive form of commodified production policy. Working class pressure would then be necessary to address the contradictions of this form of intervention, pressing toward an noncommodified production position.

The principal tasks to be performed by the progressive planner involve heightening awareness of the growing imbalance between rental housing production and need. One aspect of this is a clear alternative definition of the problem. The source of this disparity must be clearly identified as the outcome of a housing market system in which production and investment are based on the potential rate of profit. Information of production and need must be widely disseminated in efforts to publicize the dimensions of the problem. Pressures for state intervention in production have a greater likelihood for creating working class solidarity as the class-based nature of the housing market is revealed through everyday experience. The public housing program may be seized upon as an initial form of intervention, so that an alternative is available to pressures for subsidization of private production and allocation through the market.

Urban Development

The urban area plays an important role in the capital accumulation process. As David Harvey demonstrated, it constitutes the cumulative value of previous investments and provides resources for developing new forms of production and accumulation.(17) For the working class, the city is defined in terms of consumption and the provision of daily needs as well as the quality of life.

Private, commodified property structure conflicts over the type and location of development. The various factions of capital have particular interests in preserving their investment, and thus seek to influence the distribution of externalities and public expenditures for their benefit. At the same time, the working class seeks to use the built environment to satisfy its own needs – primarily for employment and consumption, rather than exchange. Competition among the different components of capital and between capital and the working class, each pursuing their own interests, propel the development and use of land.

The development of the city must respond to the particular demands of the larger economic system to accommodate its continued growth and transformation. The conflicts among economic sectors need to be resolved and mediated to serve this larger economic interest. HUD, through the local government, plays a major role in rationalizing and directing the process by supporting production and consumption facilities. These increase the productivity of labor and provide facilities and services to lower the cost of living, and hence the minimum necessary wage rates. The state has absorbed greater portions of these costs – which are essentially unprofitable – over time. The ability of the local state to maintain, and/or expand these investments is contingent on economic conditions, and is therefore threatened in periods of recession or extreme inflation. HUD intervenes to maintain a certain level of local activity to further and support accumulation.

In general it fulfills this role by creating programs such as the Community Development Block Grant program, Section 312, and Urban Renewal. These provide funds for infrastructure development and improvement, community facilities, and housing rehabilitation. HUD designs the activities in the context of the national as well as local needs of capital and the relationship of the city to them. The response of HUD to problems and dislocations in urban development is examined in the following sections through an analysis of the major development programs.

Community Development Block Grants

The Community Development Block Grant (CDBG) Program, created by the Housing and Community Development Act of 1974, constitutes the major federal program in the area of urban development. Cities of over 50,000 are classified as "entitlement" cities, which assures them a fixed amount of annual funds, determined on a formula basis. This formula takes into account population, extent of poverty, and overcrowded housing conditions. Smaller, "discretionary" jurisdictions compete for remaining funds, as long as they are deemed consistent with broad national urban development objectives. CDBG replaced eight categorical loan and grant programs, under which funds were allocated on a case by case basis.

In order to assess the significance of CDBG and its emphasis on decentralized decision making, it is necessary to examine the program as a response to the contradictions of a particular period in urban history, as well as to the categorical programs it replaced. The enormous investment represented by the urban infrastructure and the importance of the city as a center of coordination and control under monopoly capitalism, makes postwar central city decline a compelling problem. Categorical programs provided the majority of funds for state intervention in the central city during this period.

The fact that under categorical programs expenditure decisions were made at the national level reduced local political conflict to reactions to specific projects. However, such a focus provided concrete issues around which intense protest could be mobilized, such as transit programs, housing demolition, and commercial construction. The emergence of reformist organizations on the national level created pressures in these programs for greater low income benefits. The restructuring of the city for the accumulation process began to be threatened, as well as the legitimacy of the urban social order. The CDBG program, in a response to these contradictions uses the mystification of statistics to distribute its funds, thereby characterizing decisions as neutral and objective.

Under CDBG political debate on the local level is concerned with a broad range of needs rather than with the merits of a specific project. Demands must therefore be organized around more general, ongoing issues than they were under the categorical programs, the most difficult kind of organization to sustain on the local level. Overall the CDBG program has resulted in depoliticization on the national level and has transferred local level allocation decisions to a more diffuse political plane.

State intervention through the CDBG program, including nonmarket provisions such as public works and neighborhood improvement, may be characterized as occurring on the level of production. Because the state generally contracts with the private firms to produce these goods and services and does not engage in production itself, the form of state intervention is mostly commodified.

Projects funded through CDBG include street improvements, flood and drainage work, playgrounds, sidewalks, and housing rehabilitation. Because these activities maintain wage rates at a lower rate than if workers had to purchase such goods in the market, the generation of profits is supported. CDBG, therefore, may be considered generally reproductive of capitalistic social relations.

CDBG activities also further the economic position of actors such as private lending institutions and construction companies by creating opportunities for profit on projects that would otherwise be considered poor investments.

The commodified nature of most CDBG activities suggests that progressives should exert pressure for direct state production of these goods and services around considerations of need rather than exchange. One means of moving into direct state production is to integrate public sector employment programs with local activities funded under the Block Grant program.

One potentially unreproductive feature of the CDBG program is that on the local level the majority of expenditures reflect state intervention in the productive sphere, i.e., program funds are largely used to arrange for the production of goods and services. The political debate surrounding the program is therefore more likely to center on _what_ to produce and _for whom_ – reliance on the mystification of the price system is not possible as the political character of expenditure decisions becomes more evident. The potential is thus present for working class groups to gain some measure of control over social capital investment decisions. As Esping-Andersen et al. note, demands that focus on state intervention in production are less likely to fragment class consciousness because they deal with the level at which class relations are defined.

Organization around such CDBG production issues has both its problems and prospects. Relatively small physical investments and the diversity of activities funded under CDBG make it difficult to focus on concrete projects as manifestations of class-based political action. Also, local capitalists often dominate local political debate because of the city's dependence on them. Since policies that attack the premises of private appropriation risk the loss of employment and tax revenues, the potential for political conflict around production issues is present. Its organization, however, may prove difficult.

The nominal requirements of the program for citizen participation have an unreproductive potential that may be useful in organizing. Such requirements may be used to organize lower income groups, first around specific issues related to the CDBG budget and secondly, around more general class issues in the city. The process of building such coalitions necessitates bringing together different groups involved in various stages of the CDBG deliberation process. On the national level, this may mean pressuring for a higher use of CDBG funds to assist lower income persons, as well as redefining benefits so that programs in the general area of lower income concentration are not automatically assumed to be beneficial to these persons.

On the local level, it is important to establish networks between CDBG staff and groups within the community so that community viewpoints not only have formal representation but are considered in the day to day activities and deliberations of the staff. Such representation of views on an ongoing basis may help to structure the ways in which such issues are conceptualized, discussed, and analyzed.

To have a coalition with the CDBG staff, it is crucial to help organize groups within the community. A planner often needs such a constituency to justify the necessity of pursuing certain programs or directions to other parties in the city. CDBG funds may be used to help establish more formal organizations and to help them carry out various housing and development activities. In addition to the formation of such groups, coalitions must be built among existing advocacy organization so that a broadly based lower income movement acquires influence not only within the CDBG process but throughout the city.

A final coalition may be built among progressively oriented staff members in other city agencies. Maintaining contact among such persons can help provide information on a broad range of conditions within the city and help link the various activist constituencies throughout the city.

Information is a key element of the planner's attempts to form such coalitions. Knowledge of both formal and informal meetings helps insure that community groups are able to continually monitor deliberations on proposed and ongoing programs. Explanation of CDBG regulations can be of assistance in formulating proposals and evaluating programs that have been funded. This may involve not only awareness of formal regulations, but of the most current HUD interpretations, administrative decisions and guidelines. Data on program expenditures and performance should be made available on a regular basis, organized and analyzed as much as possible to clarify the distribution of benefits along class lines. More general information is also available to the CDBG planner, through the progressive planners' network, which helps community groups formulate demands and proposals on current problems.

The way in which CDBG's citizen participation requirements are met is important in structuring the power relationships that will exist in debate over its activities. Organizing advocacy groups to press for voting privileges and rights of approval of activities is a movement toward acknowledging the validity of community control over expenditures. During the period in which proposals are submitted, assistance to groups in formulating program alternatives can involve mobilization of different groups to design proposals, as well as to insure conformity to appropriate regulations. More general pressures can be placed on the program to deal with certain kinds of issues. It is especially here that information on city trends and developments can be useful. During deliberations on proposals, support organized through the various networks must be expanded to a city-wide basis, (since after the budget and its activities must be approved by the City Council.)

Housing Rehabilitation

The complex of housing rehabilitation programs attempts to serve the dual, sometimes conflicting, purpose of housing rehabilitation and neighborhood improvement and community development. HUD's four major programs focus almost exclusively on the financing of private rehabilitation through grants, low interest loans, mortgage insurance and tax advantages.

Section 312 of the Housing Act of 1964 authorized low interest (three percent) loans for the rehabilitation of single and multifamily residential and nonresidential structures in revitalization target areas. Originally designed for property rehabilitation in neighborhoods adjacent to urban renewal areas, its current objectives are to assist low to moderate income owners of single-family property to improve their homes; to complement other community development activities; and to stimulate other private investment in the community. Funds are allocated on a formula basis.

A second source of funds for housing rehabilitation is CDBG (totaling 16.9 percent of CDBG's expenditures for 1978 – second only to public works). Expenditures may be in the form of grants, loans and materials, and are primarily reserved for low to moderate income residents. HUD also encourages localities to use their CDBG funds to attract and stimulate ("leverage") private capital in order to expand the total resources available for below-market interest loans. By lowering interest rates, floating bond issues, and entering into tax-exempt financing schemes, communities buy private capital, which can then be loaned at below-market rates. Tax laws assure that lending institutions earn comparable profits and insurance protects them from default. Approximately one-half billion dollars has been leveraged in this manner.

Section 8 – Substantial and Moderate Rehabilitation – programs are the only two that attempt to serve low income tenants. Localities write down some financial costs and subsidize rents for reserved units for low income people to encourage and facilitate private participation in the rehabilitation process.

The fourth program, FHA Title I Loan Insurance, established as part of the Housing Act of 1964, provides insurance for 90 percent of all property improvement and rehabilitation loans up to $15,000. Like 202(b), the program establishes the maximum interest rates for the loan. There are no geographical or income limits on insurance distribution.

Intervention in housing rehabilitation is part of the state's general effort to redevelop and maintain portions of urban areas. Like urban renewal, it is designed to ameliorate the incipient threat to capital posed by abandonment and deterioration of the built environment. However, the form and emphasis changed in response to the sometimes violent struggle against urban renewal projects, the difficulty of justifying large capital expenditures for massive new structures, and the political and economic need to protect older, undermaintained neighborhoods from complete deterioration. Some concessions are made to low and moderate income owners who might leave the city, or who otherwise would not be able to improve their homes. Except for Section 8, there is little provision for tenants or low income owners who cannot afford to repay a loan, or whose individual allocation cannot cover the cost of the necessary rehabilitation work. Yet statistics show that 21 percent of houses valued at under $10,000 had structural deficiencies compared to 4.9 percent for units valued between $10,000 and $20,000, and less than 2 percent for those with higher values. Renters live in even worse conditions: approximately 26 percent live in substandard units compared to 11.8 percent for homeowners.

State intervention in this sphere of housing essentially reinforces the competitive, small-scale labor intensive character of construction, which dominates the productive process, and mortgage debt financing, which dominates the economic process. In almost all cases, the programs operate at the level of circulation – by distributing funds directly to individuals, their ability to consume rehabilitation services and financing increases. As a result, individuals relate separately to the state with little regard for their political or class positions or collective needs. The citizen participation requirements in 312 and CDBG provide the opportunity for social action in identifying target areas, and in proportioning available rehabilitation funds. But allocations to localities, general income requirements, and eligible activities are broadly established at the federal level.

Although the level of operation is circulation, where there is a concentration of rehabilitation activity, the effect can move closer to production. If the physical and economic character of whole neighborhoods changes, an opportunity is created to organize protests against the program to demand control of the spending process, or to ask for greater funds.

The programs are commodified due to their implementation through the private housing, construction and, in some cases, financial markets. While direct loans and grants do not rely fully on private lending institutions, they duplicate their functions in maintaining class relations and a class-based urban morphology. Rehabilitation itself is primarily performed by small local construction firms, which constitute the most competitive sector of the industry. The impact on the industry as a whole, however, is relatively small – rehabilitation constitutes less than 12 percent of total construction expenditures.

The position of labor in construction has been upheld despite continual attempts to weaken legislation requiring unionized labor on projects with more than eight units. This situation tends to maintain the competitive division between the working class at the point of production and the working class as consumer. The programs rely on financial capital to originate, service and underwrite loans, and to develop financing packages, thereby extending finance capital into the growing market of rehabilitation. FHA Title I Insurance further promotes this participation in unassisted rehabilitation.

For the most part, both the level and form of operation are reproductive of class relations and the structure of housing production. Even the state's direct role as lender offers little challenge to private sector domination of housing or to the function of housing as a commodity. In fact, loans and grants increase housing's value and life as a commodity. The conservative nature of homeownership is reinforced as recipients seek to maximize their own interest in property. The class position is solidified by added debts and increases in property investment. The Section 8 program maintains private construction industry's role as provider of rental units and the position of the tenant as renter. In short, the only modification in the relations of production is the increased role of the state in selecting contractors and determining the extent and quality of work that is accomplished.

Conceptualization of progressive changes or uses of these programs should be identified in the context of the state's role, which attempts to resolve problems arising from the imbalance in consumption and production of housing in certain low to moderate income areas in the urban housing market. The imbalance currently takes two forms: first, in neighborhoods where significant property rehabilitation and reinvestment transforms the class orientation of the housing and services, rehabilitation increases the rents beyond the ability of former residents to pay. In a growing number of cases, rehabilitation is accompanied by condominium conversions or renovation to single-family use. Thus, like urban renewal, rehabilitation effectively decreases the low and moderate income housing supply and forces more people to relocate to other low-cost areas. The state may not be directly involved in the movement, but there is little doubt that it contributes to the intensity of the dynamic. Protest against the trend in these gentrifying neighborhoods has already forced the government to respond to the situation. The reaction, however, has been minimal, for government's concern is still primarily political, not economic.

The other form of contradiction occurs in neighborhoods where deterioration of housing and services continues as a result of underproduction and disinvestment by the private market, and because state funding prefers less blighted areas with greater spatial advantages. Despite the current focus on gentrification and displacement, the dominant trend of decay and abandonment continues to escalate in older northeast and midwest cities.(18)

The potential for pushing the rehabilitation programs toward progressive solutions of these problems is limited by both the form and level of their operation. Distribution of funds to individuals according to federal guidelines provides little opportunity for class organization. In fact, it divides the working class into homeowners, renters and labor, and places them in competition with one another for resources and power. Opportunities for progressive action in the short term, therefore, lie in influencing the <u>use</u> of the programs. This would attempt to promote organization of housing producers and consumers, collective ownership, neighborhood control, and socialization of housing production. In order to develop a more progressive form it may be important to push demands beyond the state's fiscal capacity, thereby necessitating its intervention in the production process.

A first task in housing rehabilitation is to expand the possibilities for neighborhood, community, and labor organizations to: 1) obtain rehabilitation funds; 2) perform some state functions in the administration of programs; and 3) provide construction and finance services. A greater role for them would reduce the dominance of private capital in the community and begin to link housing consumers with producers. For example, a maintenance, repair, and rehabilitation cooperative in which residents contribute labor and/or money in return for service and materials socialize these aspects of housing and modifies the commodity relations that have contributed to the deterioration of housing. Depending on the form of the cooperative, it may be possible to make distributions on the basis of need, rather than solely on ability to pay.

Transformation of ownership and tenure arrangements in conjunction with the rehabilitation of both occupied and abandoned or foreclosed properties provides another opportunity for progressive action. The inability of the owner to obtain sufficient rents to pay costs, raise capital, and obtain a sufficient level of profit can provide the rationale for enabling tenants, by contributing labor and/or capital, to acquire an equity share in a rehabilitated building. Community organizations might obtain abandoned property and apply for rehabilitation funds. Long-term leases would be available to the residents. Residents would then have the advantage of stable tenancy, and the unit would become part of the community's public resources.

A second direction with progressive potential is to increase the state's role in production and ownership of rehabilitated housing in an effort to move away from the commodity form. The planner could show how this would, in long-term costs for the resident and the government, increase the state's ability to meet housing needs and, at the same time, provide employment to low income neighborhood residents. The argument would gain credibility if demands for rehabilitation assistance exceed the current fiscal capacity or political willingness to pay.

Office of Neighborhood Development

The Office of Neighborhood Development (OND) was established in 1977 to promote the participation of neighborhood and community organizations in revitalization activities. OND's primary purposes are to strengthen neighborhood groups by: 1) building their technical and administrative capacity; 2) helping them attract public and private funds to increase development activities; and 3) increasing their ability to function without state support. The strategy for providing assistance has three integrated parts: the first, to provide information on various aspects of the community development process, government programs and organizational management (current distribution of such materials reaches approximately 5,000 neighborhood organizations); second, to provide technical assistance through workshops and direct consultation to solve specific problems or to develop technical skills; and third, to provide direct funding for organizational and functional development. The twenty-nine organizations selected under this program, as part of their program building efforts, will assist other, less experienced neighborhood groups, in their development process.

OND was initially instituted without an operating budget and had to broker resources from other programs within HUD. Dependence on other programs, which were often critical of its objectives and reluctant to relinquish their funds, forced OND to operate in extremely tenuous conditions. For the first time in 1979, Congress authorized $5 million for the program to support self-help organizations, which now gives OND a more independent, secure level of operation.

The establishment of OND was a response to the needs of urban neighborhood organizations in predominantly low income and minority neighborhoods. It was established to overcome the alienation of residents from the political and economic processes in the community, and more specifically, the failure of these processes to provide adequate housing, jobs, and community facilities and services. Assistance is designed to enable the organizations to become full partners in neighborhood affairs and to compete in the economic and political market for resources and influence. The service is premised on the legal and philosophical argument that the state has an obligation to extend basic participatory rights to groups unable to take advantage of them, and therefore on the need to maintain the structure of social relations.

OND operates at the level of production, since technical assistance is given directly to recipients by HUD or its contractors. This direct service permits organization around issues of delivery and could be expanded to include housing or other community development issues.

OND's activities are distributed predominantly in a noncommodified form, i.e., they are produced for direct use rather than for exchange. While there are no subsidies involved, the state does purchase services and therefore there is a slight commodity aspect that perpetuates the existence of a certain private sector.

OND's reproductive consequences arise from the competitive process of determining who will receive technical assistance services and from the selection and contracting of individual groups to act as assistance providers. This creates a divisive framework, which rewards the development of organizational self-interest characteristic of a commodity society. Because the recipient group becomes the client of a professional, certain role distinctions can emerge. Further, establishment of acceptable management and organizational methods in return for assistance and resources may reduce experimentation with progressive forms of production and ownership.

The success of the program results in stronger community groups and therefore has some reproductive effects in the stabilization of physically deteriorating conditions and the reintegration of alienated individuals into socially sanctioned organizations. In general, the organization's activities focus on resource management and organizational power, vis-a-vis other groups rather than on coalition building and action based on class interests.

To the extent that OND or its associated nonprofit community groups produces technical assistance services, it operates outside normal profit oriented commodity relations and has unreproductive consequences.

The progressive components of OND need to be developed. The program's internal function within HUD and its external function and direct relationship to neighborhood and community based organization is rare in the federal government and, if strengthened, could serve as a mechanism to demand more direct funding and services for neighborhood organizations. An external link and a political support network is essential to sustain the existence of OND. The fate of the Model Cities program in the late sixties, and indeed, OND's own limited budget, demonstrates the weak position that working class interests have within the state.

OND may also expand its efforts by promoting a quasi-governmental role for community organizations in the provision of certain local functions. This would heighten the neighborhood organization's institutional importance in the community, increase neighborhood control, and broaden the participation of residents.

Support for a neighborhood organization's role in production may also further progressive goals. This has particular application in severely deteriorated neighborhoods with high rates of housing abandonment and public and private disinvestment. The failure of the private market to serve the community, even with public subsidy, is self-evident, and justifies support of alternative producers and systems. It becomes possible in this context to foster socialized maintenance, management, ownership, and production, based in varying degrees on need and cost, rather than profit.

The implications of the planner's position as a state agent should, however, not be neglected in defining possible roles; instead they should take advantage of state resources, while simultaneously reinforcing OND's current objectives of self-sufficiency and independence from the state.

CONCLUSIONS

In the preceding sections we analyzed selected programs conducted by the U.S. Department of Housing and Urban Development. Either as employees of that department or of another agency in close contact with it, our commitment to social change requires that we clarify HUD's general functions within American capitalist society, determine how its activities fulfill these specific historical functions, and explore the possibilities for moving its activities in a progressive direction.

Our analysis of HUD began with the department's role in mediating the contradictions that emerged in housing and urban affairs during the overall development of the society. The specific topical issues with which HUD deals, and its programmatic response to those issues, are thus placed in the broader context of the evolution of capitalist society.

Assessment of the planner's role therefore depends on adequately understanding the position of the state and its relationship to the basic structural characteristics of society, specifically those that define capitalist social relations. This includes identification of the basic structural conflicts that not only generate social change but also necessitate state mediation.

The progressive planner who has an understanding of state action can explore elements of HUD's programs that may be useful in promoting fundamental social change. The classification scheme of Esping-Andersen, Friedland and Wright provides guidelines for assessing the extent to which programs reinforce the society's structure, as well as those aspects that are potentially destructive. Again, such prospects must be surveyed within their particular historical contexts. In addition, since state action both shapes and is shaped by class struggle, it is necessary to analyze contradictions within state activities in order to identify and suggest future developments as well as to suggest general directions for unreproductive action.

A notable gap in our analysis has been our failure to develop a dynamic theory of the state. Though the scheme provides us with a powerful tool for classifying the specific mechanisms through which a given program operates, as the originators note, they do not relate their analysis to a more generalized conception of state functioning and its relationship to the production and accumulation of capital. Thus we have an essentially static scheme of state programs grounded in a given set of relationships between the state and the overall political-economic system, but we lack a theoretical model that would incorporate a variety of state-economy relationships.

James O'Connor has, however, developed a useful typology of state functions.(19) This typology classifies state expenditures according to their relationship to the overall role of the state in creating or maintaining the conditions necessary for profitable capital accumulation. The state simultaneously, though often with contradictory results, directly attempts to foster capital accumulation and to maintain and legitimate existing social relations. State expenditures, then, can be viewed as fulfilling either an accumulation or a legitimation function, though, usually it will involve both.

By looking at the relationship between the accumulation of value, the driving force behind a capitalist economy, and the programmatic functioning of the state, O'Connor presents a theoretical understanding of the state within a series of ever changing historical contexts. An integration of O'Connor's approach with that of Esping-Andersen et al. might further illuminate an analysis such as ours by offering a framework for studying the impact of structural change on the progressive potential of specific programs.

Whatever the mode of analysis, we believe that the overriding value of this paper has been in detailing the process involved in social change. Though the specific content of our analysis may only be of interest to a few individuals involved in HUD's urban housing and development issues, the process we have outlined is applicable to other progressives working within the state. Movement toward progressive social change must be based upon an educated understanding of what one is attempting to change and how one plans to make that change. It is our hope that this paper contributes to that understanding.

NOTES

(1) Esping-Andersen et al., "Modes of Class Struggle and the Capitalist State," 1976.

(2) Ibid.

(3) U.S. Department of Housing and Urban Development, HUD Statistical Yearbook, 1977.

(4) Harvey, "The Political Economy of Urbanization," 1975.

(5) U.S. Department of Housing and Urban Development, Series Data Handbook, 1978.

(6) Foard and Frantz, "Evolution of Federal Legislative Policy in Housing," 1973.

(7) U.S. Department of Housing and Urban Development, HUD, 1977.

(8) Ibid. Evaluation of Existing Housing Programs, 1978.

(9) Harvey, "Labor, Capital and Class Struggle," 1976.

(10) Bureau of National Affairs, 1978.

(11) U.S. Department of Housing and Urban Development, HUD, 1977.

(12) Ibid.

(13) Clark, Simon, Ginsburg, and Norman, "The Political Economy of Housing," 1975.

(14) Housing and Community Development Reporter, "Section 8 Leased Housing Assistant Payments Program," April 25, 1977.

(15) Piven and Cloward, Regulating the Poor, 1971.

(16) Hartman and Stone, "Housing: A Radical Alternative," 1978.

(17) Harvey, "Labor, Capital," 1976.

(18) Sternlieb, "New Regional and Metropolitan Realities," 1977.

(19) O'Connor, "The Fiscal Crisis of the State," 1973.

13 Sensitizing Planners to Organization

Howell S. Baum

Forty years ago Karl Mannheim argued that the role of planning should be one of governance because social relationships had become complex, change was increasingly more rapid, and technical tools began to pose the threat of widespread destruction. Planning was, he contended, a means of mediating potentially destructive conflicts and establishing widely legitimate rules for social decision making. He portrayed a situation in which traditional procedures for making decisions were no longer well accepted and the risks posed by many parties acting according to various procedures were extremely high.(1)

The situation that Mannheim described has not improved, and in at least two respects it is worse. First, the means of destruction available to both nations and individuals are not only more dangerous but also more widely distributed. Moreover, the likelihood that people with weapons will actually use them, either premeditatedly or impulsively, has also grown. Christopher Lasch has observed that people today are increasingly consumed with rage, which may find its expression in the use of the handgun, physical or mental abuse of spouses and/or children, and arson or looting. As a societal symptom, this rage is a complex phenomenon. Among many things, it expresses widespread feelings that people are constrained from satisfying their needs, that the rules of society are effectively rigged to prevent people from attaining what they want. Indeed, in response to this continual frustration, many people have forgotten what they may want. They want only to give vent to their rage.(2)

The inability of people to identify what they want points to a second way in which the present situation is worse than that described by Mannheim. One reason that many people cannot state clearly what they want is that politics and public opinion have become, in Habermas's expression, "scientized." A culture of scientism has persuaded people that issues of choice may be technically calculated and decided. Issues of policy are reduced to tasks for technique. Conflicts of material interest are portrayed as difficult but solvable technical problems.(3) As a consequence, people become persuaded that they have no interests that cannot be somehow served without their participation. Their troubles are, as C. Wright Mills would say, "private troubles"; they do not see them as related to public issues that require a political process for resolution.(4) Instead, people become reconciled to believing that their needs are accounted for by technicians and can be bureaucratically dispatched. And yet the rage is a sign that, whatever people have come to accept, they continue to feel that they have desires, needs, and interests that are not served.(5)

In this situation the problem of governance is complex. People have real conflicts of interest – although they often have difficulty seeing them clearly.(6) When they identify conflicts, they frequently find no legitimate rules for resolving them short of extreme violence. The problem of governance is to restore democratic politics in which individuals and groups may articulate the interests that concern them and resolve their conflicts through consensually acceptable, legitimate procedures.(7) The restoration of democratic politics becomes the challenge for planners.

To contribute to this project planners must have both intellectual insight and competence in action. They must understand the ways in which the scientization and bureaucratization of social life conceal political conflicts. They must be sensitive to the public issues that are implicit in people's private troubles. They must be sensitive to the conflicts of interest that reside in public, political issues. Finally, planners must be able to act in such a way as to make this sensitivity effective. In interpersonal relationships they must be able to understand what people really mean and to respond to real, not superficial, concerns. In the organizations in which they work they must be able to influence colleagues in order to exercise some control over the assignment of their work and the implementation of their recommendations. Most importantly they must be able to involve large sectors of affected public groups in planning decisions, and they must be able to organize political support for groups with few material or other resources. In these ways planners can contribute to the creation of democratic politics guided by a broad view of political and economic issues affecting the society.

This raises a crucial question for study. Planners have been trained and are employed to formulate social issues for decision making. Yet one strand of many planners' training suggests that these issues can and should be formulated in technical terms. Further, most planners work in or have frequent contact with bureaucratic organizations in which it is often common procedure to recommend decisions with minimal participation by affected interests. Thus both the training and the work setting of many planners may contribute to the problems in governance just described. It is important to understand whether planners are sensitive to the potential dangers in these tendencies and to assess the degree to which planners may be prepared to contribute, instead, to a restoration of democratic politics as a means of societal governance.

Planners' ability to resolve problems in governance rests on their understanding of structural issues and their competence in articulating and pressing for these issues in the organizations where they work. This study focuses on the ways in which the organizational environments in which planners work affect their views of what they do and their goals in practice. The author conducted interviews with 50 planners in Maryland. The sample, drawn from the membership of the American Institute of Planners, appears to be representative of American planners generally.(8)

The paper approaches these questions by making explicit the "cognitive map" of planners.(9) Planners, like other people, carry a mental image of the world that helps them locate themselves in space, time, and meaning. Their actual experience and the meaning that they attach to this experience depends on this cognitive map. People "see" other people and objects that are located on their maps, but they somehow fail to see others that are excluded. The content and shape of the maps change with experience; people and objects may move into and out of visibility. Functionally, a person's cognitive map also operates as a cognitive grid, screening other people and objects and altering the likelihood that they will be experienced by that person. In characterizing the effect of the cognitive map grids on experience, one may say that they make people more sensitive to certain types of phenomena while simultaneously rendering them insensitive to certain other phenomena.

By assessing planners' cognitive maps, this study investigates whether planners recognize the processes through which decisions in their organizations are made concerning the issues about which the planning staff writes reports and makes plans. Planners' interview responses will be analyzed to assess whether they reflect a clear understanding of 1) the structure of their agency or firm; and 2) the ways in which this structure affects decisions on planning issues. The responses will be examined to determine whether planners mentally locate themselves in relation to some explicit structure of power in their organization or the larger community. Do planners tend to recognize their activities as part of a network of formal and informal relationships that might be developed into a coalition of support for particular planning recommendations? This line of investigation is important for two reasons. First, planners who recognize these organizational realities are more likely to be effective in having their recommendations implemented (other things being equal), than those who do not.(10) Second, the restoration of democratic politics depends in part on the ability of planners to think in political terms and to make use of organizational decision making processes to broaden participation in planning.

PLANNERS' PERCEPTIONS OF THEMSELVES

The description of planners' sensitivity is divided into two sections. This section draws on planners' responses to several questions in order to depict what planners see themselves as doing. The next section draws on responses that fill in the details of cognitive maps in which planners mentally locate their work vis-a-vis other people and other activities.

What Planners Try to Accomplish

Responses to two questions help to develop a picture of planners' activities as they see them. The first question asked was what they try most to accomplish as practitioners. Most of the responses contained loftily phrased, often progressive sounding objectives for society: planning better communities, creating environments that meet people's needs, increasing social justice, and improving the rationality of decision making.

Most of the statements can be grouped into one of three categories. The largest group, mentioned by one-third of the sample, concern goals related to the physical environment, such as making changes in the physical environment to meet human needs, helping to balance growth and development, and contributing to physically appealing communities. The tone of these goals is expressed in the following quotes. One country planner described his concerns about the ends of his planning generally: ". . . making an environment, the things I touch, more useful to the people involved, whether they know it or not. . . enhancing the quality of life."

An administrator reflected on what he tries to do through the activities of his department: ". . . improving a community's living environment. . .seeing people receive improvements of services, physical improvements that they envision should be part of their community. . .whatever they saw as the needs of their community."

An architect-planner said that he was interested in:

> . . . solving human problems. It is the same thing as when I work as an architect. I want to be responsive to a wide range of human needs. . . .There are psychological and aesthetic needs that I feel are important to try to satisfy. I think my design background has made me aware of a wide range of human needs, and I try to meet them. What I try to do is to be more satisfied with practicing as an architect, but expanding my definition of what it is to be an architect.

Almost one-third of the sample mentioned various social goals, including increasing social justice, improving social equity and, in a number of ways, meeting human needs. For example, one planner with many years of experience commented that, "In terms of distributing benefits, I try to distribute benefits to people who are disadvantaged. I try to put the costs where people can pay for them. That is difficult because the government process is financed by a regressive process."

A planner in an urbanizing county offered the following overview of his goals in contributing to the shaping of this urbanization process:

> I think that the county is an urbanizing county. The dangers that the county will approach will be like the problem of the cities. Others may be worse because the county does not have the infrastructure that the city does. I see myself as working for the county, helping the county to become aware of some of the problems which are on the doorsteps and to develop some institutions which would help it to do that. I see this as being planning a series of employment programs. That is one of my goals.

A transportation planner in a state agency described his goals this way:

> I guess (my goals are) increasing or improving the living situation for as many people as possible through my particular field. I obviously do not have money to give to the poor. . . .Creating a better environment for as many people as I can, while simultaneously I consider freedom of mobility of the individual a high priority.

A third group of planners, representing about one-sixth of the sample, said that they work to get results, regardless of the specific content. The following statements are representative of this view. One planner of several decades' experience said he worked for, ". . .implementation of plans. (I am) not satisfied to come up with documents that go on a shelf. Attached to every planning document should be a section that shows where it can be done, how it can be financed, when it can be implemented."

A planner-developer, who first suggested that he did not have any specific goals, emphasized results as a necessity: "I am not out to change the world. I was never out to change the world. . . . I have no great humanitarian goals. Money is more important." Another planner emphasized results as important for a sense of competence and satisfaction with work: "(I look for) the success of a project. End results, unfortunately, are the only measure of your accomplishments, and everyone would try to achieve that. In architecture the success is quite short term. But in planning, you may never do that. There is a rate of achievements in planning, rather than a successful project."

There is an affective component to many responses that these statements do not convey. A number of planners confess having difficulty identifying any personal goals. For example, one planner suggested that the general status of planning is so low that individual planners may never be able to set and reach personal goals until their work acquires broad social legitimacy: "My immediate concern is with (the agency's) staff. I have a tremendous concern – maybe it grows out of personal insecurity – with having the section and department legitimized. Often we are the laughing stock. (We must) strive constantly for the credibility of our section and our section's work."

Another planner shared some of these concerns and said that he needed a position in which he could have power before it would make sense to set personal goals: "Personally, I want to have my own shop. I want to be a director. . . . I want the profession to have more respect within the local government. I think the profession is viewed as an outsider meddling in the business of local government."

A private consultant who had worked in planning for several decades expressed a sense of resignation about not having much control over his work: "I don't have any ambitions any more along these lines. I am so busy with production."

A strongly stated but broadly representative view was provided by one city planner when asked what he tried to accomplish: "Nothing. The way I see it, I'm here at my desk. I'll do whatever they ask, just as long as it's not zoning. One thing which we used to do, which no one liked to do, was land-using the city. Now it is done by a computer."

This planner singles out zoning as distasteful; other planners identify other tasks they want to avoid. Yet what this planner's statement represents is a broad sense of discouragement. This view shows a readiness by planners to do creative work, coupled with a belief that such creative work will not be expected of them. A number of planners share this feeling, even while they express the desire to serve broad ends through planning.

These statements create a picture of contrasts. On the one hand, approximately two-thirds of the planners identify some goals toward which they say that they strive in practice. Although some of these goals are vaguely stated, most might be characterized as concerned with making changes in the physical or social environment in order to meet people's needs. Many planners, however, including some who espouse these goals, say that they feel they have little power and that, consequently, goals do not mean much in practice. Even among those who identify clear goals, very few express confidence that they make much progress toward them in their daily work. Most of these planners do not see themselves as powerful.

How Planners Expect to Accomplish Their Goals

In the above statements planners portray themselves as a group whose prime goal is meeting people's needs, but also with a sense of impotence about their ability to accomplish their goals. In this light it is useful to ask what skills planners believe they need to enable them to reach their goals. It is possible, for example, that planners' goals may be reasonable in the positions they occupy but that they have chosen inappropriate skills to lead them to those goals. To analyze this possible conflict, planners were asked what they regarded as their strengths in practice.

The tone of the responses was set by one successful administrator who impulsively retorted, "I didn't know that I had any (strengths)!" A number of planners responded to the question with a long pause. Others declared succinctly, "I don't know." Following such unpromising prefaces, most planners moved ahead to provide some answer to the question.

The skills that planners did mention as strengths may be grouped into two categories: intellectual skills and interpersonal/organizational/political skills. Approximately two-thirds of the sample described their strengths in terms that emphasized intellectual skills. One-third portrayed their strengths in terms that included skills in interpersonal or political processes, sometimes combined with intellectual skills.

The planners emphasizing their intellectual strengths in practice referred to the types of expertise identified in the following statements:

> I think I am good at analysis and evaluation of the results. I am also good at developing procedures and schemes that serve the immediate needs.

> I think the thing probably is in synthesis. I am not a data freak. I enjoy getting together all the information because it is necessary. But the challenge is to say, what does it all mean? Which I could call the synthesis phase. That is when I can contribute the most.

> (I would emphasize) the ability to remove myself from the day and look at the future to get a decent reading on what is happening . . . in order to have an air of predictability which you can be relatively sure about.

These statements are representative of the two-thirds of the planners who emphasized intellectual skills as their primary strength. These planners describe their work as a rational, intellectual process and depict themselves as intellectual problem solvers. They collect information, organize it to formulate alternative solutions for problems, evaluate the alternatives in light of their likely future consequences, and make recommendations for others to follow. Earlier, these planners said that they seek to accomplish goals related to reordering society and the physical environment. Now they say that in practice they wield intellectual skills in order to achieve these goals. They imply that there is something about the force of their ideas that should make social and physical changes come about. At the same time, many of these same planners reported a sense of powerlessness in their work. Apparently they are saying that in practice their ideas alone do not give them influence to enact the ends they seek.

The planners who characterized themselves as having interpersonal or political strengths, either alone or in combination with intellectual strengths, present a contrast. In this group one skill frequently mentioned is essentially a bridge between ideas and organizational practice. A veteran planner described this skill as "my ability to deal with complex matters, to integrate them and to help other people understand them, so that they can make intelligent choices, without sacrificing too much of the detail."

Administrators are most frequently expected to work with others, and they tended to be particularly inclined to identify interpersonal skills as a strength. One administrator expressed the viewpoint of many when he emphasized his ability "as a manager, a synergist, where I can bring together different disciplines, where I can orchestrate things, and out of it comes something physical. That is what I do best."

Another administrator, with two decades of experience, emphasized, as did many planners, the importance of his ability to get along with people:

> My personal greatest strength is an ability to work with people. I am not a great administrator, and I am not a fantastic organizer. But I have been able to break through barriers and get people to talk with each other. We have to resolve differences which will occur unless we do communicate. Coordination, communication is so vital in these things.

One county planner provided a particularly articulate description of what is involved in working with others in organized decision making processes:

> I am practical. (It is) the combination of personality and training as a strategist. If there is anybody who can figure out a way to make something happen in a system as complex as this, it is me. . . . I seem to have a higher tolerance, patience. Basically being a secure person. . . . It takes coming into the situation and looking at it, understanding that there are constraints. . . . It's like, in a situation as complicated as this, the person who defines the problem is ahead of the game. If somebody has defined the problem, what they have got is one perspective on it. You work to bring about some consensus. A combination of being able to tolerate a high degree of ambiguity and yet constantly seeking to make order out of it.

These statements depict a different view of the planning process from that offered by planners emphasizing intellectual strengths. Here planning is described as a political process wherein planners contribute to social and physical changes by clarifying issues, communicating with interested actors, and facilitating agreements among parties with possible differences in interests. These planners are saying that ideas in themselves have little force to accomplish broad planning goals without the organization of coalitions in support of the ideas.

These statements suggest two observations. First, a majority of planners, describing the planning process as an intellectual one, and rarely referring to the political interests of the parties involved, do not regard themselves as social or political actors of any type. Second, the minority of planners, who describe themselves as political actors who are sensitive to other parties' interests in the planning process, are more optimistic about the likelihood of making progress, albeit marginal, toward their goals.(11)

PLANNERS' COGNITIVE MAPS OF THE ENVIRONMENT OF THEIR WORK

The preceding findings point to two reasons why it is important to explore the cognitive maps of planners, to make clear the terrain they recognize surrounding their work. First, many planners' expressions of powerlessness raise the question whether or not the various goals and strengths that planners claim are appropriately matched to the environments in which they experience themselves as working. For example, do the majority claiming intellectual strengths but expressing frustration actually describe an environment in which intellectual skills alone are sufficient for influence? Do those claiming interpersonal or political strengths go on to describe their environment in sufficient detail to relate their claimed strengths to what they actually experience in their organizations?

Second, it was argued initially that planners should contribute to a restoration of democratic politics, and yet, in describing personal strengths, relatively few planners make direct reference to political action. Accordingly, it is important to investigate whether organizational and political phenomena appear in planners' cognitive maps of the environments in which they work. Specifically, it should be asked whether planners are sensitive to the political processes that influence planning decisions. Do planners describe or refer to the structure of their agency or firm and the ways in which this structure affects decisions on planning issues? Do planners make tangible mention of the structure of power in their organization or in the larger community? Are they aware of the influence of both formal and informal organizational relationships in developing a coalition of support for a particular planning recommendation?

Planners' Difficulties in Assessing Their Work

Some evidence about the presence of organizational phenomena in planners' cognitive maps comes from responses to a question to planners about whether they ever experience difficulty in assessing their work. Planners' responses divide them roughly into two groups – one that has relatively little difficulty in assessing their work and one that has relatively common difficulty making an assessment. The similar explanations offered by planners reporting assessment difficulties are most informative for the purpose of examining the cognitive maps of planners. The tone of the comments was set by one planner who said that, with regard to the intrinsic quality of her work she rarely had problems assessing it, but that with regard to the form of presentation of that same work to others in the planning process she sometimes had difficulties. For her and other planners there was apparently something nonrational about the organizational process of planning that made assessment of work in the context of that process difficult.

Many planners describe the organizational process of planning as confusing. One city planner who said that he rarely had difficulty assessing his work emphasized:

> . . .the very complex nature of the work itself. The rules and regulations of the legislation are very complex, and so sometimes the technical complexity makes it difficult to assess. The other part is in terms of human behavior. Human behavior itself is very complex. Social scientists are just beginning to understand what makes people tick.

An administrator who claimed organizational skills observed, nevertheless:

> I think that at the beginning of any project or process you establish your goals which you want to achieve and you work from your goals down to your plan to carry out your goals. . . . By the time of implementation, it appears to be a kind of a compromise. When you implement the plan, you wonder if it corresponds to the original goals. I think that happens almost on a daily basis.

This view is echoed by a consultant who remarked that

> Projects often end up going for a great period of time, from start to when they open the doors. . . . A lot of the people I worked with will be gone by then. So there is a great separation between my early efforts and what the product looks like. It is easy to lose sight of the other things which you do along the line before you get to the final product. Or you could go through the entire thing, and the project is aborted.

These planners refer to intellectual difficulties in grasping the complexities of the planning process; they also allude to difficulties in controlling their role in this process. One county planner noted that there are difficulties related to "the stage of the thing when you pick it up. (Often) it is not clearly defined. It kind of leaves you with a lost feeling before you get into it. When it is all done, nothing becomes of it. Those kinds of circumstances."

A public agency administrator elaborated on the difficulties in controlling the planning process:

> It is that you are too close to the work. Part of the problem is that you do not have time. The job has to be done. You have to come up with quick solutions. You do not have time to sit back and reflect on how you might do it five different ways. There is a different way to answer the question (about difficulty assessing his work). . . . I could say that it would frequently be the case that you do not have the time to think about the best way of doing it. I'm convinced that winging it is not the best way to go. The biggest problem with the job is that you really do not have the time to do the breadth and analysis which you know you should do. You continually have to suboptimize. You have to use people who do not have the skills to get the job done. Or you do not have the time to do the research. The people and time constraints are significant.

In the context of this complexity, consequently, it is difficult to identify any fixed standards for evaluation, as this regional planner argued:

> There is really no fixed standard to evaluate it by, and the kinds of feedback you get are not necessarily ones which I consider valid. Half the time I don't think they know what they are talking about. Or if you think they don't want to rock the boat. . . if you are working for (a large commission), it is impossible to achieve a consensus about what you are supposed to be achieving. I think this is one of the most difficult things about working with a regional planning agency in a controversial arena. So it is rare that you get a program that it is not difficult to get everyone to agree on. Just choose whom you want to make enemies out of. You just try not to take it personally.

In describing difficulties in assessing work, planners claiming organizational or political strengths tended to report slightly less difficulty than planners claiming intellectual strengths. This difference suggests that planners who regard themselves as political actors comprehend the planning process better than planners who regard themselves as rational intellectual analysts. If this is correct, then it is clearly appropriate to see planning as a process of facilitating communication among disparate interests and organizing the efforts of numerous actors in support of a course of action which represents a compromise among the goals of many parties.

Nevertheless, even though politically oriented planners seem to understand the planning process better than others, most planners did refer to some difficulty in assessing their work, and invariably they related their frustration or puzzlement to the political organization of the process. The following experience is typical: Planners report that they perform competent intellectual work and submit it to the appropriate recipient. Then something that most have difficulty comprehending or describing – something "crazy" – happens to their work. It may be lost. It may be received but never read. It may be read but never responded to. It may be responded to, without result. Or, eventually, "something" may happen, but so much time has elapsed since the planner's input that it is difficult to know whether the results are related to the planner's work.

Most planners report that they cannot comprehend this organizational process intellectually. In addition, most indicate that they do not have the interpersonal skills to influence it politically. The result is a loss of control over their work once it becomes part of the organizational process of planning. This experience epitomizes alienation in work.(12)

How Planners Would Change the Conditions for Planning

Planners were asked what changes in the environment of planning would make it easier for them to accomplish their goals. Their responses identify phenomena to which they are sensitive in a dual sense: these are phenomena to which they are particularly attentive, and they are phenomena that irritate them. The responses provide further information about the presence or absence of organizational concerns in planners' cognitive maps.

One-tenth of the planners in the sample named specific superiors as culprits and said that their replacement would make proper planning possible. For example, one planner in a county office made this recommendation:

> Fire two, three people at the top of the department, this division, and the heads of administrations in other (related departments). Get somebody with a little desire to work closely with but not be quite so shilly-shallying about dealing with people with potentially hostile political complaints. If you're going to get something done, you have to ruffle a few feathers sometimes. But if you do it in an honest way, you get respect, and get something done.

One-fifth argued that there should be fewer bureaucratic restrictions on technical planning and that the planning process should somehow be "depoliticized." One planner said that his personal solution might be to "go from being a Planner to a planner, aligning myself to more project-, less politically-tied organizations and individuals. The county system is very politicized, very slow to move."

More concretely, another planner described his goals for changing the planning process:

> One thing would be . . . we're trying to work now . . . to change the planning process and the planners – changing the level of responsibility which planners take within the local government. We're trying to stick it to them (the planners)! Out here the

> Council are the planners. I'd like to see them not see themselves as the planners. What I see ultimately as helping us to do a better job is changing the roles and responsibilities and organizational structure of the county. I'm trying to have an effect on that.

Two-fifths said that planners in various general ways should have more power, should receive more support for their efforts, and should have a larger budget for their work. One county land use planner said simply, "We need easier and more frequent access to the County Executive's office, because that is where the power exists." Another planner argued that good planning required a larger budget than planners currently worked with:

> This (changes that should be made) gets into problems of dollars, taxes, money, income, zoning, regulation . . . and I honestly do not have any nice neat answers to any of this. Money is limited. The principal element needed is understanding on the parts of those controlling these things. I can understand the problems of the councilmen. This is not easy, because the people themselves do not understand.

A veteran of several decades underscored the need for planners to develop a constituency for their work:

> One of the biggest priorities is more responsibility for business to work with neighborhood organizations, and I guess more of a trust between government and people, especially large government. There has to be more trust on the part of government that people can do things for themselves. And the only way to do this is to build power for the people, but also to bring in business, in partnership with people power.

These recommendations have a remarkable quality. In expressing planners' sensitivity to perceived points of leverage in their work environment, they suggest components of a theory of political decision making. Planners refer to the importance of personality, bureaucratic rules, budget allocations and support from community groups. Collectively, planners seem to share some understanding of different aspects of decision making in planning organizations. Individually, however, few planners appear to have either a broad or a sophisticated understanding of organizational decision making. Most planners focus on single components of their organizations for change; they do not articulate an understanding of the relationship between tinkering with one component and changing the organization as a social and political system in order to permit them the influence they desire.

For example, the suggestion that the replacement of superiors would significantly change the planning environment implies that relations in organizations can be reduced to the interactions of specific individual personalities. At another extreme, the recommendation that the planning process be depoliticized treats the organizational process as if it were an abstraction, something that could somehow be either politicized or depoliticized while remaining substantially intact. In addition, the desire that the planning process be depoliticized stands in evident contradiction to the recommendation most frequently offered by planners calling for more power and support. This recommendation conveys a lack of appreciation for organization as a political strategy. The empowerment of planners must be a political process. Yet few planners perceive any contradiction between calling for depoliticization of the planning process and simultaneously calling for more power for planners. Further, most of the planners calling for more power do not refer in definitive ways to the organizational setting in which they presently work with less than the desired support. Nor do they specify organizational strategies that could bring them power.

Planners who claim to have organizational or political strengths do not differ significantly from planners claiming intellectual strengths in relation to the types of recommendations for changes they offer or in terms of the relative abstractness of their recommendations. These findings suggest that, insofar as planners claiming organizational skills may feel influential in the planning process, many may be focusing on interpersonal relations in the organization, rather than on the overall direction. In this respect they apparently resemble other planners in lacking an overview of the decision making process as a whole.

When describing their work, many planners characterized it as working on an assembly line while wearing blinders, in such a way that the workers on both sides of them are hardly visible. Many planners are not certain where their work comes from. They know who gave them their immediate assignment, but they do not always know what larger problem and picture their assignment fits into. Once they have carried out their assigned work, they submit their product, usually a written document, to a supervisor (generally the same one who gave them the assignment). In this process they may have some influence over how their assignment is presented to them or how they execute their assignment, but what becomes of the product of their work is for many planners a mystery.

Buffeted by political pressures, the planner's report or recommendations traverses several organizational lines of communication. But planners evidently do not have a picture of these organizational lines in their cognitive maps. Consequently, when they speak of changes, they refer to what they do see directly – namely, individuals who give assignments – or they refer abstractly to a process whose character they only dimly imagine.

How Planners Redefine Their Work in Practice

Cumulatively, these findings pose an important question. A majority of planners start out with broadly stated, often progressive goals. Yet many express a sense of powerlessness in meeting these goals. On close inspection, it appears that most planners do not have a clear understanding of the organizational environment in which they work or an understanding of the ways in which organizational change strategies might give them influence. Accordingly, it is reasonable to ask whether, in the face of this frustration and perplexity, planners may not redefine their expectations so as to find some satisfaction in their work. Planners were asked what they looked for as signs of their effectiveness in their work.

Two-fifths of the planners said that they regarded implementation as the primary criterion of their effectiveness. Either some part of their recommendation is put into practice, or, more modestly, some part of their analytic work is used by others. How much or which part of their work is accepted tends to be less important than that some portion has been accepted. For instance, one planner argued that he was "looking for on-the-ground kinds of validations (actual construction)." An administrator said that he wanted to know, "Do I get my own way? That doesn't mean that I cannot compromise at points, because I have, but I look at the percentage, of how often it goes where I thought it should go."

Another planner said that he wanted to have his work read. He looked for "its being picked up by other people. . . beyond being done by yourself. . . implementation." In a similar vein, a staff planner in a state agency emphasized,

> primarily, acceptance by the secretary of this department. Secondarily, as actual accomplishments, in terms of achieving legislation or achieving budget funds, which I initiated or helped to plan. But primarily I see my role as being a technical advisor to the head of the organization in planning-related ideas, and his acceptance of these ideas is the best evaluation I can have that I am having an impact.

A second group of planners, also comprising about two-fifths of the sample, said that they look for supportive feedback from their immediate client or from the constituency for or with whom they are planning. Although they find it most desirable to be commended for doing work that actually improved others' lives, they indicated that they also value clients' comments that they like working with the planner or respected the planner's intentions. One planner in an urban county emphasized good working relationships in the community: "(I value) being taken seriously by my director, working directly with the staff of almost every county department. The response I get from the community when I am with them tells me that they believe what I am doing."

A planner who does considerable volunteer work pointed to influence on others' thinking:

> (I look at) simply the degree to which those with whom you're working at least recognize the need to take a longer-range point-

of-view. In the case of the recreation program in the county, for example, the degree to which the County Council, the County Executive at least indicate that they know what you're talking about.

A private consultant stated that he relied completely on the client's satisfaction:

> The satisfaction of the client (is the only indicator of effectiveness). I don't judge my work. It is the client who judges my work. It is up to the client to judge if you have done his work. His satisfaction is your satisfaction. You can have any criteria – it depends on whom you get. As long as the client is satisfied, I am satisfied.

A final group, which included one-third of the planners, emphasized the importance of approval or compliments from agency colleagues as a sign of their effectiveness. The following comments are typical of this focus:

> (I look for) responses from other people, verbal responses, how people react. When I do workshops, I give out feedback sheets. I've even started doing that with our staff, after our management meetings. I have not perfected that yet, but yesterday I had good results.

> (What is primary for me is) whether my work meets criticism, praise, compliments.

> (I look for) no editing (of what I write). . . .There is not that much backslapping and congratulations. When I have done something decent, I get some congratulatory remarks from colleagues. I do not need that all the time, but now and then it is nice. Often here you feel you are being taken for granted.

These statements contrast markedly with the earlier, nebulous statements about what planners seek to accomplish in practice. More significantly, the ways in which planners redefine their aims reflect their organizational environment even while they make little mention of the organization. For example, whereas two-thirds of the planners describe themselves as practitioners with intellectual strengths, two-thirds identify interpersonal feedback from clients or colleagues as their primary criterion for effectiveness, and most of the rest identify some form of implementation requiring interpersonal effectiveness. Planning takes place in organizational settings, and planners come to evaluate themselves in terms of their ability to enact the outcomes expected of them in their roles or their ability to obtain the rewards accessible to them in their roles. The influence of the organization is similarly evident in planners' movement from the initial goals of accomplishing broad social or physical change to the striving for almost any kind of acceptance of their work and, crucially, personal approval and compliments from others with whom they work.

The influence of organizational structures on this transformation of goals is evident in an association between particular choices of criteria for effectiveness and the roles of the planners most frequently mentioning those criteria. For example, private consultants are concerned first about implementation of results and clients' approval, which translates into economic survival. Public agency administrators, working under many expectations similar to those of private consultants, consider themselves effective when they are able to contribute to implementation and when they receive praise from such clients as elected officials and community leaders. However, lower level staff are quite different. Very few are concerned about implementation. Less than a fourth are interested in a response from constituents. Rather, two-thirds look for comments from others in their agency to tell them whether they should consider themselves effective.

The very low importance that staff planners attach to implementation – including even the use of their work by someone else – is remarkable. This emphasis on interpersonal relations with agency colleagues represents a response to the feelings of powerlessness expressed by a number of planners. In this respect, the orientation of most lower level staff planners epitomizes the problem experienced by many planners. They tend to limit their influence and any resultant satisfaction as planners by mapping the setting for their work in such a way that they do not see the organizational process within which planning decisions are made. They are not aware of alternative ways in which planning problems may be formulated or the available resources that they may draw on to influence the formulation of these problems and the implementation of recommendations about them. At the same time, desiring some satisfaction in work, they turn their attention to those rewards that are accessible to them within the organization. However, because they have only a vague picture of the organization, they recognize few opportunities for influence as a source of satisfaction and turn instead to possible rewards that they can grasp – praise and compliments from colleagues. Thus, although many planners apparently do not recognize the organizational process, they are very much affected by it in redefining their work.

INTERPRETATION

Many of the comments made by planners on issues with a political or organizational dimension revealed little recognition of these issues. Many planners do not generally see decision making as a social process involving conflicts of interests and in which various political resources, including organizational skill, are necessary for influence. They may not be sensitive to the types of organizational conflicts and strategies for their resolution with which political actors are familiar. Planners may not see that the process of reaching a decision involves organizing a consensus among interests with different perceptions of what is a problem and how it may be resolved.

The cognitive map of planners may also be described positively in terms of what is included. Planners often see themselves as individual entrepreneurs working with individual clients on well-defined technical problems with definitive solutions. They have a tendency to believe that knowledge is directly transformable into power and that they will influence decision making by virtue of their possession of both a greater quantity and also more accurate information than others.

Described either positively or negatively, this cognitive map provides a poor guide to the world in which most planners work. Most are employed by, or must negotiate with, bureaucratic organizations. They collect and analyze information for actors in a political decision making process. While they are not expected to make decisions, their actual influence over decisions rests on their understanding of the organization of the decision making process and their willingness and ability to exercise political skills in that process.(13) Planners who carry the cognitive map described here will have limited influence because they are carrying a map for one world while attempting to act in another.

In the context of the discussion of governance and the restoration of democratic politics, the most important finding is that most planners do not see the world in which they practice in either political or organizational terms. They are not accustomed to looking for conflicts of interest embedded in planning problems or to seeing themselves engaged in a "politics of expertise" (14) over the definition and resolution of these problems in organizational decision making processes. One specific consequence is that planners who do espouse progressive goals may be so ineffective in working in organizational settings that they end up pragmatically redefining their expectations in terms of organizational rewards. More generally, because most of these planners are unaccustomed to thinking in political terms, the broad discussion of the restoration of democratic politics or progressive roles for planners is likely to have little meaning for them.

The implication of these conclusions for planners is clear: until they are able to see their practice in political terms, they are unlikely to have much influence over planning decisions. Yet there is another, and more serious, implication for citizens. The challenge to planners, it has been argued, is to help to restore democratic politics. However, the planners described here tend to conceptualize planning issues in technical terms and to dispatch them within the narrow bounds of bureaucratic regulations. They reinforce the scientization and bureaucratization of politics. Far from contributing to the restoration of democratic politics, most planners in effect contribute to a decay of politics and problems in governance. Consequently, the poor and the powerless whose interests are not represented in planning decisions will likely continue to be ignored. This is not simply a problem of the political weakness of a group of practitioners. More critically, it is a problem of the disenfranchisement of large numbers of citizens from decisions that could address and redress social and economic inequalities.

AN ALTERNATIVE, PROGRESSIVE ROLE FOR PLANNERS

As the preceding study indicates, there are two compelling reasons for seeking an alternative role for planners. First, planners will constrain themselves to ineffectiveness as long as they continue to eschew politics, treat issues in technical terms, and conform closely to bureaucratic norms. Second, since planners are unavoidably implicated in decisions about the distribution of both public and private goods and services, planners should be prepared to acquire the knowledge and skills that will enable them to influence the distribution of these goods and services toward the groups in society who now have few of either.

Norman Krumholz and his associates have argued similarly from their planning experience:

> Attempts to implement policies spell politics. This does not introduce politics into planning; it has always been there. The critical question is: whose politics, whose values will planners seek to implement? Planners who choose to address themselves to the roots of our nation's urban crisis must come face-to-face with the problems of our cities' most disadvantaged residents and the neighborhoods in which they live. . . .Ultimately, this calls for a change in the traditional role of a planner, one that will lead to broadened responsibilities and, hopefully, to greater influence. Planners may choose to stay within the narrow boundaries of their customary area of expertise, or they may define new roles for themselves. To opt for the former is to risk being relegated to an increasingly marginal position in urban affairs. In choosing to redefine their roles along the lines outlined above, planners may eventually find themselves in positions of leadership in urban government.(15)

This section briefly describes an alternative role that planners employed in bureaucracies might adopt to contribute to restoration of democratic politics in support of people who are now poor and powerless. (Other roles would be appropriate for planners working elsewhere.) This role would compensate for the apolitical stance of most of the planners pictured here. The next section discusses strategies for educating planners for such a role.

The goal of a progressive role for bureaucratically employed planners is to politicize the process of making decisions about planning issues. Planners should identify the issues that they analyze with the affected interests. They should be prepared to involve and provide support for the poorer and less powerful interests. This process of politicization requires changes in both planners' thinking and their actions.

Intellectually, planners should be prepared to analyze any planning issue within the broader context of economic and political interests affected by the issue. In receiving assignments or in initiating studies, planners must be prepared to carry out both the technical analysis expected of them and an analysis of the economic and political implications of the technical issues and alternative courses of action that could be taken in relation to the issue. The quality of the technical analysis should not be questionable. At the same time, the technical and political analysis should be so carefully joined that it would be difficult to separate the two in any reading of the planner's work. Put simply, any planner should be prepared to perform a "political impact analysis" routinely, as part of every assignment.

And yet the preparation of politically sensitive analyses of planning issues, no matter how competently they are prepared, is unlikely in itself to affect decision making. This is one lesson of the experiences of current practitioners, who have paid little attention to communicating their analyses with impact within a political decision making process. In short, planners must be prepared not only to think in political terms, but also to act in political terms. The political content of any planning analysis consists not only of the words in any written document but also the organization of political support behind alternative positions identified as the document.(16)

Citizen participation is a more or less acceptable component of planning processes. However, although it is ostensibly an effort to maintain linkages between technical analyses and a wide range of perceived political interests, in practice the citizens who participate actively in most planning processes tend to represent a small segment of interests affected. Yet the rhetoric of citizen participation gives planners a tacit mandate to establish a variety of formal and informal contacts with citizen groups. Planners can identify the groups they want to contact on the basis of their political analysis of the interests affected by planning issues. These groups may become both sources of information and potential users of the analyses of planning issues prepared by planners.

This role, similar to that described by the Needlemans, may have two progressive effects.(17) The first is to facilitate the participation of excluded interests in the political process of influencing planning decisions. Planners may develop constituencies for their analyses of planning issues so that their content includes the message that citizen groups are concerned about the outcomes of decisions that they perceive as affecting their interests. Their strategy makes it more likely that planners' analyses combining technical and political considerations are likely to be accepted, read, and seriously considered in the political process through which planning decisions are reached. Incidentally, whatever formal participants do with planners' analyses, in this way planners will succeed in disseminating their analyses to an audience outside the immediate planning bureaucracy, who may then use the analyses and the recommendations as guides for longer-range political action.

This role may contribute in another crucial way to progressive goals. The cumulative effect of large numbers of planners directly or indirectly bringing citizen groups into the planning process is to begin to recreate political discussion about planning issues. Technical issues may have to be translated back into clear formulations of the economic and political interests affected and may have to be identified more accurately as basic choices of policy direction. This process is likely to be a gradual but cumulative one, in which citizen groups more carefully watch planning decisions and more certainly raise political concerns in connection with them. These citizen groups clearly require continual intellectual and emotional support from the planners.

Insofar as the number of interested actors who insist on participating in planning decisions increases, it is possible that normal decision making processes may become overloaded – unable to accommodate widespread, explicitly political demand for participation. This pressure on planning decision making processes may force a recognition of the inadequacies of these processes as procedures for governance in a society with many broadly conflicting interests. Blockages in making decisions may lead to the consideration of alternative procedures for accommodating conflicting interests. This strategy is similar to that of welfare rights organizations, which seek to raise questions about the appropriateness of existing social welfare policies by organizing citizens to make legal claims on the social welfare system in an effort to overload and break the system. Such a crisis, it is hoped, would lead to a consideration of alternative policies. This strategy is, of course, a long-range one.

EDUCATION FOR PROGRESSIVE PLANNING ROLES (18)

In order to perform the progressive planning role just described, planners will need various types of knowledge, as well as intellectual and action skills, which most planners do not have. They will need an understanding of the broad political and economic context within which planning issues rest. Other papers in this volume have described this structural context.(19) In addition, planners processing such knowledge will need to be sensitive to the organizational context within which they work. They will need to understand the formal and informal operations of the specific bureaucratic organization where they are employed, as well as the larger political process through which decisions about planning issues will be made. Related to this more sophisticated mapping of organizations and their politics, planners will need to develop skills in working with and influencing significant actors in the bureaucratic organization and its environment.

The implications of the preceding discussion for education are clear. New roles for planners require that they think and act in radically new ways. In order for planners to acquire the new knowledge and skills, fundamentally new methods of educating planners are necessary. The development of new programs in planning education should begin with an identification of reasons why planners may not think and act in political terms now. First, there are strong pressures in planning work settings for planners to emphasize technical concerns and to exclude political considerations, particularly when raising political issues would hold powerful interests open to scrutiny. Nevertheless, there are many practitioners who could bring political issues to light if they had the skills, and there are many others who might raise political issues if they were aware of them. Accordingly, while acknowledging the importance of bureaucratic pressures to be apolitical, the discussion here will focus on the ways in which planners may lack the knowledge or skills to confront these pressures. It is here that planning education programs may have their most immediate effects.

The statements of planners interviewed in the study point to five types of situations in which planners may experience obstacles to understanding and acting politically in organizations.(20) These obstacles may be ordered along a continuum corresponding to their complexity and the difficulty of interventions called for to remedy them.

1. At the most complex end of the continuum are those present and future planners who have deep emotional ambivalences about power and its exercise and who will be unable to be sensitive to organizational and political issues until they can resolve this ambivalence.(21)

2. A second group may not have conflicts about the exercise of power but may be markedly uncomfortable in interpersonal and group relationships in organizational settings.

3. A third group may be comfortable with the exercise of power and comfortable in interpersonal relationships but may hold the ideological belief that they should not or need not exercise power in their roles as intellectuals.

4. Another group may be emotionally and intellectually prepared to exercise power but may lack specific skills instrumental in the use of power.

5. A fifth group may have the emotional and intellectual readiness and the interpersonal competence to be effective as organizational actors but may simply not recognize political situations and opportunities to take initiatives in influencing decisions.

These five groups do not have tight boundaries and may overlap. Any single planner may experience obstacles associated with one or several groups. Nevertheless what is valuable about this classification scheme is that it points to different types of interventions that may be necessary to make a significant number of planners more sensitive to organizational issues and prepared to act on them.

Because some obstacles to planners' understanding and acting in political settings are highly complex, educational programs to make planners sensitive to organization and politics should be both didactic and experiential. Accordingly, the needs of any class of planning students or practitioners should be met with a curriculum consisting of a variety of educational strategies. In response to the obstacles just described, a series of educational interventions may be identified as potential remedies. Corresponding generally to the ordering of obstacles from less to more complex, these interventions may be arranged along a continuum, from the more didactic to the more experiential:

1. Didactic suggestions that organization and politics are important: Being sensitive to – selectively guiding attention toward – both organization and political organizing strategies is one type of action. Didactic presentations have severe limitations in their ability to teach effective action without additional experiential learning.(22)

2. Case studies: Case studies permit vicarious participation in situations where the presence or absence of organizational sensitivity and political strategy affected the outcomes of planning decisions. Case studies may be most useful in alerting planners to the importance of this sensitivity and in pointing out some specific organizational issues and specific political skills that planners have used. Case studies may not seriously affect noncognitive or emotional obstacles to planners' becoming conscious political actors.(23)

3. Simulation games: Simulation games provide for direct participation in situations that may comprise part of a normal planner's role. Participants must become sensitive to the organizational incentive system of the game and are expected to discuss each other's behavior after the game. The value of simulations for teaching about organizational and political issues depends on their plausibility as simulations of planning situations. Further, the leader's ability to direct participants' attention to nonrational components of behavior in the game is also important.(24)

4. Role playing: Role playing involves simulation of an entire role substantially similar to what a planner normally plays. Role playing requires participants to respond to other actors and to analyze their behavior. Participants may become conscious of nonrational influences on behavior in organizational and political situations if they can be pushed away from conventional, rational, cognitive explanations for behavior. Role playing may draw participants' attention to issues involved in the specific exercise but may not provide participants with motivation to change their behavior outside the exercise setting, where a different incentive system may prevail.(25)

5. Training groups: Tavistock groups forcefully make participants sensitive to their unconscious assumptions and feelings about power in groups and about authority figures. T groups provide participants with models of effective strategies of influencing others in groups and organizations, with an emphasis on collaboration. Both types of groups help participants to become more conscious of unconscious

and nonrational obstacles to personal effectiveness in understanding and working with other people. These groups may be unique in their ability to confront noncognitive obstacles to organizational and political sensitivity, as well as to teach some political strategies consistent with personal styles. The carryover effect of groups depends on the incentive system of participants' home organizational setting.(26)

6. Supervised field instruction: The crucial component of field instruction in planning positions is the quality of supervision. Real world experience in planning by itself has no inherent educational value in teaching political understanding or skills; otherwise, the practitioners interviewed in this study would think and act differently. In field placements with supervision, the consistent questioning of a supervisor can make students sensitive to certain types of issues, such as organizational and political concerns. In addition, a supervisor can help a student to develop skills to use in dealing with these issues once they become identified as problems in practice. The similarity of the placement positions to other planning positions contributes to the likelihood that sensitivities and skills will be carried over into other planning work.(27)

Different combinations of these educational strategies may be effective in making more planning students and practitioners sensitive to the political interests and conflicts implicated in planning issues. In addition, these educational experiences may help to teach these planners political skills that can be strategically valuable in serving the interests of groups hitherto excluded from the planning process. These educational methods have relative strengths and weaknesses in relation to the learning needs of particular groups of students. The sensitivity and political skill that planners could learn in these ways should be employed along with an understanding of the political and economic structural context of planning issues.

This discussion was intended to draw attention to some problems involved in teaching political action and to identify some educational strategies for dealing with these problems. A more extensive discussion of these issues may be found in "Educating Planners for Sensitivity to Organization."(28)

CONCLUSION

A serious misunderstanding of planning practice by the practitioners who work from day to day as planners results in their feeling powerless, and they turn from seeking broad social or physical change to asking for simple reassurance from colleagues. They are powerless in part because they do not understand political decision making processes in planning organizations.

There are three increasingly serious consequences of this misunderstanding of planning practice. The first is the demoralization of planners, evident in their comments about their work. While taking at face value the statement that they are, in fact, employed to do planning, many encounter obstacles to their planning efforts, and they cannot comprehend why. Second, when planners who work on issues involving the allocation of goods and services are thwarted in their attempts to identify the political and economic interests at stake, those who fail to be identified obviously suffer. If planners do not facilitate the participation of the poor and relatively powerless in planning decisions, then the powerlessness of these groups will be reinforced. Third, if planners are unable to involve diverse interests in making decisions on planning issues, there will be no democratic planning process. Decisions will continue to be made bureaucratically, and the technical biases of planners will continue to obscure the meaning of these bureaucratic decisions. If democratic politics are not restored, there can be no legitimate procedures for societal governance. The consequences are that poorly articulated but strongly felt conflicts continue to threaten social stability and that personal security is continually imperiled.

Neither planning practitioners nor planning educators have a clear understanding of the organization and practice of planning. Establishing educational programs that will enable practitioners to better understand their practice and that will prepare practitioners to share their new understandings with professional educators is critical if the serious consequences of collective ignorance are to be averted.

NOTES

(1) Mannheim, Man and Society in an Age of Reconstruction, 1940.

(2) Lasch, The Culture of Narcissism, 1978.

(3) Habermas, Towards a Rational Society, 1970.

(4) Mills, "The Big City," 1963.

(5) This description of the "scientization of politics and public opinion" is obviously superficial. Its major features are emphasized here. Its dynamics are described in detail by Habermas in Towards a Rational Society, and Legitimation Crisis, 1975. The way in which the American political tradition has accommodated the bureaucratization of politics is well described by Wolin (1960).

(6) The nature of these conflicts of interests are described in terms of the American political economic structure by Markusen, Stone, and Hartman elsewhere in this volume.

(7) I have discussed this issue earlier in "Toward a Post-Industrial Planning Theory," 1977.

(8) Fifty randomly selected members of the Maryland Chapter of the American Institute of Planners were interviewed. The sample comprises 25 percent of the chapter membership. The A.I.P. membership was selected for sampling because it was expected to include practitioners in diverse roles and settings who would be likely to have a strong identification with planning. People interviewed worked primarily in traditional physical planning, various types of social planning, economic planning, and transportation. The sample had the following characteristics:

- 88 percent male, 12 percent female
- 94 percent white, 6 percent black and other
- age range from 26 to 78; median age of 37
- income range from $10,000 to $40,000 and over; median income between $20,000 and $24,999
- 68 percent employed in public agencies, evenly divided between administration and staff, 32 percent employed as private consultants.

In these respects the sample is representative of the population of planners enumerated in the 1970 United States Census (as summarized in Beauregard, "The Occupation of Planning," 1976) and the national membership of the American Institute of Planners (as described in American Institute of Planners, "AIP Membership has Not Changed Much Since 1965," 1974; "Membership Survey from 1976 Roster," n.d.). (The American Institute of Planners recently merged with the American Society of Planning Officials to form the American Planning Association. The new, larger organization includes many public officials and lay persons interested in planning, in addition to practitioners calling themselves planners. The study sample is probably still representative of the practicing planners in the new A.P.A., though no surveys of A.P.A. membership have yet been carried out that can substantiate this impression.) Compared to the national A.I.P. membership the sample appears to have a stronger undergraduate background in the social sciences and engineering, as well as more graduate training in planning and other areas.

(9) The term "cognitive map" was originally coined by Edward Chase Tolman to stand for the mental representation of the physical environment that people use to make their way through space. Subsequently, the meaning of the concept has been expanded to refer to the various mental images that people develop to guide them through the experienced world. Neisser, Cognition and Reality (1976) has described the development and use of the concept.

(10) Bolan, "Community Decision Behavior" (1969), has identified a number of characteristics of a planning situation that may affect the

planner's influence: (1) process roles, including the planner's motivation, opportunity, and skills; (2) decision field characteristics; (3) planning and action strategies; and (4) issue attributes. While a planner may exercise some control over some of these variables by studying the organizational "map" and acting self-consciously, some of these variables will effectively be beyond the planner's control.

(11) Meltsner, Policy Analysts in the Bureaucracy (1976), in his study of policy analysts in the federal bureaucracy, found fundamentally similar types of actors. The planners who see themselves as intellectual actors in a rational problem solving process correspond to Meltsner's "technicians," who exercise a high level of analytic skill and show minimal political skill. The second group of planners, who are concerned with their ability to "sell" their ideas to others in a political decision making process, correspond to Meltsner's "entrepreneurs," who exercise both analytic and political skills. They have varying degrees of sensitivity to what Needleman and Needleman have called "the community planning pressure system," in "Guerillas in the Bureaucracy," 1974, and they attempt to respond to organizational and political pressures in promoting recommendations. Meltsner has identified a category of "politicians" who have considerable political skills and few analytic skills. Few obvious "politicians" were found in the study of planners being discussed here; they are included in the group of planners emphasizing interpersonal and political skills.

(12) Marx, Economic and Philosophical Manuscripts, 1964 (1844), wrote that labor could be considered to be alienated insofar as workers do not have control over the products of their labor. Although Marx wrote with industrial workers in mind, the condition that he characterized as the alienation of labor appears to be equally part of the experience of planners who perform intellectual labor.

(13) Benveniste, The Politics of Expertise (1977) and Meltsner (1976) describe at length the implicitly political roles of planners within organizations and discuss alternative strategies that planners may employ to exercise some influence in these roles.

(14) This term comes from the title of Benveniste's (1977) book, in which he delves into the details of what he calls an "apolitical politics."

(15) Krumholz, Cogger and Linner, "The Cleveland Policy Planning Report," 1975, pp. 303-304.

(16) Krumholz and associates in Cleveland have similarly argued for the importance of planners to think and to act in a politically sensitive manner. Beginning with a description of a new action style, they note:

> In Cleveland, experience indicates that planners can have considerable impact on public policy if they will do two things. First, they must become activists prepared for protracted parti-

cipation and vocal intervention in the decision-making process. Too often planners have been content to assume a passive role, never making recommendations unless called upon by more powerful actors. An agency that wishes to influence decisions must often take the initiative. It must seize upon important issues and develop recommendations without prior invitation. . . .

Second, planners who wish to influence public policy must offer something that decision-makers want and can relate to. . .not rhetoric but information, analysis, and policy recommendations which are relevant to political decision-making. . . .On a daily basis, local politicians must confront growing problems without adequate information, a long-range perspective, or even a clear idea of what they wish to achieve. . .The agency and its staff must have solid data and cogent arguments to support their recommendations. "The Cleveland Planning Policy Report," 1975, p. 299.

(17) Needleman and Needleman, Guerillas in the Bureaucracy (1974), characterize the role played by many community planners as a "bureaucratic guerrilla."

(18) This section is a very brief summary of a longer paper entitled "Educating Planners for Sensitivity to Organization," (1979), available from the author.

(19) Stone, "Housing and the American Economy," 1979; Weiss, "Origins and Legacy of Urban Renewal"; and Markusen, "Regionalism and the Capitalist State," this volume.

(20) I have identified and characterized these five types of situations with the assistance of consultations with the following people who have taught and trained planners and similar practitioners to act effectively in organizations: Boris Astrachan, Amrit Baruah, Nancy Carroll, Paul Ephross, John Forester, Donald Klein, Marilyn Lammert, Melvin Levin, Charles Levine, Beryl Radin, Hans Spiegel, Stanley Wenocur, and Linda Wolf.

(21) The importance of this obstacle should not be underestimated, as Donald Klein suggests from his experiences in teaching people to understand and use power.

(22) Cook, "Graduate Education in the Management Science" (1970), and Culbert, "The Real World and the Management Classroom" (1977), are two educators who have described their conclusions that didactic discussion of the importance of political skills is inadequate to teach these skills, which, they contend, must be learned in practice.

(23) Charan, "Classroom Techniques" (1976) has noted that the use of case studies in teaching has encompassed a range of practices from didactic pedagogy to active participation of students. He observes that there is no evaluative literature on the use of this method from which to draw any consistent conclusions. He suggests that methods for using case studies in teaching organizational understanding and skills must be carefully examined in order to learn how they may be most effective.

(24) Johnson and Johnson, Joining Together (1975) and Kolb, Rubin, and McIntyre, Organizational Psychology, 1979, provide numerous stimulation exercises in areas in which planners are involved in organizations. For example, they offer exercises in decision making and the use of power. They discuss how these exercises may be structured in order to maximize the transfer of learning from the exercises to practice situations.

(25) Kidron, "The Effectiveness of Experimental Methods" (1977), has observed that role playing exercises encompass such a range of activities that evaluations of their lasting effects are not yet conclusive. Argyris and Schon's, Theory in Practice (1974), work with practitioners suggests that role playing exercises are likely to affect practitioners' subsequent actions to the degree that the exercises include systematic confrontation of practitioners' actions. In this way it may be possible to force the role players to articulate the "theories-in-use" actually governing their actions, which may be distinct from the "espoused theories" that rationally describe and justify actions. Uncovering "theories-in-use" makes it possible to identify obstacles to effectiveness implicit in customary ways of acting.

(26) Klein and Astrachan, "Learning in Groups" (1971), have systematically described and compared the Tavistock group and the T group as two theoretically well articulated approaches to understanding group processes. They identify the ways in which these training groups may enable participants to learn about the dynamic meaning of group and organizational structures and about the use of power in affecting these structures. Astrachan and Flynn, "The Intergroup Exercise" (1976), note that it is impossible to generalize about individual participants' responses to group exercises.

(27) Beinstein, "Urban Field Education" (1976), and Heskin, "From Theory to Practice" (1978) provide two accounts of field instruction experiences. Heskin is particularly helpful in indicating areas in which supervisors may be instructive to students in planning field placements by raising questions about practice issues.

(28) Baum, "Educating Planners for Sensitivity to Organization," unpublished paper, Baltimore, University of Maryland.

14 Thinking About Practicing Planning

Robert A. Beauregard

Planning practice is an undeveloped concept and a poorly understood activity. Although we have extensive knowledge concerning the problems that planners confront, the activities in which they engage, the organizations that employ them, the legislation that provides direction and funding, and the political and technical ideology that underlies their work, we do not have a differentiated set of categories for describing the meaning of planning practice. Practice is considered a singular, homogeneous phenomenon; one is either practicing planning or one is not. No distinctions are made among various types or qualities of planning practice. While vague notions of good planning and bad planning are noted in the literature, they are more colloquial than analytical. Thus, even though planning practice can be described, it has not been adequately interpreted in ways that link it with planning theory. These interpretations must overcome the differing terminology used by practitioners and theorists and, more importantly, create knowledge that is both constructive and instrumental for planning behavior. The objective of this paper is to provide one such interpretation of planning practice, a perspective infused with both theoretical and practical meaning.

To correctly understand the nature of planning practice, however, one must possess a set of categories that accurately represents what planners do. To this end, the concept of practice is explored along two theoretical dimensions, levels of consciousness and types of consequences. Rudimentary data and quotations by planners about their work are then presented in a narrative format. One problem that arises is that the ways in which planners and theorists describe their practice are incongruous. These mutual descriptions do not blend in a coherent and useful interpretation of planning activities. This is one of the problems that needs to be solved if academics who engage in progressive education are to work effectively with those engaging in progressive practice.

THINKING ABOUT PRACTICE

The notion of practice has its roots in the Greek word praxis, commonly translated as acting or doing. To think of practice as simply doing, however, is not sufficient for planning or other complex activities. Distinctions among various types or qualities of practice need to be made.(1) Therefore, "practice" will be used in a broader sense to encompass not only the characteristic activity in which a planner engages but also the kind of consciousness attached to the activity and the consequences of the activity. My purpose in this is to create a set of categories for describing practice so that the disjuncture between theory and practice, which is so characteristic of planning practice, can be bridged.

Levels of Consciousness

Consciousness is central to any extended concept of practice. A person unaware of self and of environment engages in action in a qualitatively different way than does a person who reflects upon psychological motivations about his or her place in society, and may select different actions under similar circumstances. The nonreflective person is less purposeful and more responsive to external stimuli; the reflective person is more prone to assessing actions in light of objectives and may also be better able to evaluate the efficacy of his or her behavior and thus modify it in order to act more effectively. Consciousness is thus an important determinant of how people practice. While an almost infinite range of degrees of awareness can exist, for purposes of developing a theoretical perspective on practice, three levels of consciousness are sufficient: ordinary, reflective, and radical.

Under conditions of ordinary consciousness, a person acts without reflecting upon the meaning of his or her actions. There is a perceptual knowledge of behavior but not processed knowledge.(2) That is, the person perceives what is being done but does not relate it to an external purpose or theory, and possibly not even to personal satisfaction. Even though these actions might have had an external purpose in the past, that purpose has been internalized, suppressed, or even repressed. Brushing one's teeth is such an example – once consciously engaged in, most of us now perform the task without thinking.

Not all actions that occur under ordinary consciousness are habitual, however. A more important aspect of this level of consciousness is what happens when the relation between action and purpose has been repressed. In this case, the person is alienated from the consequences of his or her actions. This is often true of that practice labeled "work." At the workplace, many people are placed in a situation of ordinary consciousness because they are alienated from control over the product of their labor. The relation between work and the full rewards of employment is severed.(3) Management controls the link between action and purpose and, for the most part, discourages reflection.(4) A laborer performs most efficiently for the capitalist manager when he or she is operating at the level of ordinary consciousness.(5) This lack of awareness and knowledge about meaning, and of reflection on purposes and consequences is characteristic of ordinary consciousness. Action is alienated from purpose.

Reflective consciousness exists when a person considers the meaning of her or his actions and uses that understanding to guide those actions toward specific ends. When a person reflects, this reflection has the potential to result in a change, possibly an improvement, of behavior. Actions are neither habitual nor aimless. But to bring about this connection between action and consequence, the person must have some control over the situation in which practice takes place. Without it, the person may be conscious of a need for change but may also feel powerless.(6) Consciousness is thereby stifled, and the person must either abandon purposiveness or consider strategies for grasping control. Reflective consciousness can thus be interpreted, in part, as the awareness of the ability to control the relationship between action and consequences.

The other part of this interpretation involves discrimination among consequences to align them with an external purpose. Only then do the consequences for others (i.e., the social consequences) become meaningful to the person who is acting. Behavior becomes purposefully social. Actions such as writing a term paper, developing a land use plan for a community, and learning diagnostic procedures so that one can better cure patients fall under the rubric of reflective consciousness. In doing these things, the person thinks about the relationship between actions and consequences and evaluates and adjusts that relationship vis-a-vis an external purpose.

Radical consciousness implies an added dimension. While acting for personal or political gain is subsumed under reflective consciousness, only actions that are reflective and purposive in terms of restructuring society, or certain key components of it, are part of radical consciousness. At this level, reflection becomes radical theory. Consequences emerge from distinctly political actions, and purpose becomes the restructuring of extant societal relationships. The person with a radical consciousness holds a vision of a "better" society, a society structured differently from what exists. This vision may be romantic – resembling an earlier, mythic world; regressive – demolishing those structures that protect individuals and groups from oppression and externally-imposed misery; reformist – retrenching the powerful and coopting the disenchanted; or progressive – lessening human misery and providing more equality through modification of the existing patterns of power and privilege. To undertake actions associated with these visions, the radical must combine a theory of societal change with actions that are theoretically guided. And since radical theory is political theory, these actions will be part of a political strategy. At the level of radical consciousness, then, purpose emerges from radical theory and reflection, actions are directed at radical alternatives, and consequences are political ends. If consciousness at this level (unless the motivating vision is a reformist one), is translated into effective actions, it will lead to the abolition of alienation and an articulation of class consciousness so that a radically different political economy is created.

Types of Consequence

So far, action has been considered from the subject's perspective; its relation to object needs to be more fully delineated. This requires investigation of the material consequences of taking action, i.e., the resultant changes in objective reality. Three types of consequences will be considered: ideological, material, and structural transformations.

Actions that bring about an ideological transformation include those that change people's psychological states and attitudes, modify the content and nature of prevailing ideas, manipulate the flow and quality of information, and restructure ideologies. Strictly speaking, these are not changes in material reality. Ideas, beliefs, information, and feelings are symbols and dispositions, not concrete objects and behaviors. Yet, in the sense that perceptions are changed, and to the extent that people adjust their actions to their interpretations of reality, then behaviors will be modified. The inclusion of this type of consequence recognizes that many actions that shift ideology and information also have ramifications in the material world. For example, a person who publicly introduces a new perspective on urban decline may find that this action becomes instrumental for policymakers or for interest groups who use the idea as justification for action. Inclusion of ideological transformation also provides a category that can encompass the actions and products of theorists and technical experts. Moreover, to deny the importance of ideological transformation is to denigrate the function of theory and its ability to advance practice. While material conditions are important for prompting men and women to act, ideology and information play an influential secondary role in determining and justifying the specific actions they will take.

The second type of consequence – material transformation – involves a change in the characteristics of a concrete object. That change may involve modifying the shape or configuration of various objects (e.g., trimming a rose bush or combining wood and canvas to make a tent), or it may involve transforming the nature of materials (e.g., combining various chemicals to produce plastic). Normally, this type of consequence is associated with manual labor.(7) Concrete objects are changed through work in order to increase their usefulness or to increase their value as a commodity. Regardless of whether use or exchange is the purpose, the point here is that the worker manipulates certain materials, performing a set of operations on them. These operations constitute the active and objective side of the worker's practice and lead to concrete consequences. The range of actions is vast and can include such human work as digging trenches, washing dishes, constructing bridges, and making drugs. It could even be extended to the transformation of humans through medical procedures (e.g., skin grafts).

The last category is structural transformation. Structures are those relatively stable relationships among social entities in which power over individuals, organizations, and institutions is used to achieve the goals of certain people. They include local school systems, hospitals, marriages, labor markets, and political economies. The consequences of these structures are directed both by the distribution of influence within them and by their influence over external relations. The process of structural transformation realigns this influence so that different individuals are in control and thus different individuals benefit. The structure may be eliminated (e.g., the dictator exiled and replaced by a representative democracy), or it may just be modified (e.g., reorganizing a police department in such a way that services are provided from a neighborhood base, rather than a central one, while control over them remains in the hands of a city-wide bureaucracy). Thus, structural transformation may range from a change in the emotional involvement of two individuals to the replacement of the prevailing political economy. Between these extremes, actions are taken to disband organizations, establish enterprises, and replace leadership. Structural transformation, then, is political action; i.e., an action that changes the distribution of control and the allocation of symbols and resources. All political action is not structural transformation however. Structural transformation is only that which changes the pattern of intersecting relationships.

While each of these types of consequences is conceptually distinct, this does not mean that they necessarily occur independently of one another. An ideological transformation may bring about a change in behavior, causing an individual to modify some concrete object in a different manner. Relationships among people may be transformed as a result of new information or new ideas. Structural transformations may cause ideological changes as rationales are brought into conformance with new power relations, and even material things may be modified because the individuals now in power require a physical environment to suit their needs and public image. These various types of consequences will most likely not occur in isolation from one another. Nor do such consequences of practice exist independently of the levels of consciousness. Engaging in activities that purposively bring about structural transformations would seem to require a somewhat radical consciousness, while manipulating materials may require only ordinary consciousness in certain settings. As a result, the intersections of these two dimensions create a number of qualities of practice. Different types of consequences and levels of consciousness combine to define the nature of practice.(8) Practice, then, is conceptually complex. Before we can fully understand it, our theory of practice must be further developed.

THINKING ABOUT PLANNING PRACTICE

The above theoretical dissection of practice is lacking in empirical content. In order to make the scheme meaningful for planning practice, the literature was searched for planners' reflections on their work.(9) These verbalized reflections were analyzed in order to identify those aspects of practice of which planners were primarily aware. When planners comment upon their work, that act in itself mirrors a level of consciousness. This consciousness, however, must be assessed and elaborated upon in terms of its content. The question that must be answered is: "What characteristics of planning practice do planners select for reflection?"

When planners think about practice, their ruminations frequently focus on the frustrations they experience in their work.(10) These frustrations are associated mainly with the problem of "getting things done" – achieving the consequences of planning and establishing an institutionalized planning process. This discouragement emanates from their role as technical experts, not implementers, and advisors, not political decision makers. Planners are aware that they function as technical advisors, and that this role positions them within the realm of public action, yet increases the distance between their decisions and the consequences of their work. Such realizations have encouraged planners to avoid measuring their success in terms of material consequences. Practicing planners have focused instead on the process of planning, particularly their contributions as technical experts to the rationalization of public decision making. These interrelated themes, expressed in the comments of many of the planners quoted herein, constitute the general content of their thinking about planning.

Commenting on their frustrations, two planners expressed the following thoughts:

> My work is something special to me, but I've had to learn to live with uncertainty and frustration. To get by, you have to redefine what you mean by success in planning. . . .

> The work isn't glamorous. After about two years you lose animation. The planning operation gets stifled. You feel you're not being challenged. Routine gets to you. There's no innovation.

The daily problems they face and the bureaucratic routines developed to deal with those problems contribute to the limitations put on planners. It is not just the perceived lack of consequences that frustrates them, but also the complexity of public decision making and the intractability of existing groups and organizations. All of these make successful planning difficult. As one planner commented, "It is so complicated to plan when dealing with community people and also when dealing with other agencies. They all have their own self-interests."

Thus, planners are capable of identifying the immediate sources of their frustrations. These sources intervene between their planning activities and the consequences they wish to achieve. The paucity of material outcomes looms large in the minds of planners. Planners enter the profession hoping to improve the world but end up settling for minor ameliorations.(11) As one planner admitted, "I can't put my finger on a single project that was generated, orchestrated, and brought to execution by the planning department. Nothing that actually sprang from this organization. There's very little tangibility to planning."

Many times this is expressed in the classic planning lament: "Too often plans sit on shelves. . . I am determined that it's not going to be another study that ends up in a drawer."

Or, as a less pessimistic and frustrated planner said: "I found that planners do get some things implemented, but began to recognize how insignificant the projects themselves are." Planners, then, relate their frustrations to the lack of material consequences and the various limitations on their decision making and actions. It is a crisis in implementation, a thwarting of the pragmatic ideal. To overcome this frustration, planners have turned to "process" and developed a different awareness of themselves, while not totally abandoning the historical commitment to reshaping the built environment.(12)

Planners claim a special competence in problem solving and this has become a hallmark of the planning profession. The planning process is seen as important, and permeates practitioners' reflections on their work. They talk of clarifying issues, increasing communication among groups and educating the public about various problems and prospects from a planning perspective. The following quotes represent these themes:

> Usually my relations are with the leaders of the most important organizations. I deal with them and try to get them to understand planning issues.
>
> I try to frame issues, I try to interpret interests on the part of the agency so they can have a clearer idea of what their options are.
>
> I perform an education function, giving information to people in the community as to how the government operates. . . .

Process, then, becomes both the content and consequence of planning. But this is not a panacea. Planners accept it simultaneously as a path to, but also an avoidance of, the achievement of material outcomes: "I'm one of those people who wants to see results. But I define results in my own way, in terms of my concept of process" and "To have community people try to get their requests processed, even if they lose, is a kind of success. Sure, you might still like to see something material happen; but looking at success in this broader way helps."

Of course, process and product are not independent of one another and there is awareness of that also: "If we are capable of communicating understanding. . . we can probably be most effective in gaining acceptance of plans we are presenting."

The residue of planning becomes the rational perspective that is instilled in citizens. Moreover, this emphasis on process, which is difficult to quantify but seems to be more dominant than that on concrete consequences, is compatible with the role in which planners view themselves.

It has been well-documented that planners perform as technical experts and advisors.(13, 14, 15) This is how they are trained, and these are the skills for which they are hired.(16) The planners studied herein reflected on their advisory role and the potential it contains for effectuating their recommendations. As two planners commented, "Most planners are sensitive to these problems, but planners don't make decisions. They provide advice and it is often neglected by the decision makers," and the "planning profession may still be in the recommendation stage. Planners don't control what happens in a city."

The role of technical advisor is seen as too constricting. Giving advice is of little consequence, unless those being advised already favor what is being proposed. This is seldom perceived to be the case in planning. Thus, planners also voice a concern about being more than technical advisors. This leads to new behaviors – modifications based upon an awareness of their limitations:

> Planners have to identify many kinds of input needed for decisions. . . .Responsibility to form (their) own views on basic policy and try to promote them in the most rational and effective way possible. At times one must be a broker because of all the factors.

> It wouldn't be a case of preparing reports and plans and not being able to follow through. . . . It is crucial to be a salesman and get the plan implemented.

The constraints on their actions and recommendations, then, generate an awareness of their role and a frustration with the paucity of material consequences and with the difficulties of establishing planning procedures. All of these are related to an understanding of those factors external to planning that hinder its success.

Two themes emerge as planners reflect on forces in their immediate environment that shape their work: politics and citizen involvement. The first is intertwined with the perspective planners have of their role – that of technical advisor searching for the best solution but without the power to guarantee its implementation. The planner is constantly thwarted by politics. Certain practitioners are likely to jump quickly to the need for adjusting to political reality:

> There is no question that good planning is good politics.

> The product is to turn out, in pieces, the state comprehensive plan. . .nothing radical or surprising. It has to be politically wise.

> Any person who believes that the means at hand will allow us to plan major changes in the city environment belongs to the "ivory tower" school of planning. He has not been through the school of

> hard knocks and political reality. . . . The planning profession is full of dreamers who, in my opinion, are a danger to the survival of our profession.

In their comments, however, planners are not always clear about what this adjustment entails and how it should proceed. (Neither are they articulate concerning the nature of politics.) Should planners learn to act in a political fashion to attain their interests or simply confine their plans and proposals to that which is politically feasible? Regardless of the path taken, it is important that planners are aware of politics as a factor in their practice.

The politics of dealing with elected officials is not the only barrier to successful planning. Citizens must also be accommodated. Here again, this source of frustration is seen both as an opportunity and as a constraint. Citizens can serve as political support, not just as opposition.

> I tend to feel that democratic involvement can be carried to an extreme, thus hindering planning.

> In this capitalistic society, for planning to play any role at all the community has to be active.

> Training did not prepare me for perhaps the most important element in a planner or designer's work – the relationship to the client and community.

Citizen involvement is also frustrating. Not only might it delay the approval of plans, but many times it leads to a questioning of the legitimacy of technical procedures and of the judgment of planners. Still, it can function in a positive way. Without citizen support, the implementation of planning proposals becomes doubtful; with it, the probability of success is increased. As planners reflect upon this, however, their consciousness does not lead to any specific actions that might assure the mutual compatibility of planning and participation.

Comments about the internal limitations that prevent successful planning are less common. While planners do make reference to funding constraints, lack of data, insufficient expertise, and the weaknesses of planning methodology, much more emphasis is given to external factors such as politics and citizen involvement. The focus of their thoughts is outward, into society, rather than inward toward the mechanics of their practice and the validity of their theories. Certainly, what is omitted from their consciousness is as important as what is included.

This awareness that planners have of their work extends beyond frustrations, role, material consequences, planning process, and limitations on success. Practitioners feel that they provide public decision making with a larger perspective; i.e., an expanded awareness of community problems. This belief reflects the notion that planners have comprehensive views and are able to synthesize various interests and orientations. But in explicating this thought planners are vague:

> I can see things in functional fields but most especially across functional fields that agencies and lay people need to focus on, and I can help to frame issues.
>
> All neighborhoods have narrow outlooks. . . . They won't recognize any connection with the rest of the area.
>
> I do a lot of mediating and interpreting between these various groups.

In effect, planners believe that they bring to community decision making a heightened sense of consciousness from which others can benefit. This comprehensiveness, moreover, subsumes the notion of consequence; it relates to an understanding of the implications of alternative choices.

This consciousness of intersecting interests and larger contextual factors does not seem to be combined with an equally expansive sense of purpose. Practicing planners are most likely to identify their purpose not in terms of some larger, abstract goal (e.g., to undertake societal guidance), but in terms of relatively specific objectives (e.g., avoiding incompatible land use arrangements). Statements of this nature convey an awareness of planning consequences:

> My goal is transportation for people who don't have any right now.
>
> What I am interested in is people, especially housing for poor people.
>
> But the real priority is the physical disease of the city – not social problems like crime or health. Housing, the physical structure, is the real priority.

In defining their purposes in these ways, planners have rejected utopian goals. "Comprehensive planning is contrary to human nature. Nobody will give up what they have" and "I think you have to work within certain realities. I wish I were a little more prepared for reality when I was in school." But, as was articulated most vociferously in the 1960s, planners question whether or not they are pursuing the right goals: "Sometimes I feel that whatever I do in the community, it's peripheral to the most pressing community problems. What the people here really need are jobs, or higher income."

Other planners have abandoned goals that involve changing the built environment or directly improving the welfare of the population. Instead, their orientation returns to process: "My work has to be professionally competent," and "I try to satisfy the professional community of which I am a part."

Thus planning behavior is directed at the things that planners can ostensibly control: the planning process and their professionalism.

Despite their claim to a larger perspective, however, planners generally do not question the status quo, or search for explanations outside the liberal reform perspective.(17) Most planners are not radicals and thus do not engage in radical commentary. But neither does one find a conservative turn in planners' thinking against the onerous imposition of government or in expressions of a need to return to an unfettered market economy. Insights concerning the larger contradictions within society, the role of the political economy in shaping planning practice, and the world that planners attempt to change are infrequently encountered among the bulk of practicing planners. The following quotations are unique:

> In the U.S. people are socially separated by economic determinations. Money prohibits the development of sound social patterns and arrangements.

> My work entails formulating policy for the mayor on environmental issues. Increasingly I am becoming aware of perceived contradictions between environmental and social concerns.

This lack of understanding concerning the larger purposes and functions of planning within the political economy should not be surprising. Planners, beginning with their institutional emergence as part of the Good Government movement in the early 1900s, have been primarily reformists, and as reformists have not engaged in radical critiques.

Planners do, however, search for relevance in their work. But this relevance is so difficult to capture that their thinking is short-lived and undirected. Some look to their colleagues for support while others evaluate the meaningfulness of their work in terms of internal criteria; e.g., the honesty of their efforts or the suitability of their techniques. Still others look to the elusive norms of the planning profession or to the positive responses of clients, administrative superiors, or elected officials.(18) In all cases, however, the significance of their work is ephemeral. This lack of permanence further exacerbates their frustrations. It is difficult to establish a planning process that will, in all probability, produce desired material consequences and guide community decision making. Planners, then, are not sure how to evaluate their planning. As a result, they do not always have confidence in the usefulness of their actions.

As planners reflect on their work, their thoughts turn to the frustrations they encounter in trying to change the environment. Implementation of the products of planning is not an automatic outcome of their efforts. Seldom are plans carried to fruition. When they are, the results are not always what was originally intended. Practitioners blame this on both politics (including their lack of influence over political decisions), and the complexity of the issues being confronted. They attend to the process of planning in hopes of establishing the conditions for the acceptance of their proposals. But in doing so they face another problem: the unpredictable and relatively uncontrollable nature of citizen support. To cope with this, planners attempt to clarify issues, discover consensus and educate people about the planning process. This not only changes the shape and content of the planning process but also the roles that planners play.

As planners focus on these concerns, they consider how these roles position them in the decision making environment. To be technical experts and advisors is compatible with their training and often congruent with the expectations of their employers. Yet planners perceive that they have little influence in these roles. Still, they are reluctant to abandon them insofar as they constitute the traditional identity of planners and have provided them with access to public policy arenas. No solutions are obvious. New roles have not been legitimized, neither by academics, employing organizations nor legislation.

Instead of turning to utopianism – substituting idealism for impact – planners continue to remain pragmatic. The goals they set for themselves and the purposes they espouse are narrowly defined and specifically tailored to making changes in the built and natural environments and to modifications of the processes of community decision making. Planning practice comes to be defined as what planning practitioners are doing currently, and they seldom look beyond this to the larger functions of planning within the political economy. Regardless of these limitations, there is a particular content to the ideas that emerge as planning practitioners think about planning. The question remains whether practical thinking can be integrated with theoretical thinking to form a synthesis of planning practice.

SYNTHESIS

The guiding premise of this work is that theory and practice are interrelated; more specifically, that theory must be based upon and guide practice. That being the case, a synthesis of the two approaches presented previously should be attempted. As presented here, this synthesis relies on both the quotations used above and on that body of planning literature on the behavior of planners.(19) The results of this integration of theory and of the data on planning practice can be used to reflect upon planning education and progressive practice.

When the data are assessed for their congruence with the first dimension of practice – levels of consciousness – one finds planners primarily exhibiting reflective consciousness. These practitioners, as expected, do not remain at the level of ordinary consciousness. Those interviewed and quoted are most likely those who are reflective. The nonreflective possibly misunderstand their roles and thus are unable to comment in pertinent ways. Radical consciousness seems to be characteristic of only a small group of leftist practitioners.

Such generalizations, admittedly, hide many of the specifics of the consciousness that planners do have. Planners think about their work and search for its meaning, purpose, and consequences. That meaning, however, is confined to the realities of planning as seen from the professional perspective, the purposes are narrowly and concretely defined in terms of specific changes in the material world or improvements in process, and the consequences are seen more in the negative; i.e., as generally nonexistent or unsatisfactory and thus frustrating. Larger purposes external to the planning profession elude them.

Similarly, planners do not reflect publicly on the meaning of planning in terms of their own personal growth and psychological well-being, except in the case of their comments on being frustrated. They are capable of reflecting upon their actions in terms of the goals of planning, but do not extend their thinking to the intersection between planning goals and political economic purposes. As they turn to the larger context of planning, they ignore its role within a reform liberal social order. Instead, their awareness focuses upon individual political actions and the constraints and potentialities they harbor for planning success. Still, planners perceive themselves to have little real power and, as a result, overlook the objective potential in their positions and roles.(20)

Also important for reflective consciousness is the extent to which such thinking produces changes in the behavior of planners. On the one hand, such changes are apparent. Planners view their role of technical advisor as inherently weak compared to the impact they want to achieve. Their response has been two-fold. First, they have advocated more politically oriented planning – more involvement with politics either in conformance with political forces or in advocacy of particular political positions. Second, they have emphasized process rather than product. Lacking the ability to bring about planned changes in the built and natural environments they have opted to focus upon the process of decision making in the hope of instilling more rationality into public decisions.

Despite this change of focus, prompted by their reflective consciousness, planners lack the control over their roles and positions that would allow them to produce more extensive and more acceptable consequences. As employees of government or in positions where they are dependent upon governmental or private consulting relations, they are subordinate to their employers. Yet their reflective consciousness has led them to modify their practice in ways open to them.

Closer to the essence of planning practice is the dimension of types of consequences. Planners generally see themselves as doers rather than thinkers and probably would prefer to have their work judged by its consequences and not by its level of consciousness. Planners do produce consequences of the ideological, material and structural varieties.(21) As technical advisors they are noted for their generation of reports containing information and advice for use in enlightening people about or offering solutions to a particular problem. The planners quoted above, however, were not that supportive of this ideological transformation. Instead, they were likely to denigrate their reports by lamenting the fact that the reports were often shelved and thus produced few concrete results. As they think about the consequences of their work they are prone to dismiss this contribution. Their products are only a means to an end – the end being material transformation.

Planners are also likely to point out the contribution they make to expanding the quantity and improving the quality of information in a community, thereby increasing the understanding that citizens, elected and appointed officials, and bureaucrats have of the planning process. These ideological transformations, however, are not viewed as emanating from or dependent upon the creation of documents. Rather, they are seen as solely a function of group interactions. The actual and potential linkage between the objectifications of analysis and the quality of the education that occurs is not recognized. Planners generally seem to overlook the usefulness of their reports, or not to exploit it. Part of this might be explained by the traditional concern with improving the built environment, and being unable to settle for anything less.

In thinking about the consequences of their work, these practitioners have no method of assessing ideological and material transformations, nor for suggesting ways in which planners could better accomplish these tasks. Planners produce reports, obtain funding, and draw together those actions of individuals and organizations that eventually lead to rehabilitated housing, new street locations, different configurations of land usage, and the many other substantive outcomes peculiar to planning. Reports, however, are not valued very highly, and those successful transformations of the built and natural environments that occur appear isolated from the initial planning activities. Planners are generally not that articulate about what it is that planning is to change and whatever material transformations do result from planning are downgraded. The actual impact of planning on the human environment is only weakly represented in the consciousness of planners.(22)

Structural transformations are also part of planning practice, though not commonly recognized as such. The imposition of planners into a community, with their ties to regional, state and federal organizations and funding sources changes the patterns of influence. For example, the establishment of a strong subdivision review process creates new relations between business and government in general and, specifically, among developers, banks, elected officials and bureaucrats. The extent to which planners are successful at instituting planning procedures might also lead to structural transformations. They could probably accomplish this to a greater extent then they do now – the potential lies in planners' concern with process. But the utility of this consequence within planning receives little consideration.

Neither the conceptual framework of practice nor the data allow a clear identification of various qualities of planning practice; i.e., particular types generated by the intersections of consciousness and consequence. The two dimensions are not specific enough to planning behavior and are couched in terminology incompatible with the expressions used by planners to characterize their practice. The data were not elicited specifically for the purpose of identifying qualities of practice and thus fit clumsily into the conceptual framework. More work, both theoretical and empirical, needs to be done. This should not, however, delay the pursuit of progressive education and progressive practice.

PROGRESSIVE EDUCATION AND PROGRESSIVE PRACTICE

The above interpretation of planning practice constitutes the starting point for recommendations regarding progressive education and progressive practice in planning. The goal is to develop methods for transferring knowledge and for taking action that bring about the transformation of the present political economy into one that is more humane, egalitarian and just. Progressive planning education would stress knowledge of the humanistic side of public policy, of distributional analysis and actions, and of democratic procedures. It would infuse students with radical consciousness, or at least provide the conditions that foster it, and provide them with radical theory that identifies the desired consequences of progressive planning and demonstrates the connections between those consequences and planning behavior. Such education would itself be democratic without abandoning or denigrating the different types of knowledge possessed by the participants. Progressive planning practice would undertake actions directed toward the redistribution of power and privilege, both on a spatial and nonspatial basis, and the establishment of the conditions for the emergence of a socialist society. It would engage radical consciousness in the production of structural transformations, encourage others to be radical in their practice, and debunk the liberal pretensions of public policy in the United States. Not to be forgotten is the need for a greater integration of progressive practice with progressive theory.(23)

These goals for progressive planning education have a number of specific implications. Greater attention should be given to contextual and structural issues, not just organizational strategies for change (24) but also investigations into the relation between the political economy and the actions and functions of planning.(25) Planners do not seem to comprehend their role as liberal reformers, nor the roles that they do not play. Any movement toward progressive practice must begin with a consciousness expanded from the reflective into the radical. Progressive education would include therefore attention to three interrelated aspects of plannng: 1) planning as a form of labor within advanced capitalism; 2) the nature of political consciousness and political actions; and 3) the types of strategies and techniques most efficacious in producing various types of material consequences, particularly structural transformations. The first would focus upon dimensions of planning practice not heretofore identified: its relation to alienation within the capitalist mode of production, the nature of the value it produces, and its contribution to capital accumulation. This would provide students with an awareness of the nature of practice and thus a basis for assessing their position within the political economy. Such knowledge could then be extended into an analysis of political consciousness and action, focusing upon various strategies for social change both within and without bureaucratic settings. This would enable the relation between radical theory and radical actions to be probed. Lastly, planning education should give more attention to how the actions of planners are linked to their consequences. Too much emphasis is currently given to the techniques themselves and not enough to the results that they are supposed to produce. This should not be treated in a narrow sense but approached in a way that reflects upon the nature of a socialist society and the "nonreformist reforms" necessary to achieve it.(26) All these concerns would provide the theoretical link from ideas and consciousness to progressive practice.

Progressive planning should be practiced by both theoreticians and practitioners. The former, as academics, must recognize education as their practice and develop a pedagogy that reflects their radical consciousness. Practitioners engaged in planning outside the university must solidify their own progressivism, raise the consciousness of other practitioners and of the community, work to produce radical consequences through political strategy, and give greater attention to the connections between radical theory and radical practice. Practitioners must act to both articulate the purposes of radical theory and provide a test of the validity of its strategy and tactics. Theory must be used to generate an objective analysis of the nature of planning within advanced capitalism in order to build a viable political planning strategy. This requires critical thinking about practice planning.

NOTES

(1) Within the writings of Karl Marx, practice takes on various qualities. It can be alienating or nonalienating, reformist or revolutionary, class conscious or not. He writes of the worker in the capitalist firm who is alienated from the means of production, the liberated worker who has overcome the capitalist division of labor, and the revolutionary who is working actively for a socialist society. See Bernstein, _Praxis and Action_, 1971; Israel, _Alienation: From Marx to Modern Sociology_, 1971; Mandel, _The Marxist Theory of Alienation_, 1970; Marx, _Capital_, 1967; and Vasquez, _The Philosophy of Praxis_, 1977.

(2) Mao Tse Tung, "On Practice," 1965.

(3) Underlying many interpretations of alienated labor is a normative model of laboring, the craftsman. See Mills, _White Collar_, 1956.

(4) Admittedly, for certain occupations in certain types of firms (e.g., researchers in highly technological firms), reflection is encouraged in order to improve productivity.

(5) Braverman, _Labor and Monopoly Capital_, 1974.

(6) The issue here is whether the person feels powerless, not whether that powerlessness is objectively true. This can only be determined through action.

(7) Braverman, _Labor and Monopoly Capital_, 1974.

(8) To actually identify these qualities, sharper categorizations of consciousness and consequence are required, not to mention finely drawn data and a theory that can detect and guide the search for such qualities.

(9) Since this is an exploratory piece, already established data sources were used to ground the discussion in existing knowledge. I decided to avoid the traditional approach of theory testing and concentrated on elaborating concepts and generating theory. My purpose was to discover the qualities of planning practice, not to quantify their statistical distribution. This procedure is discussed in Glaser and Strauss, The Discovery of Grounded Theory (1967). The following data sources were used: Altshuler, The City Planning Process, 1965; Baum, "Sensitizing Planners to Organization," this volume, 1980; Baum, "Strains Between Planners," 1978; Baum, "The Uncertain Consciousness of Planners," no date; Cole, The Role of Psychological Belief Systems in Urban Planning, 1975; Lieberman, The Practitioner Viewpoint, 1976; Needleman and Needleman, Guerrillas in the Bureaucracy, 1974; various newspaper articles, and Planners Network. In addition, I searched through all the case studies of planning I could find and even looked through back copies of Planning to see if practitioners had written letters to the editor which discussed their work. These last two sources, with the exception of Altshuler, The City Planning Process, 1965, proved fruitless. Quotations from the Baum works were used in the analysis but not specifically identified here on request of the author. Using a theoretical sampling technique, I identified quotations by practicing planners about their work. As additional quotations were discovered which reflected ideas already in the sample, they were not included. The result was a set of 127 quotations. The data were placed in various categorization schemes, some of which were based on the theoretical discussion of practice. Basic themes were then identified. The claim being made is that the interpretation given to these quotations is representative of the data and, more importantly, is credible because it is not contradicted by impressions within other commentaries on planners. The strength of the paper, I believe, lies in the confluence of theory and data; that confluence reinterprets what planners do and generates a new, though crude, approach to planning practice.

(10) In looking through the data, reading various interpretations of planning behavior, and discussing the paper with practicing planners the theme of frustration kept reappearing. It became a useful organizing element. Planners may, in fact, be frustrated and alienated, but I am only pointing out the existence of this feeling, not its distribution across the planning population.

(11) Dyckman, "What Makes Planners Plan," 1961.

(12) Scott, American City Planning Since 1890, 1969.

(13) Altshuler, The City Planning Process, 1965.

(14) Benveniste, The Politics of Expertise, 1977 ed.

(15) Rabinovitz, City Politics and Planning, 1969.

(16) Beauregard, "The Occupation of Planning," 1976.

(17) Even a search through all the issues of Planners Network, a newsletter for various left-leaning activists and academics produced little in the way of commentary which linked planning practice to critical analyses of the political-economy.

(18) Baum, "The Uncertain Consciousness of Planners," n.d.

(19) In addition to the data sources listed in footnote 9, the following books and articles were consulted: Benveniste, The Politics of Expertise, 1977 ed.; Dyckman, "What Makes Planners Plan," 1961; Forester, "What Do Planning Analysts Do?" 1978; Jacobs, Making City Planning Work, 1978; Meltsner, "Bureaucratic Policy Analysts," 1975; Meyerson and Banfield, Politics, Planning, and the Public Interest, 1955; and Rabinovitz, City Politics and Planning, 1969.

(20) Benveniste, The Politics of Expertise, 1977 ed.

(21) Most likely, planning activities produce multiple consequences, a fact which adds even greater complexity to this investigation. Throughout their history, planners have given emphasis to all three. See Scott, American City Planning Since 1890, 1969.

(22) It should be recognized that much of what planners do is preventive; i.e., acting to arrest and even halt actions which bring about detrimental transformations. The concern with externalities highlights this reactive orientation.

(23) Frankel, "The Relation Between Theory and Practice," 1968.

(24) Baum, "Strains Between Planners," 1978.

(25) Beauregard, "Planning in an Advanced Capitalist State," 1978.

(26) Gorz, Strategy for Labor, 1967.

15 Critical Theory and Planning Practice*

John Forester

PRACTICAL PLANNING THEORY

A "critical theory"(1) of planning practice can be not only empirical, interpretive, and normative in its content, but it can be practical as well.(2) Critical theory can help us anticipate and correct for: 1) public resentment and mistrust of planners, 2) unintentionally counter-productive technical planning practice, and 3) obstacles to effective design review and democratic planning processes.

My remarks are based upon my observations of a metropolitan city planning department's office of environmental review, whose duty it was to assess building plans for the city, review them for "significant adverse environmental impact," and then issue either a "negative declaration" or a requirement of an environmental impact report. Some cases reviewed were without significant impacts while a few others did require environmental impact reports. Most proposals, though, fell in between these two groups. In these cases, the planners had to check the likely impacts carefully and often negotiate with the project sponsor or developer for design changes to assure minimal adverse environmental impacts. In such cases, the planner had two roles. He or she was reviewing and also participating in project planning and redesign. By drawing on examples from this context, I hope to show that a critical theory of planning practice may be at once practical, factual, economical, and ethically instructive as well.

My thesis is as follows: Critical theory gives us a new way of understanding action (what a planner does) as attention-shaping (communicative action) rather than more narrowly as a means to some end

*A substantially revised and elaborated version of this chapter will appear as "Critical Theory and Planning Practice," in The Journal of the American Planning Association, forthcoming.

(instrumental action).(3) If planners do not recognize how their ordinary actions may have subtle communicative effects, they may be well-meaning but nonetheless counterproductive. They may be sincere but mistrusted, rigorous but unappreciated, reassuring yet resented. Where they intend to help, they may create dependency; where they intend to express good faith, they may unrealistically raise expectations. These problems are not inevitable, though. By recognizing the practical, communicative character of planning actions, we can suggest strategies to avoid these problems and to improve practice as well. In addition, we can understand structures of action, e.g., the organizational and political contexts of planning practice, as structures of selective attention (systematically distorted communication). For example, developers and neighborhood residents are likely to withhold information. Access to information and the ability to act on it, which constitutes expertise, are unequally distributed, as is the ability of citizens to participate effectively.(4) And the agendas of decision making (and planning department work programs as well) are politically and selectively structured. Such a view leads us to ask additional and more specific questions of the planner than whose ends or interests are being served. How does the planner politically shape attention and communicate? How does the planner provide or withhold information about project alternatives to affected people? Does the planner speak in a way that people can understand, or are they mystified? Does the planner encourage people to act or rather discourage them with a (possibly implicit) "leave it to me?" What can planners do to prevent unnecessary, disabling distortions of communication? How can planners engender learning, participation, and self-determination?

PLANNING PRACTICE AS ATTENTION SHAPING: COMMUNICATIVE ACTION

In practice any action works not only as a tool but also as a promise, shaping expectations. Planners may be effective not because they put words on paper, but because they may alter expectations by doing so. The planner's formality may tell a city resident more than the actual information provided. The quality of the communication counts; without it, technical information would never be trusted, and cooperation would be impossible. With no one listening, effective work in the planning office would grind to a halt.

Consider a local planner's description to a neighborhood group of a proposed shopping center project. If the planner describes the project in predominantly economic terms, the audience will envision something different than if the planner described it in mostly political terms. And again, they would envision something different if the project were described in the most ordinary language – as if for a Sunday supplement. But each of these descriptions would be about the same project. Which account should be given? Which account should be believed?(5) Choices must inevitably be made.

The problem is this: the planner's ordinary description of a project, a meeting, what someone has said, etc., is a communicative action in itself. Like all action, it depends upon intentions, and interests and an audience. Without an audience, a description would be like a play on opening night when no one came. Without intentions and interests setting it up, a description would be worthless. But with interests making something worth describing, and intentions making the describing worth doing, and an audience to listen, the planner's description of a project may actually help get ordinary work done.

Planners do much more than describe, of course. They warn others of problems; they present information to other staff, neighborhood residents, developers, and others; they suggest new ideas; they agree to perform certain tasks or meet at certain times; they argue for particular efforts; they report relevant events; they offer opinions, and they comment upon ideas and proposals for action. And these are only a few of the minute, essentially pragmatic and communicative acts that planners ordinarily perform. These acts are the atoms out of which any bureaucratic, social, or political action is constructed. When they are verbal, we can call them "speech acts."(6) If these social acts were not possible, we couldn't even ask one another "what did the project sponsor say?" Precisely because such communicative acts are effective, a warning such as "Watch out – he doesn't like planners" has pragmatic meaning: you watch out.(7) Without these communicative acts, the intelligibility and common sense of our ordinary social world could not exist. Planning problems would be inexpressible and practical action would be impossible.(8)

These elementary communicative actions are at the heart of the possibility of ordinary, cooperative working relationships – in everyday life, in planning, in political movements, and in society more generally. Communicative acts are fundamental to practical life; without them there is no understanding, no common sense, no shared basis, even for disagreement or conflict.(9) Without shared, commonly structured communicative abilities – communicative competence – we could not say "hello" and be understood. And the planner could not say, "The meeting's Wednesday at 7:30 – come prepared" and be understood either. These communicative acts are ordinary, often taken for granted, but they are politically potent as well.(10) The planner's speech acts perform both technical and political work.

FROM ENABLING RULES TO ORGANIZING PRACTICES

Enabling Rules

These essential communicative acts of ordinary planning practice do not grow automatically from natural conditions. They are not biological. They are social actions, rooted in languages we can speak together. Words and noises don't just come from our mouths. We tell, or ask, or promise, or greet, or argue – we act. And when we speak, we don't just make noises, we participate in a structured form of social action that is historical, normative and rule structured.(11) And it's not up to us to decide whether or not we want to follow the rules of ordinary language use – if we want someone else to understand what we say, what we promise, or warn of, or call attention to, or ask. If we want to tell someone that a project review meeting is likely to be especially important, we can't just make up a special word to get the point across – we have to say what we mean, using the language and whatever frame of reference we share. If we want to be understood when we speak, we have to work through the rules structuring ordinary language – or what we really mean to say won't be what anyone listening thinks we mean. The rules here are not restrictions; they enable us to know what one another means.(12) They help the planner know that "please check out the proposal" does not mean "we're all done with it."(13) We can communicate pragmatically – though there are exceptions – because we presuppose and anticipate, that a set of implicit rules will ordinarily be followed.(14)

We ordinarily (but not always!) try and expect others:(15)

1. to speak comprehensibly. If we didn't ordinarily presuppose this norm, we'd expect babble and never listen.

2. to speak sincerely, truthfully. If we did not presuppose this norm, we could not trust anything we heard – or even trust that we could check to see what was really meant;(16)

3. to speak legitimately and in context. We don't expect building developers to give biblical interpretations in front of the Planning Commission or clergy to propose planned unit developments before their congregations.

4. to speak the truth. If we didn't generally presuppose this norm, we'd never believe anything we heard, even if we knew the best of intentions were involved. We'd never be able to check or test the truth of a story or hypothesis if we generally expected falsehood to pervade communication. Only by presupposing and mutually fostering this norm is it possible to tell the difference between reality and ideology, between fact and sheer fantasy. Those skeptical about this norm of truth might consider if they presume less when they speak of the realities of poverty, sexism, or cruelty. (Of course exceptions to the generally presupposed norm exist. We can lie, but even the lie only works because the listener is ordinarily bound by the norm to expect truthfulness in ordinary communication.)

These norms of pragmatic communication are usually taken for granted. They are part of the subtle foundations of common sense. If we violate them, we are confronted by confusion, mistrust, anger, and disbelief.(17) As these pragmatic norms are broken, our shared experience and our social and political world disintegrate.(18) These problems have special importance in planning for two reasons. First, since planners often have little formal power or authority, the possible effectiveness of their communicative acts has increased importance. Second, public serving planners face certain special, private, or class interests (e.g., corporate development interests) that may work systematically to violate these norms of ordinary communication. Planners then face the results: a community group "snowed" by a developer's consultant, an inquisitive citizen confused by apparently "necessary" public works cut-backs, a working class community organization led to accept delays as "better" neighborhoods receive more attention from city government. Planners need to anticipate the practical effects not only of class-based communicative acts, but of their own communicative practices as well.

Meaning More (In Practice) Than Intended

When planners tell a neighborhood group about a proposed project they inevitably communicate more than they intend.(19) They may lapse into bureaucratic language and so confuse and mystify people.(20) They may present information but have no way of knowing what it will really mean to the audience. They may be trying to gain acceptance, but their professional or formal manner may lead residents to doubt their sincerity. Pragmatically effective communication is never guaranteed.(21) The four norms of "universal pragmatics" discussed above are just that: pragmatic guides and standards for practice.(22) As they are violated, mutual understanding, trust, and cooperation will suffer. We can take these four norms of ordinary communication, our universally presupposed pragmatic abilities, and pose them as practical questions for planning practice.

1. Is the planner's communication comprehensible, so others can understand what is happening around them or to them?

2. Is the planner's communication sincere and uttered in good faith, or are the listeners being manipulated, misled, fooled, or misguided?

3. Is the planner's communication legitimate, given the planner's role and the participation of other interested parties, or is the planner taking unfair advantage of professional status? (If a planner tells a developer or community organization member, "You'll have to live with this design, there's nothing you can do," this may be, for example, a personal judgment in professional clothes.)

4. Is the planner's communication true? Can we believe it? Is there evidence supporting it? What do other accounts of the situation

tell us? Are the listeners being offered information upon which they can act, or are they being misinformed, however unintentionally?

Practical Distortions of Communication: Political Costs and Corrective Strategies

Realists might aver that it would be foolish for planners to always be sincere or always tell the truth. But this avoids the real issue. For if we are to trust and rely upon planners, it is important to know not only when and why insincerity and falsehood may at times be justified, but also to know what results such practices have.(23) These issues of distortion are particularly important because of the bureaucratic and political pressures operating upon planners.(24) They will often feel compelled to be less frank or open than they might wish, but then we should not be surprised when we find members of the public at times suspicious, resentful, or angry.

The four questions raised just above ask how the norms of ordinary communications are met or violated in practice. There are also, however, systematic distortions of communication that planners themselves face. Consider, for example, the politically selective channelling of information, the unequally distributed ability to engage in political and planning processes (of citizens with or for whom the planning staff work), the professional status (or stigma) of the planner's deeds, conflicting interpretations of cases and their significance, scarce information and fluid networks of contacts, and a maze of bureaucratic rules for noninitiates to navigate.

How, then, does the organizational and political structure of private interests and public agencies foster or retard open, unmanipulated communication (and so participation) by affected persons? To answer this question, we must assess the socially and politically structured distortions of communication faced every day by citizens and planners (see table 15.1). When ordinary communication is unnecessarily or deliberately distorted, responsible political action will be crippled.(25)

For each entry in table 15.1, we are to ask a practical question: "How can planners work with others to prevent such distortions of communication?" Table 15.2, equally schematic, suggests strategies of response to counter the distortions of table 15.1.

These strategies of response are varied, but they can be summarized in one word – organizing. This is the planner's pragmatic response to a political reality of effectively disabling distortions of ordinary communication: organizing which corrects or compensates for these distortions.(32) Not only do these strategies address the basic obstacles to open democratic political processes, they are pragmatic as well. They seek to marshall information, cultivate support, work through informal channels, make use of expertise, and so forth.(33) Thus, the analysis of the distortion or violation of the norms of ordinary communication leads logically to questions of response.

Table 15.1. How We Experience Distortions of Communication
Norms of Pragmatic Communication

(Practical level)	Comprehen-sibility	Sincerity	Legitimacy	Truth
face to face	lack of sense ambiguity confusion	deceit insincerity	meaning out of context	misinformation
	"What?"	"Can I trust him?"	"Is this right?"	"Is this true?"
organizational (e.g. hospital proposing expansion)	public exclusion by jargon	conflicts of interest between hospital/ client	unresponsive-ness assertion of rationalizations professional dominance	information witheld responsibility obscured need mis-represented
	"What's this mean?"	"Can we trust?"	"Is this justified?"	"Is this true?"
political economic	mystification tion complexity	misrepre-sentation of the public good	lack of accountability legitimation by line not by active participation	policy possibilities obscured/witheld/or misrepresented idelogy as: public ownership is always inefficient
	"You think <u>they</u> under-stand what that means?"	"That's their line."	"Who are they to say?"	"What they never tell us about is. . ."

Table 15.2. Responses Correcting Distortions of Communication: Organizing Distortion Type (Pragmatic Norm Violated)

(Practical level)	Comprehen-sibility	Sincerity	Legitimacy	Truth
face to face (26)	revealing meaning	checking intentions	determining roles and contexts (27)	checking evidence
	"What does that mean?"	"Does she mean that?"	"I don't need to accept that. . ."	"I'll check to see if this is really true."
organizational (28)	minimizing jargon; creating public review committees	organizing counter advocates; checking with networks	making decisions participatory; checking with affected persons	utilizing independent/ critical third party expertise
	"Clean up the language so people can understand it"	"Check with Stu to see if we can trust this."	"What's the neighborhood association had to say about this?"	"Check Cathy's analysis to see if these figures are really right."
political economic (29)	demystification; counterskills	exposing interests	democratizing the state; politicizing planning (30)	institutionalizing debate, political criticism; democratizing science; politicizing planning (31)
	"All this really means is. . ."	"Of course they say that! They're the big winners if no one speaks up."	"Without political pressure, the bureaucracy will continue to serve itself. . ."	"We have to show what can be done here"

PRACTICAL PLANNING: ORGANIZING (ENABLING) AND DISABLING PRACTICE

As we broaden our understanding of the planner's action (from technical to communicative), we come to a new understanding of the practical organizational problems planners face. It becomes evident that problems will be solved not by one expert but by pooling expert and nonprofessional contributions; not by formal procedure alone, but by informal consultation and involvement; not predominantly by strict reliance on data bases, but by careful use of trusted "resources," "contacts," "friends" as well; not through formally rational management procedures, but by internal politics and the development of a working consensus; not by solving an engineering equation, but by complementing technical performance with political sophistication, support-building, liaison work, and, finally, intuition and luck.

Only in the most isolated or the most routine cases will future-oriented planning proceed smoothly.(34)

The planner's technical acts may be instrumentally skilled, but may be politically inept. A formal economic calculation may be impeccably performed, but the planner's client may "not really trust the numbers." Any technical action (calculating a solution, making a demographic prediction, reviewing architectural plans for flaws) communicates to those it serves, "this solution (etc.) serves your needs" or "now, this much done, you may still wish to. . .(change this parameter, devise another scenario, look and see for yourself)." In planning contexts, this metacommunicative character of technical action has often been overlooked.(35) Its practical implications, too, particularly its costs, have often been neglected. The most well-meaning professional activities of planning staffs have at times communicated, if unintentionally, "Leave the analysis to me; I'll give you all the results when I'm through. You can depend on me." At times this has reflected an agreed upon division of labor. At other times the political and practical consequences of such communication have been to separate planners and planned-for, to reduce the accessibility to information of those affected by plans, to minimize the planner's capability to learn from design review criticism, to engender public mistrust for planning staff, and to reinforce the planner's apprehensions of what seems to be necessarily disruptive public participation. As long as this practical communicative dimension of (even the most technical) planning is ignored, planners will pay such costs.(36)

Furthermore, planning organizations may – against their best intentions – immobilize or disable responsible public political participation and action. By ignoring the effects of bureaucratic language, planning organizations may perpetuate the exclusion of all but those who already "know the language." If they are not perceived as speaking truthfully, planning organizations will breed distrust, suspicion, and a growing hostility to professional public servants – to say nothing of the posible cooperation that is thwarted. More subtly, if planning organizations preempt community involvement by defining problems as overly technical or as too complex for nonprofessionals to understand, they may engender political passivity, dependency, and ignorance.(37) And if they do not systematically search for design alternatives and possible political solutions through regular processes of community consultation, pooling expertise, and project reviews (extending from brainstorming to collective criticism), planning organizations are likely to "satisfice" too quickly, inefficiently, and miss real program or design opportunities.

Ironically, then, technically oriented planning may effectively but unintentionally communicate to the public the message that, "you can depend on me – you needn't get involved. I'll consult you when appropriate." While such a message may simplify practice in the short run, it may also lead to inefficiency and waste by separating planners from the political constituency they serve, weakening them both in the face of the designs and agendas of powerful economic forces in their neighborhoods and cities.(38) It subverts the accountability of planners and keeps the public uninformed about events and local decisions affecting their lives. Planning that is predominantly technical in focus may also neglect its political friends. When action is at stake – not to mention the planners' jobs – this can be costly. Planners can find opportunities to increase their productivity and effective community involvement by attending to the practical communications that function either to discourage or alternatively encourage cooperative and critically constructive and supportive organizational and community bases. Technical acts should not be seen in a vacuum. To avoid counterproductive "leave it to us" messages which these acts may (meta-) communicate, planners have several options, as indicated in figure 15.1 below.

The statement "planning is political" need not mark the end of the discussion; it could, instead, be a fruitful beginning. By anticipating the interests and commitments of affected groups, planners could build political support in addition to producing technically sound documents. To be effective, rigorous analysis would still have to be used (if not always appreciated) by politically influential groups or the staff of other agencies; technical analysis in planning cannot stand alone. Numerous studies show that the technical role of planning analysis is often frustrating and ineffectual if divorced from pragmatic considerations of political communication – lobbying, maintaining trust, addressing the specific concerns of the decision making audiences, and so on.(39) Attention to the practical communications structuring planning practice contexts can save wasted time and effort; otherwise, technical reports may be destined for the shelf.

Concluding Note

Practical organizing strategies (suggested in figure 15.1) may provide opportunities for planners seeking to improve local planning practice and avoid the disruptive, frustration producing problems of organizationally distorted communications (suggested schematically in table 15.1). Planning actions are not only technical, they are also communicative – they shape attention and expectations. These com-

Planners can:

1. cultivate community networks of liaisons and contacts rather than depending on the power of documents, both to provide and disseminate information;
2. listen carefully to gauge the concerns and interests of all participants in the planning process to anticipate likely political obstacles, struggles, and opportunities;
3. notify less-organized interests early in any planning process affecting them (the more organized groups whose business it is to have such information won't need the same attention);
4. educate citizens and community organizations about the planning process and the "rules of the game";
5. supply technical and political information to citizens to enable informed, effective political participation;
6. work to see that community and neighborhood nonprofessional organizations have ready access to public planning information, local codes, plans, notices of relevant meetings, and consultations with agency contacts and specialists supplementing their own in-house expertise;
7. encourage community-based groups to press for open, full information about proposed projects and design possibilities;
8. develop skills to work with groups and conflict situations rather than expecting progress to stem mainly from isolated technical work;
9. emphasize to community interests the importance of effective participation in informal processes of project review, and take steps to make such design change negotiation meetings equitable to professionally unsophisticated groups;
10. encourage independent, community-based project reviews and investigations; and
11. anticipate external political economic pressures shaping design decisions and compensate for them – soliciting "pressure" countering vested antipublic interests rather than minimizing external pressure altogether.

(These actions are all elements of organizing practices of mobilizing concerned and affected persons, in addition to technically calculating problem solutions.)

Fig. 15.1. Communicative Strategies Complementing Planners' Technical Work

municative effects are often unintentional, but they are nevertheless pragmatic; they make a difference. Presenting technical information to a community organization, a planner's manner may communicate as much as his or her words.

These practical communicative effects can be counterproductive for planners if they are ignored. If they are recognized, planners can complement their technical activities with strategies (suggested schematically in table 15.2) designed to open effective communication to those persons and groups affected by proposed projects and plans. These practical communication strategies may be organizationally economical as they reduce the unnecessary disruption of the planning process, cultivate support for planners' actions, and reduce the likelihood that planners' efforts will be overwhelmed by the larger political process in which any planning is embedded.

The focus on the pragmatic aspects of such communicative planning actions is rooted in the recent literature of critical theory, especially as developed by Jurgen Habermas. A critical theory of planning practice calls our attention 1) empirically to concrete communicative actions and organizational and political economic structures; 2) interpretively to the meanings and experiences of persons performing or facing those communicative actions; and 3) normatively to the respect for or violation of fundamental social norms of language use, norms making possible the very intelligibility and common sense of our social world. By recognizing planning practice as normatively rule structured, communicative action distorting or revealing to the public the prospects and possibilities they face, a critical theory of planning aids us practically as well as ethically. This is the contribution of critical theory to planning: pragmatics with vision – to reveal true alternatives, to correct false expectations, counter cynicism, foster inquiry, spread political responsibility, engagement and action. Critical planning practice, technically skilled and politically sensitive, is an organizing and democratizing practice.

NOTES

(1) By "critical theory" I refer predominantly to the work of Jurgen Habermas and the interpreters of his recent Toward a Rational Society, Knowledge and Human Interests, Theory and Practice, Legitimation Crisis, and Communication and the Evolution of Society, 1970; 1971; 1973; 1975; and 1979 respectively. The best interpreters of Habermas's critical theory are Bernstein, The Restructuring of Social and Political Theory, 1976, McCarthy, The Critical Theory of Jurgen Habermas, 1978, and Schroyer, The Critique of Domination, 1973. For the broader development of critical theory, see Jay, The Dialectical Imagination, 1973.

(2) Bernstein completes his review of the apparent restructuring of modern social and political theory with the challenge: "An adequate social and political theory must be empirical, interpretive, and critical." (Restructuring, p. 235).

(3) For one distinction between instrumental and communicative action, see Habermas's Toward a Rational Society, from p. 91 on. Weber's concept of "meaningful social action" can be understood as communica-

tive action, as Schutz has shown. See, for example, Schutz, Phenomenology and Social Relations, 1970. Also important for an understanding of the concepts of systematic structuring of attention (e.g. distortions of communication) is Peter Berger and Thomas Luckmann's Social Construction of Reality, 1966.

(4) Compare Lukes's Power: A Radical View, 1974 for the treatment of the structural distortions of communication and information considered by E.E. Schattscheider, Peter Bachrach, and Morton Baratz; Murray Edelman's work, e.g. The Symbolic Uses of Politics and his recent Political Language, provides another view of distorted communications. Schroyer's Critique of Domination and Claus Mueller's Politics of Communication (cited below) are attempts to bridge Habermas's analysis of communicative action and its distortions (on the one side) and the more traditional treatments of power and political structure (on the other side). See also, for example, the lengthy introduction to Habermas's Theory and Practice. Cf. Alvin Gouldner's very narrow reading of systematic distortions of communication as "censorship," in his Dialectic of Ideology and Technology, 1976.

(5) This question is especially important to the extent that the listener has no opportunity to engage the speaker and question the given description – thus enabling a richer account to be given. But when the listener is uninformed and trusting, even the recourse to conversation and interaction may not change matters. The offered account, selective as it must be, will effectively stand (e.g. the planner may say to the community organization member/developer, "There's just nothing much you can do."). It's helpful to remember, of course, that planners are not omniscient, and that such statements, like others, may or may not actually be true.

(6) The classic analysis of "speech acts" appears in the work of Austin, How to Do Things With Words, 1961, and more recently, Searle's direct treatment in Speech Acts, 1969.

(7) Nonverbal communication is also important. In face-to-face interaction, nonverbal communication takes the form of tone, gesture, deadpan or lively facial expressions. At the organizational level, nonverbal communication is effective in the structuring of agendas, meetings, work-programs, and the character (e.g. more or less formal, comprehensible, encouraging) of the planning or policy formulation process. At both levels, what remains unsaid may be as important and effective as what is said. See Watzlawick, et al., Pragmatics of Human Communication 1967. See also note 35.

(8) Habermas calls the theory of these speech acts "the theory of universal pragmatics": universal because all social communication seems to depend on the structure and possibility of such acts, and "pragmatic" because these acts are concretely practical – they make a

difference in our lives. See "What is Universal Pragmatics?," 1979. See also note 7, above.

(9) See, for example, Apel's "The Priori of Communication and the Foundation of the Humanities," 1977.

(10) Watzlawick shows that even a threat depends upon effective communication; to be successful, a threat must "get through" and it must be believable, as minimal conditions. See his How Real Is Real?, 1976, p. 107.

(11) See Cavell's Must We Mean What We Say? 1969 especially the essay with that title. Also see Pitkin's Wittgenstein and Justice, 1972.

(12) See Searle's Speech Acts for the difference between regulative and constitutive rules. Charles Taylor develops some of the political implications of these differences for politics and the study of politics in his "Interpretation and the Sciences of Man," (Searle, cited above, note 6).

(13) "Please check out the proposal" may have many nonliteral, practical meanings too. For example, it may mean, "this proposal isn't documented properly." But our understanding of such nonliteral meanings presupposes that we know how to apply the ordinary rules of language use. Otherwise, we wouldn't, at the first level, be able to recognize the literal meaning, its possible implications, and then at the second level, its fit or possible mis-fit with the context of its use (i.e., whether or not we should take it literally).

(14) Extended analysis of such presupposition and anticipation of the "universal pragmatic" norms of speech can be found in McCarthy's Critical Theory of Jurgen Habermas; Schapiro's "Reply to Miller's Review of Habermas's Legitimation Crisis," Spring 1976 is also helpful.

(15) See Habermas's "What is Universal Pragmatics?," p. 2, in Communication and the Evolution of Society, 1979.

(16) A recent analysis of this presupposition of the principle of veracity and the instances of its justified violation appears in Sissela Bok's Lying, 1978.

(17) "Since our ability to cope with life depends upon our making sense of what happens to us, anything which threatens to invalidate our conceptual structures of interpretation is profoundly disruptive." Marris, Loss and Change, 1975, p. 13.

(18) Dallmayr argues that the violation and respect of these universal pragmatic norms of communication may be taken to ground a "communicative ethics" and a normative political vision. See his "Toward a Critical Reconstruction of Ethics and Politics," 1974. I develop the

implications of a "communicative ethics" for planning in "What Do Planning Analysts Do? Planning and Policy Analysis as Organizing," 1978. See also, Schroyer's Critique of Domination, pp. 162-3, for the argument that Habermas's critique of systematically distorted communications is a refined form of the classical critique of ideology.

(19) Cavell distinguishes the semantic meaning of an uttered sentence from the pragmatic meaning of the same utterance, and he argues that as speakers and actors we are responsible for both. Good intentions are not enough; pragmatics count. See Must We Mean What We Say? 1969.

(20) From the journal of a young planner in California: "Sitting in on Environmental Review Committee meetings, I notice how the applicants interact with the Committee – the "slickies" know the genre. They speak with professional language, e.g. "that's correct" for "that's right." Others come in and get bounced around by the strange terminology and the unfamiliar process. What a humiliating experience for them. . ." Fall, 1978.

(21) For example, a public health department director, facing a planning commissioner's proposal of additional formal interagency meetings: "What you're proposing is a formal structure that'll look great on paper, but won't be operational. What we need is ongoing informal consultation and communication so we know what each other's doing – that's what works!" (K.G., Tompkins County H.S.A. Subarea Council, 3/21/79).

(22) "The normative foundation of a critical theory is implicit in the very structure of social action that it analyzes." Bernstein, Restructuring of Social and Political Theory, p. 213, quoting McCarthy.

(23) See Bok, Lying, cited above, for an extended discussion.

(24) Assessing the distorted communications prevalent in modern bureaucracies, Ralph Hummel argues that bureaucratic organizations are characterized not by two-way communication, but by one-way information. "Bureaucracy separates man from his language. . . .The 'language' through which a bureaucracy speaks to us is not a language designed for problem-solving. Bureaucratic language is a language for passing on solutions. . ." The Bureaucratic Experience, 1977, pp. 157-9.

(25) See Mueller's The Politics of Communication, 1973.

(26) I treat the problems of distorted communication and political response at the level of face-to-face interaction in my "Listening: The Social Policy of Everyday Life (Critical Theory and Hermeneutics in Practice)," 1978.

(27) McGuire writes, ". . .insofar as systems of rules and norms contribute to systematically distorted communication, insofar as they

exist as systematic barriers to discursive will formation, they are irrational. . .And insofar as (communication structures) create a fiction of reciprocal accountability, concomitantly creating ideologies by sustaining the 'legitimacy' of these very structures they are irrational. . . and hence illegitimate – involving no moral obligation." ("Speech Acts, Communicative Competence, and the Paradox of Authority," Winter 1977.)

(28) Several sources provide insight and suggestions for those seeking to correct distortions of communication at the organizational level: Wilensky's Organizational Intelligence; Needleman and Needleman's Guerrillas in the Bureaucracy; Alinsky's Rules for Radicals; also helpful may be Benveniste's Politics of Expertise, and Freire's Pedagogy of the Oppressed and Education for Critical Consciousness, 1970, 1974.

(29) The political economic ethic or vision of "opening communications" is the ethic of the critique of ideology. Embodied in actions seeking to correct distorted communication, the distortion of attention to actual possibilities, this is a call for political organizing, for democratizing public policy.

(30) To politicize planning does not mean to "make trouble." This is the misreading of "politics" that perpetuates a narrow, technically focused, politically inept planning practice. To politicize planning along the lines called for by critical theory means to broaden the basis of consideration of alternatives, to foster participation and spread responsibility to nonprofessional citizens; to balance the reliance upon technique with the attention to regular political debate and criticism.

(31) "The ultimate objective of repoliticization. . . should be to resurrect the notion of democracy, which is far too important an ideal to be sacrificed to capitalism. . . .The problem is not that capitalist societies accumulate, but the way in which they do it. In order for the beneficiaries of accumulation to remain a narrow group, a boundary is established beyond which democracy is not allowed to intrude. . . .(T)he time has come to think, not about demolishing accumulation, but about democratizing it. The way to eliminate the contradictions between accumulation and legitimation is to apply the principles of democracy to both – to give people the same voice in making investment and allocation decisions as they theoretically have in more directly political decisions." (Wolfe, Limits of Legitimacy, 1977.)

(32) The normative goal or ideal of "organizing" and "opening communications" ought not be dismissed as romantic or utopian, a call for infinite gentleness or "listening forever" – for it is a practical call to prevent noise, misinformation, unnecessary ambiguity, the misleading elevation or lowering of citizens' expectations.

(33) We must beware, when we speak of "opening communications," that this is not understood so narrowly as "getting more citizen input," getting more bodies to meetings. This is precisely how "input" misleads us, for it is not input, but reponsibility and constructively critical political participation that are at issue.

(34) See for example, Benveniste's The Politics of Expertise, 1977.

(35) When the context of a planner's description or evaluation is technical, that description or evaluation may have a pragmatic political effect in addition to that of its technical message. Paul Watzlawick writes, "The paramount communicational significance of context is all too easily overlooked in the analysis of human communication, and yet anyone who brushed his teeth in a busy street rather than in his bathroom might be quickly carted off to a police station or a lunatic asylum – to give just one example of the pragmatic effects of nonverbal communication." from Pragmatics of Human Communication 1967.

(36) Illich argues, "Paradoxically, the more attention is focused on the technical mastery of disease, the larger becomes the symbolic and nontechnical function performed by medical technology." from Medical Nemesis, 1977.

(37) Galper writes of professional social work practices: "In every interaction in which we engage, we encourage certain responses in others and discourage other responses. Workers who are themselves politicized. . . will offer suggestions and interpretations from this perspective. . . (These interpretations) must clearly be offered in service to the client and not in service of political ends that are somehow separate from the situation and well-being of the client." from The Politics of the Social Services, 1975.

(38) Ibid.: "In one sense, the virtual death of a formal welfare state organizing role is a benefit because it forces us to develop the organizing role for persons in all service-delivery positions." In the face of fiscal conservatism and austerity budgets, planners too must work as organizers.

(39) See, for example, Meltsner's Policy Analysts in the Bureaucracy, 1976; and Norman Krumholz, et al., "The Cleveland Policy Planning Report," 1975; see also the analysis of interviews with local planners in Baltimore by Howell Baum, School of Social Work and Community Planning, University of Maryland, Baltimore, Maryland 21201. Harold Wilensky, Organizational Intelligence, 1967. See note 28.

16 Teaching Radical Planning

Edward Bergman
Jean-Louis Sarbib

THE CHALLENGE FROM CONSERVATISM

The political climate in the United States in the late 1970s is one of retrenchment and conservatism leading to a reaffirmation of the virtues of laissez-faire capitalism. These virtues are viewed as the tested certainties that made America into the world's most powerful nation and to which the country must return to regain its strength. In this atmosphere, government bureaucracy is perceived as an overgrown intruder, solely preoccupied with its own (wasteful) survival; most unions are viewed as obstacles to personal freedom and to solutions to problems of inflation; the benevolence and positive nature of free enterprise is reaffirmed in theoretical publications and in countless advertising campaigns of monopoly corporations.

The much heralded tax revolt is generally seen as a call to limit government spending and to cut social services. Though the taxpayers' anger could also be interpreted as a desire to see social services administered and delivered in a drastically different way, the conservative interpretation remains unchallenged. A different analysis could provide the rationale for progressive organizing of communities based on increasing local control of and participation in the drafting of social legislation supported by federal funds. This is however a delicate and potentially dangerous route to take. The consequences of Nixon's "New Federalism" underline the importance of combining such decentralized spending with effective control of policy mechanisms by a majority of the population (and not by the local elite).

In the absence of such an alternative explanation, the apparent public discontent with the form of welfare liberalism typical of big government and its accompanying pageant of professional bureaucrats has lent credence to neoconservative theorizing.

In intellectual circles influential in molding the most recent philosophy of public policy, neoconservatives have taken the offensive. Most are failed liberals who are reentering the establishment by repudiating their earlier beliefs on the basis of their rediscovery of the dark side of human nature and of their ambivalent faith in technology.

The question of technology, however, is one where the conservative ideology does not speak with a single voice. If traditional conservatives denounce the illusion of technique, joining the countercultural radical critics, the neoconservative has not given up the capitalist faith in technology. In that sense, neoconservatism is much closer to a corporate view of the world than traditional conservatism ever was. The contrast between Adam Smith laissez-faireism and the neoconservatives' acceptance of domination by large corporations is important and could lead to considerable difficulties in translating neoconservatism into a set of widely acceptable public policies.

Beyond the breakdown of the regulatory mechanisms of welfare state liberalism under the pressure of the international economic crisis, two factors are further contributing to the neoconservative wave.

On the one hand, orthodox Marxism is not directly addressing the issue of the nature of class relations in the Soviet state and socialist countries, hence obscuring the traditional Marxist theoretical and organizational treatment of the nature of the state, the role of the party, of the proletariat, of intellectuals etc. Neither is it addressing the question of international relations within the Communist world. The answers that the Chinese Cultural Revolution provided to these questions have lost creditability due to shifts in China and renewed conflicts in South East Asia in 1978 and 1979. Although a good deal of study is devoted to these matters in radical circles, there is as yet more controversy than agreement on how to analyze these problems and on defining an acceptable way of dealing with them. This crisis of Marxism has provided the neoconservatives with valuable allies, such as France's "new philosophers."

On the other hand the ideological response of traditional liberals to the neoconservative challenge to liberal domination in policy circles has been practically nonexistent. Their political strategy seems to consist in waiting for pluralist politics to provide a providential leader to lift them out of their depression.

Neoconservatism has triggered a series of reactions (both organizational and ideological) from a broad spectrum of people, ranging from leftist liberals and the militant wings of some labor unions to scattered remnants of the radical Left of the 1960s, who are often badly split by arguments generated by the crisis of orthodox Marxism. Among this loosely defined group there is no agreement, either on the nature of the problems facing the Left or on a proper strategy to follow. This lack of agreement raises a number of theoretical and organizational questions that must be addressed.

THE IDEOLOGICAL CONTEXT OF PLANNING EDUCATION

Planners will increasingly face dilemmas as their function in society is modified to fit new circumstances and to conform to the neoconservative challenge. Raising such questions in planning schools is not automatically met with approval or support (to say nothing of enthusiasm) either by the majority of planning students or teachers. In this paper we will explore the role of the self-proclaimed radical academic in planning schools.

In dealing with this issue as such, it is important to analyze, however briefly, the impact of the general economic and ideological context on students and on radical academics.

The graduate students of the late 1970s came of age in an era of shrinking opportunities. But they still want "the good life" – professional jobs, gourmet foods, European vacations, foreign films, and gentrified cities in which their main responsibility is assuring their own happiness. While in college most looked to professional school as the key that would open the door to this good life. In the process they learned to see their education as an instrument rather than an experience. Upon arrival in professional school, this attitude is translated into a demand for acquiring skills capable of securing good jobs in a competitive market. While stronger in medical, business or law school, this trend is also noticeable in planning schools, especially when tracing the socially induced evolution of student concerns over the last ten years. But it is important to underline the fact that, although influenced by the larger societal context, planning students seem to remain more concerned than their peers in other professional schools with questions of social justice or at least with the possibility of improving society. However, the amount of time and effort they are prepared to devote to these goals and their resilience to generally adverse conditions are the characteristics most affected by their general preoccupation with self: even more than the American students of the 1960s, they want to see results now or they will change direction.

Most radical academics teaching in today's planning schools came of age during (or have been influenced by) the social turmoil of the 1960s. The crisis of the 1970s, while leading some of these academics to adopt conservative views, has confirmed in others their criticism of liberalism. This has underlined their need to refine an understanding of the role of planning in American society in order to define new practice related roles for themselves and for field practitioners. The 1978 conference in Blacksburg helped us see the convergence of many isolated efforts and may have influenced some radical academics to be more secure about teaching.

The decade separating many students from faculty has engendered an apparent paradox: radical faculty members are teaching students in what are increasingly depoliticized schools of planning. Table 16.1 summarizes this situation.

The paradox works as follows: faculty tends to note as most important to their practice the substantial changes that have affected instructional materials, planning problems and curricula; students tend to focus on the current low levels of social concerns found in overall curricula, future practice settings and among their peers, and to favor in what they perceive to be marketable skills. Each is a realistic view

Table 16.1. Receptivity to Radical Planning Ideas

	1968-9	1978-9
Faculty	Nil	Low to Moderate
Instructional materials, literature, research, models	Low	High
Range of Planning Problems	Low to Moderate	Moderate to High
Formal Instructional curricula	Nil	Low to Moderate
Planning Practice settings	Moderate	Low
Students	High	Low

but we contend that faculty members are at least responsible for analyzing how these viewpoints differ, why they have come to diverge in the recent past, and how an historical account of planning thought, planning practice and planning education can place these comparatively recent events in a larger perspective. Such an analysis occurs at the University of North Carolina in a planning theory class where the history, theory and functions of planning are discussed as the logical consequence of state intervention in advanced capitalist development processes, particularly the processes related to neighborhoods, consumption, etc., that Marxists call social reproduction or "reproduction of the labor force." The teaching of this and related courses creates a certain dilemma for students and teachers alike. These dilemmas raise some important questions to which we now turn.

THE DILEMMAS OF TEACHING AND LEARNING RADICAL PARADIGMS

When radical faculty and students, molded by different sets of societal experiences, come together in the classroom, a complex process of interaction is set in motion. At the most immediate level, students perceive the teacher as an authority figure and tend not to question the views presented for fear of risking a poor grade. This is particularly true during the first semester when entering students carry into graduate school their behavior as grade-minded undergraduates. Since most courses aimed at the socialization of planners are taught in the early stages, a consuming concern for grades could represent a significant problem in actually engaging the students. The problem, however, can be reduced by opening up the classroom discussion, and making clear that personal views, provided they are informed by at least a minimal amount of fact and history are perfectly acceptable though subject to challenge.

Another problem arises from the nature of the radical analysis of the role and function of planning in American society. There seems to be an emerging agreement on the role of planning as an instrument to legitimize the capitalist state. Historical reviews of various kinds of planning efforts usually lead to the conclusion that planning has often resulted in the maintenance (or sometimes the reinforcement) of the status quo, even when planners saw themselves as promoters of reform and change. When planning is seen in this light it often discourages those students who chose planning school because of their interest in social change. These students usually face two kinds of hurdles: one is peer-related and involves breaking the barrier of "cynical cool" that many students affect. The second hurdle is more significant. Most of the students interested in change first conceptualize their roles as that of professional planners working to induce change within the confines of the welfare state in order to achieve a better distribution of goods and services. The radical critique of the welfare state, however, creates a problem for them because it denies a progressive role for individuals committed to change. Radical planners have so far been unable to provide such students with a vision of alternative roles that can be personally fulfilling, politically progressive and immune from the fallacies of liberal reformism. The general climate of retrenchment and apparent ascendancy of neoconservative ideas makes this problem particularly acute.

Confronted with the difficulty of having to reconcile their interest in change with a vision of the welfare state as a custodian of the poor, and unable to direct or to change significantly the future direction of American society, students react in a variety of ways. Their reactions parallel those of planners who are confronted with delicate political problems in the real world of planning agencies or state bureaucracies. In that sense, teaching socialization courses such as planning theory (or, to a lesser extent, planning methods) from a radical standpoint represents a rough approximation of a first exposure to the politics of planning. Admittedly, what is missing in the classroom, but could be crucial in a real situation, is the dialectic of planner/agency and planner/client and the resulting high level of personal involvement on the part of the planner.

The various student reactions underline different types of problems that together set an agenda for study by radical academics. Three types of reactions can be identified.

1. One consists of considering the radical analysis to be interesting and intellectually challenging in an otherwise dry and technical curriculum, but ultimately rejecting it as utopian, too critical or unable to offer viable alternatives in the present situation. Most students react this way, to a greater or lesser extent, depending on their previous

experiences or ideological presuppositions. The rest of their planning education is devoted to acquiring skills: they work hard and see themselves as technicians. They experience a rapid transition, once described by John Friedmann, of going from "planning as a vocation" to "planning as a job."

2. The second reaction consists of a reaffirmation of the possibility of reconciling a radical consciousness with the existing pattern and nature of planning jobs. Such an approach raises a series of important research and strategy questions that must be addressed by radical academics in planning schools. This position ultimately leads to an affirmation of the possibility of effecting change from within the state apparatus. It raises important theoretical questions about the autonomy of the state and about the nature, function and class position of professionals in modern capitalist societies. The development and the nature of state intervention after World War II, the growth of a stratum of professional managerial bureaucrats, and the increased importance of the role of the state in production as well as reproduction processes have led some to affirm that the state is no longer simply "the executive committee of the bourgeoisie," but can affect the direction of the future evolution of society in a progressive way. A growing volume of material is available on these topics and it is important to find ways of discussing these theories in light of the experiences of practitioners who try to follow the path of radical action from within the state.

The passive acceptance of the conservative challenge to the liberal welfare state has two aspects. First, most traditional liberals have deserted the ranks of the advocates of the welfare state and second, they have been replaced by radicals who, while seeing the need to maintain a minimum level of social services, nevertheless reject a wholehearted belief in the benevolence of the liberal state. The radicals (as they still define themselves), who are serving in the upper reaches of the social service bureaucracies of the Carter administration are a good example of this social phenomenon. Their presence often gives bureaucratic affairs an incongruous atmosphere, with the official speaker offering an articulate political critique of the policy being presented in the name of his or her agency. Is the institutionalization of cynicism a positive step?

Besides the theoretical questions about the autonomy of the state and the class structure of advanced capitalism, the choice of working within the state raises some related strategic questions. What type of organization, if any, do self-proclaimed radical professionals need? Should they act as whistleblowers? Information sources? Should they form unions? Should such unions be professional unions or unions formed in conjunction with other state employees, professional and nonprofessional? Why types of links should radical professionals maintain with their clients? What kinds of support networks can they most effectively use? Can planning schools (and their alumni) play any particular role in establishing, maintaining and feeding such support networks?

The theoretical and the strategic questions outlined above set up a research agenda for radical planning academics that could help them establish contact with like minded field practitioners. They also have obvious implications for involvement in curriculum development.

3. The third type of reaction consists in rejecting the possibility of structurally reconciling professionalism and radicalism and can lead to a student leaving school. Such students say that there are only radical individuals and deny the significance of talking about radical planning. In professional circles, a similar attitude manifests itself in the form of schizophrenic lifestyles where most meaningful political activity takes place after hours in openly political settings where the professional participates as an individual.

These three types of reactions (insofar as they approximate choices made by field practitioners) show the need to pursue the research questions mentioned above not simply as a way to advance knowledge but because answers to such questions can help outline role expectations for those planning students who react positively to the presentation of radical paradigms. We believe that radical teachers have a responsibility to follow up on their classroom presentations and on their academic research through a close involvement in various aspects of the life of their departments and communities. These responsibilities comprise the practice that may unite us and provide the major reason for continuing to hold conferences on radical planning. With this in mind we now turn to a discussion of the responsibilities of radical planning academics.

RESPONSIBILITIES OF RADICAL PLANNING ACADEMICS

The possibility of specifying a radical practice for planners and for planning academics necessarily hinges upon some real or potential degree of state autonomy from capitalist processes of material production and social reproduction. We point this out as a key assumption – not as a defended proposition – which is essential to the further exploration of corollary responsibilities for radical planning academics. (This is, of course, an assumption deserving of specific, explicit theoretical attention and of testing in suitable practice situations.)

Assuming then that a radical academic practice can be envisioned, what are the responsibilities that academics should acknowledge? Three in particular that come to mind are research and scholarship, the development of theory, and pedagogy. If we were to be graded by the progress made to date in each of these areas, the grade spread might be B+ through C-.

Research and Scholarship

First, radical scholarship and research have significantly contributed to our understanding of some planning problems (e.g., labor processes and economic dependencies in local economies), but less work has been undertaken in many other areas of planning concern (e.g., land use and environment). This uneven development of radical scholarship may be traced, in part, to the varying degrees of interest among current academics in applying alternative or radical analysis to the full range of planning concerns.

In addition to broadening the realm of radical scholarship in planning, academics must also come to terms with basic epistemological questions. By what means is knowledge expanded as an academic practice? What is the proper role for empirical studies and findings? Are such issues in planning essentially comparable to those faced by radical academics from related disciplines, or does, for example, the development of knowledge applied to processes of social reproduction single out planning epistemologies as peculiar or unique?

Theory Development

Second, radical academics have a continuing role to play in the development of planning theory. Theory development in planning seems to have increased recently. The stream of papers and articles has expanded measurably in the last half decade and this flow will doubtless increase in the wake of the 1978 and 1979 conferences held in Blacksburg and Ithaca. The significance of the two conferences does not reside so much in the fact that they have provided a place for the presentation and discussion of theoretical developments, but that they have signaled the maturity of planning theory as an identifiable field of inquiry. Further, the conferences clearly established that radical academics and practitioners have taken the initiative in advancing this field as a project. Since planning theory can only be tested by practitioners, this will of necessity be a joint project undertaken by both radical planners and planning academics. Although the responsibility for theory development is a joint one, radical academics by virtue of their detachment and institutional ties are best situated to elaborate theoretical propositions for subsequent testing and revision.

Joint efforts are to be encouraged. Maintaining contact among academics and practitioners must go beyond the infrequent conferences that foster discussion of works in progress. Strong support of the Planners Network (360 Elizabeth St., San Francisco, CA 94114) and similar associations by radical academics is a valuable way of maintaining contacts, particularly if such support includes active involvement with practitioners in theory development. Furthermore, joint research efforts conducted in specific, concrete planning situations afford suitable opportunities for theory development at a practical level. Particularly valuable are continued contacts between radical academics and alumni from planning schools; work begun earlier in an academic setting can then mature naturally among peers and provide the basis for a continuing dialogue.

Pedagogy

Without belaboring the obvious, responsible pedagogy seems to us highly dependent upon serious research, scholarship and theoretical work. But the unique role of planning academics should be acknowledged here: we are responsible for producing society's professional managers (whether or not they represent a specific stratum or class). As such, our practice is of a dual nature: as discussed above, we are engaged in the production of social knowledge and in creating awareness of planning as a principal technical force in the process of organizing our lives outside workplaces, in neighborhoods, schools, etc. (what Marxists call social reproduction). But we are simultaneously producing embodied knowledge in the form of trained practitioners. We are, so to speak, closely involved with reproducing the technical means for society to reproduce itself. It is vitally important that this be fully understood, for otherwise students cannot readily distinguish their brief academic experience as practitioners in training, which necessarily reflects the concerns of radical academics, from the students' subsequent field practice as agents of the state, working in various aspects of social reproduction. Nor can planning academics do much to resolve legitimate student concerns about the nature of radical field planning practice if attention becomes focused solely on narrow issues of instruction, curricula, etc. as they affect radical academics.

Other radically inclined students, enrolled in nonvocational, liberal arts programs or in graduate programs that lead to research and teaching posts, can more eagerly absorb critical radical analyses, because the immediacy of such insights does not necessarily threaten their life prospects or sense of purpose. But the situation of students (and faculty) in planning schools is qualitatively different, particularly if their class backgrounds are such that entry into the professional managerial class in some way legitimizes the mobility assumptions that they hold. Here the central responsibility of radical planning academics becomes clear: In developing a critical consciousness among planning students, a radical academic must constructively dispel some of the naive or unwarranted elements of social change optimism that may have initially brought students into the program; at the same time we must be careful not to administer a disabling dose of cynicism or cause students to seek recourse in unreflective versions of orthodox planning.

Radical academics should help to prepare people who are politically aware and sophisticated, who have a realistic set of expectations about what they can accomplish, an agenda of what needs to be done, some ideas on organizational issues so that they are less likely to be easily and quickly burned out in the process of confronting powerful bureaucracies.

What pedagogical measures might be pursued by academics who seriously take on such responsibilities? Several come to mind:

1. Academics should alter their full repertoire of courses to reflect a radical analysis. This responsibility is not met by teaching a token radical planning course for the sake of curriculum balance. If the radical perspective is to have any validity, its philosophy must be inherent in every course.

2. A full repertoire of radical planning courses should incorporate a well developed planning paradigm, where the term paradigm is meant to convey the notion of an elaborated view of radical planning as a practice. Strong, closely argued criticism is an essential beginning, but coursework should also develop a coherent view of planning practice as a radically different enterprise.

If we focus on planning and its role in social reproduction, promising ways of developing a more fully elaborated planning paradigm may emerge. For example, we know that contradictions in processes of social reproduction are increasing and that planners are often responsible for managing these processes. To the degree that such contradictions are caused by popular demands and that continuing or amplifying such contradictions leads to increases in political awareness and sophistication among citizens, radical planning may play an important social role. A more fully developed theoretical and experimental understanding of planning for social reproduction will help in the development of such a paradigm, particularly if social reproduction is understood to occur mainly in the decentralized community contexts so familiar to planners. And if our state of understanding is too limited, or available instructional materials seem inadequate, these needs should further help establish research and scholarship priorities for radical academics.

3. Expansion of curricula should include courses that orthodox planning education often overlooks. Every planning school has differing needs, but most could use, for example, additional course offerings in historical analyses of planning thought and practice, or on the class structure of planning and planning situations.

4. We must define a radical planning methodology to aid in the design and teaching of planning methods. It is necessary but scarcely sufficient to criticize the origin and current use of planning methods without also considering their alternative uses or the existence of alternative methods. Much like the initial assumption we made concerning some degree of state autonomy, we must also assume that not all social technologies and methods necessarily lead to social domination. Some methods can be taught because they are analytically revealing, others because they provide common baseline descriptions that continuously recur in practice, and still others because radical planners must be prepared to legitimize their involvement in serious planning problems or to deploy such methods as defensive tactic. Much work remains to be done along these lines.

If radical planning academics do not meet this responsibility directly, i.e., develop an affirmative set of methodologies, then we risk being thought of as irrelevant by students who must justify their eventual practice to peers and to the public. Moreover, we may forego genuine opportunities to engage our more orthodox colleagues in a shared concern about appropriate methods and a discussion of their underlying assumptions.

Beyond the issue of working with colleagues on appropriate methods, we should take the initiative to engage other faculty in various colloquia and panels or to coteach courses and seminars with them. This allows students and other faculty the opportunity to view planning and planning situations from the perspective of two or more competing paradigms. One should not expect that other faculty will come to share a radical perspective (although this too may infrequently occur); rather, colleagues more fully exposed to well presented radical paradigms are more likely to appreciate the complexity and saliency of such insights and therefore be less likely to dismiss out-of-hand poorly understood or vulgarized versions of radical planning.

In revising courses, curricula and other pedagogical instruments to reflect radical planning perspectives, we should be cautious not to isolate ourselves from the full student body. It is always tempting to treat radical topics in full detail with a group of like minded students, but one must also be aware of "preaching to the clergy" and of isolating the laity. To this end, it is perhaps prudent that radical academics teach at least one or two courses with fairly broad appeal (i.e., problem-based workshops, hands-on methods, history). Such courses provide a healthy mix of divergent positions that radical planners are certain to encounter in practice; but they also provide a safe period of incubation during which radical consciousness among some members of the wider student body might be nurtured and developed. At the very least, such courses provide conventionally inclined students with an opportunity to test their views in a critical setting at the same time that academics are able to keep in touch with orthodox reactions and conventional criticisms; these opportunities may be exercised in and out of the classroom. This caution should not be overdrawn, but it does merit concern, particularly in departments with a small number of radical faculty and students.

Extracurricular learning opportunities for students also deserve support from radical academics. Since orthodox planning philosophy dominates the curriculum in nearly every planning school, radical planning students must take fullest advantage of extracurricular opportunities. This may imply the establishment of a student organization (i.e., Radical Planning Alternatives at the University of North Carolina - Chapel Hill) or joining Planners Network as student affiliates. Once established, these mechanisms can provide the necessary environment to provide mutual support, engage others outside planning schools, and become involved in community projects. To the degree that supportive groups in the local community are amenable to working with radical planning students, they too provide a continuing base for student involvement and extracurricular learning. Since these groups also need help, which student and faculty can provide, enduring reciprocal arrangements often emerge. Finally, academics are best able to keep track of radical alumni to maintain student-practitioner ties. Radical Planning Alternatives at UNC-CH recently hosted a panel with alumni who reported on their current involvements. While students gain much from such contacts (including job leads), alumni also benefit from the opportunity to reflect on their current practice and to keep in touch with recent developments in planning as well as in related fields of radical scholarship.

Bibliography

Aaron, Henry J. Shelter and Subsidies: Who Benefits from Federal Housing Policies? Washington, D.C.: Brookings Institution, 1972.

Abrahamsson, Bengt. Bureaucracy or Participation: The Logic of Organization. Beverly Hills: Sage Publications, 1977.

Abrams, Charles. The City is the Frontier. New York: Harper & Row, 1965.

______. The Future of Housing. New York: Harper & Row, 1946.

Achtenberg, Emily N. Critique of the Rental Housing Association Rent Control Study: An Analysis of the Realities of Rent Control in the Greater Boston Area. Cambridge, Mass.: Urban Planning Aid, 1975.

Achtenberg, Emily N.; and Stone, Michael. Tenants First! A Research and Organizing Guide to FHA Housing. Cambridge: Urban Planning Aid, 1974.

Alinsky, Saul. Rules for Radicals. New York: Vintage Press, 1971.

Allen, Robert. "Racism and the Black Nation Thesis." Socialist Revolution 6 (1976): 145-50.

Altshuler, Alan. The City Planning Process. Ithaca: Cornell University Press, 1965.

American Institute of Planners. "Membership Survey from 1976 Roster." Washington, D.C.: American Institute of Planners.

Annuai Housing Survey: 1975, United States and Regions. Current Housing Reports, Series H-150-75. Washington, D.C.: Government Printing Office, 1977.

"The Apartment Market." National Real Estate Investor 15 (1974): 41.

Apel, Karl Otto. "The Priori of Communication and the Foundation of the Humanities." In Fred Dallmayr and Thomas McCarthy, Understanding and Social Inquiry. Notre Dame: Notre Dame Press, 1977.

Appelbaum, Richard. Size, Growth and U.S. Cities. New York: Praeger Publishers, 1973.

______; Bigelow, J.; Kramer, H.; Molotch, H.; and Relis, P. The Effects of Urban Growth: A Population Impact Analysis. New York: Praeger, 1976.

Arendt, Hannah. "Action." In The Human Condition. New York: Doubleday Anchor, 1959.

Argyris, Chris; and Schon, Donald A. Theory in Practice. San Francisco: Jossey-Bass, 1974.

Astrachan, Boris M.; and Flynn, H.R. "The Intergroup Exercise: A Paradigm for Learning about the Development of Organizational Structure." In Erie J. Miller, ed., Task and Organization. London: Tavistock Publications, 1976.

Austin, John. How To Do Things With Words. London: Oxford University Press, 1961.

Banfield, Edward. "Means and Ends in Planning." In S. Mailick and E.H. Van Ness, Concepts and Issues in Administrative Behavior. Englewood Cliffs, N.J.: Prentice Hall, 1962.

______. The Unheavenly City. Boston: Little Brown, 1970.

Barkin, David. "A Case Study of the Beneficiaries of Regional Development." International Social Development Review, no. 4 (1973).

______. "Regional Development and Interregional Equity: A Mexican Case Study." In Wayne A. Cornelius and Felicity M. Trueblood, eds., Latin American Urban Research Review no. 5. Los Angeles: Sage Publications, 1975, pp. 277-301.

______. "Confronting the Separation of Town and Country in Cuba." In W. Tubb and L. Sawers, eds., Marxism and the Metropolis. New York: Oxford, 1978.

Barnett, Richard; and Mueller, Ronald. Global Reach. New York: Touchstone, 1974.

Bauer, Catherine. "Is Urban Redevelopment Under Existing Legislation?" Planning. Chicago: American Society of Planning Officials, 1946.

______. Modern Housing. Boston: Houghton Mifflin, 1934.

______. "Redevelopment and Public Housing." Planning. Chicago: American Society of Planning Officials, 1950.

______. "Redevelopment: A Misfit in the Fifties." In Coleman Woodbury, ed., The Future of Cities and Urban Redevelopment. Chicago: The University of Chicago Press, 1953.

Baum, Howell S. "Strains Between Planners' Expertise and Their Autonomy: Implications for Professionalization." Baltimore: School of Social Work and Community Planning, University of Maryland, 1978.

______. "Toward a Post-Industrial Planning Theory." Policy Sciences 8 (1977): 401-21.

______. "The Uncertain Consciousness of Planners and the Professional Enterprise." Baltimore: School of Social Work and Community Planning, University of Maryland, no date.

Bay Area Kapitalistate Collective, "Introduction to the Special Issue on Class Struggle and the State." Kapitalistate 7 (Winter 1979).

Beauregard, Robert A. "Planning in an Advanced Capitalist State." In Robert Burchell and George Sternlieb (eds.), Planning Theory in the 1980's. New Brunswick: Center for Urban Policy Research, 1978.

______. "The Occupation of Planning: A View from the Census." Journal of the American Institute of Planners 44 (1976): 187-92.

Beinstein, Judith. "Urban Field Education: An Opportunity for Enhancing Students' Personal and Social Efficacy." Human Relations 29 (1976): 677-85.

Bell, David. The Coming of Post-Industrial Society. New York: Basic Books, 1973.

Bellush, Jewel; and Hausknecht, Murray, eds. Urban Renewal: People, Politics, and Planning. New York: Anchor Books, 1967.

Benello, C. George and Roussopoulos, eds. The Case for Participatory Democracy: Some Prospects for a Radical Society. New York: Grossman, 1971.

Benveniste, Guy. The Politics of Expertise. 2nd ed. San Francisco: Boyd and Fraser, 1977.

Berger, Peter and Luckmann, Thomas. Social Construction of Reality. New York: Anchor Press, 1966.

Berliner, Howard. "The Emerging Ideologies in Medicine." The Review of Radical Political Economics 9 (1977): 116-123.

Berliner, Howard S. and Salmon, J. Warren. "The Holistic Health Movement and Scientific Medicine: The Naked and the Dead." Socialist Review 34 (1979).

Bernstein, Richard. The Restructuring of Social and Political Theory. Philadelphia: University of Pennsylvania Press, 1976.

_______. Praxis and Action. Philadelphia: University of Pennsylvania Press, 1971.

Blumberg, Richard E., Robbins, Brian Quinn, and Barr, Kenneth K. "The Emergence of Second Generation Rent Controls." Clearinghouse Review, August 1974, pp. 240-249.

Blumenthal, Hans. "Comment." Monthly Review 29-30 (June 1978).

Bobbio, Norberto. "Why Democracy?" Telos, no. 36 (1978), pp. 43-54.

Bok, Sissela. Lying. New York: Pantheon, 1978.

Bolan, Richard S. "Community Decision Behavior: The Culture of Planning." Journal of the American Institute of Planners 35 (1969): 301-310.

Bookchin, Murray. Post-Scarcity Anarchism. San Francisco: Ramparts Press, 1971.

Booth, Richard. "The Adirondack Park Agency: A Challenge in Regional Land-Use Planning." George Washington Law Review 43 (1975).

Bowly, Devereaux. The Poorhouse: Subsidized Housing in Chicago, 1895-1976. Carbondale: Southern Illinois University Press, 1978.

Boyer, Brian D. Cities Destroyed for Cash. Chicago: Follett Publishing Company, 1973.

Boyer, Christine. "National Land Policy: Instrument and Product of the Economic Cycle." In Judith de Neufville, ed., Land Use Policy: The Theories and the Choices. Berkeley: University of California Press, forthcoming.

Boyle, Godfrey, and Harper, Peter. Radical Technology. New York: Pantheon, 1976.

Boyte, Harry C. "The Populist Challenge: Anatomy of an Emerging Movement." Socialist Review 32 (1977).

Bradley, John M. "Volunteer Education: Key to Building an Effective Planning Process." Health Law Project Library Bulletin 4 (1979): 164-172.

Braverman, Harry. Labor and Monopoly Capital. New York: Monthly Review Press, 1975.

Brecher, Jeremy. Strike! San Francisco: Straight Arrow Books, 1972.

Brenner, Joe, and Franklin, Herbert. Rent Control in North America and European Countries. Washington, D.C.: Potomic Institutes, 1977.

Brenner, Robert. "The Origins of Capitalist Development: A Critique of Neo-Smithan Marxism." New Left Review 104 (1977) 25-92.

Brodsky, Barry. "Tenants First: FHA Tenants Organize in Massachusetts." Radical America 9 (1975): 37-48.

Brous, Ira et al. Democracy in the Workplace. Washington, D.C.: Strongforce, 1977.

Burdell, Edwin. "Rehousing Needs of the Families on the Stuyvesant Town Site." Journal of the American Institute of Planners 11 (1945): 15-19.

Burlage, Robb. "ARC's First Six-Year Plan: A Critical Interpretation." People's Appalachia 1, no. 4 (1970): 14-29.

__________. New York City's Municipal Hospitals. Washington, D.C.: Institute for Policy Studies, 1967.

Burton, Dudley J. The Governance of Energy: Conditions, Prospects, and Underlying Issues. New York: Praeger, 1979.

Butler, Cecil. "Strategies for Neighborhood Economic Revitalization and Community Economic Development." Economic Development Law Project Report VI, Issue 1 (1976).

California Housing Council, Inc. The Case Against Rent Control. San Mateo, California: The Council, 1977.

California State Reconstruction and Reemployment Commission. Blighted! Commission Pamphlet #10. Sacramento, California: The Commission, 1946.

California Statewide Housing Plan, 1977. Sacramento, California: Department of Housing and Community Development, 1977.

Carlisle, Rick et al. Community Participation in Selecting Worker Ownership; ESOT: A Local Development Strategy. Final Report on the National Science Foundation. Chapel Hill, N.C.: Department of City and Regional Planning, University of North Carolina, 1978.

Caro, Robert. The Power Broker. New York: Random House, 1974.

Castells, Manuel. The Urban Question. Cambridge: MIT Press, 1977.

______. "The Wild City." Kapitalistate 4-5 (1976).

Cavell, Stanley. Must We Mean What We Say? New York: Scribner's, 1969.

Center for Community Economic Development. A Review of the Abt Associates, Inc., Evaluation of the Special Impact Program. Cambridge, Massachusetts: Abt Books, 1977.

Charan, Ram. "Classroom Techniques in Teaching by the Case Method." Academy of Management Review 1 (1970): 116-23.

Chinitz, Benjamin. "Toward a National Urban Policy." In B. Chinitz, ed., Central City Economic Development. Cambridge, Massachusetts: Abt Books, 1979.

City and County of San Francisco Board of Supervisors. Public Hearing on Redevelopment of the Western Addition. San Francisco: The Board, 1948.

Cizman, Paula L. "Steelyard Blues." Mother Jones, April 1978, pp. 36-42.

Clark, Simon and Ginsburg, Norman. "The Political Economy of Housing." In Political Economy and the Housing Question. London: Conference of Socialist Economists, 1975.

Clavel, Pierre. "Planners and Citizen Boards." Journal of the American Institute of Planners 34 (1968): 130-39.

Coalition for Housing. Rent Control and the Housing Crisis in Southern California. Los Angeles, California: The Coalition, 1977.

Cole, David. The Role of Psychological Belief Systems in Urban Planning. Ann Arbor, Michigan: University Microfilms Incorporated, 1975.

Colean, Miles. Renewing Our Cities. New York: The Twentieth Century Fund, 1953.

Collective for the Special Regional Issue. "Uneven Regional Development: An Introduction." Review of Radical Political Economics 10, no. 3 (1978).

Congressional Research Service. The Theory of Rent Control. Washington, D.C.: Library of Congress, 1978.

Cook, S.L. "Purpose and Quality of Graduate Education in the Management Sciences." Management Science 17 (1970): B5-B12.

Cooper, Terry L. "The Hidden Price Tags: Participation Costs and Health Planning." American Journal of Public Health 69, no. 4 (1979): 368-378.

Coraggio, Jose Luis. "Towards a Revision of the Growth Pole Theory." Viertel Jahres Berichte, no. 53 (1973).

Crenson, Matthew. The Unpolitics of Air Pollution. Baltimore: Johns Hopkins Press, 1971.

Culbert, Samuel A. "The Real World and the Management Classroom." California Management Review 19 (1977): 65-78.

Dahl, Robert A. Who Governs? New Haven: Yale University Press, 1961.

Dallmayr, Fred. "Toward a Critical Reconstruction of Ethics and Politics." Journal of Politics 36, no. 4 (1974): 926-957.

Dallmayr, Fred, and McCarthy, Thomas. Understanding and Social Inquiry. Notre Dame: Notre Dame Press, 1977.

Danziger, Sheldon; Haveman, R.; Smolensky, E.; and Taouber, K. "The Urban Impacts of the Program for Better Jobs and Income." Madison, Wisconsin: Institute for Research on Poverty, 1978.

Davies, Richard. Housing Reform During the Truman Administration. Columbia: University of Missouri Press, 1966.

Davis, Horace B. Toward a Marxist Theory of Nationalism. New York: Monthly Review Press, 1978.

Davis, Karen and Schoen, Cathy. Health and the War on Poverty. Washington, D.C.: Brookings Institution, 1978.

De Jouvenel, Bertrand. No Vacancies. Irvington-on-Hudson, New York: Foundation for Economic Education, Inc., 1948.

Deutsch, Karl. Nationalism and Social Communication. Cambridge, MIT Press, 1966.

Dewey, John. The Public and Its Problems. Denver: Swallow, 1927.

Diamond, Arnold H. The Supply of Mortgage Credit: 1970-74. Washington, D.C.: U.S. Department of Housing and Urban Development, 1975.

Domhoff, G. William. Who Really Rules? New Brunswick, New Jersey: Transaction Books, 1978.

Downe, Anthony. "Interest Rate Rise Erodes Leverage and Appreciation." National Real Estate Investor 16, no. 10 (1974).

Dreier, Peter. "The Politics of Rent Control." Working Papers VI, no. 6, (1979).

Dubos, R. Man, Medicine and Environment. Harmondsworth: Penguin Books, 1968.

Dyckman, John W. "What Makes Planners Plan?" Journal of the American Institute of Planners 27 (1961): 164-67.

Economic Development Administration. "Employee Ownership." Washington, D.C.: U.S. Department of Commerce, 1977.

Economic Development Law Project. "Coordinating CDC and Block Grant Community Development Programs: An Evaluation of 1975 and 1976." Economic Development Law Project Report 7, Issue 1 (1977).

Edel, Matthew. "Urban Renewal and Land Use Conflicts." The Review of Radical Political Economics 3, no. 3 (1971): 76-89.

Edelman, Murray. Political Language. New York: Academic Press, 1977.

________. The Symbolic Uses of Politics. Urbana: University of Illinois Press, 1964.

Ehrenreich, Barbara and Ehrenreich, John. "Hospital Workers: Class Conflict in the Making." International Journal of Health Services 5, no. 1 (1975): 43-51.

_______, eds. The American Health Empire. New York: Random House, 1970.

Elkin, Stephen. "Cities Without Power: The Transformation of American Urban Regimes." In D. Ashford, ed., State Power and Urban Choice. Chicago: Maroufu Press, forthcoming.

Elmstrom, Harry. Rent Control. Chicago: National Association of Realtors, 1977.

Emmanuel, Arghiri. Unequal Exchange. New York: Monthly Review Press, 1972.

Engels, Frederick. The Housing Question. Moscow: Progress Publishers, 1970. Reprinted from the 1877 edition of articles originally published in 1872.

Esping-Andersen, Gosta; Friedland, Roger; and Wright, Erik Olin. "Modes of Class Struggle and the Capitalist State." Kapitalstate 4-5 (1976): 186-220.

Federal Housing Administration. A Handbook on Urban Redevelopment for Cities in the United States. Washington, D.C.: U.S. Government Printing Offices, 1941.

Feinstein, Roger. "Policy Development in a Federal Program: A Case Study of the National Politics of Urban Renewal, 1949-1960." Ph.D. dissertation, Columbia University, 1974.

Feldmann, Marshall M.A. "Manuel Castells' The Urban Question: A Review Essay." Review of Radical Political Economics 10, no. 3 (1978): 136-144.

Finley, M.I. Democracy: Ancient and Modern. New Brunswick, N.J.: Rutgers University Press, 1972.

Fitch, Robert. "Planning New York." In Roger Alcaly and David Mermelstein, eds., Fiscal Crisis of American Cities. New York: Vintage, 1977.

Fleetwood, Blake. "A New Elite and an Urban Renaissance, Rediscovering the City." New York Times Magazine, January 14, 1979, pp. 16-28.

Foard, Ashley and Fefferman, Hilbert. "Federal Urban Renewal Legislation." In James Q. Wilson, ed., Urban Renewal: The Record and the Controversy. Cambridge: The MIT Press, 1966.

Forester, John, "Critical Theory and Planning Practice." Journal of the American Planning Association, forthcoming, 1980.

Forester, John. "Listening: The Social Policy of Everyday Life (Critical Theory and Hermeneutics in Practice)." Ithaca, N.Y.: Cornell University, Department of City and Regional Planning, Working Paper #6, 1978. A.

________. "Questioning and Shaping Attention as Planning Strategy: Toward a Critical Theory of Planning." Ithaca, N.Y.: Cornell University, Department of City and Regional Planning, Working Paper #7, 1978. B.

________. "What Do Planning Analysts Do? Planning and Policy Analysis as Organizing." Ithaca, N.Y.: Cornell University, Department of City and Regional Planning, Working Paper #8, 1978. C.

Form, W. and Miller, D. Industry, Labor and Community. New York: Harper and Row, 1960.

Frankel, Charles. "The Relation of Theory to Practice: Some Standard Views." In Herman D. Stein, ed., Social Theory and Social Invention. Cleveland: The Press of Case Western Reserve University, 1968.

Freire, Paulo. Education for Critical Consciousness. New York: Seabury, 1974.

________. Pedagogy of the Oppressed. New York: Seabury, 1970.

Fried, Marc. "Grieving for a Lost Home: Psychological Costs of Relocation." In Leonard Duhl, ed., The Urban Condition. New York: Simon and Schuster, 1970.

Frieden, Bernard J. and Kaplan, Marshall. The Politics of Neglect: Urban Aid from Model Cities to Revenue Sharing. Cambridge: MIT Press, 1975.

Frieden, Bernard J. and Solomon, Arthur P. The Nation's Housing: 1975 to 1985. Cambridge, Massachusetts: Joint Center for Urban Studies, 1977.

Friedland, Roger; Piven, Frances; and Alford, Robert. "Political Conflict, Urban Structure and the Fiscal Crisis." In Douglas Ashford, Comparing Public Policy: New Approaches and Methods. Sage Yearbook in Politics and Public Policy. Beverly Hills, California: Sage, 1978.

Friedman, Lawrence. Government and Slum Housing. Chicago: Rand McNally and Company, 1968.

Friedman, Milton. Capitalism and Freedom. Chicago: University of Chicago Press, 1962.

Friedman, Milton, and Stigler, George. "Roofs or Ceilings? The Current Housing Problems." Popular Essays on Current Problems 1, no. 2 (1946): 3-22.

Friedmann, John. "The Public Interest and Community Participation: Toward a Reconstruction of Public Philosophy." With comments by Robert Nisbet and Herbert Gans, Journal of American Institute of Planners (1973): 2-12. A.

_____. Retracking America. Garden City: Anchor Press, 1973. B.

Friedmann, John; and Weaver, Clyde. Territory and Function: The Evolution of Regional Planning. London: Edward Arnold, 1978.

Funigiello, Phillip. The Challenge to Urban Liberalism. Knoxville: The University of Tennessee Press, 1978.

Galbraith, John K. The New Industrial State. Boston: Houghton Mifflin, 1967.

Galper, Jeffry. The Politics of the Social Services. Englewood Cliffs, N.J.: Prentice Hall, 1975.

Gans, Herbert. "The Human Implications of Slum Clearance and Relocation." Journal of the American Institute of Planners 25 (1959): 15-25.

Garn, Harvey A.; Tevis, Nancy L.; and Snead, Carl E. Evaluating Community Development Corporations – A Summary Report. Washington, D.C.: The Urban Institute, 1976.

Garrigon, Richard T. "The Case for Rising Residential Rents." Real Estate Review 7, no. 2 (Fall 1978).

Gelfand, Mark. A Nation of Cities. New York: Oxford University Press, 1975.

Gerth, Hans, and Mills, C. Wright, eds. From Max Weber: Essays in Sociology. New York: Oxford University Press, 1958.

Giddens, Anthony. The Class Structure of Advanced Societies. New York: Harper and Row, 1973.

Gilderbloom, John. "The Impact of Moderate Rent Control in New Jersey." Thesis, University of California at Santa Barbara, 1979.

_____. The Impact of Moderate Rent Control in the United States: A Review and Critique of Existing Literature. Sacramento, California: Department of Housing and Community Development, State of California, 1978.

_____. "Report to Donald E. Burns, Secretary, Business and Transportation Agency, on the Validity of the Legislative Funding of AB 3788 and the Economic Impact of Rent Control." State of California, Department of Housing and Community Development. Sacramento, California: Department of Housing and Community Development, 1976.

Glaser, Barney G., and Strauss, Anselm L. The Discovery of Grounded Theory. Chicago: Aldine Publishing Company, 1967.

Glickman, Norman J. "Methodological Issues and Prospects for Urban Impact Analysis." In Glickman, ed., The Urban Impacts of Federal Policies. Baltimore: Johns Hopkins Press, forthcoming.

Glucksman, Andre. Les Maitres Penseurs. Paris: Grasset, 1977.

Goldsmith, William W. "The War on Development." Monthly Review 28 (1977): 50-57.

______. "The Ghetto as a Resource for Black America." Journal of the American Institute of Planners 40 (1974): 17-30. A.

______. "Some Thoughts on Teaching Regional Planning." Proceedings of the Colloquium on Comparative Urbanization, UCLA, 1974. B.

______; and Derian, Michael J. "Is There an Urban Policy?" Journal of Regional Science 19 (1979): 93-108.

______; and Siy, Robert Y., Jr. "More on Third World Development." Journal of the American Institute of Planners 44, no. 4 (October 1978).

______; and Vietorisz, Thomas. A New Development Strategy for Puerto Rico: Technological Autonomy, Human Resources, A Parallel Economy. Ithaca, N.Y.: Cornell University Program on International Studies in Planning, 1978.

______. "Operation Bootstrap, Industrial Autonomy, and a Parallel Economy for Puerto Rico." International Regional Science Review 4, no. 1 (Fall 1979): 1-22.

Goldstein, Harvey A. "Special Impact Program – Three Views." In Journal of the American Institute of Planners 44 (1978): 346-347.

Goldstein, Harvey A.; and Rosenberry, Sara A., eds. The Structural Crisis of the 1970's and Beyond: The Need for a New Planning Theory. Blacksburg, Virginia: Division of Environmental and Urban Systems, Virginia Polytechnic Institute and State University, 1978.

Gordon, David. "Capitalist Efficiency and Socialist Efficiency." Monthly Review 28 (1976): 19-39.

Gorz, Andre. Strategy for Labor. Boston: Beacon Press, 1967.

Gouldner, Alvin. Dialectic of Ideology of Technology. New York: Seabury Press, 1976.

Greenberg, Edward; Leven, Charles L.; and Little, James T. Methods of Urban Analysis: Neighborhood Self-Help Development. Washington, D.C.: U.S. Department of Housing and Urban Development, Office of Policy Development and Research, 1978.

Greer, Guy; and Hansen, Alvin. Urban Redevelopment and Housing. Washington, D.C.: National Planning Association, 1941.

Gruen, Claude; and Gruen, Nina. Rent Control in New Jersey: The Beginnings. San Mateo, California: California Housing Council, 1977.

Habermas, Jurgen. Communication and the Evolution of Society. Boston: Beacon Press, 1979. A.

______. "What Is Universal Pragmatics?" Communication and the Evolution of Society. Boston: Beacon Press, 1979. B.

______. Legitimation Crisis. Translated by Thomas McCarthy. Boston: Beacon Press, 1975.

______. Theory and Practice. Boston: Beacon Press, 1973.

______. Knowledge and Human Interests. Boston: Beacon Press, 1971.

________. Toward a Rational Society. Translated by Jeremy Shapiro. Boston: Beacon Press, 1970.

Hall, Ellen. Inner City Health in America. Washington, D.C.: Urban Environment Foundation, 1979.

Harnappe, P. "Spatial Aspects of Industrial Development in Western Europe: Economic and Political Areas." Environment and Planning 7, no. 4 (1975): 439-48.

Harrison, Bennett, Urban Economic Development: Suburbanization, Minority Opportunity, and the Condition of the Central City. Washington, D.C.: The Urban Institute, 1974.

Hartman, Chester. "The Big Squeeze." Politics Today (May-June 1978): 40.

______. Yerba Buena. San Francisco: Glide Publications, 1974.

______. "The Housing of Relocated Families." Journal of the American Institute of Planners 30, no. 4 (1964): 266-86.

Hartman, Chester; and Stone, Michael. "Housing: A Radical Alternative." In Raskin, Marcus (ed.), The Federal Budget and Social Reconstruction. New Brunswick, N.J.: Transaction Books, 1978.

Harvey, David. "Labor, Capital and Class Struggle Around the Built Environment in Advanced Capitalist Societies." Politics and Society 6, no. 3 (1976): 265-295.

______. "The Political Economy of Urbanization in Advanced Capitalist Societies: The Case of the United States." In Gary Gappert and Harold Rose, eds., The Social Economy of Cities. Beverly Hills: Sage Publications, 1975.

______. Social Justice and the City. Baltimore: Johns Hopkins Press, 1973.

______. "The Urban Process Under Capitalism." International Journal of Urban and Regional Research 2, no. 1 (1978).

Havemann, Joel; Stanford, Rochelle; and Pierce, Neil. "Federal Spending: The North's Loss is the Sunbelt's Gain." National Journal (June 1976): 878-91.

Hays, Samuel P. Conservation and the Gospel of Efficiency. New York: Atheneum, 1969.

Hayward, J.; and M. Watson, eds. Planning, Politics and Public Policy: The British, French and Italian Experience. Cambridge: Cambridge University Press, 1975.

Health-PAC Bulletins. New York: Health Policy Advisory Center.

Hechter, Michael. "The Persistence of Regionalism in the British Isles, 1865-1966." American Journal of Sociology (September 1973): 319-42.

Hemmens, George; Bergman, Edward; and Moroney, Robert. "The Practitioner's View of Social Planning." Journal of the American Institute of Planners 44 (1978): 181-192.

Heskin, Allan David. "From Theory to Practice: Professional Development at UCLA." Journal of the American Institute of Planners 44 (1978): 436-51.

Hesseltine, William. "Regions, Classes and Sections in American History." Land Economics 20 (1944): 35-44.

Hill, Richard Child. "Fiscal Collapse and Political Struggle in Decaying Central Cities in the United States." In Larry Sawers and William Tabb, eds. Marxism and the Metropolis. New York: Oxford University Press, 1978.

Hirschman, A.O. Strategy of Economic Development. New Haven: Yale University Press, 1958.

"An Historical Analysis of Tenants' First Coalition." Shelterforce (Summer 1977).

Hobsbawm, Eric. "Some Reflections on 'The Break-up of Britain.' " New Left Review 105 (1977): 3-24.

Hoselitz, Bert F. "The Market Matrix." In W. Moore, and A. Feldman. Labor Commitment and Social Change in Developing Areas. New York: Social Science Research Council, 1960.

Housing and Community Development Reporter. "Section 8 Leased Housing Assistance Payments Program." Washington, D.C.: Bureau of National Affairs, April 25, 1977.

Hulchanski, John David. "Citizen Participation in Planning: A Comprehensive Bibliography." Toronto: Department of Urban and Regional Planning, University of Toronto, 1974.

Hummel, Ralph. The Bureaucratic Experience. New York: St. Martin's Press, 1977.

Hunter, Floyd. Community Power Structure. Chapel Hill, N.C.: University of North Carolina Press, 1953.

Hunter, Oakley. "Realities of the Marketplace Forcing Smaller Units on U.S. Home Buyers." The Money Manager 4, no. 21 (1975).

Huntington, Samuel P. "The United States." In M. Crozier; S. Huntington; and J. Watanyki, eds., The Crisis of Democracy: Report on the Governability of Democracies to the Trilateral Commission. New York: New York University Press, 1975.

Hyman, Herbert. Regulating Health Facilities Construction. Germantown: Aspen Systems Corporation, 1977.

Hymer, Stephen. "The Multinational Corporation and the Law of Uneven Development." In J.N. Bhagwati, ed., Economics and the World Order from the 1970's to the 1990's. New York: Macmillan, 1972.

Illich, Ivan. Medical Nemesis. New York: Bantam Books, 1977.

Institute of Real Estate Management. Income/Expense Analysis: Apartments, Condominiums and Cooperatives. 1975 edition. Chicago: The Institute, 1975.

Israel, Joachim. Alienation: From Marx to Modern Sociology. Boston: Allyn and Bacon, 1971.

Jackson, Anthony. A Place Called Home. Cambridge: The MIT Press, 1976.

Jacob, Mike. Understanding Landlording. Santa Barbara, California: Rent Control Alliance, 1978.

Jacobs, Allan B. Making City Planning Work. Chicago: American Society of Planning Officials, 1978.

Johnson, David W., and Johnson, Frank P. Joining Together. Englewood Cliffs, N.J.: Prentice-Hall, 1975.

Kain, John F. "Failure in Diagnosis: A Critique of Carter's National Urban Policy." P-78-2. Cambridge, Massachusetts: Department of City Planning, Harvard University, 1978.

Katznelson, Ira. "The Crisis of the Capitalist City: Urban Politics and Social Control." In W. Hawley et al. Theoretical Perspectives on Urban Politics. Englewood Cliffs, N.J.: Prentice-Hall, 1976.

Keating, Dennis. Rent and Eviction Controls: A Selected Annotated Bibliography. Exchange bibliography 1136. Monticello, Ill.: Council of Planning Librarians, 1976.

Keith, Nathaniel. Politics and the Housing Crisis Since 1930. New York: Universe Books, 1973.

Kelman, Sander. "The Social Nature of the Definition Problem in Health." International Journal of Health Services 5, no. 4 (1975): 625-642.

________. "Toward the Political Economy of Medical Care." Inquiry, September 1971.

Kidron, Aryeh G. "The Effectiveness of Experiential Methods in Training and Education: The Case of Role Playing." Academy of Management Review 2 (1977): 490-95.

Klarman, H. "Health Planning: Progress, Prospects, and Issues." Milbank Memorial Fund Quarterly (Health and Society) 56, no. 1 (1978): 78-112.

_______. "Planning for Facilities." In Eli Ginzburg, ed., Regionalization and Health Policy. Washington, D.C.: DHEW, Health Resources Administration, 1977.

Klarman, H; Rice, D.P.; Cooper, B.S.; and Stettler, H.L., III. "Sources of Increase in Selected Medical Care Expenditures, 1929-69." Staff paper No. 4. Washington, D.C.: Social Security Administration, Office of Research and Statistics, April 1970.

Klein, Edward B., and Astrachan, Boris M. "Learning in Groups: A Comparison of Study Groups and T Groups." Journal of Applied Behavioral Science 7 (1971): 659-83.

Klein, Woody. Let in the Sun. New York: Macmillan, 1964.

Koeppel, Barbara. "The New Sweatshops." In The Progressive 46 (1978): 22-26.

Kolb, David A.; Rubin, Irwin M.; and McIntyre, James M. Organizational Psychology. 3rd ed. Englewood Cliffs, N.J.: Prentice-Hall, 1979.

Kolko, Gabriel. The Triumph of Conservatism: A Reinterpretation of American History 1900-1916. New York: The Free Press, 1963.

Kotelchuck, David, ed. Prognosis Negative: Crisis in the Health Care System. New York: Vintage, 1976.

Kotelchuck, Rhonda. "Government Cost Control Strategies: Futile Monitors." Health-PAC Bulletin, no. 75 (1977).

_______. "The Depression and the AMA." Health-PAC Bulletin, no. 69 (1976), p. 13-18.

Kotz, Nick; and Kotz, Mary Lynn. A Passion for Equality. New York: W.W. Norton, 1977.

Kramer, Ralph M. Participation of the Poor: Comparative Community Case Studies in the War on Poverty. Englewood Cliffs, N.J.: Prentice-Hall, 1969.

Krause, E. "Health Planning as a Managerial Ideology." International Journal of Health Services 3, no. 3 (1973): 445-463.
Kravitz, Alan. "Mandarinism: Planning as Handmaiden to Conservative Politics." In T. Beyle and G. Lathrop, eds., Planning and Politics: Uneasy Partnership. New York: Odyssey Press, 1970.
Krumholz, Norman; Cogger, Janice M.; and Linner, John H. "The Cleveland Planning Policy Report." Journal of the American Institute of Planners 41 (1975): 298-304.
Lander, Louise. "HSA's: If You Don't First Succeed." Health-PAC Bulletin 70 (1976): 1-15.
Lasch, Christopher. The Culture of Narcissism. New York: W.W. Norton, 1978.
Laslett, Peter. The World We Have Lost. New York: Monthly Review Press, 1972.
Lee, R.J.; and Jones, L.W. "The Fundamentals of Good Medical Care." Publications of the Committee on Costs of Medical Care 22 Chicago: University of Chicago Press, 1933.
Lett, Monica. Rent Control: Concepts, Realities, and Mechanisms. New Brunswick, N.J.: Center for Urban Policy Research, Rutgers University, 1976.
Levy, Bernard-Henri. La Barbarie a Visage Humain. Paris: Grasset, 1977.
Lieberman, Susan Abel. The Practitioner Viewpoint: An Exploration of Social Policy Planning Practice and Education. Chapel Hill, N.C.: Department of City and Regional Planning, University of North Carolina, 1976.
Lindbeck, Assar. The Political Economy of the New Left: An Outsider's View. 2nd ed. with commentaries. New York: Harper and Row, 1977.
Lindblom, Charles. Politics and Markets. New York: Basic Books, 1977.
______. The Intelligence of Democracy. New York: Free Press, 1965.
Lowe, Jeanne. Cities in a Race with Time. New York: Random House, 1967.
Lowi, Theodore. The End of Liberalism. New York: W.W. Norton, 1969.
Lubove, Roy. Twentieth Century Pittsburgh. New York: John Wiley and Sons, 1969.
Ludlow, William. "Land Values and Density Standards in Urban Redevelopment." Journal of the American Institute of Planners 11, no. 4 (1945): 5-10.
Luebke, Paul; McMahon, Bob; and Risberg, Jeff. "Selective Recruitment in North Carolina." Working Papers for a New Society (1979): 17-20.
Lukes, Steven. Power: A Radical View. London: MacMillan, 1974.
Lustig, R. Jeffrey. "On Organization: The Question of the Leninist Party." In Politics and Society 7, no. 1 (1977): 27-67.
Lynd, Robert S.; and Lynd, Helen M. Middletown in Transition. New York: Harcourt Brace, 1937.
Mackintosh, J.P. The Devolution of Power. London: Chatto and Windus, 1968.
"Major Conspiracy Suit Threatens Tenants' Right to Organize Union." Civil Liberties Union of Massachusetts, Docket, December 1976.

Mandel, Ernest; and Novack, George. The Marxist Theory of Alienation. New York: Pathfinder Press, 1970.

______. On Practice. Peking: Foreign Language Press, 1965.

Manicas, Peter. "The Democratic Community." In P. Manicas, ed., The Death of the State. New York: G.P. Putnam's Sons, 1974.

Mannheim, Karl. Freedom, Power, and Democratic Planning. Edited by Hans Gerth and Ernest K. Bramstedt. London: Routledge and Kegan Paul, 1950.

______. Man and Society in an Age of Reconstruction. Translated by Edward Shils. New York: Harcourt, Brace and World, 1940.

Marcuse, Herbert. One Dimensional Man: Studies in the Ideology of Advanced Industrial Society. Boston: Beacon Press, 1964.

Marcuse, Peter. Rental Housing in the City of New York: Supply and Condition 1975-1978. New York: City of New York, 1979.

______. "Housing in the History of Early City Planning." New York: Graduate School of Architecture and Planning, Columbia University, 1978. A.

______. "Housing Policy and the Myth of the Benevolent State." Social Policy 8 (1978): 21-26. B.

______. "The Political Economy of Rent Control: Theory and Strategy." Papers in Planning, no. 7. New York: Columbia University Division of Urban Planning, 1978. C.

Markusen, Ann. "Regional Political Economy," forthcoming.

______. "Class, Rent, and the State: Uneven Development in Western U.S. Boomtowns," Review of Radical Political Economics 10, no. 3 (1978).

______. "Federal Budget Simplification: Preventive Programs vs. Palliatives for Local Governments with Booming, Stable, and Declining Economies." National Tax Journal 30, no. 3 (1977).

Markusen, Ann, and Fastrup, Jerry. "The Regional War for Federal Aid." The Public Interest 53, (1978): 87-99.

Marris, Peter. Loss and Change. New York: Anchor Press, 1975.

Marmor, Theodore R., and Marone, James A. "HSAs and the Representation of Consumer Interests: Conceptual Issues and Litigation Problems." Health Law Project Library Bulletin 4, no. 4 (1979): 117-128.

Marx, Karl. Capital. (3 vols.) New York: International Publishers, 1967.

______. The Economic and Philosophical Manuscripts of 1844. Edited by J. Struik and translated by Martin Milligan. New York: International Publishers, 1964.

Massey, D., and Meegan, R. "Industrial Restructuring Versus The Cities." Urban Studies 15, no. 3 (1978): 273-88.

McCarthy, Thomas. The Critical Theory of Jurgen Habermas. Boston: MIT Press, 1978.

McClosky, Herbert. "Ideology and Consensus in American Politics." American Political Science Review 74 (1964): 361-82.

McConnell, Grant. "The Environmental Movement: Ambiguities and Meanings." Natural Resources Journal 11 (1971): 479.

McGuire, R.R. "Speech Acts, Communicative Competence, and the Paradox of Authority." In Philosophy and Rhetoric 10 (1977): 30-45.

Meltsner, Arnold. Policy Analysts in the Bureaucracy. Berkeley, California: University of California Press, 1976.

______. "Bureaucratic Policy Analysts." Policy Analysis 1 (1975): 115-131.

Mermelstein, David. "Austerity, Planning, and the Socialist Alternatives." In Roger E. Alcaly and David Mermelstein, eds. The Fiscal Crisis of American Cities. New York: Vintage, 1977.

Meyerson, Martin. "Building the Middle-Range Bridge for Comprehensive Planning." Journal of the American Institute of Planners 22 (1956): 58-64.

Meyerson, Martin; and Banfield, Edward. Politics, Planning and the Public Interest. Glencoe: The Free Press, 1955.

Michelson, Stephan. "Community-Based Development in Urban Areas." In B. Chinitz, ed., Central City Economic Development. Cambridge, Mass.: Abt Books, 1979.

Milio, Nancy. "An Ecological Approach to Health Planning for Illness Prevention." American Journal of Health Planning (October 1977).

Mills, C. Wright. "The Big City: Private Troubles and Public Issues." In Power, Politics, and People. New York: Ballantine Books, 1963.

______. The Power Elite. New York: Oxford University Press, 1957.

______. White Collar. New York: Oxford University Press, 1956.

Mollenkopf, John. "The Postwar Politics of Urban Development." In Larry Sawers and William Tabb, eds., Marxism and the Metropolis. New York: Oxford University Press, 1978.

______. "Community Organization and City Politics." Ph.D. dissertation, Harvard University, 1973.

Molotch, Harvey. "The City as a Growth Machine: Toward a Political Economy of Place." American Journal of Sociology 82, no. 2 (1976): 352-355.

Morris, Richard T.; and Murphey, Raymond J. "A Paradigm for the Study of Class Consciousness." Sociology and Social Research 50 (1966): 297-313.

Moskovitz, Myron; Warner, Ralph; and Sherman, Charles E. California Tenants Handbook. Occidental, California: Nole Press, 1974. A.

______. Reapportion Housing and Rents. Albany, N.Y.: New York State Temporary Commission on Living Costs and the Economy, 1974. B.

Moss, Robert. The Collapse of Democracy. London: Temple Smith, 1975.

Mowtiz, Robert; and Wright, Deil. Profile of a Metropolis. Detroit: Wayne State University Press, 1962.

Moynihan, Daniel P. "The Politics and Economics of Regional Growth." The Public Interest 51 (Spring 1978).

______. The Politics of a Guaranteed Income. New York: Random House, 1973.

Mueller, Claus. The Politics of Communication. New York: Oxford University Press, 1973.

Nathan, Richard P.; and Dommell, P.R. "The Cities." In Joseph Pechman, ed., Setting National Priorities: The 1978 Budget. Washington, D.C.: The Brookings Institution, 1977.

National Commission on Urban Problems. Building The American City. Washington, D.C.: U.S. Government Printing Office, 1969.

National Council for Urban Economic Development. Coordinated Urban Economic Development: A Case Study Analysis (10 volumes). Washington, D.C.: National Council for Urban Economic Development, 1978. A.

________. Community Economic Development Demonstration Program Issue Papers. Washington, D.C.: National Council for Economic Development, 1978. B.

________. National Resources Development Report for 1943, Part 1: Post-War Plan and Program. Washington, D.C.: U.S. Government Printing Office, 1943. A.

________. National Resources Development Report for 1943, Part 2: Wartime Planning for War and Post-War. Washington, D.C.: U.S. Government Printing Office, 1943. B.

________. Better Cities. Washington, D.C.: U.S. Government Printing Office, 1942. A.

________. National Resources Development Report for 1942. Washington, D.C.: U.S. Government Printing Office, 1942. B.

________. Urban Land and Planning Policies. Washington, D.C.: U.S. Government Printing Office, 1939.

________. Our Cities – Their Role in the National Economy. Washington, D.C.: U.S. Government Printing Office, 1937.

Navarro, Vicente. "Political Power, The State and Their Implications in Medicine." Review of Radical Political Economics 9, no. 1 (1977): 61-80.

Needleman, Martin; and Needleman, Carolyn. Guerrillas in the Bureaucracy. New York: John Wiley and Sons, 1974.

Neisser, Ulric. Cognition and Reality. San Francisco: W.H. Freeman and Company, 1976.

Noyelle, Thierry. "The Crisis of the 1970s: Capital Dilemmas in the Snowbelt." In H. Goldstein and S. Rosenberry, eds., The Structural Crisis of the 1970s and Beyond: The Need for a New Planning Theory. Blacksburg, Va.: Division of Environmental and Urban Systems, Virginia Polytechnic Institute and State University, 1978.

O'Connor, James. "The Democratic Movement in the United States." Kapitalistate, 7 (1979).

________. The Fiscal Crisis of the State. New York: St. Martin's Press, 1973.

Offe, Claus. "The Abolition of Market Control and the Problem of Legitimacy." Kapitalistate 2 (1973-74): 73-76.

O'Malley, Joseph, ed. Karl Marx: Critique of Hegel's Philosophy of Right. Cambridge: Cambridge University Press, 1970.

Parish, F.W. "The Economics of Rent Restriction." Lloyds Bank Review (April 1950): 1-17.

Peattie, Lisa. The View from the Barrio. Ann Arbor: University of Michigan Press, 1968.

Pennace, F.G. "Introduction." Verdict on Rent Control. London: Institute of Economic Affairs, Cormorant Press, 1972.

Perlman, Janice. "Grassrooting the System." Social Policy 7 (1976): 4-20.

Perry, Clarence Arthur. The Rebuilding of Blighted Areas. New York: Regional Plan Association, Inc., 1933.

Perry, David C., and Watkins, Alfred J., eds. The Rise of the Sunbelt Cities. Beverly Hills: Sage, 1977.

Pitkin, Hanna. Wittgenstein and Justice. Berkeley, California: University of California Press, 1972.

Piven, Frances Fox. "The New Urban Programs: The Strategy of Federal Intervention." In R. Cloward and F.F. Piven, The Politics of Turmoil. New York: Vintage Books, 1975.

______; and Cloward, Richard A. Poor People's Movement. New York: Pantheon Books, 1977.

______. Regulating the Poor. New York: Vintage Books, 1971.

Powles, John. "On the Limitations of Modern Medicine." Science, Medicine and Man 1, no. 1 (1973): 1-30.

President's Advisory Committee on Government Housing Policies and Programs. Recommendations on Government Housing Policies and Programs. Washington, D.C.: U.S. Government Printing Office, 1953.

President's Conference on Home Building and Home Ownership. Slums, Large-Scale Housing and Decentralization. Washington, D.C.: National Capital Press, 1932.

Pressman, Jeffrey. Federal Programs and City Politics. Berkeley: University of California Press, 1975.

Rabinovitz, Francine F. City Politics and Planning. New York: Atherton Press, 1969.

Rafuse, Robert. "The New Regional Debate: A National Overview." Washington, D.C.: National Governor's Conference, April 1977.

Rainbook, Resources for Appropriate Technology. New York: Schocken, 1977.

Raskin, Marcus, ed. The Federal Budget and Social Reconstruction. Washington, D.C.: The Institute for Policy Studies, 1978.

Renaud, Marc. "On the Structural Constraints to State Intervention in Health." International Journal of Health Services 5, no. 4 (1975): 559-572.

Restoring Credit and Confidence: A Reform Program for New York State and Its Public Authorities. A Report to the Governor by the New York State Moreland Act Commission on the Urban Development Corporation and Other State Financing Agencies, March 31, 1976.

Review of Radical Political Economics (RRPE). Special Issue on Regional Uneven Development in Advanced Capitalism 10, no. 3 (1978).

Rifkin, Jeremy. The North Will Rise Again. Boston: Beacon Press, 1978.

______. Own Your Own Job. New York: Bantam Books, 1976.

Roberts, Milton C., Jr. "Federal Community Revitalization Efforts – What Targets, What Focus?" In G. Whittaker, ed., Community Revitalization. Ann Arbor, Michigan: Division of Research, Graduate School of Business Administration, University of Michigan, 1979.

Rodwin, Lloyd. Nations and Cities. Boston: Houghton Mifflin, 1970.

Rohrer, Margaret; and Frame, Douglas. Rent Control. Berkeley, California: Bureau of Public Administration, 1947.

Rondinelli, Dennis. Urban and Regional Development Planning. Ithaca, N.Y.: Cornell University Press, 1975.

Rostow, Walter. "Regional Change in the Fifth Kondratieff Upswing." In David C. Perry and Alfred J. Watkins, eds., The Rise of the Sunbelt Cities. Beverly Hills: Sage, 1977.

Rowen, James, ed. "Public Capital: Using Public Money in the Public Interest." In New Directions in State and Local Public Policy. Washington, D.C.: Conference on Alternative State and Local Public Policies, 1977.

Sale, Kirkpatrick. "The World Behind Watergate." New York Review of Books 20 May 3, 1973, pp. 9-15.

Sandberg, Ake. "Planning, Democracy, and Socialism." In The Limits to Democratic Planning. Goteborgs Offsettyekeri: AB, 1976.

Sanders, S.E.; and Rabuck, A.J. New City Patterns. New York: Reinhold Publishing Corporation, 1946.

San Francisco City Planning Commission. Western Addition District Redevelopment Study. San Francisco: The Commission, 1947. A.

San Francisco City Planning Commission. New City: San Francisco Redeveloped. San Francisco: The Commission, 1947. B.

Savings and Loan Fact Book 1977. Chicago: United States League of Savings Associations, 1977.

Sawers, Larry. "Cities and Countryside in the Soviet Union and China." In W. Tubb and L. Sawers, eds., Marxism and the Metropolis. New York: Oxford, 1978.

_______. "Urban Form and the Mode of Production." Review of Radical Political Economics (Spring 1975): 52-68.

Sawers, Larry; and Wachtel, Howard M. "The Distributional Impact of Federal Government Subsidies in the United States." Kapitalstate, no. 3 (Spring 1975): 56-70.

Schaar, John B. "Legitimacy and the Modern State." in P. Green and S. Levinson, eds., Power and Community: Essays in Dissent. New York: Pantheon, 1970.

Schechter, Henry B. The Residential Mortgage Financing Problem. U.S. Congress, House Committee on Banking and Currency, Subcommittee on Housing, 92nd Congress, 1st Session, 1971. Washington, D.C.: U.S. Government Printing Office, 1971.

Schroyer, Trent. The Critique of Domination. Boston: Beacon Press, 1977.

Schulkin, Peter A. Commercial Bank Construction Lending. Federal Reserve Bank of Boston Research Report No. 47. Boston: Federal Reserve Bank of Boston, 1970. A.

_______. "Construction Lending at Large Commercial Banks." New England Economic Review, (July/August 1970). B.

Schulze, R. "The Bifurcation of Power in a Satellite City." In M. Janowitz, Community Political Systems. New York: Free Press, 1961.

Schumpeter, Joseph. Imperialism and Social Classes. New York: Meridian Books, 1955.

_______. Capitalism, Socialism and Democracy. New York: Harper and Row, 1942.

Scott, Mel. American City Planning Since 1890. Berkeley: University of California Press, 1969.

Searle, John. Speech Acts. London: Cambridge University Press, 1969.

"The Second War Between the States." Business Week, May 17, 1976, pp. 92-114.

Securities and Exchange Commission. Real Estate Investment Trusts: A Background Analysis and Recent Industry Developments 1961-1974. Washington, D.C.: Securities and Exchange Commission, 1975.

Seeman, Melvin. "On the Meaning of Alienation." American Sociological Review 24 (1959): 783-91.

Sennett, Richard. The Uses of Disorder. New York: Knopf, 1970.

_______; and Cobb, Jonathan. The Hidden Injuries of Class. New York: Random House, 1972.

Shapiro, Jeremy. "Reply to Miller's Review of Habermas' Legitimation Crisis." Telos 27 (1976): 170-5.

Shearer, Derek. "Catalog." Mother Jones (April 1978): 36-52.

Shelton, John P. "The Cost of Renting versus Owning a Home." Land Economics 46 (February 1968): 205.

Shils, Edward. "Centre and Periphery." In The Logic of Personal Knowledge: Essays Presented to Michael Polanyi. London: Routledge and Kegan Paul, 1961.

Shonfield, Andrew. Modern Capitalism. New York: Oxford University Press, 1965.

Shonick, William. Elements of Planning for Area-Wide Personal Health Services. St. Louis: C.V. Mosby Company, 1976.

Sieverts, Steven. Health Planning Issues and Public Law 93-641. Chicago: American Hospital Association, 1977.

Simon, Richard. "The Labor Process and Uneven Development in the Appalachian Coalfields." Available from author, P.O. Box 1261, Morgantown, West Virginia, 1978.

Smelser, Neil. Social Change in the Industrial Revolution. Chicago: University of Chicago Press, 1959.

Snell, Bradford. American Ground Transport: A Proposal for Restructuring Automobile, Truck, Bus, and Rail Industries. Presented to the Subcommittee on Antitrust and Monopoly of the Committee on the Judiciary, United States Senate, February 26, 1974. Washington, D.C.: U.S. Government Printing Office.

Source Catalog Collective. Organizing for Health Care: A Tool for Change. Source Catalog No. 3. Boston: Beacon Press, 1974.

Special Analyses: Budget of the United States Government, Fiscal Year 1978, Part 1.F. Washington, D.C.: Government Printing Office, 1977.

Spring, Joel H. Education and the Rise of the Corporate State. Boston: Beacon Press, 1972.

Sternlieb, George. The Realities of Rent Control in the Greater Boston Area. New Brunswick, New Jersey: Center for Urban Policy Research, 1974.

______. The Urban Housing Dilemma: The Dynamics of New York City's Rent Controlled Housing. New Brunswick, New Jersey: Center for Urban Policy Research, 1972.

______; and Hughes, James. "New Regional and Metropolitan Realities of America." Journal of the American Institute of Planners 43 (1977): 227-241.

Stone, Michael. "Federal Housing Policy: A Political Economic Analysis." In Jon Pynoos, Robert Schafer, and Chester Hartman, eds., Housing Urban America. Chicago: Aldine, 1973.

______. "Gimme Shelter!" in U.S. Capitalism in Crisis, edited by the Crisis Reader Editorial Collective. New York: Union for Radical Political Economics, 1978.

______. "The Housing Crisis, Mortgage Lending, and Class Struggle." Antipode 7, no. 2 (1975): 22-37.

______. People Before Property: A Real Estate Primer and Research Guide. Cambridge, Massachusetts: Urban Planning Aid, 1972.

______. Shelter Poverty: A New Approach to Defining and Measuring the Housing Cost/Income Problem. Boston: University of Massachusetts, College of Public and Community Service, 1979.

Stone, Michael; and Achtenberg, Emily. Hostage! Housing and the Massachusetts Fiscal Crisis. Boston: Boston Community School, 1977.

Straus, Nathan. The Seven Myths of Housing. New York: Alfred A. Knopf, 1944.

Strongforce, Democracy in the Workplace. Washington, D.C.: Strongforce, 2121 Decatur Place, N.W., 1977.

Sundquist, James. Dispersing Population. Washington, D.C.: Brookings Institution, 1975.

______; and Davis, David. Making Federalism Work. Washington, D.C.: Brookings Institution, 1969.

Sweezy, Paul M. "Cars and Cities." Monthly Review 24 (1973): 1-18.

Tannen, Louis. "Health Planning as a Regulatory Strategy: A Discussion of History and Current Uses." International Journal of Health Services, forthcoming.

Tarrow, Sidney. Between Center and Periphery. New Haven: Yale University Press, 1977.

Tenth Annual Report on the National Housing Goal. Washington, D.C.: U.S. Department of Housing and Urban Development, 1978.

Terkel, Studs. Working. New York: Avon, 1972.

Therkildson, Ole. "Regional Development in Western Europe: A Study of the Locational Behavior of Large Industrial Enterprises." Master's thesis, Cornell University, Department of City and Regional Planning, October 1976.

Turner, Frederick Jackson. The Significance of the Section in American History. New York: Henry Holt and Company, 1932.

Unger, Roberto Mangabeira. "The Theory of Organic Groups." In Knowledge and Politics. New York: Free Press, 1975.

U.S. Bureau of the Census. "Housing Starts and Building Permits in September 1977." CB77-201, October 19, 1977. Washington, D.C.: U.S. Government Printing Office, 1977.

______. "September 1977 Construction at $173.7 Billion Annual Rate." CB77-210, Nov. 1, 1977. Washington, D.C.: U.S. Government Printing Office, 1977.

______. Historical Statistics of the United States, Colonial Times to 1970. Bicentennial Edition. Washington, D.C.: U.S. Government Printing Office, 1976.

______. "Property Subject to Local Taxation Assessed at More than $1 Trillion in 1975, Census Bureau Reports." CD76-212, October 6, 1976. Washington, D.C.: U.S. Government Printing Office, 1976.

______. Statistical Abstract of the United States: 1976. 97th edition. Washington, D.C.: U.S. Government Printing Office, 1976.

U.S. Bureau of Labor Statistics. Rent or Buy? Evaluating Alternatives in the Shelter Market. Bulletin 1823. Washington, D.C.: U.S. Government Printing Office, 1974.

U.S. Congress, Joint Economic Committee, Subcommittee on Fiscal and Intergovernmental Policy. Central City Businesses – Plans and Problems. Washington, D.C.: U.S. Government Printing Office, 1979.

U.S. Congress, Joint Economic Committee, 95th Congress, 1st Session. Financing Municipal Needs. Washington, D.C.: U.S. Government Printing Office, 1977.

U.S. Department of Health, Education and Welfare. Health, United States, 1976-77. DHEW Publication No. HRA77-1232. Washington, D.C.: U.S. Government Printing Office, 1977.

______, Public Health Service, Health Resources Administration. Consumer Participation in Health Planning: An Annotated Bibliography. Washington, D.C.: U.S. Government Printing Office, 1976.

U.S. Department of Housing and Urban Development. Nationwide Evaluation of Existing Housing Program (Section 8), and technical supplement. Washington, D.C.: U.S. Government Printing Office, November 1978.

______. HUD News, HUD No. 78-241, July 26, 1978.

______. Decentralizing Community Development: Second Report of Brookings Institution Monitoring Study of CDBG Program. Washington, D.C.: U.S. Government Printing Office, June 2, 1978.

______. Third Annual CDBG Report. Washington, D.C.: U.S. Government Printing Office, March 1978.

______. Series Data Handbook. Washington, D.C.: U.S. Government Printing Office, 1978.

______. HUD Statistical Yearbook. Washington, D.C.: U.S. Government Printing Office, 1977.

______. First Annual CDBG Report. Washington, D.C., December 1975.

______. HUD News. HUD No. 75-361, Sept. 10, 1975, Table 8.

______. Housing in the Seventies: Report of the National Housing Policy Review. Washington, D.C.: U.S. Government Printing Office, 1974.

U.S. Department of Housing and Urban Development – Independent Agencies Appropriations for 1976. Hearings, Subcommittee of the Committee on Appropriations, House, 94th Congress, 1st Session, 1975.

U.S. Executive Office of the President (1978). A New Partnership to Conserve America's Communities. A Status Report on the President's Urban Policy. Washington, D.C., June 1978.

U.S. House Select Committee on Lobbying Activities, 81st Congress, 2nd Session, 1950. Hearings Part 2: Housing Lobby. Washington, D.C.: U.S. Government Printing Office, 1950.

U.S. House, Committee on Banking, Currency and Housing, Subcommittee on Housing and Community Development. Evolution of the Role of the Federal Government in Housing and Community Development, A Chronology of Legislative and Selective Executive Actions, 1892-1974. 94th Congress, 1st Session, 1975.

U.S. House of Representatives. The Ninth Annual Report on the National Housing Goal. House Document 95-53. Washington, D.C.: U.S. Government Printing Office, annual.

U.S. League of Savings Associations. Savings and Loan Fact Book. Chicago: U.S. League of Savings Associations, annual.

U.S. National Commission on Urban Problems. Building the American City. Washington, D.C.: U.S. Government Printing Office, 1968.

U.S. President's Committee on Urban Housing. A Decent Home. Washington, D.C.: U.S. Government Printing Office, 1968.

U.S. Senate, Special Committee on Post-War Economic Policy and Planning, 79th Congress, 1st Session. Hearings Pursuant to S. Res. 102: Housing and Urban Redevelopment. Washington, D.C.: U.S. Government Printing Office, 1945.

U.S. Senate, 92nd Congress, 2nd Session, Committee on the Judiciary. Competition in Real Estate and Mortgage Lending. Hearings before the Subcommittee on Antitrust and Monopoly. Washington, D.C.: U.S. Government Printing Office, 1971.

U.S. Senate, Select Committee on Small Business. The Role of the Federal Government and Employee Ownership of Business. Washington, D.C.: U.S. Government Printing Office, 1979.

Upton, Letitia and Lyons, Nancy. Basic Facts: Distribution of Personal Income and Wealth in the United States. Cambridge, Massachusetts: Cambridge Institute, n.d.

Urban Land Institute. Prospects for Rental Housing Production Under Rent Control: A Study of Washington. Research Report No. 24. Washington, D.C.: The Institute, 1976.

_______. Nine Cities: The Anatomy of Downtown Renewal. Washington, D.C.: The Institute, 1969.

_______. The City Fights Back. New York: The Citadel Press, 1954.

_______. "Discussion of Principles to be Incorporated in State Urban Redevelopment Enabling Acts," Technical Bulletin No. 2. Washington, D.C.: The Institute, 1945. A.

_______. Statement by Seward Mott Before The Urban Redevelopment Commission, Columbus, Ohio, 12/6/45. Washington, D.C.: The Institute, 1945. B.

________. Proposals for Downtown Detroit. Washington, D.C.: The Institute, 1942. A.

________. Proposals for Downtown Louisville. Washington, D.C.: The Institute, 1942. B.

________. "Urban Land Institute Adopts Huge Post-War City Replanning Program," Press Release, 2/1/42. Washington, D.C.: The Institute, 1942. C.

________. Outline for a Legislative Program to Rebuild Our Cities. Washington, D.C.: The Institute, 1942. D.

________. Decentralization in New York City. Chicago: The Institute, 1941. A.

________. Proposals for Downtown Cincinnati. Chicago: The Institute, 1941. B.

________. Proposals for Downtown Milwaukee. Chicago: The Institute, 1941. C.

________. Proposals for Downtown Philadelphia. Chicago: The Institute, 1941. D.

________. The Urban Land Institute. Washington, D.C.: Urban Land Institute, 1940. A.

________. Decentralization: What Is It Doing To Our Cities? Washington, D.C.: Urban Land Institute, 1940. B.

________. Proposals for Downtown Boston. Washington, D.C.: Urban Land Institute, 1940. C.

Vasquez, Adolfo Sanchez. The Philosophy of Praxis. New Jersey: Humanities Press, 1977.

Vernon, Raymond. Metropolis 1985. New York: Vintage, 1960.

Vietorisz, Thomas; Mier, Robert; and Harrison, Bennett. "Full Employment at Living Wages." Annals of the American Academy of Political and Social Science 418 (1975): 94-107.

Vinton, Warren J. "A New Look at the Role of Public Housing in Urban Redevelopment." Planning. Chicago: American Society of Planning Officials, 1949.

Vladeck, Bruce C. "Health Planning – Participation and Its Discontents." American Journal of Public Health 69, no. 4 (1979): 331-32.

________. "Interest-Group Representation and the HSAs: Health Planning and Political Theory." American Journal of Public Health 67, no. 1 (1977): 23-29.

Wagner, Helmut. Phenomenology and Social Relations. Chicago: University of Chicago Press, 1970.

Walker, Mabel. Urban Blight and Slums. Cambridge: Harvard University Press, 1938.

Walker, Richard. "Two Sources of Uneven Development Under Advanced Capitalism: Spatial Differentiation and Capital Mobility." Review of Radical Political Economics 10, no. 3 (1978).

Walton, John. "The Vertical Axis of Community Organization and the Structure of Power." Social Science Quarterly 48 (December 1968).

Warren, Roland L. et al. The Structure of Urban Reform. Lexington, Mass.: D.C. Heath, 1974.

Watzlawick, Paul. How Real Is Real? New York: Vintage Press, 1976.

______ et al. Pragmatics of Human Communication. New York: Norton Press, 1967.

Webb, Lee, ed. Public Policies for the 80's. Washington: Conference on Alternative State and Local Public Policies, 1978.

Weinstein, Bernard, and Firestine, Robert E. Regional Growth and Decline in the U.S. : The Rise of the Sunbelt and the Decline of the Northeast. New York: Praeger, 1978.

Weinstein, James. The Corporate Ideal in the Liberal State. Boston: Beacon Press, 1968.

The Welfare Fighter. October 1972, "Congress Kills FAP." Washington, D.C.: The National Welfare Rights Organization, 1972.

Westaway, J. "The Spatial Hierarchy of Business Organizations and its Implications for the British Urban System." Regional Studies 8, no. 2 (1974): 145-55.

Wheaton, William L.C. "The Evolution of Federal Housing Programs." Ph.D. dissertation, University of Chicago, 1953.

Whittaker, Gerald F., ed. Community Revitalization. Ann Arbor, Michigan: Division of Research, Graduate School of Business Administration, University of Michigan, 1979.

Whisnant, David. Talk on the State and the Arts. Institute for Policy Studies. Washington, D.C.: June 1977.

Wildavsky, Aaron. "If Planning Is Everything, Maybe It's Nothing." Policy Sciences 4 (1973): 127-53.

______. "Why Planning Fails in Nepal." Administrative Science Quarterly 17 (1972): 508-28.

______. "Does Planning Work?" The Public Interest 24 (1971): 95-104.

Wilensky, Harold. Organizational Intelligence. New York: Basic Books, 1967.

Williams, William Appleman. "An American Socialist Community." In C. Benello and D. Roussupoulos, eds., The Case for Participatory Democracy: Some Prospects for a Radical Society. New York: Grossmans, 1971.

Williamson, Jeffrey. "Regional Inequality and the Process of National Development: A Description of the Patterns." Economic Development and Cultural Change 13, Part II (July 1965).

Willis, John W. "Short History of Rent Control Laws." Cornell Law Quarterly 36 (1959): 54-92.

Wilson, Patricia A. "The Political Economy of Regional Development in Peru: 1968-1977." In La Cuestion Regional en America Latina, Jose Luis Coraggio, ed. Siglo XXI and Moulton, forthcoming.

______. "From Mode of Production to Spatial Formations: The Regional Consequences of Dependent Industrialization in Peru." Ph.D. dissertation, Cornell University, Department of City and Regional Planning, 1975.

Wolfe, Alan. The Limits of Legitimacy: Political Contradictions in Contemporary Capitalism. New York: Free Press, 1977.

______. "The Capitalist Distemper."

Wolin, Sheldon. "Carter and the New Constitution." New York Review of Books 25 (June 1, 1978): 16-19. A.

______. "The State of the Union," New York Review of Books 25 (May 18, 1978): 28-31. B.

______. Politics and Vision. Boston: Little, Brown and Company, 1960.

Woodyatt, Lyle. "The Origin and Evolution of the New Deal Public Housing Program." Ph.D. dissertation, Washington University, St. Louis, 1968.

Yousem, Joseph. "Rent Controls Destructive in Principle and Practice." In Rent Control, Report of the National Association of Realtors. Chicago: Institute of Real Estate Management, 1977.

Zwerdling, Daniel. Democracy at Work. Washington, D.C.: Association for Self-Management, 1978.

Index

About the Contributors

PIERRE CLAVEL teaches planning at Cornell University. Before that he taught planning and public administration at the University of Puerto Rico and did local planning work in New England and upstate New York. His special interests are politics, administration, and economic development programs. His chapter in this volume is a condensed version of part of a book in progress on opposition planning in Wales and Appalachia.

JOHN FORESTER is an assistant professor in the Department of City and Regional Planning at Cornell University. Having received his Ph.D. in city and regional planning from the University of California at Berkeley in 1977, he teaches and writes in areas of social policy planning, the behavior of planning analysts and planning organizations, planning theory, and critical theory.

WILLIAM W. GOLDSMITH studied at Berkeley and Cornell. In Ithaca he co-founded the nonprofit corporation – Tompco Better Housing. Now he directs and teaches courses in the Program on International Studies in Planning at Cornell. He has worked in Latin America and recently published _A New Development Strategy for Puerto Rico: Technological Autonomy, Human Resources, A Parallel Economy_.

RICHARD P. APPELBAUM is associate professor of sociology at the University of California at Santa Barbara. He holds a B.A. from Columbia University, an M.P.A. from Princeton University and a Ph.D. from the University of Chicago. He is co-author of _The Effects of Urban Growth_ and author of _Size, Growth and U.S. Cities_ (both published by Praeger) and articles in _Working Papers_, _Society_, _Urban Affairs Quarterly_, the _American Sociological Review_ and other journals. He currently holds a National Science Foundation Public Service Science Residency to work with community groups on problems of rental housing.

HOWELL S. BAUM teaches social planning at the University of Maryland School of Social Work and Community Planning. He has studied and written about the ways in which planners' cognitive maps and assumptions about social action affect their practice. The paper in this volume is part of a larger study of planners' consciousness as practitioners. He is now working on a more detailed description of the organizational issues to which planners should be sensitive in practice. He is also examining didactic and experiential methods for teaching planners to be sensitive to these issues.

ROBERT A. BEAUREGARD teaches planning theory, social policy, and urban theory in the Department of Urban Planning and Policy Development at Livingston College, Rutgers University. He received his Ph.D. in city and regional planning from Cornell University. His current work focuses on the development of a practice-oriented planning theory, the relations among dependency, social policy and labor market participation, and the role of the private sector in urban revitalization. He is co-author of A Human Service Labor Market.

EDWARD M. BERGMAN is an associate professor in the Department of City and Regional Planning, University of North Carolina at Chapel Hill. His teaching and research is focused on planning theory and local economic planning, with particular emphasis on the role of community based enterprises, worker ownership and labor market inequalities in providing the basis for community consciousness. He is currently co-authoring a text on urban economic planning and writing a primer intended for citizens to use in gaining control of local economic development processes.

ROBB BURLAGE is assistant professor of urban planning in the Graduate School of Architecture and Planning at Columbia University and director of the Joint Health Planning Program. He is founder of the Health Policy Advisory Center in New York City, author of New York City's Municipal Hospitals, and is Health-PAC Bulletin national policy columnist. He is on the board of the Public Resource Center and convenes the Washington Labor and Health Roundtables. Burlage co-founded Peoples Appalachia journal and was formerly state planning research director in Tennessee.

DUDLEY J. BURTON teaches social theory and planning at the University of California at Santa Cruz. He is the author of The Governance of Energy (Praeger, 1979) and is now engaged in further work with Brian Murphy on the issues of democratic planning.

PETER DREIER is assistant professor of sociology at Tufts University. He holds a B.A. in journalism from Syracuse University and a Ph.D. in sociology from the University of Chicago. He has been a newspaper reporter and community organizer. Currently he works with Massachusetts Fair Share and a number of housing and tenant groups in the Boston area. His articles have appeared in Social Policy, Working Papers, the Columbia Journalism Review, Insurgent Sociologist, Dollars and Sense, Society, Socialist Review, and In These Times. His textbook (co-authored with Roberta Ash Garner) on socialist sociology will be published by Winthrop in 1980. He previously taught at the universities of California and Oregon.

JOEL FRIEDMAN presently works as a researcher on neighborhood issues in the Office of Policy Development and Research in the Department of Housing and Urban Development in Washington, D.C. He holds a masters degree in urban planning from the College of Architecture and Urban Planning at UCLA. He is also involved in local housing issues in the Washington, D.C. area.

JOHN INGRAM GILDERBLOOM is a Ph.D. candidate in sociology at the University of California at Santa Barbara and a fellow of the Foundation for National Progress. He has been a staff person with, and is currently consultant to, the California Department of Housing and Community Development, where he authored a major study of the effects of rent control. He recently edited a guide on rent control for public officials and housing activists published by the Conference on Alternative State and Local Public Policies.

HARVEY A. GOLDSTEIN teaches in the Division of Urban Planning, Columbia University. He has written numerous articles and professional reports on aspects of urban and community economic development and is the co-editor of _The Structural Crisis of the 1970's and Beyond: The Need for a New Planning Theory_, the proceedings of the Conference on Planning Theory held in May 1978 at Blacksburg, Virginia. He received a Ph.D. in city and regional planning from the University of Pennsylvania.

CHESTER HARTMAN is an urban planner living in San Francisco. He holds a Ph.D. in city and regional planning from Harvard and has taught there, at Yale, and at the University of California, Berkeley. His books include _Housing and Social Policy_, _Yerba Buena: Land Grab and Community Resistance in San Francisco_, and _Housing Urban America_ (co-edited with Jon Pynoos and Robert Schafer).

SANDER KELMAN is currently a visiting assistant professor in the Department of City and Regional Planning at Cornell University, Ithaca. He is the author of numerous articles on the political economy of health. He was formerly on the faculties of the Department of Preventive Medicine, University of Illinois Medical Center in Chicago and the Sloan Program in Hospital Administration at Cornell. He holds a Ph.D. in Economics from the University of Michigan.

LOUANNE KENNEDY is associate professor of health care administration at Baruch College, City University of New York and Mt. Sinai College of Medicine.

JUDITH KOSSY is a rehabilitation specialist in the Office of Community Planning and Development in the Department of Housing and Urban Development in Washington, D.C. She works on local housing issues in the Washington area and has written on urban planning in China. She has a Master of Urban Planning degree from the College of Architecture and Urban Planning at UCLA.

ANN R. MARKUSEN is assistant professor of city and regional planning at the University of California, Berkeley, where she teaches regional planning and works on regional development issues in the American west.

M. BRIAN MURPHY teaches political theory and American politics at the University of Santa Clara. He has written articles on the tax revolt and the legitimacy of the state. He writes for the journal, Kapitalistate, is currently working on a film about culinary and service work, and is continuing to work with Dudley Burton on the problems of democracy in advanced capitalism.

MITT REGAN works in the Community Development Block Grant Office in Alexandria, Virginia. He has a masters degree in urban planning from UCLA's College of Architecture and Urban Planning. He is involved in work with local housing issues.

JEAN-LOUIS SARBIB teaches in the Department of City and Regional Planning at the University of North Carolina, Chapel Hill. He is working on an intellectual history of the concept of planning in modern American society and is interested in developing a dialectic approach to the study of the future. He has taught at the University of Pennsylvania and has worked on international economic problems in the French Ministry of Industry. He has contributed articles to Le Monde Diplomatique and L'Architecture d'Aujourd'hui. His publications include La Division Internationale du Travail (co-author) and La Societe Francaise dans La Division Internationale du Travail: deux scenarios prospectifs (with Pierre Maclouf).

MICHAEL E. STONE teaches in the Center for Community Planning, College of Public and Community Service, University of Massachusetts in Boston. He has worked with community groups in New Jersey and Massachusetts as an advocacy planner, researcher, technical assistant, trainer, and organizer. He is the author of People Before Property: A Real Estate Primer and Research Guide and co-author of Tenants First: A Research and Organizing Guide to FHA Housing and Hostage! Housing and the Massachusetts Fiscal Crisis. He received his A.B. from UCLA and his Ph.D. in astrophysics from Princeton.

MARC A. WEISS is a Regents Fellow in City and Regional Planning at the University of California, Berkeley. He is co-author of A House Divided, a book about American politics in the 1960s, and has published articles on many aspects of urban political and economic life. A former community organizer, he is working on a Ph.D. dissertation on the history of city planning in the United States.